THE REAL RUNABOUTS V
by Robert Speltz

THE REAL RUNABOUTS Vol. V

Copyright 1984 by Robert Speltz
ISBN 0-932299-40-0
First Printing 1984
Second Printing 1993
Third Printing 2000
Printed by Stoyles Graphic Services
Mason City, Iowa 50401

DEDICATION

I wish to dedicate this book, *Volume V* of *The Real Runabouts*, to my wonderful aunts and uncles and to their children and grandchildren. I thank God for having such loving, supportive relatives who have kept encouraging me through my health problems and the writing of these five volumes over the last ten years.

The photo on this page shows seven of my aunts and uncles, whose names are listed here. A special dedication goes to my deceased aunt and uncle, Helen and Bob Bagan of Waseca, Minnesota, and to their children and grandchildren as well. I was named after my uncle Bob, and both of these great people passed away close to when my twin brother Art died in late 1977, early 1978. May God bless you and thanks for being you.

Left to right:
Dorothy and William Keefe—Austin, Minnesota
Donald Rieland—Mankato, Minnesota
Catherine Campion—Albert Lea, Minnesota
Marcella Rieland—Mankato, Minnesota
Angela Speltz (my mother)—Albert Lea, Minnesota
Robert Speltz—Albert Lea, Minnesota
Lauretta and James Bean—Springfield, Minnesota

DESCRIPTION OF COVER PAINTING
Painting and captions by Fred Craig

From left to right:

No. 1: A 38' Taylor Craft Cruiser. Extinct from late fifties—Taylor Boat Works, the harbour Toronto. This particular model, their second largest, and last of only 5 or 6 produced, was ordered by the RCMP 2 craft in 1959 or 1960. This one, The "Lady Alva" was owned by a visitor to Stoney L. in 1968—and still looked like new, beautiful graceful vessel fully appointed with a stateroom and accommodation in luxury for 6. She was Kermath powered. I don't remember the exact horsepower.

No. 2: The white launch with auto-touring top is the "Auto Car" trademarked from out your way which the Peterborough Canoe Company built a number of, under license in the 1920's. We had nine of them under various owners for 20 years or longer here on Stoney L. They were roomy, seaworthy and comfortable, at 16 m.p.h. usually with a Kermath or Buchanan 6 cylinder engine. Very reliable and great performers. Usually 24'-26' and a beam of approximately 6'5".

No. 3: In front of it tied alongside, one of "Aud" Duke's Port Carling Boat Works and Duke Boat Works' in the early 1940's up until mid-1970's. I have no idea how many of this model he built, there is a photo of it in Volume 3 with himself at the wheel. It was 17' Honduras Mahogany Deluxe Model, usually a 4 or 6 cylinder. Buchanan or choice of Kermath in rear—speeds up to 38 m.p.h. very similar lines to my 1950 Deluxe 17' Chris-Craft.

No. 4: The Deluxe International Model 26'-28' Sheppard (1958 and 1959 years) Twin V-8. Chrysler V-drive speeds to 38 and 42 m.p.h. Very roomy, deep hulls (birds eye maple wide strip from windshield area on top sides, sometimes ordered white enameled) naugahyde upholstering, in varied colors to order, 24 oz. white duck folding top, 12 volt system twin remote spotlights, map lights, floor foot lights, wipers and heater (optional). Siren—a trademark.

No. 5: In the boathouse slip, the white cedar lapstrake 22' Mason overnighter inboard or outboard or IBO unit usually in late 1960's. Built or finished by Mason Boats, Smith Falls, Ontario, but the hulls were Nova Scotian built and shipped to Mason. Very simple, but nicely finished seaworthy, light deep hulls. A good friend here has a 1968 model in excellent shape with a Waite heater built in, as well as an auxiliary battery charger and alternator. He runs a microwave oven from, and extras like side wipers as well as windshield. We have cruised comfortably in her in November snows, these last two autumns. It has an 185 OMC IBO and can make roughly 42 m.p.h. but the deep v hull makes her dig at that speed slightly. Beautiful performer at about 3.2-5 m.p.h. Stable, smooth traveler.

No. 6: The Greavette Streamliner (your favorite or one of them — 1937, 1938 and 1939) or specially built in the late 1960's to order at Gravenhurst. Usually a 6 cylinder Kermath or 8 cylinder Chrysler Crown. Speeds up to 45 m.p.h. according to the particular owners power choice. The totally reconditioned 1939 model here on the lake (currently listed at $50,000.00 by owner) is a beauty. I saw it twice last August at around 38 m.p.h. Quiet, level, and a showboat for certain. They plane very levelly!

No. 7: In the left foreground, The Grew 24' Sea Master Inboard Deluxe Buchanan V-8 Interceptor powered V-drive. Clinker built for heavy water, sturdy deep hull with beautiful lines. Much in preference on Georgian Bay waters and many other places. They were built in great numbers and in overnighters up to 30' as well as outboard models in the 1950's through the mid-1960's, when production stopped due to costs. (I would cherish one today as they are scarce in our district of Kawarthas.)

No. 8: Minett Shields pride and venerable octogenarian. This one is 38'. They went up to 40' on order and the craftsmanship was superb as photos attest.

No. 9: Last, but first here, the venerable *Dispro, this one an early Ditchburn, who built a good number of them as well as the original. Johnson the patent holder on the power source, Greavette and Duke Port Carling Boat Works also built them, and The Old Lindsay Boat Company under joint orders. The famed St. Lawrence 1 cylinder, 4-6 h.p. engine, and the patented lifting shaft tunnel.

Preface

by William (Bill) Morgan

I was very honored when Bob suggested that I write the preface for his new book. I am indebted to Bob for the tremendous work he has done on the preparation of these books.

Up until now, there has been no real history on the evolution of the "Antique Boats," as we have come to call them. The volumes that Bob has come up with have become "The Bible of the antique boating industry." They have brought invaluable information and details to the novice boater who is trying to upgrade his boat. Without these books, it would be an impossibility.

I have personally been involved in antique boats for the past 40 years, and in business for the past 30 years. I have seen the interest of wooden boats go downhill up until the mid-60s, and have been aware of a complete reversal ever since that time. In the early 1970s the Antique and Classic Boat Society came into existence. In those early days we felt that the potential membership of the Society would be about 1,000 members. Within a 10-year span the membership has grown to about 3500 members with 20 chapters springing up all over the country.

Twenty years ago the antique boats were thrown away and discarded. Now there has been an increasing demand to save and preserve any old boat. The future, as far as I can see, "is endless with the birth of the fiberglass era." The modern trend has been to make roomy, wide boats, that are practical and free of maintenance and upkeep, but also free of the warmth and looks and feel that antique boats possess. I have been very happy to see this sport grow in the direction that it has. In the last five years I have seen an increase in demand for boats that were in dire need of total restoration. These boats have been picked up by individuals who are willing to devote, time-wise, a couple of years, and become very involved with the complete restoration of their boats. I think from this work a special group of people will evolve who will be very knowable about woodworking fundamentals of the wooden boat construction. This certainly has prolonged the boat building industry.

We have seen some of these people open small repair shops that will help preserve the wooden boats we are all so proud and fond of.

Clayton was the "Grand Daddy" of the boat shows 20 years ago. This has grown so that some weekends are now getting two or three shows throughout the summer. We have seen the caliber of boats upgraded yearly, and there is a constant need for technical assistance. The shows have been a good meeting place for the novice who is in the process of restoration.

The Antique and Classic Boat Society has been working on judging formats, which are so necessary to set the standards of judging throughout the country.

It is very satisfying to see the interest in the vintage of Gold Cup Racing boats coming alive. It has saved many of the old hulls, and currently there is a trend to reproduce the famous Gold Cup boats. Many of the original boats have been destroyed because they were so lightly built and framed. By the time their racing career was over they were in such bad shape that their usefulness had ended.

Through new methods of boat building, one-of-a-kind reproductions have been built. We can look forward within the next ten years to having almost all 1920 to 1940 boats reproduced. I would hope that at some future time the owners would donate them to museums for display in the years to come.

Bill Morgan operates the Hacker Boat Company. He is involved in building new Hackers and in all areas of this sport!

CONTENTS

PREFACE v

INTRODUCTION x

I. MORE AMERICAN SPEEDBOAT BUILDERS FROM THE PAST 1
A. The Albright Boat & Marine Co.
B. Dunphy Boat Co.
C. Vanguard Power
D. Thompson Brothers Boat Co.
E. Midwest Boat Co.
F. Stan Craft Corp.
G. Morehouse Boat Co.

II. MORE CANADIAN SPEEDBOAT BUILDERS OF THE PAST 32
A. Mac-Craft Corp. Ltd.
B. Wallace Boat Works
C. Ontario Boat & Engine Works
D. Lacaille Boat Co.
E. Fetthall Boats
F. Scott Boat Co.
G. George Vandenbossche Boats Inc.

III. MATERIAL APPLYING TO VOLUME I 64
A. Chris-Craft Corp.
B. Hacker Craft Boat Co.
C. Century Boat Co.
D. Dee Wite
E. Gar Wood
F. Hafer Boat Co.
G. Curley Craft Boat Co.
H. Ramaley Boat Works
I. Streblow Boat Co.
J. Hutchinson Boat Works
K. Speedboat Builders in Canada
L. Greavette Boat Co.
M. Shepherd Boats Ltd.
N. Peterborough Canoe Co. Ltd.
O. Riva Boat Co.
P. Nautica Rio

IV. A COLLECTORS GUIDE TO CLASSIC CHRIS-CRAFT SPEEDBOATS 1961 THROUGH 1968   183

V. ONE-OF-A-KIND REAL RUNABOUTS   198
A. 1935 15½ foot Chris-Craft Utility
B. 1951 Chris-Smith Boat Crib
C. 1955 29 foot Greavette Day Cruiser
D. "Super Speedboat Seated 125 Passengers"
E. 1934 19 foot Phelps & Cornell Runabout
F. 1949 23½ foot Miss Comet Custom Inboard Runabout
G. 1938 Chris-Craft 29 foot Sportsman
H. 1947 19 foot Deluxe Higgins Runabout
I. 1965 24 foot Greavette Streamliner Runabout
J. "The Merry Go Round"
K. 1928 40 foot Custom Runabout, The Typhoon
L. "Thumpin' Again" 1962 26 foot Budych-Hacker Custom Utility

VI. LITTLE THINGS YOU MAY NOT KNOW ABOUT CONCERNING YOUR "REAL RUNABOUT"   216
A. Breaking in a New Engine
B. Watch the Instruments
C. Lubrication of Your Engine
D. Reduction in Speed & Why This Occurs
E. Care of the Bottom of Your Boat
F. Reconditioning Wooden Bottoms
G. Care of Varnished Surfaces
H. Care of Stuffing Boxes
I. Installing a Propeller Wheel
J. Water Proofing Hulls
K. Fiberglass Your Inboard
L. Hard Glueing
M. Grouting
N. Restoring Instrument Faces
O. Steering Wheels Used On Various Century Inboard Speedboats From 1957 Through 1977
P. Care & Feeding of Vacuum-Type Automatic Bailer
Q. Winter Storage of the Wooden Runabout and/or Utility

VII. SPEEDBOAT RIDE OPERATIONS AND OLD-TIME WOODEN BOAT DEALER SHOWROOM PHOTOS   227
A. Speedboat Ride Operations
B. Old-Time Wooden Boat Dealer Showroom Photos

VIII. NEW LISTINGS FOR PARTS, DEALERS & RESTORATION SHOPS, ETC. 251

  A. Outboard Motor Parts Dealers
  B. Inboard Engine, Parts and Motor Manual Sources
  C. Convertible Tops, Canvas Work, Upholstery and Flooring
  D. Paint and Varnish Suppliers
  E. Instruments and Instrument Repairs, Etc.
  F. Steering Wheel Repairs, Etc.
  G. Antique Boat Insurance
  H. Lumber and Fastenings, Etc.
  I. Clothing, Gift Items, Etc.
  J. New Eastern Restoration Shop Listings
  K. New Canadian Restoration Shop Listings
  L. New Midwestern Restoration Shop Listings
  M. New Southern Restoration Shop Listings
  N. New Western Restoration Shop Listings
  O. Props and Prop Repairs
  P. Replacement Rubber Products, Etc.
  Q. Hardware, Windshield Brackets, Rubber Moldings, Etc.
  R. Miscellaneous New Listings
  S. Decals, Nameplates, Etc.
  T. Miscellaneous New Listings
  U. Clubs, Magazines and Books of Interest
  V. Additional New Clubs
  W. Boat Magazines of Interest To Wooden Boat Enthusiasts
  X. Current Magazine Articles of Interest—Outboards
  Y. Current Magazine Articles of Interest—Inboards

IX. CURRENT BUILDERS OF MAHOGANY INBOARD RUNABOUTS 279

  A. The Ace Speedboat Co.
  B. Hacker Boat Co.
  C. Julius Marinacci
  D. Black Bottom Runabouts, Inc.

CONCLUSION 288

ACKNOWLEDGEMENTS 289

INTRODUCTION

Once again it is my pleasure to share with you, my readers and friends, new materials on one of our favorite subjects: real wooden inboard runabouts. Work on this volume has been in progress since January of 1983. After starting this book I soon realized that the amount of new materials I had gathered would produce too large a book, so I decided to split it into two volumes rather than make one large book. Therefore, I wish to announce that there will be another book written following this one, to be known as *The Real Runabouts: International Edition*. Volume VI will cover all new material, including stories on current and former runabout builders in Sweden, Germany, England, the United States, Canada, and Italy. But more about that book later; our task here is to discuss *Volume V*.

In Chapter One we look at seven American runabout builders. The first, Albright Boat Company, was best known for its futuristic-styled plywood outboards but they also turned out some fine inboard utilities. Dunphy Boat Company of Wisconsin, best known for their molded plywood and lapstrake outboards, also built a variety of beautiful mahogany inboards during the 1930s. You will be surprised how beautiful the old Dunphy inboards really were. The third builder is Vanguard Power Boat Company of Indiana. This firm once built many custom racing inboards, plus a unique Water Wagon utility that you will find different from other utility inboards. Thompson Brothers Boat Company of Wisconsin turned out a few inboard models in the early 1930s as well. Though best known for canoes and outboards of all types and sizes, Thompson did build a couple of sleek little beauties. Midwest Boat Company of Neenah, Wisconsin was a very small firm that built a few mahogany inboard runabouts. My good friend Ed Lewin of Mound, Minnesota, shares information on his unique split-cockpit model. From the far west, Stan-Craft Boat Company of Montana really built some fine looking inboard runabouts, utilities, and even cruisers. I know you will be surprised as you survey their various offerings up through the early 1960s. Finally, Chapter One ends with a discussion of Morehouse Boat Company and their inboards that were built on the Finger Lakes of New York State.

Chapter Two deals with Canadian builders, ones we have not looked at before. The first firm we review is Mac-Craft Boat Company of Canada. You will note, after looking at Mac-Craft photos in that section, that their boats closely resemble Chris-Crafts that were built nearby. There are reasons for this occurring which you will find out as you read about Mac-Craft. The second Canadian firm is Wallace Boat Works. Their story was new to me also. A reader some time ago advised me of them and was good enough to really dig out the facts and photos on these beautiful, old varnished "woodies" that will warm the hearts of us all. Ontario Boat & Engine Works were discussed in *Volume IV* concerning their outboard runabouts. They also produced several different models of the Canadian Wildcat inboards that closely resembled the American Hacker Craft. LaCaille Boat Company, formerly located in the province of Quebec, built some nice inboards in their day too. This section shows photos of and talks about perhaps the last LaCaille inboard still in existence today. I think you are going to like LaCaille. FettHall Boats of Canada built some rather unique inboards, though they did not remain in business too many years. The use of an engine that did not provide dependable service finally brought the firm to its knees. Both owners of the old FettHall Boat Company went on to work for other boat builders after their firm folded. Scott Boat Company of Toronto, Ontario started out strictly as a kit boat builder, one of the first in Canada, but later branched out into ready-to-use hulls in both outboard as well as inboard types. To date I have yet to hear of any Scott boats still in use, but who knows? There may be some up in Canada somewhere still providing good service to their owners. Our last Canadian firm is Van-Craft, located in the same city where Mac-Craft used to be built. The Van-Craft owner formerly worked for Mac-Craft but stayed in Wallaceburg, Ontario, when his old employer moved elsewhere. Van-Craft Boats built a popular mahogany utility along with some larger wooden cabin cruisers.

Chapter Three covers new material received on firms listed in *Volume I* written seven years ago. If you are a fan of Chris-Craft, Hacker, Gar Wood, Century or other major builders, you will really enjoy this chapter. Near the end of the Gar Wood section is a new and exciting feature of *The Real Runabouts*. Sixteen pages of full-color photos mark their first appearance in *Volume V*. I am really excited about this and hope you enjoy the varied selection of boats shown. Look closely; perhaps your boat or boats grace this new, colorful feature.

Chapter Four covers all modern Chris-Craft runabouts and utilities built in the years from 1961 through 1968. A photo of each boat, along with pertinent details on each, are shown in Chapter Six. Remember, these modern speedboats deserve your respect since, down the road, they shall be the antiques of tomorrow.

All of us dream of owning *Lockpat II* or *Pardon Me* or loads of other "one-of-a-kind" inboards, don't we? Well, Chapter Five reviews 12 different one-of-a-kind inboards ranging from a tiny model built by Chris-Smith for his grandchildren up through a Super speedboat built from the remains of a former PT boat that could carry as many as 125 paying customers at once. I think you will enjoy the good variety of boats appearing in this chapter. (*Volume VI* will include additional one-of-a-kind speedboats that I could not include in this book.)

Chapter Six gives facts on how to care for your inboard once you "take the plunge" and buy one. Some of the subjects covered are taken from a Chris-Craft owners' manual.

In Chapter Seven we take a look at the good ol' days when almost every lake or river of any size had at least one "Speed Boat Rides" operator located on it. Most of the material came from a friend of mine who used to drive speedboats for one of the leading ride operators in our area. I hope this section will lead to the unearthing of other materials on old speedboat ride operations where you live. I would love further old photos and stories on this aspect of inboards to possibly appear in future books or articles.

Chapter Eight contains pages and pages of all new listings for restoration shops, boat dealers, parts sources, etc. I have included many listings that appeared in *Volume IV* for a complete list. This chapter should be of interest to almost everybody. I try to keep it as up-to-date as possible. New listings come to my office almost every day. I plan to include them in *Volume VI*. Most firms listed prefer to talk to you by phone rather than by the mail. Most are small operations and the owners are far too busy to answer the numerous letters they receive every day, but they will take care of you faster over the phone. As long as we are talking about using the mail, I must confess to you that my mail has reached the point where postage is my second highest expense, following that of printing costs. May I ask you to please enclose a self-addressed, stamped envelope for my use when you write me for information? I welcome all your letters, questions, and comments but those folks including the s.a.s.e. will get priority service.

Our final chapter, Chapter Nine, takes a brief look at four current builders of mahogany inboard speedboats. The first, Ace Speedboat Company, have built a sleek, old Hacker design which looks like something right out of the late 1920s. This glistening honey will turn heads wherever it appears. Hacker Craft inboards are the ultimate runabout to own for most speedboat buffs. Hacker Crafts are being built once again by none other than Bill Morgan, the "dean" of Hacker Craft restoration persons. Bill purchased the Hacker name, and over the last few years has again started building three different mahogany Hacker runabouts. These beautiful runabouts are dead ringers for the Hackers of old on the outside, but the inside features many improvements, construction-wise, over the older Hackers. (Bill has also built a goodly number of "replica" Gold Cup race boats. We shall look at a few of them in *Volume VI*.) Julius Marinacci was the original builder of the Fairliner Torpedo inboard that was built out in Washington state. Since then, Julius has come out with a longer, wider and more highly powered Torpedo which is a very beautiful runabout. If you like the sleek, torpedo-styled runabout, then maybe you should take a closer look at this firm. Our final builder in Chapter Nine is the Black Bottom Runabout Company. This eastern builder currently restores wooden speedboats, and also builds and markets a sporty, split-cockpit runabout patterned after the popular Gar Woods of the early 1930s. (Such firms as Grand Craft, Morin Mahogany Marine, Stan-Craft Runabouts, and Gar Wood Speedsters, plus others, will be discussed in *Volume VI*.) More and more Americans as well as people throughout the world prefer the look of the old days with the modern space age building products of today when it comes to their inboard speedboats.

Well, that's what lies ahead. It is now time to plunge into *The Real Runabouts, Volume V*. I hope you will enjoy it.

CHAPTER I

More American Speedboat Builders from the Past

As in the former volumes of *The Real Runabouts,* we shall proceed in Chapter One to take a look at a selection of seven more firms who built wooden inboard runabouts and utilities years ago. You probably will recognize the names and remember at least something about a few of the firms; others will probably be new to many of you. I am the first to admit, there are still many firms that I wish to cover in future books and if it were not for the people who shared material used in this chapter and elsewhere throughout this book, there would not have been more than maybe one or two volumes in this set.

The first company we shall look at is the Albright Boat Company located originally in Charlotte, North Carolina. Though their boats were mahogany plywood, not planked hulls, I think you are going to really enjoy the Albrights after you see them on the next few pages. Without further ado, we shall now start our review of Albright, perhaps the all-time best builder of plywood hulled inboards, bar none.

THE ALBRIGHT BOAT & MARINE CO.

Though most of the firms discussed in this book built mahogany planked, varnished inboards, there were some very outstanding plywood inboards also available back in the 1950's as well.

The Albright Boat Company had its start in 1953 when D. C. and W. D. Marsh of Charlotte, North Carolina, began operating a small boat factory in that city owned by Mr. Albright. The Marsh boys were locally quite famous for their award-winning wooden outboard hydroplanes. Before Albright Boat Company began, the two Marsh brothers operated a little boat construction and repair shop at Lake Wiley. By the spring of 1953, the new Albright Boat plant was finished and the Marsh brothers were busy building and selling small 12-, 13-, and 14-foot flat-bottom fishing boats. These new fishing boats were planked with plywood rather than the conventional strip planking that most firms were still using back then. By using plywood, labor costs were reduced as plywood made a stiffer, lighter boat that could be completed in much less time. As time went on, several more deluxe utility outboards were added to the lineup. In 1954 the first true Albright outboard runabout, the 15' Falcon, was introduced. This model was finished with routed and striped decks like more expensive inboards and was available in a rainbow of color combinations. The Falcon continued in the Albright lineup every year and was one of the firm's all-time best sellers.

1955 Albright Ad.

The first Albright inboard was offered in 1955. An ad for that 17-foot Catalina inboard is shown here. Power was provided by a 60 or 110 h.p. Gray engine, and the boat had a suggested retail price of from $2,195 to $2,595. If you look very closely at the boat shown in that ad, you will note the windshield and top shown there are the same ones used by Century and Hacker-Craft at that same time.

With the good acceptance of the first Albright inboard, the firm in 1956 introduced another 17-footer. This one had a Gray Fireball and could reach speeds of

1956—The 17' Falcon Fireball with optional power gives speeds to 50 m.p.h., and is one of the many boats built by the Albright Boat and Marine Company, Charlotte, North Carolina.

50 m.p.h. One of the great features pioneered by Albright was the colorful paint jobs that were available by the firm year after year. Below is a list of just a few colors available that owners could select from when they bought their new Albright inboard or outboard:

White and red	Yellow and black	2-tone green
Pink and grey	Red and white	Other custom bottom and
White and black	White or mahogany	side colors available

All Albright inboards were built of AA grade African mahogany plywood sides and bottom. Sides were 3/8" thick while bottoms were double-planked 1/4" plywood with 3/8" 5-ply over that. The larger inboards were even built of heavier materials. Framing and ribs were all of Philippine mahogany.

I have photos here showing various Albright inboards from different years. Jim Templeton, who worked for the firm for six years, dug these out of the files but was unable to pinpoint their exact years. If not mistaken, I am quite sure the ones shown above were from 1956 or early 1957; however, I am positive that for 1957 four Albright inboards and 12 outboards were built. I shall list below the specifications on those four boats, starting with the least deluxe model and going up.

17' Falcon Albright Inboard with painted decks.

1957 16'6" Imperial Albright utility—top speed, 38 m.p.h.

Falcon 17' Albright Inboard utility

16' Riviera Inboard,	70 H.P. Graymarine Engine	List $2,480.00
16' Riviera Inboard,	85 H.P. Graymarine Engine	List $2,670.00

16' Falcon Inboard,	70 H.P. Graymarine Engine	List $2,820.00
16' Falcon Inboard	85 H.P. Graymarine Engine	List $3,010.00
16' Falcon Inboard	109 H.P. Graymarine Engine	List $3,120.00

1957 Albrights

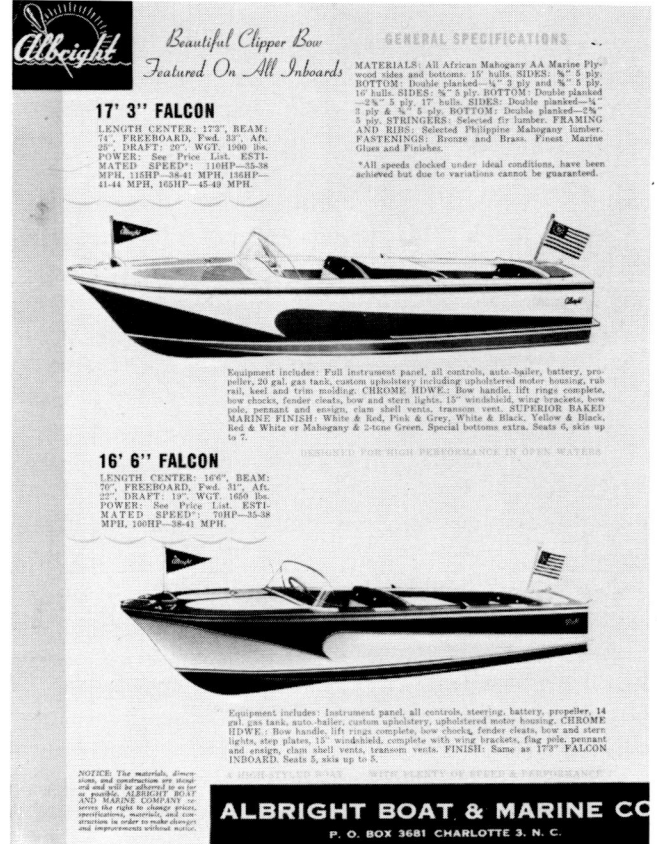

1957 Albrights

MODEL	LENGTH	ENGINE OPTIONS	SPEEDS	FINISH COLORS
Catalina Skier	15'	70 h.p. Gray	38 m.p.h.	Blue, green or white sides, varnished decks
Falcon	16½'	Up to 100 h.p. Gray	41 m.p.h.	All colors shown on earlier chart
Falcon	17'3"	Up to 136 h.p. Gray	49 m.p.h.	Same as above model
Imperial	16'6"	70 h.p.	38 m.p.h.	Gold, white and black

As you can tell by the photos, the 16'6" Imperial was a most stylish inboard. In fact, when first displayed at the marine dealer national boat show, crowds around the Albright booth were so great that other manufacturers complained, saying things were too congested for others to walk through the aisles.

The closeup photo here, showing the 1957 Imperial Albright utility resting on the trailer, will show you the

ALBRIGHT OUTBOARD INBOARD BOATS for '58

famous for
✓ QUALITY ✓ PERFORMANCE ✓ BEAUTY

Power and beauty combined with latest engineering advances make the "Falcon" 17' 3" inboard a leader in '58. Baked marine enamel finish over African and Philippine Mahogany add striking new beauty in a wide range of colors. Gray power to 225 hp V-8. Also a 16' 6" Falcon, 70 to 109 hp.

**VISIT THE ALBRIGHT DISPLAY — BOOTHS 34 & 35
CHICAGO NATIONAL BOAT SHOW
Floyd Harper and Bob Girard
February 7th - 16th**

ALBRIGHT BOAT & MARINE CO. P. O. BOX 3745, CHARLOTTE 3, N. C. PHONE: FR 6-3596

actual Packard car rear tail lights that did operate and were back-up lights as well when you backed from your slip. Not too many boats could boast such a feature, could they? Well, Albright hung in there even as fiberglass boats began to take more and more of their business away. Albright even built some fiberglass outboards patterned after their wooden boats but they were never very popular. In 1959 Albright Boat Company was sold and moved to Pineville, North Carolina, where it continued in business until 1961, when building of all small boats finally came to an end during the Recession of that time. A new 26' fiberglass cruiser was then built in the old plant, but its tooling was soon sold to Wheeler Cruisers who built the boat for a while.

Jim Templeton started his own firm in 1959, building a 27' White Hawk inboard cruiser. At that time it was one of the largest fiberglass boats being built. Today Jim operates Southeastern Glas Laminates, a firm specializing in design, tooling, production and consulting of fiberglass products. Templeton has been working on and off to produce a fiberglass hulled inboard along the lines of a wooden Riva with all wood decks. There is a drawing of the planed boat shown here. Good luck, Jim, and thanks for shedding some light on an old favorite of many of us wood boat buffs, Albright of Charlotte, North Carolina.

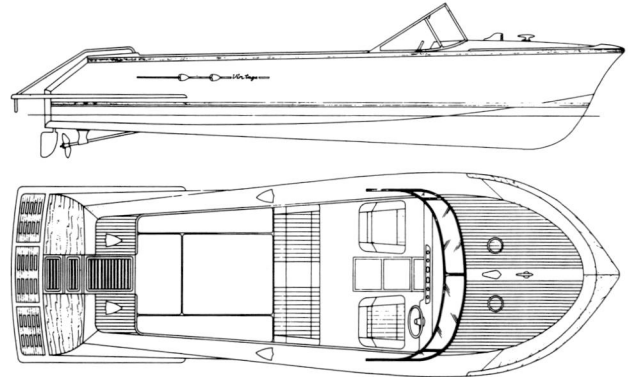

From sunny North Carolina we head north and a little west to the state of Wisconsin, home of the former famous firm of Dunphy Boat Company of Eau Claire and later, Oshkosh. Dunphy was by far most famous for their molded plywood outboards and later on, lapstrake outboard and I.O. runabouts and cruisers. Back in the middle 1930s Dunphy offered a selection of all varnished runabouts that will probably surprise you as much as they have me.

DUNPHY BOAT COMPANY
of Oshkosh, Wisconsin

If you were a kid back in the early to mid-1950s and were a "boat nut," you more than likely will recall Dunphy molded plywood boats. Dunphy molded plywood hulls were among the best ever built, and if you wish to read more on them, I recommend Chapter Two, p. 106 plus in Volume IV for the complete Dunphy outboard story.

While working on Volume III, I believe it was, I came across a small ad showing a beautiful split-cockpit Dunphy mahogany runabout that was 17½' long. I tucked this ad away, hoping someday to find more material on this famous midwestern builder with hopes of including it and their inboards in a future volume. Well, that time has finally come, as this past year I was able to pick up two beautiful old Dunphy catalogs from the years around 1934 to 1936. There are no dates on either issue, but I am sure that is about when the boats we shall look at were built.

I wonder just how many, if any, Dunphy mahogany inboards still exist? If you have one or know of one, drop me a note and let me hear about it. If you have one you have a rare boat, that's for sure. First of all, though, let's take a look at a little of the early history on Dunphy before we "feast" on their runabouts.

Dunphy Boat Company traces its beginnings back to 1854.[1] In that year, young John Dunphy was a busy man, freighting supplies for James J. Hill on barges and scows prior to the Civil War. Hill was busy constructing his famous Great Northern Railroad which would eventually stretch across the northern part of the U.S. all the way to the West Coast. When the Great Northern was finally completed here in the Midwest and James J. Hill and the rest of his crew moved on West, Dunphy was left in Eau Claire, Wisconsin. At that time, Dunphy decided, because of his closeness to a cheap lumber supply and power sources, he would open a small boat shop in Eau Claire. From the start, Dunphy build good boats of all types, both powered and nonpowered, and he became quite well known here in the Midwest. To give you an idea of just what the firm built, by 1921 they offered the following types of pleasure craft: high grade inboard launches, rowboats, canoes, plus fishing and outboard motor boats.

Let's take a look at two of the 1921 Dunphy inboards in a little more detail. First of all, even as early as 1921, Dunphy was pioneering the "Fast V-bottom runabout." Three models were being built that year in sizes of 20', 25' and 30' in length. Each boat was equipped with a modern 4-cylinder, 4-cycle engine while the cockpits were provided with two built-in seats forward and one stern seat aft with cushions, etc. Two wicker chairs, linoleum floors and electric lights were also standard fare. Included in the price were such items as horn, flag staffs, steering wheel, electric starter, and 6 rope fenders. People always enjoy old-time prices, so here are samples of what a 1921 Dunphy inboard sold for:

20' runabout	Beam 58"	w/12 h.p. Kermath engine	$ 975.00
25' runabout	Beam 72"	w/25 h.p. Gray engine	$1,350.00
30' runabout	Beam 76"	w/35 h.p. Gray engine	$2,275.00

If your preference back in '21 was for slower, more casual cruising, then the series of three Dunphy family runabouts were just what you needed. These three models were built along the lines of the older launch-type inboards. Engines were mounted forward of the passenger compartments and these craft were equipped, even down to the 6 rope fenders, identical to the V-bottom inboards we just looked at. The main difference between the V-bottom runabouts and the family runabouts would be the latter had smaller engines and were flat-bottomed. Again, to share old-time prices with you, here is what the 1921 Dunphy family runabouts sold for:

23' runabout	Beam 5'	w/12 h.p. Kermath engine	$1,060.00
26' runabout	Beam 5'6"	w/16 h.p. Kermath engine	$1,275.00
30' runabout	Beam 5'10"	w/20 h.p. Kermath engine	$1,950.00

[1]Speltz, Robert, *The Real Runabouts, Volume IV* (1982), p. 106.

1921 "V" bottom Dunphy inboard

Typical 1921 Dunphy launch

I have here several ads showing various inboard models built by Dunphy for the years 1926 and 1927. You will note the gradual transition to the more modern, typically runabout designs shown in these ads.

The most unusual of the models shown probably was the 26-foot three-cockpit runabout. An enlarged photo of that boat is shown here. Some unique features found on her were the following: the front cockpit featured two large leather upholstered seats, while the aft seating area sported twin wicker chairs plus another leather-covered seat. A 100 h.p. marine inboard engine was standard equipment with an advertised speed of 30 m.p.h. A larger engine could be ordered that guaranteed a speed of 45 m.p.h. for the young at heart. This beauty sold complete for $3,150 f.o.b. Eau Claire, Wisconsin.

1927 Dunphy Ad.

1927 26' 3-cockpit runabout by Dunphy, powered by a 100 h.p. engine and sold for $3,200 F.O.B. Eau Claire, Wisconsin.

Performance
—that you've always wanted

In these two motor boats you're offered the kind of performance that you've always wanted. They're *popularly priced, too*—and backed by the most exacting standards of craftsmanship. Note the facts.

The New Dunphy Sand Dab
18-foot shallow draft tunnel stern, with room for nine passengers. Runs in 11 inches of water. Beaches anywhere, lands anywhere, goes anywhere, the propeller is protected. Eases into coves, streams, and inlets where others cannot enter.
Equipped with 4-cylinder, 15 H.P. Universal Motor, with electric starter. Makes 15 miles an hour. Hull is cedar planked, brass and copper fastened, mahogany finished.
$1,150 *F.O.B. Eau Claire*

The New Dunphy 26 Foot Runabout
Roomy cockpit forward with two leather upholstered seats. Rear cockpit has one leather upholstered seat and two wicker chairs. Comfortable capacity for five in each cockpit.
Equipped with 6-cylinder, 100 H.P. Marine Motor, with electric starter. Makes better than 30 miles an hour, and on special order equipped to do 45 miles guaranteed. Steering wheels and all controls operated from forward seat. Hull is double planked mahogany, brass and copper fastened.
$3,150 *F.O.B. Eau Claire*
Remember, we are equipped to design and build any boat to your entire satisfaction. Write for illustrated catalog on launches, outboard motor boats, canoes, row boats. All boats ready for immediate shipment. Buy from Dunphy and save money.
Chas. W. Young, Atlantic City, N. J., Representative

DUNPHY BOAT MFG. CO.
Dept. C6   Eau Claire, Wis.

"famous for boats for forty years!"

Some of the 1926 Dunphy Inboards offered.

Note These Specifications
Salt water equipped. Shallow draft tunnel stern. Length—18 feet. Runs in 11 inches of water. Beaches anywhere. Protected propeller. Plenty of room for 9 passengers.
Hull is cedar planked, brass and copper fastened, mahogany finished. Equipped with 4-Cylinder 15-H.P. Universal Motor, with electric starter. Makes 15 miles per hour. (Windshield and automobile top optional equipment.) Ready for immediate delivery, $1275 F. O. B. Eau Claire.

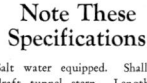
"famous for boats for forty years!"

A Great Boat for Florida
It's easy to handle—comfortable and seaworthy—the new Dunphy Sand Dab. Ready to go wherever you want to go—eager for the fishing trips or the scenic cruises along the coast or bays. Only Dunphy builds the Sand Dab—an outstanding motor boat value. Write for catalog on all Dunphy Boats. Or send your specifications—we are equipped to design and build any type of boat to your entire satisfaction.
Standardized runabouts, 21-foot and 26-foot models, in stock ready for immediate shipment.

DUNPHY BOAT MFG. CO.
Dept. C 12, Eau Claire, Wis.

1926 Ad.

By 1929 Dunphy was offering even more inboards. I have an excellent ad from 1929 that shows three new models. Perhaps the two of most interest is the 17-footer with steering in the rear cockpit. It could reach speeds up to 22 m.p.h. The 21-foot split-cockpit could be ordered as a runabout as shown, or as an open utility. It was powered by a Universal 6-cylinder engine and topped out at 30 m.p.h.

Eventually the Dunphy family members all died out, and the firm was taken over by a native of Denmark, James Larsen. During both World War I, and later in World War II, Dunphy Boat Company built large numbers of wooden craft for the army-navy. In the mid-1930s, Larsen moved the entire Dunphy Boat Company over to Oshkosh, Wisconsin, on the shores of Lake Winnebago. A new 10,000 square foot plant was erected at Oshkosh, and Dunphy continued to expand their offerings.

The next portion of this review will deal with Dunphy mahogany inboards built during the years from about 1933 through 1937 or so. I cannot be more exact than that, as none of the catalogs from which I gathered the following information had any years listed on them, but I am quite sure the period I mention is close enough to be authentic.

THREE Fast Sturdy Sea-Worthy Inboard RUNABOUTS

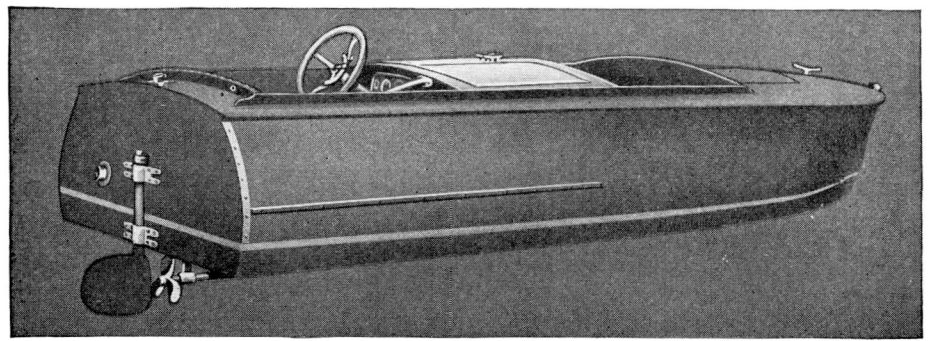

A 17-FOOTER
A real runabout for those who don't need too much carrying capacity. Double cockpit. Plenty of room for 5. Better than 22 miles per hour with the Universal Flexifour. Mahogany decks and planking... *Completely equipped* **$1,095.00**

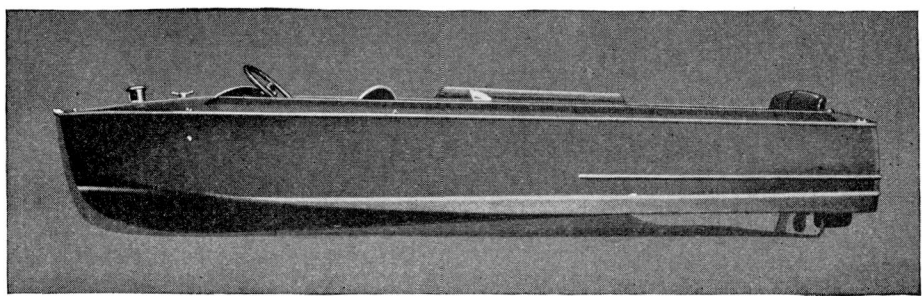

AN 18-FOOTER
18 feet, 6 inches, to be exact. Speeds up to 25 miles an hour. Six passenger roominess. Seaworthy yet only draws 11 inches. Known far and wide as the Dunphy Sand Dab. Powered by Universal... *Priced from* **$1,195.00**

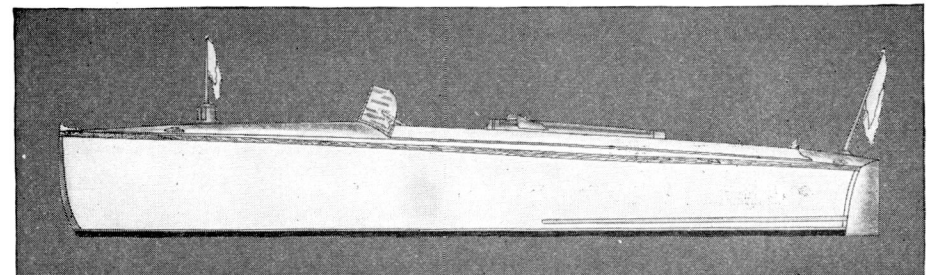

A 21-FOOTER
Plenty of beam, plenty of freeboard. She's built for fishing in open water. Can be had either with double cockpit—room for six, or with single cockpit and swivel chairs. Mahogany deck and planking. Powered with the Universal Six. She will do 30 miles per hour. **$1,850.00**

Complete specifications upon request.

OUR 1929 CATALOG is ready—a copy is yours for the asking

DUNPHY BOATS

Dealers: Write for our attractive dealer plan

DUNPHY BOAT MANUFACTURING COMPANY · Dept. MBG-3 · EAU CLAIRE, WISCONSIN

1929 Ad.

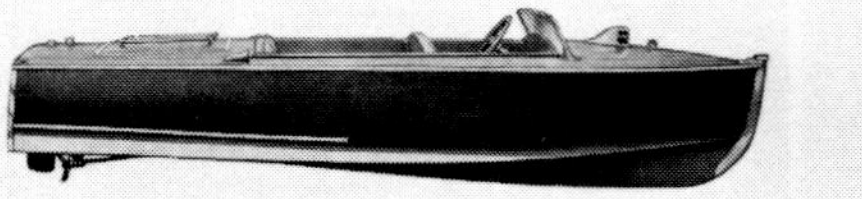

Junior Runabout

Fortunate, indeed, are those who live near or have access to small lakes and rivers. And doubly fortunate are they if they have a Junior Runabout at their command. This little aristocrat of the water is ideal for entertaining guests on lazy afternoons, exploring new channels or bays or just looking at the scenery; for quick trips to favorite hunting or fishing grounds or for the hundred and one uses that every owner of such a craft can immediately think of.

An ideal choice for smaller lakes and rivers. Its liberal beam and high free board insure seaworthiness and dryness in the rough and choppy waters. Comfortable accommodations for six passengers are provided in the roomy two-seated cockpit forward of the motor compartment.

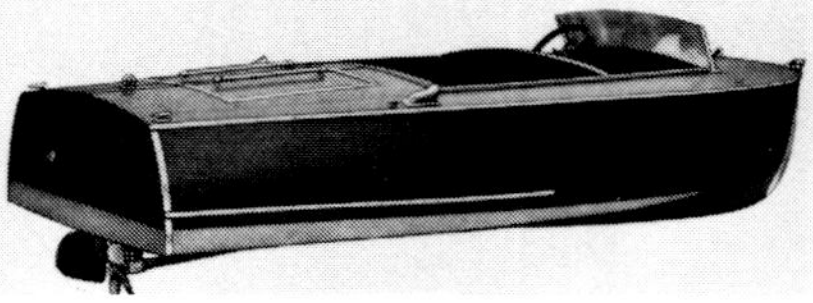

Junior Runabout

Length, over gunwales	16 feet
Beam	5 feet 4 inches
Freeboard Bow	23 inches
Freeboard Stern	20 inches
Draft	16 inches
Seating Capacity	6 passengers
Speed	22 to 24 miles per hour
Shipping Weight	1250 pounds

Construction: Keel, 1¾" x 3¾" white oak, frames, ⅞" x 2½" white oak; spaced 24"; small frames, ½"x⅞" white oak.
Side Planking: ⅝" Philippine mahogany, screw fastened.
Bottom Planking: ⅜" mahogany.
Inner Planking: Cedar, canvas between, laid in marine glue.
Fastenings: Brass and copper.
Stringers: 1½"x8", fastened through floor timbers with galvanized bolts.
Motor: Gray Light Four, 4-cylinder, 30 horsepower; V-Drive Morse Gear.
Propeller Shaft: ⅞" tobin bronze.
Propeller: 2 blades, 10x10.
Rudder: Bronze.
Strut: Bronze.
Shaft Log: Erico Type.
Gas Tank: 20 gallons.

Finish: Deck and interior cockpits natural spar varnish. Inside of hull, three coats lead and oil. Outside, black enamel above water line, red below water line and white stripe.
Deck Trimmings: Nickel silver.
Upholstering: Red Russialoid.
Steering Wheel: Auto type, connected to rudder with steel tube.
Floor: Linoleum covered.

Accessories: Combination bow running lights, flag and flag poles, 2 tie lines, 4 fenders, 1 Pyrene fire extinguisher, step plates, automatic bilge bailer, lifting rings, tool kit. Tachometer and drive shaft, $25.00 extra.

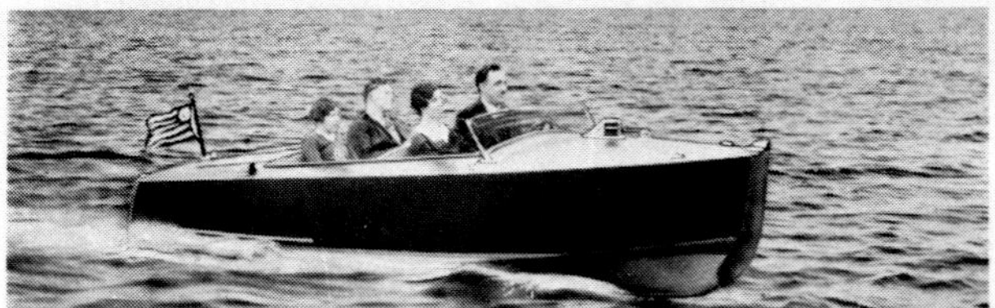

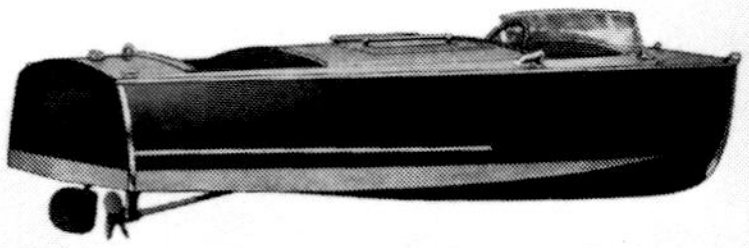

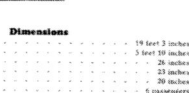

Victory

You will like this little speed demon. It is built especially for those who like a boat that will go fast, look good and with it all, be comfortable. Wherever you find smart craft assembled you will find this one prominently in attendance. It challenges attention; it's light and speedy and "level riding," comfortable seats, plenty of foot room and a high freeboard. Nothing has been overlooked.

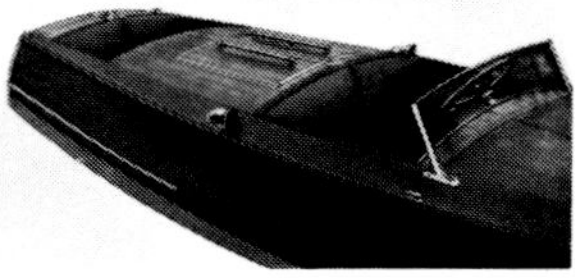

Dimensions

Length, over gunwales	16 feet
Beam	5 feet 4 inches
Freeboard at Bow	23 inches
Freeboard at Stern	20 inches
Draft	18 inches
Seating Capacity	6 passengers
Speed	32 miles per hour
Shipping Weight	1450 pounds

Construction

Keel, 1⅜"x3⅜" white oak.
Frames, ⅞"x2½" white oak.
Spaced 24".
Ribs ½"x⅝".
Spaced 8", mortised into keel and chine.
Side Planking: Philippine mahogany, ⅝", screw fastened to frames and oak battens.
Bottom: Double planked, canvas between in marine glue.
Outer Planking: ⅜".
Inner Planking: ⅜", screw fastened to ribs and frames.
Fastenings: Brass and copper.
Engine Stringers: 1⅝"x8", fitted and bolted to oak floor timbers extended from transom to forward deck.
Motor: Gray, four cylinder, fifty horsepower, with starter and reverse gear.
Propeller Shaft: 1" monel metal.
Propeller: Three blade, 11x12.
Rudder: Bronze.
Strut: Bronze with Goodrich rubber bearing.
Shaft Log: Erico type.
Gas Tank: 25 gallons capacity.

Finish: Decking sides and interior of cockpits are finished natural with 5 coats of marine spar. Inside of hull painted 3 coats antifouling paint with white stripe above.
Upholstering: Seats and backs are capoc filled and covered with blue Russialoid. Floor, covered with Battleship linoleum.

Accessories

Steering Wheel: Auto type, connected to rudder with steel tube.
Instrument Panel: Indirectly lighted, with tachometer, motometer, ammeter and oil gauge, choke and remote starter button and ignition and light switch. Deck hardware, fender moulding and cutwater, chromium plated.
Regulation running lights; flags and flag poles; tie lines, Pyrene fire extinguisher; four fenders; anchor and anchor lines; automatic bilge bailer; lifting rings; horn; tool kit.

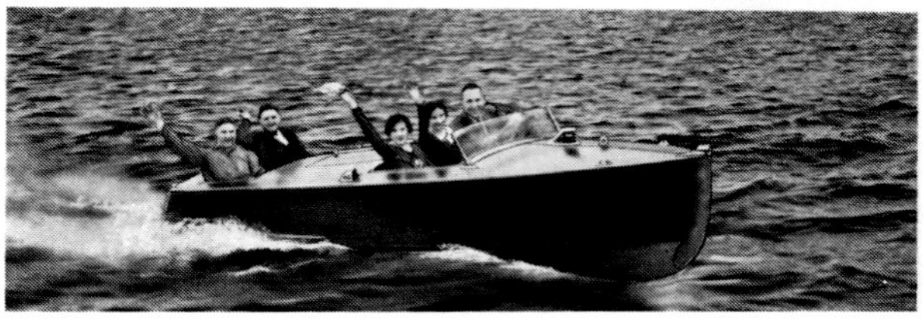

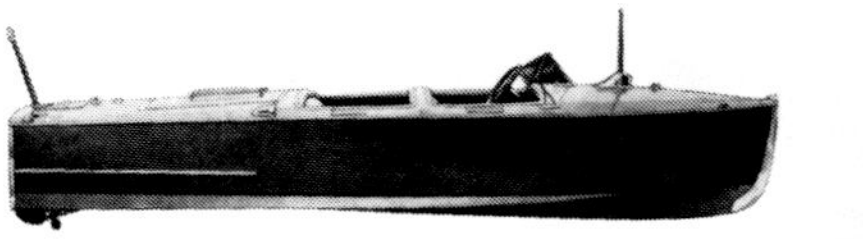

Imperial

An ideal boat for the person who has a fancy for "something better" and who can indulge that fancy. The kind of a craft that makes people sit up and take special notice as it glides swiftly by. A beautiful high quality runabout with two forward cockpits, "level riding," speed, comfort, seaworthiness and easy riding. Absolutely free from flying spray while riding at high speed.

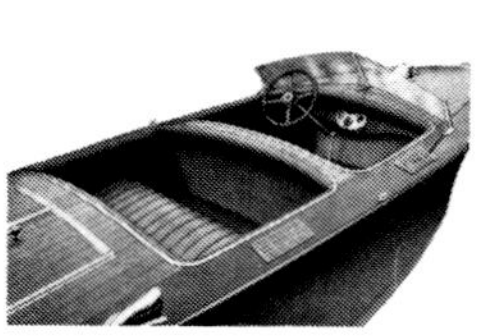

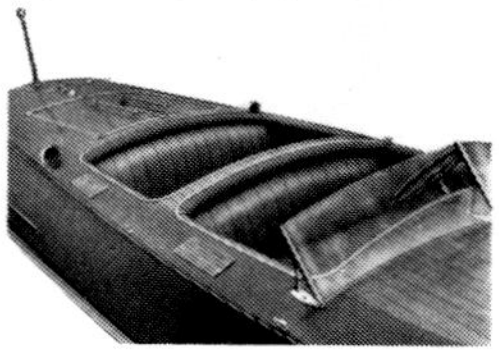

Dimensions

Length, over all	19 feet 3 inches
Beam	5 feet 10 inches
Freeboard at Bow	26 inches
Freeboard at Stern	23 inches
Draft	20 inches
Seating Capacity	6 passengers
Speed	32 to 37 miles per hour
Shipping Weight	1850 pounds

Construction

Keel, 1⅜"x3⅜" white oak.
Frames, ⅞"x3" white oak.
Spaced 24".
Ribs, ½"x⅝".
Spaced 8", mortised into keel and chines.
Side Planking: Honduras mahogany, ⅝", screw fastened to frames and oak battens.
Bottom: Double planked, canvas between, laid in marine glue.
Inner Planking: [illegible].
Outer Planking: [illegible], screw fastened to ribs and frames.
Fastenings: Brass and copper.
Engine Stringers: 1⅞"x8", fitted and bolted to oak floor timbers extended from transom to forward deck.
Motor: Gray 6-66 or Gray 6-93, with starter and reverse gear.
Propeller Shaft: 1" monel metal.
Propeller: Three blade, 12x13.
Rudder: Bronze.
Strut: Bronze with Goodrich rubber bearing.
Shaft Log: Erico type.
Gas Tank: 30 gallons capacity.

Finish: Decking sides and interior of cockpits are finished natural with 5 coats of marine spar. Inside of hull painted 3 coats lead and oil. Bottom below water line painted 3 coats antifouling paint with white stripe above.

Upholstering: Seats and backs spring upholstered and covered with blue Russialoid. Floors covered with Battleship linoleum.

Accessories

Steering Wheel: Auto type connected to rudder with steel tube.
Instrument Panel: Indirectly lighted with tachometer, motometer, ammeter, oil gauge, ignition and light switch, choke and remote starter button. Deck hardware, fender moulding and cutwater, chromium plated.
Regulation running lights; flags and flag poles; tie lines; Pyrene fire extinguisher; four fenders, anchor and anchor lines; automatic bilge bailer; lifting rings; horn and tool kit.

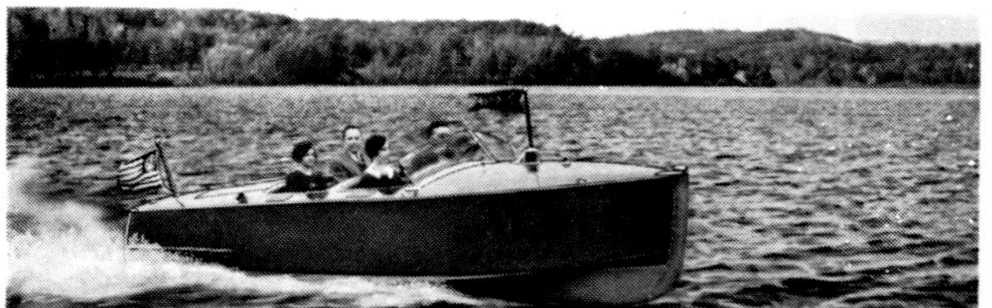

DUNPHY BOATS

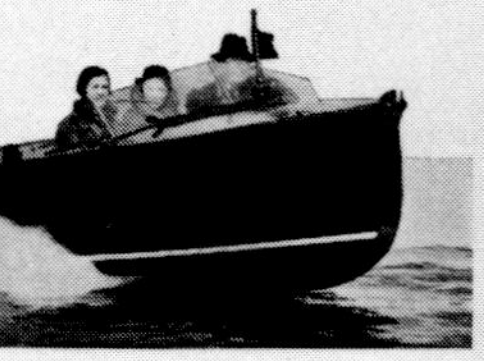

Water Phaeton

The Water Phaeton is the first boat with shock absorbers. The rounded chines break the jar of the waves. The flush deck, V-type windshield, chromium plated fittings and deep, roomy cockpits are parts of its unparalleled finish. Frames are one piece, gunwale to gunwale. Strips are continuous stem to stern. Each strip is hollowed and rounded as shown. Pounding seas only tighten the seams more. The Water Phaeton is exhaustively complete. It's seventeen and one-half feet of beauty and riding quality. Gray Six Sixty-Six or Gray Six Ninety-Three.

Equipment: Automatic bilge bailer, steering wheel, automobile type with spark and throttle control and electric horn installed on the wheel; 2 cork fenders; 2 manila tie lines; anchor; anchor line; fire extinguisher; tools; step pads; bow flag pole; stern flag pole and light and yacht ensign.

General Specifications

Length over all, 17 feet 6 inches. Beam, 5 feet 8 inches. Freeboard; Bow, 26 inches. Stern, 22 inches. Draft, 16 inches. Width of transom, 57 inches.

Keel, stem, sternpost frames and stringers of selected white oak.

Frames are steam bent in one length from gunwale to gunwale, spaced 6 inches center.

Planking: Clear selected mahogany in one length from stem to transom, compress seams, narrow strips fastened to ribs with brass screws.

Full length bilge stringers, notched over ribs extend from stem to stern.

Outside above water line finished in black, below water line bright orange and white stripe above.

Seats and back rests are capoc filled and upholstered with blue Russialoid.

Deck trimmings: Chromium plated nickel silver.

Seating capacity: Six passengers.

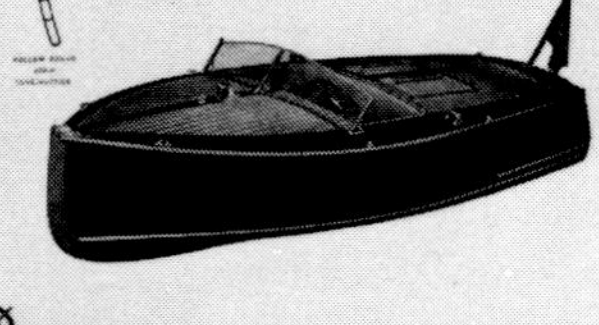

Ten

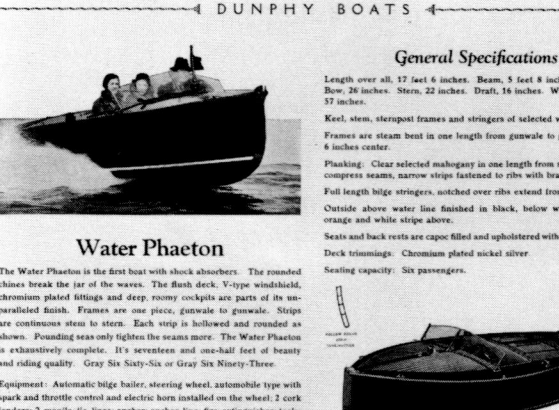

The first runabouts we shall look at were built in Eau Claire, Wisconsin, so I think these were from 1933. The first inboard offered for that year was known as a Pullman inboard cruiser. This 20-footer was a sedan cruiser with cooking and sleeping facilities for two. Runabouts of the inboard variety made up most of that 1933 model selection. Rather than list all the information on the four models, I shall list only their specifications and you can read all else in the description with the photos.

MODEL	LENGTH	BEAM	FREEBOARD	DRAFT	SEATING CAPACITY	SPEED	WEIGHT
Junior Runabout	16'	5'4"	23", bow	16"	6	22 to 24	1,250
Imperial Runabout	19'3"	5'10"	26", bow	20"	6	32 to 37	1,850
Victory Runabout	16'	5'4"	23", bow	18"	6	32	1,450
Water-Phaeton Runabout	17'6"	5'8"	26", bow	16"	6	25 to 35	—

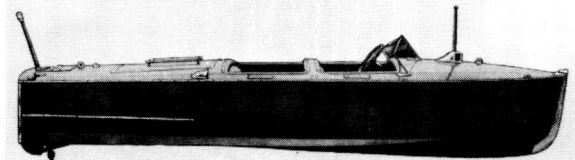

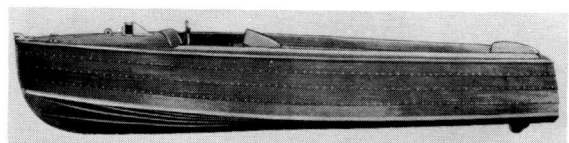

Imperial Runabout

Swanky, trim and fast, this well groomed thoroughbred can bank on the turns with a wide open throttle or come down the straight away like a thunderbolt and be absolutely free from flying spray. We believe our hull design superior to any — and racing records prove it! The double cockpit forward is roomy and the soft spring cushions and back are as muscle relaxing and nerve soothing as your favorite chair. Because of its design, we believe it to be the safest, level riding fast boat on any waters. Double planked and staunchly braced, it is the aristocrat of America's fine runabouts. If appearance and speed combined with safety and comfort are what you are looking for — the Dunphy Imperial Runabout has all these qualifications — plus.

Utility Runabout

Dunphy builds two beautiful Utility Runabouts, as keen a pair of boats as can be found anywhere. All the skill and experience of Dunphy craftsmen have been utilized to produce a boat within the price range of those who want not only appearance but a full measure of all the features which go to make the perfect boat.

As the name implies, this is a useful boat — a boat for the fisherman, the camper, the outdoor family, yet it is as smart as pepper! Low in first cost, it is practically as economical to operate as an outboard. The roomy, open cockpit permits freedom of movement and plenty of space for luggage.

Spray hood and folding top equipment can be furnished — ideal accessories for dad and son to sleep under on their next exploring trip. This lap-strake all Mahogany craft will deliver years of real boating pleasure.

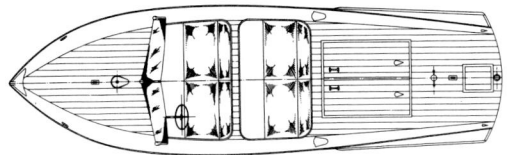

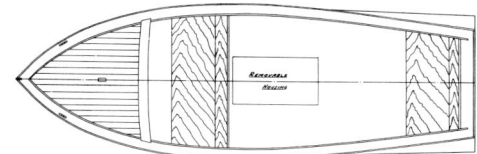

SPECIFICATIONS — IMPERIAL RUNABOUT

SPECIFICATIONS — UTILITY RUNABOUT

I think you will agree with me, any of the above Dunphy runabouts would be a treasure to own today. I guess my favorite of the four shown would be the 19'3" Imperial model, how about you?

After Dunphy moved over to Oshkosh, they built fewer inboard models, and more rowboats and outboard runabouts. About 1936 they offered the following selection: a 20-foot Cuddy cruiser that looked more like an open utility with an added hardtop roof with bunks for two inside the cabin. The Imperial runabout had been lengthened by 3 inches, though the price had been lowered to $1,295. Many boat builders had to do this during the middle 1930s to entice boat buyers back into the market after the disastrous Depression years prior to that time. Dunphy's first true utility came out in 1936 as well. She is shown here and was rather plain, without any windshield or even upholstered seats. Three models of the utility were built in 16-foot as well as 20-foot versions. The utility runabout was designed for the camper, fisherman and cabin owner. Lapstrake planking, of all mahogany, was used on this single model.

Following World War II, Dunphy stopped all inboard speedboat construction and began to switch from strip boat building to all molded plywood models by about 1955. As molded plywood faded from the scene with the advent of more and better fiberglass and aluminum hulls, Dunphy switched over to all lapstrake wooden outboards and inboard-outboards.

Here in the Midwest it is not uncommon to see a nice older Dunphy lapstrake outboard or inboard-outboard model still in use. If you would like to read more about this facet of Dunphy Boat Company, please refer back to Volume IV, Chapter Four, page 228 plus, for more information.

Dunphy was one of only a handful of builders who never came out with fiberglass boats. In 1964-65 they built their last inboard, not a runabout but kind of a revolutionary styled utility. I have seen four of these Dunphy utilities over the years, and when they are restored to their original elegance, they are quite the boat. Here is more specific information on this rather rare inboard:

In 1964 Dunphy introduced its 17-foot X-55 inboard. There is a factory photo shown here of the boat running at top speed. All were powered by 215 h.p. Interceptor engines with direct drive. Mahogany varnished plywood was used for the hull sides over mahogany frames with oak keel, chines and stringers. Fastenings were all silicon bronze, along with the use of DuPont poly-

urethane bedding compounds. It delivered a top speed of 55 m.p.h. and could seat six in comfort on rolled and pleated vinyl foam rubber bucket seats. Standard equipment included 12-volt lighting system; single lever controls; a padded dash with ammeter, tachometer, fuel, oil and temperature gauges; an 18-gallon fuel tank; Michigan Wheel cupped propeller; and all chrome-plated brass hardware, including ski tow bar. As you will note by the factory photo, the X-55 had a single step built into the bottom just ahead of the stern. These boats handle like a dream. They ride flat as a board going across water, and look like "speed" even when tied to the dock.

1965 17' Dunphy with 215 h.p. Interceptor owned by Ralph W. Williams, Jr., Atlanta, Georgia.

A thanks goes out to Ralph Williams, Jr., of Atlanta, Georgia, for sharing two photos of his X-55 completely restored. Ralph says he wouldn't trade that Dunphy for any boat, regardless of what it was.

About 1965-66 Dunphy closed due to the Recession which caused big decreases in all wood boat sales, and a fire that destroyed their plant. For over 100 years Dunphy Boats enjoyed national acceptance, and I hope the material just discussed will do at least partial justice to the many fine inboard speedboats this noted builder turned out from both of their locations—first in Eau Claire, Wisconsin, followed later by Oshkosh, where they remained until they closed.

The state of Indiana is much better known for automobiles and racing than it is for boats, but the next firm we shall look at, Vanguard Power Boats of Auburn, quietly for 10 years built some very unique racing as well as pleasure craft. It is my distinct pleasure at this time to introduce you to this little known builder, and share with you photos taken directly from the family photo albums of this interesting boat builder.

VANGUARD POWER BOATS
of Auburn, Indiana

Years ago this nation was criss-crossed with a network of small local and regional boat builders who turned out all varieties and styles of small pleasure craft. The city of Auburn, Indiana, probably is best known for the former Auburn automobile, but there was also a boat builder located there.

A special thanks goes out to Mahlon E. and Duane Rieke who provided the following items concerning the Vanguard Power Boat Company of Auburn, Indiana. I must admit, I was unfamiliar with Vanguard until about two years ago. At that time Duane & Mahlon Rieke sent me two photos of a very uniquely-styled mahogany utility, as well as an all varnished cruiser. After corresponding with the fellows for a year or so, it was decided we would include material on Vanguard Power Boats in the next book I would do on inboards. Well, here we are, and now I shall "lift the curtain" on Vanguard and share with you what I have learned about this interesting firm.

Vanguard Power Boats was begun in the year 1940 by Mahlon Rieke.[2] In those days most of the boats built by the firm were of custom runabouts and raceboats. Mahlon has provided a nice selection of old photos showing some of the racing and pleasure runabouts built prior to the start of World War II. My own personal favorite is the 1940 21-foot 2-passenger Sport

---
[2]Letter, Mahlon Rieke, 11/8/83, p. 1.

1946 24' Sedan utility

1940 21' 2-passenger 3-point Sport Hydro—360 h.p. modified Hispano Suiza aircraft engine.

1946 18'4" Hydro-Wagon by Vanguard Boats of Auburn, Indiana.

hydroplane powered by a modified V-8 Hispano-Suiza aircraft engine. That power plant developed 360 honest horsepower, and the little gem would top out at 55 m.p.h.—very fast for more than 40 years ago. The photo shown here was color tinted and it looks as though the decks and sponsons were all varnished with a gold-colored engine hatch, deck area, and what to me looks like an automobile windshield. Mahlon did not advise me if this boat is still around, but more than likely it is long gone by now. Another nifty 1940 model was a 14-foot Sport hydroplane "steeped" and powered by a Ford 100 h.p. V-8 engine. Its top speed was 40 m.p.h.

plus. The color scheme was white decks and hull sides, red bottom, varnished transom, and yellow unholstery. I am not sure of the current status of this craft either.

Another 1940 Vanguard runabout was the 22-foot 4-passenger 2-cockpit 3-point Sport Hydroplane. Some of the photos used here are from old factory files and a few were badly creased. I think though, you will still get the basic idea of just what these futuristic inboards looked like. The 22-foot runabout just mentioned above was powered by a 180 h.p. supercharged Lycoming (Cord Auto engine) which propelled this semi-racer at an estimated speed of 45 m.p.h. In 1941 the firm built a

1940 14' Sport Hydroplane "Stepped"—Ford 100 h.p. V-8, 40 m.p.h.+.

1940 22' 4-passenger, 2-cockpit 3-point Sport Hydroplane—180 h.p. Supercharged Lycoming (CORD Auto Engine) 45 m.p.h.

1941 15' Sport-Hydro—3-point suspension—91 cu. inch Gray 4-cycle engine—42 m.p.h.

1946 23' 3-passenger 3-point Sport-Hydroplane powered by (2) 160 h.p. 6-cycle Gray Fireballs, speed—50 m.p.h.

15' 3-point Sport Hydro powered via a 4-cylinder Gray 91 cu. inch power plant. That little 2-seater topped out at 42 m.p.h.

The final racing boat we shall look at in this section was built in the year of 1946. This runabout was 23' long and could carry three passengers with ease. It, amazingly enough, was powered by (two) 160 h.p. 6

Side view of totally restored Vanguard 18' utility. Note the wood trim on back half of hull sides.

cylinder Gray Fireball engines. Top speed was 50 m.p.h. As I said, I doubt if many of these boats are still around. In a lot of cases, racing boats enjoyed very short lives, as their use for racing often was extremely hard on their staying in one piece year after year.

So you think Vanguard built only racing boats? I want to show you examples of this firm's straight pleasure craft as well. Starting after the close of World War II, Rieke began building both 18' and 24' utility inboards. The first photo here shows an old family photo showing one of the first 18-footers going through trials before delivery to her new owner. The Vanguard utility built in those years, at first appearance, looks very similar to most other inboards of that day. However, if you will look closely at the next 3 or 4 photos, you will note some unusual design features found on no other inboard runabout or utility I have ever seen. *The Sadie-T* was built in 1946 and is 18'4" long and 6'6" wide. It was powered by a 140 h.p. Gray Fireball and totally restored by Duane Rieke some years back.[3] The most unique feature is the "station wagon" design, using the wood trim like the popular "woody" station wagon automobiles which were so popular back then.

Also, note the life ring mounted on the transom, just like the spare tire was mounted on the wood trim station wagon cars. A close look at that same view will reveal small seats facing aft, built in just ahead of and off to each side of the motor box. The interior of the Station Wagon or Hydro Wagon was upholstered in a sort of off-white and rust or orange-red color. This restored

Interior view of Vanguard *Sadie-T*. Note unusual mounting of ring-buoy on transom similar to spare tire on older car.

utility sports a white painted bottom with a bright red waterline.

A larger 24-foot utility was also offered. A restored and modified version is shown here. It is powered via a 140 h.p. Gray Fireball. To me, it is not as stylish as is

---
[3]Letter, Mahlon Rieke, 11/8/83, p. 1.

Original factory view of 1946 18' Vanguard utility out of Auburn, Indiana.

the Hydro Wagon, but that's just my own view.

Vanguard Power Boat Company stopped building wooden boats back in 1950. Fiberglass boats spelled the end of this firm's turning out wooden racers and pleasure craft. However, I am very pleased to advise you that Duane Rieke has again opened the family business, Vanguard Power Boats, and has as his purpose the restoration of classic boats and eventually the manufacture of modified mahogany runabouts and utilities.

Thanks again to Duane and Mahlon Rieke for sharing material on Vanguard inboards with us. The current address for Vanguard Power Boats will be found in the back of this book under "Midwestern Restoration Shops."

Our next firm is the Thompson Brothers Boat Works of Peshtigo, Wisconsin, and Cortland, New York. Thompson, as it usually was known at one time, built and sold more small wooden boats and canoes than any other single major boat builder. Since this book concerns itself with only inboards, we shall review samples of a few Thompsons built especially in the early 1930s. Though perhaps not as fancy as a lot of other boats discussed in these volumes, Thompson, nonetheless, definitely deserves review here. If you wish to read more about Thompson outboards, canoes and rowboats, I recommend Volume IV as a must.

THOMPSON BROTHERS BOAT CO.
Peshtigo, Wisconsin and Cortland, New York

The Thompson Brothers Boat Company at one time was one of the largest boat building concerns in the world. The firm still exists, though no longer owned by the Thompson family. For those who have not read Volume IV of *The Real Runabouts*, I shall briefly discuss here the early history of Thompson.

Back in the year 1904 Peter and Chris Thompson, two Wisconsin farm boys, began building a few flat-bottom rowboats and canoes during the winter months on the home farm.[4] By the spring of 1905 so many orders began rolling in from friends and neighbors that neither of the fellows could help their family plant the crops for that year. Before too long the following family members were involved in the business: Peter, Chris, Ed, Tom and Richard.[5] To start with, the bulk of boats and canoes built were sold to resorts and residents right around the Peshtigo, Wisconsin, area. Outboard motors were still in their infancy until another Wisconsinite, Ole Evinrude, came out with a relatively good outboard engine that increased interest in Thompson Boats even more.

The year 1911 saw a new factory for Thompson being built in the nearby village of Peshtigo. This original plant was expanded several times, but finally the main proportion was destroyed by a massive fire in the winter of 1953. Our goal here is to take a brief look at some of the Thompson inboard boats built over the years. Thompson was never that well known for inboards, but they did build a few up through 1934 or so.

By the 1920s Thompson produced seven different models of inboard runabouts. The Runabout Launch-Style "U" is shown here. In 1921 Thompson offered open launches in lengths of 16', 18', 20' and 24' long. According to the firm's catalog, the Style "U" was built for anyone who wanted a stable and useful inboard powered motor boat. The boats were built with long front decks and short decks aft with seats equipped with lazy-backs for comfort. Prices back in 1921 ranged from $309 for a 16' launch with a 4 h.p. Lockwood-Ash inboard up to $623 for a big 24-footer with a 8 h.p. Lockwood-Ash power plant. If you wished a more deluxe runabout of the inboard variety back in '21, then you would be interested in the Auto Express-Style "X" by Thompson.

Hunting Boats, Canoes, Rowboats, Fishboats and Motor Boats. Catalog Free. Save Money. Order by Mail. Please state what you are interested in.
THOMPSON BROS. BOAT MFG. CO.
1907 Ellis Avenue   Peshtigo, Wis.

1920 magazine ad.

---

[4]Speltz, Robert, *The Real Runabouts, Volume IV* (1982), p. 3.

[5]"Thompson Boat," *Boating Industry* (December '69), p. 104.

1921 18' Thompson Style "U" runabout launch

Auto Express-Style X runabout—20 footer

1927 16' Beach model cedar-strip Thompson inboard launch.

The Auto Express-Style "X" greatly resembles the basic inboard launch of that period. Engines were mounted forward of the passenger area and these boats sported a straight sheer line, flaring bow, and plenty of freeboard which made her dry in the roughest sea. Specifications for a typical Thompson inboard for that time would be as follows: ribs, keel, skeg, stern post, transom and stern of selected white oak, fastened in place in the most substantial manner; planking was cedar; covering boards, lazy-back combing partners and seat trimmings of selected oak; cockpit lined with clear white cedar; deck was covered with canvas which was filled, rubbed smooth and brought to a perfect finish; outside of the boat was finished white above the waterline and green below; inside of cockpit combing, lazy-backs, covering boards and fenders were finished in golden oak with the best grade of spar varnish; fittings such as vents, chocks, and cleats were polished brass; steel plate; balance-type rudder was controlled by a polished brass launch wheel.

Here are the specifications on the 3 Auto Express-Style "X" launches:

Close-up of engine compartment on 1927 16' Beach model inboard by Thompson of Peshtigo, Wisconsin and Cortland, New York.

You will note the Auto Express-Style "X" was not equipped with windshields in those years. Engine size was small back in those days, and speeds were less than 10 m.p.h. at best.

Six years later Thompson Boat Company had greatly expanded their outboard and canoe offerings while inboard offerings were about the same as 1921. For the fisherman, a new 16-foot Beach Model Motor Boat for $125 was offered. With its propeller mounted above the keel, this unique little inboard could travel the shallow

LENGTH	BEAM	DEPTH AMIDSHIPS	WEIGHT	SEATS	PRICE W/0 ENGINE	PRICE W/12 H.P.
18'	51"	26"	625 lbs.	2	$247.00	$666.00
20'	54"	30"	850 lbs.	3	$310.00	$729.00
24'	58"	32"	1,200 lbs.	4	$552.00	$969.00

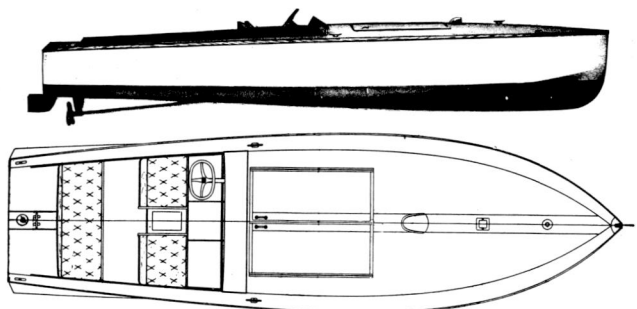

1927 20' Thompson inboard runabout.

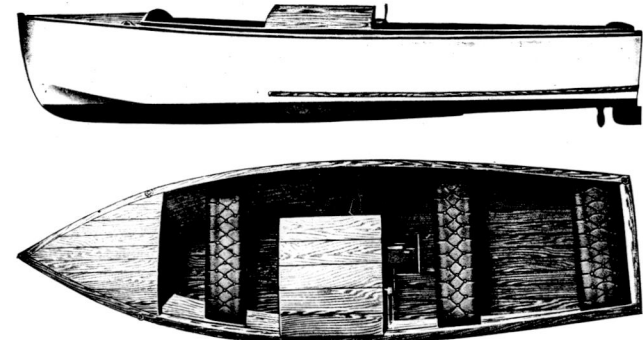

1927 18' Thompson fishing rig—powered by 15 h.p. universal engine.

lakes and creeks of the midwest and east. Her engine was mounted aft under a deck; she was steered by a rudder mounted aft and controlled by tiller ropes near the back seat. Engine size offered included 2 h.p. to 5 h.p. twin cylinder models that pushed the retail price up to just under $265 for a complete rig. There are two photos shown here.

Thompson offered a new V-bottom runabout in 1927. It was more streamlined than the old 1921 versions we just looked at. The first photo here shows a side view of this 2-seater. To show you how dimensions had changed in just six years, I shall list the 1927 specifications for you now.

up into the boat bottom, thus allowing the boat to safely operate in any depth as long as the bow of the boat was able to float over the lake or river bottom below it. Actual depth of water needed for the tunnel stern model would have been 11 inches or so. This boat came with a 15 h.p. Universal engine and retailed for $645 complete in 1927. She, too, was painted white on the hull sides with a green bottom, and varnished decks, interior and trim.

Thompson entered the era of all mahogany inboards about 1931 when they first offered the Thompson

LENGTH	BEAM	DEPTH BOW	DEPTH STERN	WEIGHT, HULL	SEATS	CAPACITY	ENGINE
18'	60''	35''	19''	675 lbs.	2	5	15 h.p.
20'	69''	36''	20''	950 lbs.	2	5	20 h.p.
26'	72''	38''	22''	1,600 lbs.	2	6	50 h.p.

Prices ranged from $685 to $1930 for the large 26-footer. The "V" hull was so designed to ride on plane, with less displacement and more speed per horsepower. If you are interested in the color scheme of these old Thompsons like I am, here is how they were finished: All hulls were painted white above the waterline with anti-fouling green bottom paint. Decks, fenders, combing and inside of cockpits were finished with the best then available spar varnish. The two brands of inboard power plants offered in 1927 by Thompson were Kermath and Universal. A new plant was built about that same time in Cortland, New York, to help take care of Thompson orders on the East Coast of the U.S. If you wished something a little less fancy, Thompson also offered an 18-foot V-bottom River model in 1927. This boat had its engine mounted amidships, and for an additional $30 the hull could be built with a tunnel stern. A tunnel stern allowed the propeller to be basically built

Scoop, a 16-foot 5-passenger family motor boat.

The new Scoop, as it was called, sold for just $760 f.o.b. Peshtigo, Wisconsin, or Cortland, New York. This little beauty came with either a standard Lycoming 40 h.p. motor or a larger Universal Blue Jacket 45 h.p. motor. The firm guaranteed their inboard did not squat in the stern at high speed or nose dive when you slowed her down after a high speed run. Speeds were suggested to range from 30 to 35 m.p.h., depending on passenger load and water conditions. The Scoop was varnished totally on decks, transom and hull sides, with red bottom and a black waterline; interior seats were red in color.

In 1933 Thompson changed the name of Scoop to Thompson Sixteen-TVB Inboard Motor Boat, and the engine size that year was increased to a 50 h.p. Universal Blue Jacket. Dimensions of the Thompson 16' inboard were:

LENGTH	WIDTH AMIDSHIPS	WIDTH STERN	DEPTH	HULL WEIGHT	SEATING	PRICE
16'	65''	54''	34''	630 lbs.	6	$760.00

Thompson Sixteen - TVB Inboard Motor Boat $760
LEVEL RIDING

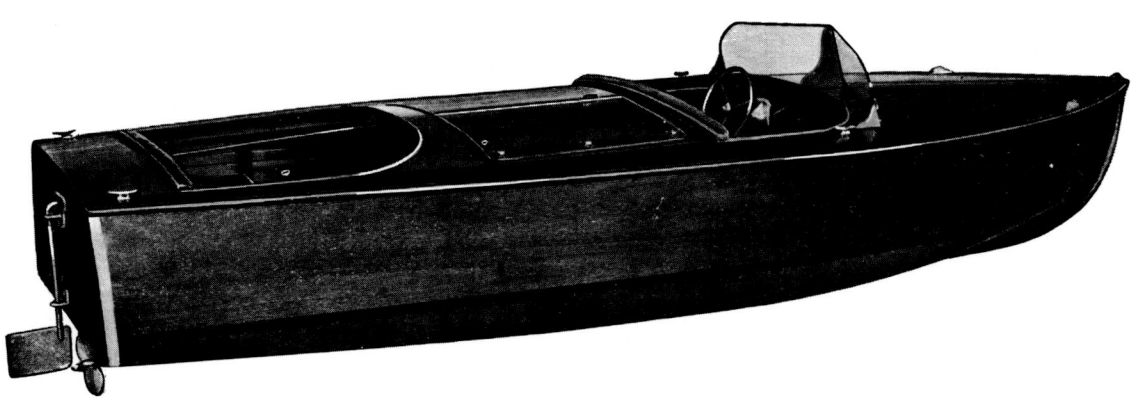

With the ever increasing speed attained with outboard motor boats, manufacturers of inboard motors have been developing high speed, four cycle, four cylinder engines to compete in price and speed with ing larger outboards. Some of the engines brought out have been developed to the point of perfection, but the designing of 16-foot hulls suitable for the installation of high speed engines has been in a transitory stage, and only the very latest models brought out have proven entirely satisfactory.

We have been watching the development of 16-foot high speed motor boats very carefully, and when the THOMPSON SIXTEEN was designed, we had the advantage of being thoroughly familiar with the merits and demerits of the various motor boats of this size brought out during the past two years.

The THOMPSON SIXTEEN was designed with painstaking care to eliminate the faults found in the performance of other small high speed motor boats. It planes easily and rides level, with the bow just above the surface so that it does not cut the water until it is under the boat. This not only makes the boat perfectly dry, but it eliminates pounding and increases the speed. The THOMPSON SIXTEEN does not settle at the stern regardless of the speed attained or the load carried, neither does the bow plunge down into the water when the boat is brought to a sudden stop. It is a strong, staunch and durable boat—extra wide and extra deep. This not only makes it roomy and comfortable—absolutely safe, seaworthy and perfectly dry—but makes it very buoyant on choppy water and rides over large waves instead of cutting through them.

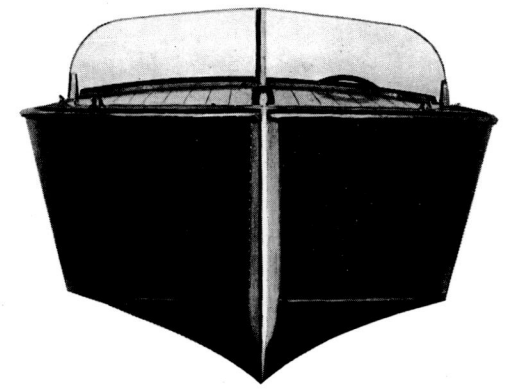

Specifications
Keel and stem .... White Oak
Frames and battens .... White Oak
Chine .... White Oak
Bottom planks, ½-inch .... Cedar
Side planks, ½-inch .... Mahogany
Deck and trim .... Mahogany

Lazy backs upholstered with moleskin artificial leather. Loose cushions made of the same material, and filled with moss, furnished for the seats.

All fastenings copper and brass. Nickel plated cut water and polished brass fittings.

It has a four cylinder, 50 H. P. Universal Blue Jacket engine, complete with electric starter (including battery) and reverse gear, installed. A speed of 34 miles an hour can be attained with this engine.

THOMPSON SIXTEEN-TVB MOTOR BOAT WITH 50 H. P. UNIVERSAL ENGINE INSTALLED

Order No.	Overall Length	Width Amid	Width Stern	Depth	Weight, Hull	Seating Capacity	Price
347	16 ft.	65 in.	54 in.	34 in.	630 lbs.	6 adults	$760.00

N. B.: When comparing the "Thompson Sixteen" with other boats of the same length, compare the width and depth carefully, especially the width at stern because the extra wide stern is one of the main reasons why the "Thompson Sixteen" rides right with any load, at any speed.

Something Entirely New—An Extraordinary Value

16-Foot TVT Motor Boat, $645

With Full Length Spray Rails

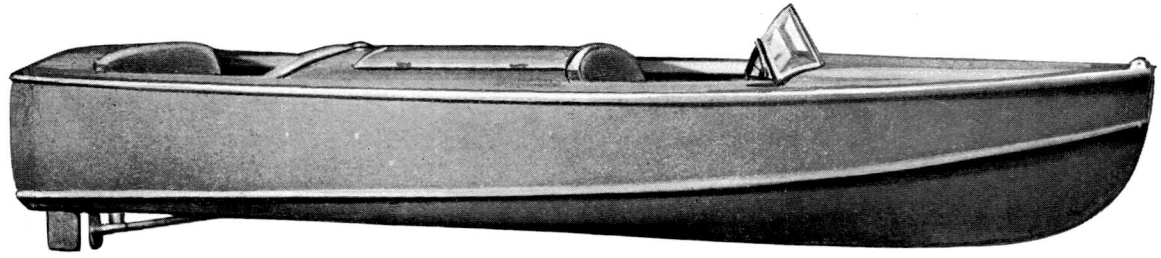

The Thompson V Type (TVT) motor boat is very similar in design and construction to our TVT outboard motor boats, and is just as superior in performance to regular V bottom motor boats, as the TVT outboard motor boats are to boats of any other type. They are made with a round bilge, but have a V type bottom, which gradually works into a flatter underbody and is perfectly flat on the bottom, at the stern.

They are absolutely safe and seaworthy—smooth riding—level riding—perfectly dry—and—bank on the turn. They not only ride right and trim right at any speed, but they carry up better and attain greater speed with a full load in both seats, than any other boat of the same size, we know of.

Perfectly Dry—Smooth Riding—Level Riding

Full length spray rails are something entirely new on motor boats. They were originated by us and used on our TVT outboard motor boats during the past season with decided success. Spray rails ride close to the surface of the water and catch the broken water created at the bow of the boat and turn it down into the solid water again before it is turned into foam. This eliminates white water and spray along the sides and keeps the boat perfectly dry from bow to stern. It is the only boat of its size we know of in which the passengers in the stern seat stay perfectly dry, when running along at a high rate of speed in a cross wind.

Spray rails also act as shock absorbers which makes this boat an unusually smooth riding boat, and they also cause the boat to plane with a heavier load, and keep the boat riding level with any load, at any speed.

Unequalled Performance—Speed Unsurpassed

We contend that the Thompson Sixteen TVT motor boat is superior in performance—smoother riding—and—the driest boat of its size on the market today, regardless of price, where, or by whom it is made.

Specifications

Ribs, keel and stem—white oak. Stern and deck—mahogany. Compressed seam cedar strip planking. All exposed fastenings copper or brass. The entire inside of the boat and the deck is finished in the natural wood with Marine varnish. The bottom of the boat below the spray rails is enameled moss green. The sides of the boat above the spray rails are enameled light brown. The spray rails are finished in black.

Order No.	Length	Width Amid	Width Stern	Depth Amid	Seating Capacity	Weight, Hull	Price
	16 ft.	65 in.	54 in.	34 in.	6 adults	550 lbs.	

345 16 foot TVT Motor Boat with 50 H. P. 4 cylinder Universal Blue Jacket engine, with reverse gear, electric starter, generator and battery, installed. Speed up to 34 miles an hour_____**$645**

346 16 foot TVT Motor Boat with 54 H. P. Phantom Gray engine installed, with reverse gear, electric starter including battery _____**$662**

Mahogany planking above the spray rails, finished in the natural wood, if wanted, **$5.00** extra.

Windshield, upholstered lazy backs and loose cushions for seats are included at the prices quoted above. Running lights are not required most places where boats of this size are used and these are optional at **$6.00** extra.

N. B.: The length of this boat is sixteen feet long measured from the bow to the stern, along the gunwale. It is made in this way so that sixteen foot lumber will make full length planking.

1931 ad for new 16 foot 5-passenger mahogany Thompson inboard.

Another model built in 1933, though not shown here, was a plain 16-foot utility inboard that sold, with engine installed, for just $395. The largest engine available in the utility was a 54 h.p. Gray Phantom Four power plant. 1934 found the Thompson 16-foot inboard unchanged except a four-cylinder engine—a 54 h.p. Gray Phantom—was being used. The 1934 price also took a healthy drop, as the model that season sold for $625 complete. Many boat builders took healthy cuts in price toward the end of the Depression just to keep sales going and stay in business. Here is a full-size photo from the 1934 catalog showing you the Level Riding 16-foot runabout. A 16-foot cedar strip slit-cockpit runabout was also offered in 1933-34. The cedar strip model was 16-feet long and came with either a 50 or 54 h.p. Universal or Gray engine. That boat sold complete for $645. An enlargement of the catalog material for that boat is shown here.

By 1937 Thompson had dropped all inboard building in favor of more popular and less costly sailboats. In the remaining years of Thompson's heyday, they built mostly outboard and I.O. power boats. Wooden canoes disappeared eventually, and the firm went heavy into wooden lapstrake boats and cruisers.

Today all Thompson boats are "glass" but the hull sides resemble lapstrake designs, probably a fall back to the late 1950s and '60s when Thompson lapstrake wooden boats were big time.

Thompson Brothers Boat Mfg. Company never built the variety of inboards like Dunphy, Century or Chris-Craft, but they did at least build some.

The next firm we shall review will be the Midwest Boat Company that was located also in Wisconsin, at Neenah, on the shores of Lake Winnebago.

MIDWEST BOAT COMPANY
of Neenah, Wisconsin

Here we go again, friends, to another one of those tiny, unknown boat builders that built a fine looking "Real Runabout." My very good friends, Ed and Marcella Lewin of Mound, Minnesota, back in 1978 picked up a rather unique split-cockpit runabout. If you will look at the photo shown here you will see a nice varnished runabout that at first glance resembles a Century or Chris-Craft from about 1940 or so. Well, this little runabout is neither of those brands, but was built by the Midwest Boat Company of Neenah, Wisconsin.

Say you never heard of that brand of boat? Well, neither had I. Ed has tried researching the firm a little, but has not had the best luck in doing so. Here are the facts as he knows them.[6] The boat was built starting in 1941 but not completed until 1946, after the end of World War II. The owner before Lewin only knew the boat was a one-of-a-kind, and it was supposed to be a scaled down version of a 1928-29 27-foot Hacker-Craft runabout.

Ed tells me the woodwork and general workmanship on the boat is excellent. I saw the boat back in 1979,

1947 17' Midwest Boat Company of Neenah, Wisconsin 100 h.p. (flat-head) Mercury motor.

---
[6]Letter, Ed Lewin, 8/26/79.

when it took part in our Land-O-Lakes Chapter of ACBS, Inc. Boat Show up at Lake Minnetonka, where it drew plenty of attention. The hull currently is finished all natural, with no stain. Ed plans to refinish the boat soon and at that time he plans to stain the hull sides, decks and transom, and finish the king plank and covering boards in black walnut. The 100 h.p. Flat-Head Mercury V-8 engine is the original power plant. At idle speeds the engine does like to overheat a little, which makes it a little difficult to operate the boat in water parades, etc. All in all, though, Ed and Marcella are proud of their "Midwest," and I am very happy they shared material on it with us.

From the short review of Midwest Boat Company we now move on to Stan Craft Corporation of Polson, Montana. Stan Craft boats have to be among the most unique-looking inboards ever built. Most stayed right in Montana or nearby, as all were sold factory-direct over the years. Interest in antique boating has taken hold again out in Montana, with their second annual antique and class wooden boat show being held in July, 1984. Of all boats I have reviewed in a long time, the Stan Crafts, especially the Torpedo designs, have really caught my fancy. I hope you will be as impressed with Stan Crafts as I have become, and wait until you read at the end of the article what is happening to the son of the founder of the firm today! You can be assured that in Volume VI you shall read more about Stan Craft inboards, but the runabouts discussed in Volume VI will be *new* Stan Crafts, not old ones restored.

STAN-CRAFT CORPORATION
of Polson, Montana

If you are like this writer, Montana conjures up visions of buffalo, Indians and beautiful scenic lands, correct? Well, that's just what I thought, but over the last three or four years, a close friendship has developed between myself and the Reverend Gary Cockrell of Kalispell, Montana. Gary and his wife manage a Lutheran Summer Youth Camp on the shores of beautiful Flathead Lake in far northwestern Montana. Now, I tell you, Flathead Lake has to be one of the all-time best kept secrets in this whole 50 states. By the time you read this, I hope to visit Flathead Lake to take part in their second annual wooden antique boat show. Reverend Cockrell was one of the "spark plugs" of the club, getting a small group of wooden boat fans together there to put on a show that would rival many held in much more populous locations—but more about that later.

I am not sure how many of you recall seeing the small photo on page 178 of Volume II of *The Real Runa-*

Stan Young shown enjoying his own 62' ketch. He built the craft himself and sails in lower Baja waters.

bouts. It is a side view of a 1947 22-foot Stan Craft torpedo runabout. At that time I knew some day I wanted to cover that firm in more detail, when and if I could find the material and photos to use. Well, it took almost five years before connections were made through the following good friends: Gary Cockrell, Stan Young (founder of the original Stan Craft Boat Company), and his son Sydney H. Young now of Post Falls, Idaho. It's people like the three named above who make my work so interesting as well as exciting every day. Syd, as he is known by his friends, interviewed his dad, Stan, and I shall just retell the story here mostly in his own words, with a few added bits of information that Gary provided me. I think you are going to find the Stan-Craft story an exciting one when you see the vast selection of models, sizes and designs the Youngs turned out during the 33 years they built wooden pleasure boats.

In the year 1933 Stan Young, then in his Senior year of High School, completed construction on his own

1933 25' Stan-Craft *Arrow* 3-cockpit runabout—powered by a Buick straight 8 engine. This first 1933 *Arrow* hauled passengers on Flathead Lake for about six years.

Special · See Flathead Lake by Boat

This fast ten passenger Runabout will take you on a 30 minute trip ❖ Evening or day

Rates for Some of the Trips From Elks' State Camp

Angel Point - - $ .25
Flathead River - .50
Wild Horse Island 1.00
Melita Island - - 1.25
Polson - - - 2.00
Around Flathead Lake, Down East shore returning West shore 2.50

These rates are per person for party of ten.

Special trips by reservation.

Flathead Lake is the largest body of fresh water west of the Great Lakes. You will enjoy every minute of your trip on this beautiful body of water. The evening and moonlight trips in the "Land of the Shining Mountains" you will long remember. Don't go through the Flathead and miss one of these trips.

For further information write, phone or wire

Elks' State Camp or Stanley Young, Somers, Montana

sleek, 25-foot 3-cockpit runabout. Little did that young man know that the original Arrow, as he called her, would eventually lead to a lifetime in boat building.

That first boat was powered by a Buick straight eight engine. Because of the placement of that huge engine, there was a single front cockpit, rather than the usual two seats, then the engine with two cockpits behind that. When you look at the photo shown here of a rare old poster used by Stan in those days to advertise his speed boat rides, you may fail to notice the unusual cockpit layout, just as I did. Note the prices Stan charged back then. Wish we could get speedboat rides for those rates today! The Arrow continued to be operated by Stan Young until 1936 or so.

In 1937 the Stan-Craft Boat Company was formed, owned and operated by Stanley C. Young for a period of time from 1937 until about 1970. Mr. Young built his very first boat in 1929, a class "B" Hydroplane of the outboard variety. Stan was one of the founders of the Montana Boat Racing Association in 1935. During the years from 1935 through 1937, Stan built a number of very fine mahogany runabouts as well as some racing craft. In 1937 a new shop was built by Stan, and his boat

RARE 1935 18' runabout pulling someone on a "Free-Board."

21

1933 Stan-Craft *Arrow* 25' runabout

1937 18' Stan-Craft runabout

1935 19' Stan-Craft Honduras mahogany runabout powered by a Scripps V-8.

1944 21' 8" original Stan-Craft Torpedo built in Seattle, Washington. Designed and built by Stan Young, driver.

Beautifully restored 1948 21' 8" Stan-Craft Torpedo owned by Chad and Frank Thomas of Kalispell, Montana. Powered by 115 h.p. Chrysler.

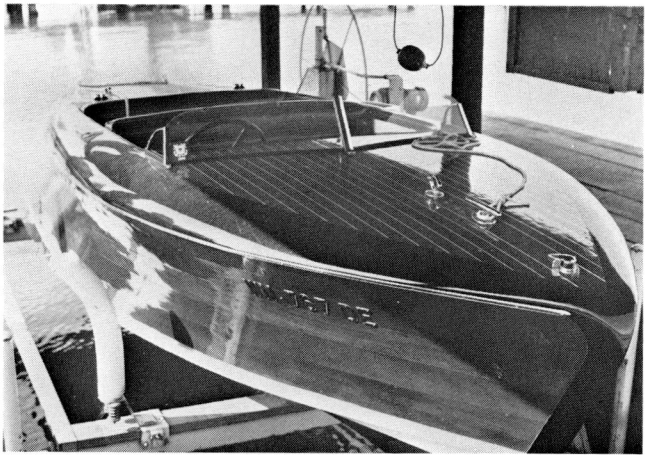

Possibly first Stan-Craft Torpedo built, still in use near Seattle, Washington.

Full speed ahead! 1946 21', hull #01 Stan-Craft—160 h.p. Gray Fireball on Flathead Lake, Montana.

1946 21' Stan-Craft Torpedo

Custom Stan-Craft Torpedo built during 1951-52.

business was "launched" in a formal manner. At first he built several different styles of inboard runabouts, as well as Snipe class sailboats. With the advent of World War II in 1941, the boat business closed down and Stan went to Seattle, Washington, where he became general manager of Shain's Boat Yard. At that location Young helped build 26', 38', 45' and 65' vessels used in the war effort. Following the eventual conclusion of the war, Stan returned back to Flathead Lake, Montana, and re-opened his boat business once more. In the years right after the war, Stan built and sold beautiful 21'6" Torpedo runabouts, along with 25' cabin cruisers.

For you readers not familiar with Flathead Lake, here are some facts on its site. The lake is 28 miles long, 15 miles across, and has a shoreline of 185 miles, so you can tell this is no pond. Boats used on Flathead have to be big, deep, fast and safe. Like Tahoe to the west, Flathead, too, can go from a perfect calm to 5-foot seas in just minutes under adverse weather conditions. Sur-

Snappy Stan-Craft Torpedo shows her stuff—1954 model.

1956 21' 8" Stan-Craft Torpedo, Hemi powered.

1954 Torpedo by Stan-Craft

Beautiful 21' 8" Stan-Craft Torpedo with blonde covering boards and king planks.

Another sleek Stan-Craft 21' 8" Torpedo equipped with planing extensions on the aft section—1954-'56.

Idling along aboard one of the last Stan-Craft Torpedo runabouts, 22 feet long and built in 1954, now owned by Gary Cockrell.

prisingly enough, Stan-Craft boats built over the years stayed right there or close by. Few ever got far away from their home lake. Gary Cockrell spends whatever free time he may have, when not busy with the camp operations, trying to track down the old boats. To date he has found some and has leads on others. Stan Young, now retired, has been very kind in helping provide Gary with company sales records, etc., to help complete the story of this firm.

From 1937 through 1966 (when Stan-Craft no longer built wooden boats), Stan Young said the company had built about 250 mahogany boats of various sizes. I hope you enjoy the photos following, tracing the revolution of the Stan-Craft from 1933 up through the middle 1960s. I have included a few cabin cruiser photos in this section also to show how versatile the Stan-Craft builders really were. In fact, Gary Cockrell tells me there are quite a number of older cruisers built in the

1938 18' double cockpit Stan-Craft runabout powered by Chrysler Ace.

Stern-view of 1938 18' Stan-Craft runabout.

1938 19' Stan-Craft—original owner, R. B. Frazier of the Annaconda Copper Company in Butte, Montana.

Late 1930s 15' mahogany Stan-Craft outboard runabout.

Stan-Craft Marina during season of 1937-38. Lots of activity taking place!

Late 1930s 20' Stan-Craft runabout—one-of-a-kind.

1939 Stan-Craft split-cockpit runabout powered by a 160 h.p. Gray Fireball.

1951 view showing 21' aluminum-clad work boats built for the National Park Service. Marina and boat plant in back of boats.

1951 18½' utility by Stan-Craft, powered by a Chrysler Crown.

1939, Stan-Craft's docks and harbor are protected at all times from wind and storms. The lake has 300 miles of shoreline.

Here are Stanley Young and two of his creations, powered by Scripps V-8 direct-drive engines in 1939.

18½' Stan-Craft utilities built from 1948 through 1954. Most powered by Chrysler Crown and Ace engines.

One of about 30 18½' Stan-Craft utilities built in the years from 1955 to 1965. Nearly all powered by Interceptors.

A hit of the first Flathead Lake, Montana, Wooden Boat Show in 1983. Gary Cockrell is the proud owner of this beauty!

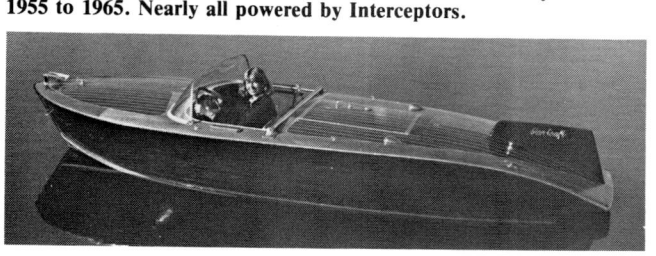

Rare and nicely restored 1954-55 17-foot Stan-Craft Beaver Tail runabout. Hidden rear seat covered by hatch just ahead of tail fin.

17' Beaver Tail Stan-Craft runabout. Clocked at 50 m.p.h. with 215 h.p. Interceptors. Designed in 1946, built three *each* in 1954-'55.

1957 21' Deluxe Sedan runabout, powered by a 215 h.p. Interceptor.

1957 26' Day Cruiser—Twin Chrysler Crowns.

1958 26' Express Cruisers powered by Twin Chrysler Crowns.

1949 25' Stan-Craft enclosed cabin cruiser.

1951 25' Stan-Craft Day Cruiser single Chrysler Crown, 115 h.p..

1951 34' Twin ACBS Dual Station Cruiser.

1953 32' twin-screw Stan-Craft Sedan cruiser.

1957 34' Dual Station, twin Chrysler Crown powered Express Cruisers.

late '40s through the late '59s still in use every year on Flathead with excellent results.

Stan-Craft also built hundreds of 14-foot fishing boats, as well as many 21-foot metal-clad work boats for the national parks, plus Sea Plane tenders for the navy and over 500 M-2 Assault boats for the army. A full-service marina was also operated by Stan-Craft from 1937 through 1980.

In 1969 the business was taken over by Sydney H. Young, oldest son of Stan. In the years from 1970 to 1980, Syd sold 100 each of 19' and 26' fiberglass boats. Then because of a depressed boating industry, Syd sold the firm and went into other work. Thus, another fine, regional wooden boat business disappeared forever—or did it?

I will tell you right here, that Sydney Young of the new Stan-Craft Boat Company, Inc. of Post Falls, Idaho, is now back in the wooden boat business. Syd has begun building a 25-foot 3-cockpit mahogany Arrow runabout along the lines of his dad's first Arrow, with many advanced features not found on that first boat. I shall cover the "new" Stan-Craft runabout in Volume VI, but will tell you here and now that it is a beauty! If you want more details now, why not write or call Syd at the following address? Tell him you read about his boats in *The Real Runabouts, Volume V*.

> Sydney H. Young
> Stan-Craft Boat Company, Inc.
> North 865 Highland Court
> Post Falls, Idaho 83854

A big thanks once more to Stan, Syd and Gary for all their help on Stan-Craft. I think everyone will agree that they made some very interesting speedboats during their years in business. Our next stop will be the Morehouse Boat Company located in upstate New York who also built a lot of fine power boats.

MOREHOUSE BOAT COMPANY
Cayuga Lake, New York

I love to keep learning about new, smaller regional boat builders which dotted the map all over this country 40 or 50 years ago. Charles Knight of Saratoga Springs, New York, took it upon himself to provide me with history on Morehouse boats that were made on the shores of Cayuga Lake, New York.

According to Charles Knight,[7] Bob and Dick Morehouse (now deceased) took over the family restaurant and boat livery business after the end of World War II and began building boats about that same time. Their dad had built some boats in earlier days, but Dick and Bob went into it on a much larger scale. They started out building 14-foot rowboats and small outboard cedar strip runabouts. Like Century, Thompson, Wolverine, and a lot of others, the fellows also built Lightning and Comet sailboats, plus an inboard utility on special order.

---
[7]Letter, Charles Knight, March, 1983.

18½' Morehouse standard utility inboard.

Only 22' Morehouse twin cockpit runabout ever built.

20-foot Morehouse cedar strip inboard utility, mid-1950s.

1982 view of Charles Knight's 18' Morehouse utility.

Charles Knight's 18½' Morehouse mahogany utility.

Charles Knight's 18½' Morehouse with newer windshield.

All inboards built over the years were 18'6" or 20' models, with the exception of the one 22' twin-cockpit model shown here. The 22-footer was powered with a 145 h.p. Hercules ML engine. The 18' and 20' models had 95 h.p. 6-cylinder Hercules K engines. Most of the inboards were built of solid mahogany, though some were cedar hulls painted white and red, with mahogany decks which were varnished.

Morehouse boats have become quite rare, with most being found on the New York Finger Lakes and elsewhere in that general area. Charles Knight owns the 18' Morehouse all-varnished utility shown here. He tells me that many of the older Morehouse inboards had their old "V" style windshields replaced with Taylor-Attwood wraparound plastic windshields over the years. All the varnished Morehouse inboards and most of the painted ones were equipped with bright blue upholstery that contrasted nicely with the varnished decks, hull sides and transoms. Charles Knight advises that maybe a hundred Morehouse inboards still exist, while outboards of various types are a bit more numerous than that. Chris-Craft instruments were used with all Morehouse inboards.

I really hope you enjoy material on these lesser known inboard builders as much as I do. Thanks, Charles Knight, for sharing material on your fine Morehouse, as well as others.

With the completion of our reviews of Chapter One, we shall now move on to Chapter Two where we will review eight more Canadian runabout builders, all of which were basically small, regional builders, but firms who built various types of launches and runabouts that I am sure everyone will find of interest. I appreciate all our Canadian friends who have shared with us photos, history and news of antique boating and boat builders north of the border. I only hope they enjoy reading about many of the U.S. boat builders we have reviewed in these last four inboard volumes. Let's now head north. The firm we shall first look at was located across the river from Algonac, Michigan. Mac Craft Boat Company is really a unique story. You will note that photos showing their boats looked almost like twins with Chris-Crafts of the same vintage and design. I think you will really enjoy Mac-Craft; they are a rare boat today. No more than a handful are known to be still in running order.

CHAPTER II
More Canadian Speedboat Builders of the Past

About five years ago a very dear man from Wallaceburg, Ontario, wrote to ask whether or not I had ever heard of a Mac-Craft inboard. Well, being honest, I had to say "no." I was familiar with Mac Bay Boats and a Mac Boats formerly of Des Moines or Ames, Iowa, but no Mac-Craft line of Canadian mahogany inboards.

Since that first letter Alan Mann, his son Blake, and I have become good pen pals, keeping in touch quite regularly through the mails. Al has taken it upon himself to be my "eyes and ears" up in the Wallaceburg, Ontaria, area and the following article, reproduced here in Al's own words, is the result of several years of diligent research and writing. This story is so well done and well illustrated that I feel it can stand on its own. You be the judge.

One of the most exciting things about Al Mann's interest in old wooden boats is that he and Blake found an old 21' Mac-Craft utility, and during 1982-83 completely restored the boat and use it every year up in their beautiful portion of Canada. Mann recently reported that he has since discovered a very rare Mac-Craft runabout which he hopes to also buy and restore to its former glory and make it the No. 2 boat in his "fleet." It's news like that which really excites me! My work on these books is all worth the hours, days, weeks and months spent on them when I hear from folks who were encouraged after reading these books to go out and buy their first "woody" to restore and now they wouldn't trade it for all the "plastic" boats ever built.

If you know of any Mac-Craft inboards available—in any condition, good or bad—please contact the Mann's at the following Club address as they hope to catalog material on every possible Mac-Craft that still exists.

MAC-CRAFT BOAT CLUB
171 Margaret Avenue
Dept. #5
Wallaceburg, Ontario, Canada N8A 2A3
(519) 627-3296

Well, on to the Mac-Craft story. If you are like me you will be amazed when you read the interesting history of the firm who said, "Builders of Canada's Finest Motor Boats."

MAC-CRAFT CORPORATION LTD. WALLACEBURG, ONTARIA

Eric MacDonald of Wallaceburg, Ontario, saw the need for a Canadian-built pleasure craft that would speedily transport boaters to the many recreational areas within the St. Clair River and Lake area. In addition, he felt there were wide possibilities for the sale of such craft across the country. As a result he explored the feasibility of establishing a local boat building firm that would fill the apparent need. He was convinced of the ultimate success of such a venture, thus in 1938 he established the Mac-Craft Corporation Ltd., with headquarters in Wallaceburg, a few short miles from the "giant" of the industry, the Chris-Craft Corporation of Algonac, Michigan.

J. Eric MacDonald, Company Founder

Mac-Craft Wallaceburg, Ontario

BUILDERS OF CANADA'S FINEST MOTOR BOATS

Mac-Craft Stationery Head

Beginning in a modest way, the company began operations on August 8th, 1938, in a small building on the banks of the Sydenham River near downtown Wallaceburg. John Laba, now retired and living in the Toronto area, recalled that he was the first "local" hired by the firm. Roy Solgot of Marine City, Michigan, was named as superintendent and layout man, while Harold "Tony" Welser, another former Chris-Craft worker, joined the staff at the same time.

The first Mac-Craft plant opened in 1938 was extremely small allowing the completion of only one boat at a time. Soon, company founder Eric MacDonald realized that larger quarters were needed. As a result the firm moved to a new location on Nelson Street.

1940 Mac-Craft (Wallaceburg) some of the workers in front of recently completed runabout. Photo in front of Nelson Street plant.

A pool of skilled boatbuilders was readily available in the area. A decade previously, the Ontario Boat & Engine Works, producers of the "Wild Cat" series of runabouts, was in operation in Wallaceburg. In addition, skilled craftsmen were available from the nearby Michigan area. Wallaceburg itself has been a shipbuilding center during the last century and the first quarter of the 20th century, thus creating a maritime heritage that began during the lumber boom days and has continued ever since.

In addition to several local craftsmen, two more Marine City residents, Fred Stevenson and Fred Johnston, were soon brought into the Mac-Craft fold. Before his death in 1983, Roy Solgot, the first superintendent, recalled that all the Marine City men involved with Mac-Craft had many years of accumulated service With Chris-Craft of Algonac and were skilled in various aspects of boatbuilding.

Within two months of the company's opening the first prototype was ready for launching. Founder Eric MacDonald designed the first craft, a 17-foot mahogany runabout. On October 27, 1938, a large crowd of interested townsfolk watched as the first Mac-Craft slid into the waters of the nearby Sydenham River. Proud plant workers clapped with approval as the 4-cylinder Gray Phantom power plant was turned over. Mac-Craft was off and running!

Two Mac-Craft 17-foot utility runabouts are shown during publicity photographs taken in connection with a brochure. They were powered by four-cylinder Gray motors and cruised comfortably at 20 m.p.h.

Eric MacDonald saw the potential for the ultimate success of the firm as he traveled to various boat shows, promoting the Mac-Craft line of pleasure boats. An open line of communication was maintained with the Smith brothers, owners of Chris-Craft Corporation, with the interchange of ideas common. All the shafts and props for Mac-Craft products were purchased from Chris-Craft. In fact, close scrutiny of both Mac-Craft and Chris-Craft products of the late 1930s reveals marked similarities. Several decades later purists insist that Mac-Crafts were direct copies of the Chris-Craft line of boats. Whether this came about by accident or otherwise cannot be determined; however, there is no doubt they

The popular 26-foot enclosed cruiser built by Mac-Craft, closely resembled the 25-foot Chris-Craft Streamline Cruiser. This model christened Helen Rose was built for H. W. Burgess, founder of the Wallaceburg Brass and Iron Manufacturing Company, a firm that supplied the hardware accessories for the Mac-Craft Company. Daniel Oliver of North York, Ontario, recently purchased the Helen Rose and is presently restoring her.

Paris Lee was a direct descendant of James Paris Lee, inventor of the world famous Lee-Enfield rifle. He was test driver for Mac-Craft and is shown trying out a new 18-foot utility. Dean MacDonald, son of the company founder is in the rear seat in this 1939 scene.

Company founder Eric MacDonald rides in the rear seat during a demonstration run in a 21-foot utility built for the Martin brothers, Ray, left and Lawrence. This craft was hull No. 2 and was restored in 1983 by Alan and Blake Mann.

17' Mac-Craft utility posing for brochure photograph.

were at least "international cousins."

Eric MacDonald soon realized that his time would be best spent with the promotional and business end of the operation. An office staff was hired, also three more skilled boatbuilders formerly with Greavette Boats Ltd. of Gravenhurst in northern Ontario. One of the new workers was George Vandenbossche who later left Mac-Craft and formed his own boat building plant in Wallaceburg—"Van-Craft." The most important new addition to the staff was another Marine City resident, Napolean "Nap" Lisee. Recently retired from Gar Wood's employ after 30 years, Lisee was hired as Mac-Craft's marine architect and designer. Lisee was known internationally as the designer of all of Gar Wood's Miss America racing hulls, long time holder of the Harmsworth Trophy and world unlimited speed record holder. With the hiring of Nap Lisee, the "Marine City Connection" was formed with Mac-Craft, as several residents of this old St. Clair River town became associated with the Wallaceburg operation. Garnet DeCou and "Cap" Belfor, also of Marine City, worked during the day shift at Chris-Craft and in the evening "moonlighted" by crossing over to Wallaceburg to work at Mac-Craft as finishers. A unique situation developed with citizens from both sides of the international border combining to establish an industry in the area "where it all began."

By 1939 it became obvious that the popularity of the Mac-Craft boats coincided with the need for larger facilities. Thus the new firm moved into larger quarters on the north side of Wallaceburg at the same location where the Ontario Boat & Engine Works was centered a few years before. The Mac-Craft Corporation was now ready to compete on a larger scale with its competitors.

In the summer of 1939 the company opened a new line of operation: the production of cruisers. Lisee had designed a 26-foot enclosed cruiser that closely resembled Chris-Crafts 25-foot Streamline Cruiser. The new Mac-Craft cruiser featured white hull sides with Philippine mahogany natural finished decks, cabin sides, trimming and interior. The cabin top canvas was finished with special Bermuda blue deck paint while ample brass hardware and fitting gave the cruiser an air of elegance. With headroom of 6½ feet, nealy 9 feet of beam, and a dining nook that could easily be converted into sleeping quarters, the new cruiser was a sight to behold! In addition, Mac-Craft introduced a beautiful 31-foot cruiser with prospects for additional models later. The 31-foot model basically resembled the 26-foot version.

The runabout phase of Mac-Craft offered a wide range including utilities that proved adaptable for the many fishermen in the area. Nap Lisee's 1939 designs included 15-, 17-, and 21-foot utilities and 19- and 21-foot runabouts, the latter two models featuring a sporty tapered stern. A 22-foot hard top utility was available, as well as optional special mahogany-framed windshields and top supports on the utilities. Both Gray and Chrysler Marine power plants were utilized in Mac-Crafts with varied power options available in all models. The runabouts featured fold down styled windscreens as well as dark king planks on the decks. Mac-Crafts had white oak frames, keels (which were hand chiseled) and chines. Three-quarter inch Philippine mahogany was used for the bottoms while five-eighths inch planking formed the sides. MacDonald owned the nearby Consolidated Lumber Company where all wood was supplied. A contract was negotiated with the Wallaceburg Brass Company to design and produce the necessary hardware and fittings.

A local sales outlet was opened in the front portion of the Nelson Street factory. The first "out of town" agency was opened in Windsor, Ontario (across from Detroit). Tony Welser, now retired and living in Marine City, recalled that his role at Mac-Craft was twofold: he was in charge of motor installations and mechanical aspects, as well as responsible for delivering the completed hulls to the Windsor sales outlet.

Napolean "Nap" Lisee was designer of the Mac-Craft line of boats. He was associated with Gar Wood for 30 years designing all the Miss America's of racing fame and in addition designed the Gar Sr., the world's fastest express cruiser in its time.

The "J.J.J." a sporty 18-foot sport runabout built by Mac-Craft in 1940. Powered by a 125 h.p. Gray, this speedy craft was one of the most popular of the Mac-Craft line.

"J.J.J." owned by Alex McIntyre, Wallaceburg, Ontario—a 1940 18-foot Mac-Craft sports runabout.

The popular 21-foot utility is shown shortly after its purchase in 1938. Forty-five years later she was restored and brought back to her original appearance and can be seen regularly in the St. Clair River area. Restored by Blake and Alan Mann, 1982-83.

The Royal Canadian Mounted Police, Marine Patrol used a 21-foot Mac-Craft utility in connection with their patrol duties in the Wallaceburg area. The officers are shown patrolling in the Sydenham River, Wallaceburg, in 1942 during a visit by the Detroit Yacht Club.

It became obvious that owning a Mac-Craft was a symbol of prestige. Several Wallaceburg and area boat lovers placed orders, including the president of the Wallaceburg Brass Company who ordered a specially fitted enclosed 26-foot cruiser. Even government officials realized the meticulous workmanship and stability of Mac-Crafts. Both the area game warden and the local detachment of the Royal Canadian Mounted Police utilized Mac-Craft highly powered utility runabouts in the course of their duties.

With the world conditions worsening in late 1939, a gloom soon pervaded the pleasure boat industry across North America. However, this turned out to be somewhat of a blessing in disguise for Mac-Craft albeit for a short period of time. William G. Ogilvie was a well established yacht broker in Toronto since 1938. With the onset of war, the importation of foreign-built craft was prohibited, so Ogilvie was suddenly deprived of his main item of trade—Chris-Crafts. On a chance visit to Wallaceburg in 1939, Ogilvie heard about the new line of pleasure craft being produced by the Mac-Craft Corporation. The firm's credibility was unquestioned when Ogilvie heard that Nap Lisee was company designer. Ogilvie recalled in a 1983 interview that he was duly impressed upon seeing the Mac-Craft line. The style and workmanship was very similar to Chris-Crafts that he had been retailing in the Toronto area for years. Soon a contract was signed and a continued cordial relationship was begun with Wallaceburg's Mac-Craft Corporation. Ogilvie became distributor, thus filling a void in his business and at the same time giving Mac-Craft welcome exposure in Toronto, Canada's large metropolitan area. William Ogilvie retired in 1974 after a wide range of experience in boating, including manager of the Disappearing Propeller Boat Company in Port Carling, Ontario. His yacht brokerage founded in 1929 continues under the banner of Ogilvie-Bloss Ltd., Port Credit, Ontario.

Through 1940 and early 1941 the firm continued production. However, it was obvious that pleasure boating would have to take a respite while the more important matters on the war front were considered. The government of Canada urgently required smaller craft for coastal surveillance, rescue work and auxiliary duties. The long standing skill of the various pleasure boat builders was recognized when contracts were awarded to various companies. The Midland Boat Works, J. J. Taylor of Toronto, Grew Boat Works of Penetanguishene, as well as Port Carling Boat Works and Greavette Boats of Gravenhurst assisted in this effort. Mac-Craft Corporation of Wallaceburg was included when the contracts were doled out.

Launching of Fairmile QO62 at Sarnia, Ontario, 1942. Built by Mac-Craft Corporation.

22-foot Hardtop Utility Sedan, being shipped out of Mac-Craft Wallaceburg plant in 1941.

Mac-Craft workers on deck of completed QO63, 1943.

Eric MacDonald's first love, the pleasure boat line, had enjoyed tremendous success in the 3½ years of the company's operation. However, he was eager to do his part for the war effort. Mac-Craft was given a contract to build two 112-foot "B" class fairmiles to be used in convoy duty between Newfoundland and the mainland of Canada. As the relatively narrow confines of the Sydenham River in Wallaceburg presented a problem with the building of vessels so large, it was decided to move the firm to Sarnia, Ontario, 33 miles north. Site chosen was a former Sarnia distillery conveniently located in the harbor area where launching facilities were readily available. In addition, nearby Lake Huron was convenient for test runs. All machinery, equipment, parts and partially completed craft at the Wallaceburg operation were shipped to Sarnia in 1941. The new site was close enough for the Wallaceburg workers to commute although several decided to take up residence in Sarnia. Nap Lisee maintained his Marine City residence and commuted to Sarnia daily.

Mac-Craft, Sarnia, Ontario ad—1942.

QO62—trial run on St. Clair River, Sarnia, Ontario, 1943.

The pleasure boat phase of Mac-Craft, however, was not neglected as the new war vessels took shape. Mrs. Ada Furtah of Wallaceburg recalled in a 1983 interview that her husband's new 26-foot Mac-Craft cruiser was started in Wallaceburg, transferred to Sarnia with the move, and eventually completed there. She recalls that during the summer of 1942 their cruiser christened *Elzette*, was launched from the Mac-Craft stocks in Sarnia and proudly headed south on the St. Clair River. A beautiful 18-foot utility, formerly owned by a

Sarnia Mac-Craft plant completed QO62 in foreground, 1943.

The last Mac-Craft produced was finished in the Sarnia plant in 1946. Formerly owned by a retired court judge in Marine City, Michigan, the 18-foot utility runabout was purchased by Brad and Steve Randall of Corunna, Ontario and restored in 1981. 1982 view.

magistrate judge in Marine City and restored in 1982 by the Randall brothers of Corunna, Ontario, was the last Mac-Craft pleasure boat completed by the Sarnia firm in 1946.

Ill health forced Nap Lisee to resign his position in 1942. In his place Martin Beebe of Port Huron was named as general superintendent. Beebe and his father John Beebe, a former Gar Wood official, supervised the installation of engines at the Sarnia Mac-Craft operation. The firm continued the production of pleasure craft but on a much reduced scale with the war contract taking due precedence. Martin Beebe designed the remaining Mac-Crafts produced in the Sarnia plant.

In 1942, William Ogilvie closed his Toronto yacht brokerage for the duration of the war. He was then appointed to the staff of the Federal Inspection Board which included supervision of the various boat building firms in Ontario that were engaged in war contracts. Mac-Craft in Sarnia was under his jurisdiction. Upon Ogilvie's recommendation, company owner Eric MacDonald hired Bert Minett, founder of the Minett-Shields Boat Building firm of Bracebridge, Ontario (see *The Real Runabouts, Vol. III*). Minett was hired as layout man at Mac-Craft and was known far and wide for his fastidious workmanship while producing those beautiful Muskoka Lakes craft that are coveted by collectors today. His skill and expertise lent a brilliant touch to the Mac-Craft operation although his emphasis was now on speed of production which contrasted with a long time philosophy of careful and meticulous workmanship.

Annual Speedboat Races on Sydenham River, Wallaceburg, Ontario, 1943. July 1st, Dominion Day. All local Mac-Crafts took part.

As World War II wound down, Mac-Craft indeed had made an important contribution to the war effort. Two fairmiles, six vessels of the "Q" series, and two minesweepers, a total of 10 craft were produced. As well the company produced numerous pontoon bridgings, a most impressive total contribution to the ultimate success for the Allied victory. As a humorous sideline late in the war, Mac-Craft was converged upon by the Royal Canadian Mounted Police as well as F.B.I. High frequency equipment used in connection with the glueing process was emitting radio impulses that for some reason was jamming air craft communication over New York City. It was thought by U.S. officials that someone was sabotaging the communication network, thus a thorough investigation was launched in attempts to pinpoint the source. Eventually Mac-Craft of Sarnia was determined as being responsible, and once the situation was explained the problem was soon rectified.

Following the cessation of hostilities, Mac-Craft completed a few more pleasure boats. Restoration and repair work, however, now formed the bulk of the firm's operations. In 1947 Mac-Craft Corporation was purchased by General Products Manufacturing of London, Ontario. A new corporation named "Macrolite" molded 16-foot outboard hulls and became involved in other non-marine lines of work. During this period, *Miss Supertest II*, an unlimited class racing hydroplane, was

BOATING SERVICE
COMPLETE FACILITIES TO SERVE YOU AT OUR
Open May 24th **MARINA** 7 a.m.-11 p.m.

Gasoline, Diesel Oil, Lubricants, Ice and Water at our Docks.
MARINE HARDWARE AND ACCESSORIES

See Our New 20-foot Runabouts
Make This Your Boating Headquarters

MAC CRAFT INDUSTRIES
AND
BOX 180 **MARINA** TEL. 3172
SARNIA, ONTARIO
(At the Grain Elevator)
A Division of General Products Mfg. Corporation, Limited

1950 Mac-Craft Ad

built in the Mac-Craft plant, utilizing the expertise of plant personnel. *Miss Supertest II* represented Canada in the Gold Cup and Harmsworth racing competitions.

As a testimony to the skill of the two phases of the Mac-Craft operation between 1938 and 1947, several remnants of the firm still exist today. At this writing, 6 runabouts and two cruisers are known to have survived the many years since production ceased. In addition, one of the former 112-foot fairmiles operates each summer as the Sarnia-based excursion vessel *Duc D'Orleans*. Along with the general upsurge of interest in wooden boats, the search for original Mac-Crafts continues by those interested in bringing back the good old days when beautifully finished wooden hulls sliced through the waters. Mac-Craft historian Alan Mann and his son Blake restored hull #2, a 1938 21-foot Mac-Craft utility. A beautiful 18-foot utility owned by Shirley McIntyre of Toronto is used daily in traveling to and from her Browning Island cottage in picturesque Lake Muskoka. Used continually by her family since being purchased from William Ogilvie in 1941, the McIntyre Mac-Craft does not have to hold second place to any of the beautiful Greavettes, Ditchburns or Minetts that are so familiar in the Muskoka district.

Shirley McIntyre's 1941 18' Mac-Craft utility. Photo taken about 1950 shows original wood frame windshield and protective top frame.

This beautiful 18-foot Mac-Craft is owned by Shirley McIntyre who lives on Browning Island in Lake Muskoka, Ontario. It was purchased in 1941 from Toronto marine broker William Ogilvie and has served the McIntyre family faithfully ever since. Original purchase price was $1200 for the hull and $600 for accessories. This runabout is in immaculate condition and is a testimony to the skill of the Mac-Craft boatbuilders.

Misty-Two, 1938 21' Mac-Craft utility under full power. Owned by Alan and Blake Mann. Snye River (Chenal E Carte).

Alan and Blake Mann's 1938 21' utility with folding canvas top.

Alan and Blake Mann's 1938 21' utility without folding canvas top.

Mac-Craft has been served by many influences. Another country and particularly the community of Marine City had a great deal of positive effect on the company. Other boat building firms—Chris-Craft, Gar Wood, Greavette and Minett—all had their influence on Mac-Craft. The second war brought wide recognition of the skill of the Mac-Craft boat builders. The faith and perseverance of company founder Eric MacDonald

Early Mac-Craft step pad design.

Carl Lisee of Marine City, Michigan is son of Mac-Craft designer Nap Lisee. On first seeing Al Mann's 21-foot utility, Lisee remarked, "I can tell right away she was designed by my dad. He liked lots of beam and was constantly at odds with Gar Wood who preferred his boats long and narrow." Scene is at the 1983 Marine City Antique and Classic Boat Show.

doggedly brought the firm to its inevitable success both in peace and wartime.

"Builders of Canada's Finest Motor Boats" was the dream that was fulfilled and ultimately realized.

From Mac-Craft our next stop will be the Wallace Boat Works which was located at Rice Lake, Ontario. A special thanks goes out to Cameron W. Wilcox,, my friend who lives at Cobourg, Ontario, who gathered all the material on Wallace used here. I think you will find the following story, as relayed by Cameron Wilcox, to be a most interesting one.

WALLACE BOAT WORKS
RICE LAKE, ONTARIO

Thomas Henry Wallace was born in the year 1872 and built mostly rowboats and canoes during the early years of the his career. Tom was heavily involved in the design and building of the famous Rice Lake Canoe. He built many large, trapping canoes in his small shop in Gores Landing, Ontario, but was best known for his racing canoes of the early 1900s. Tom won his class in the North American Canoe Championships, paddling a canoe of his own design and construction while smoking his pipe and stopping for a drink of water from the lake while the race was being held.

Fortunately, a lot of Tom Wallace's accomplishments are preserved for future generations in a museum in the Ottawa, Ontario, area. 1932 saw the first Wallace mahogany runabout being constructed. That craft was a 25-foot displacement runabout fitted with three cockpits. Two other runabouts of similar design were built by Wallace prior to the start of World War II. During the war Tom went back to building canoes; he also purchased a piece of lakefront land where he eventually located the Wallace Boat Works in the marine business which included storage and repairs. A photo here shows the firm's location before signs, docks and sheds were built.

1932 25' 3-cockpit displacement runabout built by Thomas A. Wallace.

Left to right: Thomas Henry Wallace, Lyle Wallace (son), close friend who worked at Wallace Boat Works, George Harris—still alive and builds canoes on Rice Lake.

1950 launch built by Lyle Wallace being removed from shop.

Early view of Wallace Boat Works, about 1935, before "Wallace" signs and docks were built.

Finally loaded on the trailer and ready for the water.

After Thomas Wallace's death in 1947, the business was taken over by his son Lyle who had been working at a nearby boat works, building service dinghies for the Canadian Navy. Lyle added several new docks, improved the original marine railway, and added a gas pump for the sale of fuel for boats on Rice Lake—the first gas pump on that lake.[1]

In 1950 Lyle designed and built a 20-foot modern planing mahogany inboard runabout. This runabout featured a double skin ¼" plywood bottom. It was powered by a 100 h.p. Kermath Sea Prince and traveled at an honest 35 m.p.h. That very same year another 25-foot displacement hull runabout was built by Wallace Boat Works to act as a means of travel between the Boat Works and one of the many island summer homes on Rice Lake. The 25-footer was also powered by a 100 h.p. Kermath and traveled up to 28 m.p.h. That same runabout (called *Spook Island*) still resides on Rice Lake. Cam Wilcox tells me he hopes to buy it shortly and

1950 25' 3-cockpit Wallace runabout powered by a 100 h.p. Kermath with top speed of 28 m.ph.h.

---
[1] Letter, Cameron Wilcox (Feb. 24, '84).

July 12, 1953, busy day at the docks and sheds of Wallace Boat Works.

A beautiful wooden cruiser built by Wallace Boat Works, date unknown.

Custom-built boat built by Wallace Boat Works, Rice Lake, Ontario, Canada. Note extreme amount of tumblehome.

totally restore it to its original state. Wallace inboards always featured a round bottom design which enabled the boat to bank well in the turns. One of Lyle's favorite tricks was to turn the boat sharply at high speed and run the water right along the gunwale. The above-mentioned 25-foot runabout was the last displacement hull built by the Wallace Boat Works.

During 1951-52 two 20-foot runabouts per year were completed and sold to local customers. 1953 saw Lyle design and build a 17-foot plywood runabout. This inboard was a utility model and was powered by a Ford Flat-head V-8 engine. This little baby topped out at 38 m.p.h. A 25-foot custom express cruiser was also built in 1953. The bottom was all planked of plywood while the hull sides were full length spruce. Acceptance of the 17-foot plywood utility inboard kept Wallace Boat Works busy for the next two years, completing and selling seven of that particular model. Power options for the 17-footer included either a 92 h.p. Chrysler Ace or the more familiar Kermath Sea Prince 100 h.p. model. One 20-foot version of the same plywood utility was also built, but by then boat building at Wallace Boat Works became a secondary thing as a healthy increase in boat sales, dockage and storage took up most of the firm's time.

One other plywood inboard was built. It was designed by a Higgins owner who wished for a more pronounced "V" bottom design which was always best for rough water use anywhere. In 1954 the last mahogany runabout was built by Wallace Boat Works. That boat was 20 feet long and was built for a very close family friend.

As we have seen countless times before, fiberglass and aluminum boat sales really killed off most small boat builders, starting about 1955 or so. The same thing occurred at Wallace Boat Works on Rice Lake. The last

Several Wallace launches and other inboards, taken July 12, 1953.

17-foot plywood 1953 model inboard built by the Wallace Boat Works. Very popular, well built—gave a smooth ride. Powered by Ford Flathead V-8, 38 m.p.h.

Lady Gilda being launched without engine. Built by Wallace Boat Works.

A varied assortment of Wallace boats at the firm's docks, September 6, 1953.

Beautiful all-varnished cruiser, make unknown. Photo from early 1950s.

Wallace display at Cobourg Arena. Note Kermath engine on display as well as Brydon hardware off to far right of photo. About 1953 or 1954.

20-foot plywood runabout built by Lyle Wallace about 1954. Lyle took great pride in his paint finishes.

A number of Wallace boat owners going on a picnic on August 2, 1953.

wooden boat built at Wallace slid down the railway during the summer of '55. Both Lyle and his dad had the same habit of looking down and shaking their head when things went wrong. Both men always felt wooden boats were the only way to go, neither man having much time for fiberglass pleasure boats.

Between Thomas Henry and Lyle Wallace the two men built 39 inboard runabouts. Cam Wilcox says he knows the whereabouts of at least four old Wallace inboards, and he plans to begin looking for others this summer.

The following specifications are typical of many Wallace Boat Works launches. The boat described here is the 1950 25-foot launch, *Spook Island*, that Mr. Wilcox hopes to restore.

Hull: displacement type
MATERIAL: ¾" Honduras mahogany sides
⅞" Honduras mahogany bottom
½" Honduras mahogany decks
Used ½" mahogany plugs on most all boats.
Finished with varnished decks, sides and transoms, white waterline and blue bottom paint.

Other features: brass fasteners, 100 h.p. Kermath power plant, Brydon marine hardware, stainless steel shaft, and Federal bronze props.

I hope you have enjoyed this story on Wallace Boat Works. Cameron Wilcox is to be congratulated for the fine job he has done in gathering this material. There is nothing I would rather do than learn about other boat builders. The old factory and family photos sure add a lot to these stories.

Our third Canadian builder in *Volume V* will be the Baby Wildcat Runabout that was also built in Ontario, back at Wallaceburg where Mac-Craft Boatss was also located.

ONTARIO BOAT & ENGINE WORKS
WALLACEBURG, ONTARIO

BUILT BY
ONTARIO BOAT & ENGINE WORKS
WALLACEBURG, ONTARIO

Logo used by firm.

If you have read *Volume IV* you will recall the discussion concerning the Baby Wildcat mahogany outboard runabouts made up in Canada, correct? Well, that interesting firm also built a number of mahogany inboards during their short tenure, and our job here is to look at that part of the business as well.

First of all, hats off to my good Canadian friend, Alan Mann, who has done the bulk of the research for me on the Ontario Boat & Engine Works, as he also did on Mac-Craft. I must not fail to mention that Alan's dad owned a Baby Wildcat inboard years ago, and we shall look at material on that boat.

The name Canadian Wild Cat denotes sleekness, beauty, speed and adventure. These terms appropriately described a line of pleasure craft produced by the Ontario Boat & Engine Works of Wallaceburg, Ontario, beginning in 1926. This regional firm in the St. Clair River area was close to the "hot bed" of the pleasure boat industry, the nearby Chris-Craft and Gar Wood operations located at Algonac, Michigan. In addition, the well known Hacker Crafts were produced in Mt. Clemens, another integral operation in the area often referred to "where it all began."

John Beebe, formerly of Algonac, established the new Wallaceburg industry. A skilled artisan, Beebe spent more than 30 years gaining his expertise, working under two of the "giants" of the industry, Chris Smith and Gar Wood. Eager to branch out on his own, Beebe felt that an Ontario-based operation offered many advantages, including an unlimited field for development. The Ontario Boat & Engine Works was in a position to supply Canadian lovers of boating with the highest type of speed and pleasure craft at the same prices quoted in the United States, but without the added cost of duty. In addition, a large pool of skilled woodworkers were in the immediate Ontario-Michigan area.

1927 24' Beebe "Baby Wildcat" runabout. 1940 view shows *Al* owned by Frank Mann, powered by Curtiss O-X5 Jenny.
Scene in Sydenham River, Wallaceburg (in photo my father Frank Mann, sister Mary and brothers Don and Bob. I was on the shore with my mother).

Under Beebe's guidance the Ontario Boat & Engine Works, the only operation of its kind in Ontario, began production in a former garage building. The numerous contacts John Beebe had built up over the years proved to be advantageous. Within a short time, orders came pouring in from across Canada as well as the United States. The first exported craft was a 24-foot runabout for Frank A McHugh of Wilmington, Delaware. A publicity campaign as well as participation in boat shows at Hamilton, Montreal, and Toronto brought the products wide acceptance in a short time.

C.J.B., 24-foot Wildcat built by Ontario Boat & Engine Works. Owned by Harry and C. R. Jackson.

CANADIAN WILDCAT

QUEEN OF THE WATERS
35 to 60 miles per hour

Three Standard Models, built from the finest selected Mahogany. The last word in high class Concave **V** Botton Speed Boats, powered with motors that have won a world's wide reputation.

No Duty Added to Selling Prices in Canada

3 Passenger 35 mile 17 ft Baby Wildcat Fronty motors **$1750**
7 Passenger 40 mile 24 ft. Wildcat 100 H.P. Capitol
                                   Curtis Motor complete **$2950**
10 Passenger 40 mile 31. ft Wildcat Senior 150 H.P.
                                  Scripps Motor complete **$6000**

Ontario Boat and Engine Wks.
Wallaceburg, Ont.

Late ad run by Canadian Wildcat.

The stock models of the firm included 16-foot three- and four-passenger craft with an outboard motor enclosed within a well just ahead of the transom. This phase of the firm was detailed in *The Real Runabouts, Vol. IV*. The craft, sleek in appearance and exceptionally maneuverable, was the Baby Wild Cat Jr.

A 24-foot runabout called the Wild Cat was powered with a Curtiss O-X-5 8-cylinder engine, guaranteed to speed along at 40 m.p.h. It sold for $2800 complete. The top line was the Super Wild Cat, a 28-foot runabout, powered by a 150 h.p. Scripps engine capable of speeds close to 50 m.p.h., a remarkable speed for that period of time. This model sold for $4000 complete.

All Wild Cat models were built with butternut and black ash frames, mahogany plank and decks, copper fastened and finished inside like a high grade automobile. The craft was ornately adorned with beautifully chromed brass hardware produced by the Wallaceburg Brass Company.

The 24-foot Wild Cat, referred to in publicity brochures as the "Queen of the Waters," resembled closely the Hacker Dolphin built by the Hacker Boat Company of Mt. Clemens, Michigan. Truth of the matter is, that an associate of Beebe, Harry Jackson, happened to visit Mac McCready, a friend and employee of the Hacker Company in Mt. Clemens. Conversation between the two revealed that the Hacker firm had just discontinued production of the 24-foot Dolphin model. Jackson left a deposit of $25 on two sets of frames, carted them to Wallaceburg, and turned them over to Beebe. The result was that the Wild Cat model produced by the Ontario Boat & Engine Works was basically a Dolphin look-alike. The Hacker Company was not duly concerned because the Wallaceburg firm was centered in Canada and would not be a competitive threat!

The Ontario Boat & Engine Works also produced 31-foot custom-built craft. Their prize was a 1927-built highly powered 31-foot runabout. Test driver Bob Houtekier was reputed to have coaxed a speed of 60 m.p.h. out of this prototype on the Sydenham River test course. Houtekier not only tested the various Wild Cat models but was in charge of the transport firm that carted the craft to their destinations. A record six Wild Cats were transported to the Gordon Boat Works in Bobcaygeon, Ontario, in one single transit.

Canadian boat lovers had the opportunity to view the beautiful Wild Cats at the 1927 Toronto boat show. In addition, the craft were displayed at smaller shows in Western Ontario. The craft were reputed to be second to none in design, workmanship and performance. A staff of 31 full-time workmen formed the 1928 work force of the firm. Advertisements were placed in area want ads seeking additional skilled boat builders. The assembly line of production first perfected by Chris Smith of

Algonac was utilized at the Ontario Boat & Engine Works plant. All indications pointed towards a bright future for the firm.

Tragedy struck on April 22, 1928. A devastating fire of unknown origin raced through the plant of the Ontario Boat & Engine Works. The new industry was just beginning to establish itself a very high reputation, the splendid workmanship placed in manufacturing of highly prized pleasure craft. Unfortunately, the conflagration was uncontrollable and the firm was virtually wiped out.

Thirty-five Wild Cat models had already been sold in the three and a half months of 1928. Many more orders were on the books with 115 models in various forms of production at the time of the fire. An insurance settlement allowed $125 per craft to remove smoke and minor flame damage. Several hulls had been rescued from the licking flames. Within a month the distraught John Beebe did resume production of the Wild Cats at another location, with the limited resources allowing the reduced production of two craft per day. However, the firm had suffered irreversible damage. The remaining orders were completed and within a year the firm was out of production.

As far as can be ascertained, not one hull produced by Wallaceburg's Ontario Boat & Engine Works still exists. The company that boasted "The World's Finest and Fastest Pleasure Craft" did live up to its billing, but unfortunately for all too short a time.

The fourth firm we shall review was a small one that used to be located at Magog, Quebec. The company's name was LaCaille Boat Company.

Lorne MacPherson's 1937 22' LaCaille runabout and boat house.

Last remaining LaCaille runabout built from 1920 to '39 at Magog, Quebec, Canada.

LACAILLE BOAT COMPANY
MAGOG, QUEBEC

I love to learn about interesting, new boat builders located across the world who in their day turned out some beautiful mahogany inboards. Well, Lorne C. MacPherson feels the same way and some months ago wrote me to ask if I was familiar with LaCaille inboards. I had to say I was not, so Lorne took it on himself to get material on this little known firm that was located in his home town of Magog, Quebec.

Felix LaCaille owned a local marina there in Magog, and between the years 1920 through 1939 he built a number of fine wooden boats.[2] In normal times about

---
[2]"LaCaille Boat Works Material," letter from L. C. MacPherson (Aug. 12, '83).

LaCaille Boat Works hoist with launch suspended. Early 1920s—Magog, Quebec, Canada.

1937 22' LaCaille runabout—85 h.p. Lycoming.

View of LaCaille Boat Works plant. Went out of business in 1939. Built all types and sizes of small craft.

one inboard runabout and a number of smaller outboards, rowboats, etc. were built per year. Lorne MacPherson believes his beautiful 1937 22-foot runabout is the last LaCaille runabout still in existence. Power is by a Lycoming 85 h.p., and the boat is unique for several other reasons too. First of all, there is no seam compound; between each plank Felix installed $3/16$" clear spruce spacers. The boat came equipped with electric bell, siren and retractable bumpers. It appears on the original photos sent me by Lorne, which were in color, that the King plank and covering boards are finished in a light blue color. Looking at the three photos of the restored LaCaille, one might mistake it for a Chris-Craft, except for the windshield and the split walk through front seat backs.

Two additional photos show the homemade boat lift taken in early 1920s at the LaCaille Boat Works shop. The launch in the slings is not a LaCaille however, but a launch built by a local, Philip Cummins, still alive at this writing at 98 years plus.

Though not as much history as we might like, the material on LaCaille Boats was very interesting. Canadian readers have advised that quite a few fine inboard speedboats were built in the Quebec area too, not just in the Ontario Province, so I hope to unearth further material to include in this book, if time and material arise within my schedule.

Fett Hall Boat Company of Gravenhurst, Ontario, will be our next "port o' call."

FETTHALL BOATS
GRAVENHURST, ONTARIO

Gravenhurst, Ontario, not only was the home, once, for Ditchburn and Greavette but also a smaller, lesser known inboard builder, FettHall Boats. I was unfamiliar with this particular brand of boat, but stumbled across it quite by accident while doing some other research for this book. A big "thanks" here goes out to Wm. G. (Bill) Ogilvie, one of the true "deans" of wooden boating in all of Canada. Bill has been involved in all aspects of the industry, including building and selling the Dippy Boats back in the 1920s, as well as being a yacht broker and new boat dealer down through the years. Though being retired since 1973, Bill still keeps a weather eye on boats and boating in his beloved nation, Canada. Through several very interesting letters, Bill Ogilvie helped fill me in on the study of this little known Canadian builder of wooden inboards.

The two men who formed FettHall Boats in 1929 were Bill Hall (his name was actually Wilfred) and Dave Fettes. Bill designed and built the boats while Dave handled the engine installations. In 1929 the two men concentrated on producing just one model, a 17-foot V-bottom mahogany runabout powered by a Van Blerck Jr. 25 h.p. I.O. type engine. This first twin cockpit runabout could reach speeds of 25 m.p.h. As Bill Ogilvie told me, those first 25 h.p. Van Blerck engines worked out very well and FettHall sold quite a few of that first 17-foot runabout. In 1930 Van Blerck upped the horsepower of the engine to 35 and all kinds of trouble began to occur. The added horsepower was more than the lightweight, aluminum Van Blerck could stand, and before very long customers were waiting in line to return damaged or destroyed engines. FettHall Boats stood behind their product which eventually caused them to fold all together. More about that a little later . . .

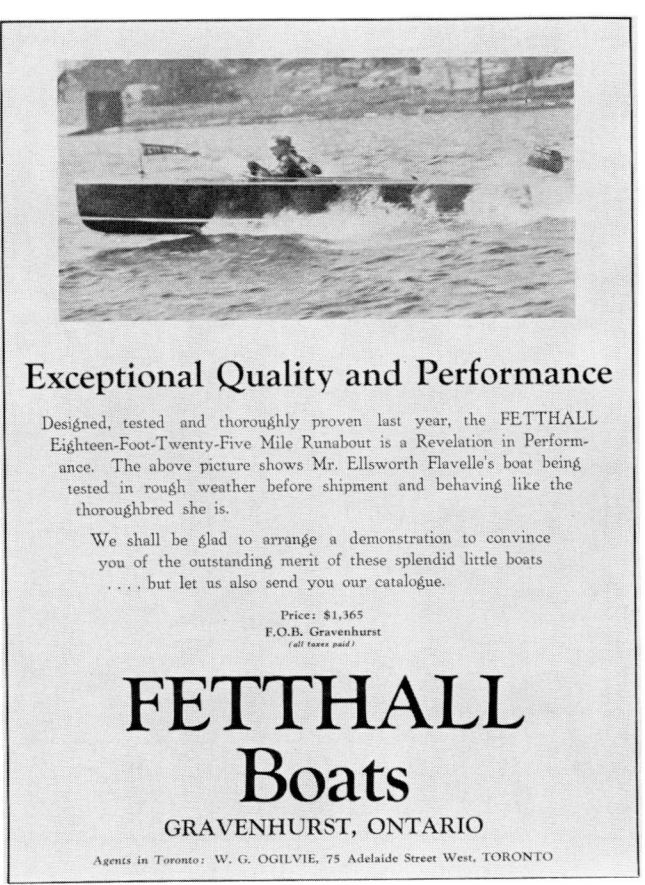

FettHall Boats ad from May 1930.

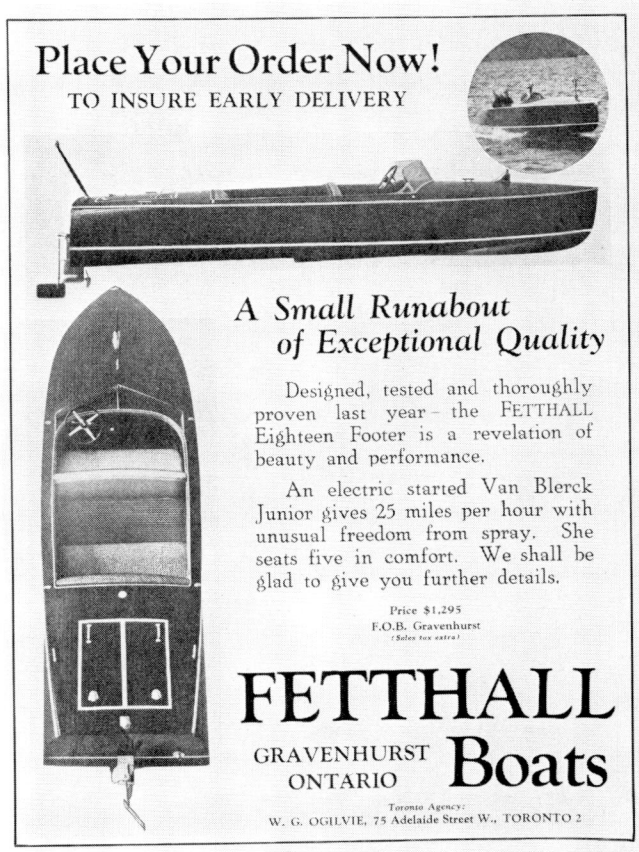

FettHall Boats ad from April 1930.

1930 would see FettHall Boats expand their model selection to two models. A sleek new 20-foot V-bottom runabout with one step was introduced. This new runabout was powered by a 4-cylinder 70 h.p. Niagara engine connected to a Columbian I.O. drive. FettHall guaranteed 36 m.p.h. on this new 1930 model. If you wished even a larger FettHall, the 28-foot by 7-foot 3-cockpit runabout was powered by a supercharged 230 h.p. 8-cylinder Niagara power plant.

This big FettHall sped along at 45 m.p.h. and was equipped with a conventional inboard drive, not the I.O. units as were used in the two smaller models. I am sorry I have been unable to find any photos of a 28-foot FettHall from 1930, but several ads for the small 17-footer are shown in this part of the article. Interestingly enough, Bill Ogilvie sold FettHall boats when he was young; his photo is shown here with a model built by FettHall Boats used by salesmen to show potential customers what a FettHall really looked like. Bill Ogilvie remembers how helpful the model boat was; he said it was beautifully made, and oftentimes children of potential customers hated to have to return the boat to Ogilvie after they looked it over.

For 1931, FettHall Boats offered two different 17-foot runabouts as well as their first 3-cockpit model, a 21-foot runabout. The firm ran a full 4-page ad in the February, 1931 issue of *Canadian Power Boating* magazine. A complete reproduction of those ads appear here. In January of 1931, FettHall tested one of their new 17-foot Family runabouts and began to lay down the keels for another six of these runabouts.[3] It was also stated that runabout production would go on through the rest of that winter. The Family runabout was powered by a 25 h.p. Falcon engine. Also in that same year, June to be exact, two of the 21-foot FettHall runabouts were delivered to their owners in Montreal, and both boats were said to have been operating well.[4] Eight people could ride in comfort aboard the 21-foot FettHall, and standard power was a 75 h.p. Chrysler.

FettHall boats enjoyed a brief but good acceptance with Canadian boat buyers of that era. Bill Ogilvie recalls selling quite a few of their boats before he became Chris-Craft dealer for Toronto Hamilton and the

---

[3]"Ontario Builder Starts Production," *Power Boating* (Jan. '31), p. 41.

[4]"FettHall's 21 Foot Model," *Canadian Power Boating* (June '31), p. 53.

Scale Models Show Features

Progressive Boat Builder Using Models to Interest Customers During Winter

By A. D. MONK

(Cuts by courtesy of Boating Business)

R. WILLIAM HALL of the Fetthall Boat Company, Gravenhurst, has a new, but very logical and successful method of demonstrating his boats when the lakes are frozen.

A beautiful scale model of their phenomenally successful eighteen footer was made with great care—and provided with a suitable carrying case—has been seen by many interested in the purchase of a motor boat last winter.

Not everyone can understand a blue print and unless, at least, half a dozen photographs are available—it is hard for the average man to picture the boat offered him by the salesman.

Although scale models cost from fifty to several hundred dollars, they have proven themselves not only as convincing sales arguments but the boat when delivered—perhaps months later—is exactly as represented by the salesman.

The prospective owner can take the model home and show it to his family—and will doubtless have a serious tussle with his son to prevent it becoming the property of said young gentleman.

The Fetthall eighteen footer has been tested and proven and the builders can guarantee the speed and performance from actual data obtained last summer—it rests, therefore, with the model to show the seating and interior arrangements to full advantage. Next to an actual demonstration a scale model backed up by proven performance figures is about the best way the owner can judge what the boat builder has to offer.

The Fetthall eighteen footer is powered with a Van Blerck Junior motor of 30 horse power and is fitted with an electric starter and reverse gear. The so-called inboard-outboard drive is used.

It is understood that tests will shortly be made with the supercharged Niagara motors—the smallest of which develop over

Mr. Hall and his model of the Fetthall 18 footer.

sixty horse power with the phenomenal low weight of less than four hundred pounds.

It is understood that excessive pounding has been largely eliminated in the Fetthall boats and even—with large power—comfortable riding in a chop is possible.

As the waterways grow in popularity so does the method of selling boats change. Two years ago the prospective customer could not see anything but rowboats and canoes on display in a city show room. To-day, in Canada, at least half a dozen large show rooms carry two or more large runabouts for the public's inspection.

The manufacture of stock boats on a large scale in the United States has induced many automobile dealers to display motor boats on their floors alongside Packards, Buicks and the rest.

Next year, it is rumoured, several Canadian automobile show rooms will have high grade stock runabouts on display and a large motor boat mart building is contemplated for Toronto's waterfront—a place where the public can see many boats and engines of all types and sizes.

In the near future Canadian boat builders may have no direct dealings with the buying public.

Bill Ogilvie, yacht broker; Alex Gilchrist, printer to the boat trade; and his partner Mr. Wright; admiring the Fetthall model.

FettHall Boats ad from May 1930.

FettHall Boats ad from May 1931.

FETTHALL
1931
MODELS

♦

FETTHALL BOATS » Gravenhurst, Ont.

A 17 ft. Family Runabout
$1285

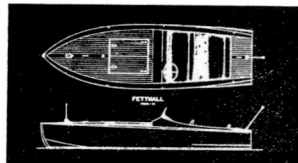

This new V-bottom runabout fills the demand for an inexpensive and smart family boat. It seats five in comfort and has speed enough to cover many miles in a day. Simplicity of control is a feature which makes it well adapted for the use of children.

Great care has been exercised to produce a boat that will be perfectly seaworthy and perform properly day in and day out with the minimum of attention and at a low operating cost.

The dimensions are: Length 17', Beam 5' 3", Draft 16". It is constructed entirely of mahogany and each part is of ample size to ensure a strong and seaworthy craft. With the Falcon 25 H.P. motor speeds from 17 to 20 miles are obtained.

Deck fittings are of nickle-plated brass. An instrument panel with ignition and light switch (with lock), ammeter and oil gauge is mounted conveniently on the dash. Automobile type steering. Seat backs and cushions are upholstered with dark blue art. leather, the cushions are Kapok filled and are fitted with life lines. The motor controls are positive, without annoying play, which ensures perfect control of the motor. Color is rich brown mahogany finished to a piano-like lustre. Equipment consists of: 3 fenders, tie lines, fire extinguisher, paddle and tool kit. Ventilating windshield is also standard equipment.

FETTHALL BOATS
Gravenhurst

FettHall Boats folder from February 1931.

A 21 ft. Standard Runabout
$2190

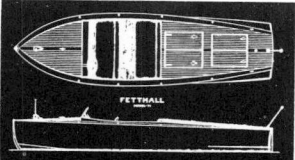

A luxurious boat for those who wish more passenger accommodation, greater speed and refinement of design and equipment. The two seats forward of the motor comfortably seat six persons, provision for two more passengers may be had in the aft cockpit as optional to the above plan. This arrangement gives equal capacity to boats of from 22 to 26 feet in length with more speed per horse power. A Chrysler Crown motor of 75 H.P. produces speed up to 30 miles per hour.

Drag link steering is provided, and as in all models particular care is taken to ensure trouble-free operation of all mechanical equipment.

The dimensions are: Length 21', Beam 6', Draft 20". Constructed of mahogany except the bottom which is two thicknesses of cedar with canvas between laid in marine glue. Color is rich brown mahogany finished with high grade spar varnish to ensure a lasting and lustrous surface.

Cushions and back are deep spring covered in a beautiful green or blue antique finish art. leather which are the utmost in comfort and appearance. Deck fittings are Chromium plate. The windshield is adjustable. The beautifully finished instrument panel is indirectly lighted and contains a tachometer oil gauge, gasoline gauge, temperature gauge, and ammeter; light and ignition switches and cigarette lighter are included on the dash-board.

We believe that this is the finest boat of the year in design, finish, and refinement of fittings and equipment, and at such a moderate price.

Fenders, horn, tie lines, fire extinguisher, boat hook and pump complete the equipment.

FETTHALL BOATS
Gravenhurst

A 17 ft. Sport Runabout
$1335 and $1535

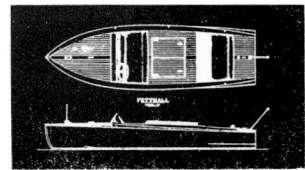

A beautiful little boat built to our high standard of material and workmanship. It is 17' long, 5' 3" beam and 18" draft. Forward drive and plenty of power with the Falcon 25 at $1335, or with the Falcon 40 at $1535, Makes a sporty little ship any one would be proud to own. Speed range with the 25 H.P. motor is from 17 to 20 miles per hour, and with the 40 H.P. motor, 22 to 25 miles per hour.

There is seating capacity for five persons. The upholstery is antique green, with Kapok cushions and upholstered backs. Ventilating windshield, instrument panel, positive steering nickle-plated fittings, electric horn, fire extinguisher, paddle, fenders and tie lines are standard equipment.

SPECIAL

For those who want maximum speed with minimum power we can furnish on special order an 18' hydroplane runabout capable of over 40 miles per hour. Prices and details on request.

Prices quoted are F.O.B. Gravenhurst, Sales tax included, and are subject to change without notice.

FETTHALL BOATS « Gravenhurst, Ont.

SPEED APLENTY IN THE NEW FETTHALL RUNABOUTS POWERED BY CHRYSLER MARINE ENGINES

Fetthall's new 8-passenger Sports Runabout is shown above. At the right — skimming over the water.

FettHall runabout photos from June 1931.

THREE NEW MODELS

SEAWORTHY - RELIABLE ECONOMICAL

In producing our new models these points in the above order were prime considerations in designing, materials and mechanical equipment. These qualities coupled with pleasing lines high grade workmanship and finish make these the outstanding boats of the year in their particular field.

17 FT. FAMILY RUNABOUT
$1285

An inexpensive all mahogany V-bottom boat to comfortably seat five. Powered with a Falcon 25 it is capable of speeds from 17 to 20 miles per hour. An ideal boat for children.

"SEE HOW THEY RUN"

17 ft. Family Runabout

17 FT. SPORTABOUT
$1535

Double cockpit and forward drive with the Falcon 40 for power make a trim craft with speed from 23 to 26 miles per hour.

STANDARD 21 FT. RUNABOUT

An outstanding boat exceptionally well appointed. Full spring upholstery is just one of the many refinements which make for comfort and convenience of those aboard. A Chrysler 75 H.P. motor gives speeds up to 30 miles per hour.

6 or 8 passenger accommodation optional.

Write for complete details of our line

FETTHALL BOATS
GRAVENHURST

FettHall Boats ad, January 1931.

(Photo by BOATING)

FETTHALL BOATS
GRAVENHURST » ONTARIO

The 21 Ft. Runabout — A Fine Boat in Design, Refinements and Performance

The 21 ft. Fetthall Standard Runabout is a luxurious boat for those who wish more passenger accommodation, greater speed and refinement of design and equipment. The dimensions are: Length 21', Beam 6', Draft 20". Seats 8 passengers. A Chrysler Crown Motor of 85 H.P. produces speeds up to 31 miles per hour. Priced at $2,190. Other Fetthall Models — 17 ft. Family Runabout at $1,285 and 17 ft. Sports Runabout at $1,360 and $1,465. (Prices subject to change without notice.)

4% Sales Tax paid.

Luxury Tax Extra.

FettHall Boats ad, June 1931.

Muskokas. The over rated Van Blerck engines eventually led to the folding of FettHall as the firm was deluged with unhappy new owners returning boats with bad engines. Since FettHall guaranteed their rigs, FettHall eventually went broke trying to keep up with replacing bad engines. The Great Depression was going full bore then, too, and that didn't help much either.

Following the closing of FettHall Boats, Bill Hall joined Greavette Boat Company, also of Gravenhurst, while Dave Fettes joined Scott Boat Company of Toronto. In fact, Scott Boats will be the next firm we shall review. In closing, FettHall Boats built some good quality boats during their three years in business, but the use of an unsound engine caused their eventual demise.

Our next firm we shall look at will be Scott Boat Company of Toronto, Ontario, Canada.

SCOTT BOAT COMPANY
TORONTO, ONTARIO

Our next firm, Scott Boat Company of Toronto, Ontario, actually first was a well established pattern-making firm that decided to go into boat building about 1932 or thereabouts. The firm hired Dave Fettes, formerly one of the owners of FettHall Boats, to be in charge of the whole operation. At first Scott Boat Company offered just kit boats for the home builder, but later went into the construction and sale of completed inboards and outboards as well. The J. C. Scott Company Ltd. were woodworkers dating back to 1879. Their reputation was among the highest in all of Canada.

In January of 1932 the firm advertised a new 20-foot 3-cockpit runabout called the Ranger. It could be constructed at home and featured such things as latest V-bottom design, seating for 9 people, a cast aluminum stem, ease of construction, and more. You could also buy the Ranger completed or as a bare hull into which the owner could install his own power plant or modify the boat to his own design. All Scott kit boats were "assembly tested," meaning that boat frames were put together so that alignment and fairing would go much better for the home builder as he built his boat. The frames were assembled at the plant and then again disassembled at the factory before they were delivered to the customer. In that way the firm was sure that all frame members were cut and made properly, saving the owner countless possible hours of headaches if various frame members were cut incorrectly. Scott Boats also offered outboard and hydroplane models as well.

For 1932 the Scott lineup of kit boats included the

Another
"SCOTT" Ready to Assemble Motor Boat

Easily Constructed at Home

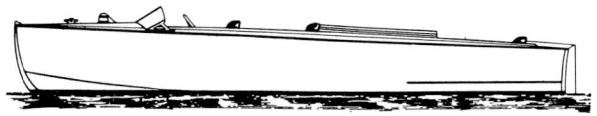

Custom Designed for "Scott" by Bert H. Hawker

"RANGER"

. . . . a Beautiful 20-Foot Family Runabout seating 8 to 9 persons . .

Make this winter pleasant and profitable. Enjoy the thrill of accomplishment. Construct this sturdy, seaworthy, modern runabout "Ranger" for next summer.

—seats 8 to 9 persons
—high speed with moderate power
—Assembly tested "Scott" boat units for great ease in construction
—beautiful lines
—Latest V-bottom design
—Cast aluminum stem
—Mahogany finish

COMPLETE HULLS. "Ranger" is also offered in complete hulls or bare hulls for those who wish to install their own power plants, at a great saving in cost!

"ASSEMBLY-TESTED." To eliminate the problem of alignment and fairing every set of "Scott" boat frames is "ASSEMBLY TESTED" right to the point of planking. An outstanding feature that tremendously simplifies the assembly of a motor boat.

LOW PRICES. Quantity production in our well-equipped plant enables us to offer you these quality boat units at remarkably low prices that are well worth investigation.

Send This Coupon for Detailed Information

I am interested in building a boat. Please forward more detailed information at no obligation to myself whatever.

Name ....
Address ....
                                    Outboard   ☐ Please
Town .... Hydroplane   ☐ Check
PB3   Runabout

The J. C. SCOTT CO. Limited
90-108 RIVER ST. » TORONTO
Woodworkers Since 1879

J. C. Scott Boat Co. ad, January 1932.

A 14-foot hydroplane under construction at the J. C. Scott Company plant in Toronto, where boats are built and sold in various forms of construction from assembly units to completed boats.

following models:
17' x 5'4" 2-cockpit runabout Gadabout
20' x 6' 3-cockpit runabout Ranger
17½' x 6½' Knockabout (utility type) inboard
16' x 4½' Outboard runabout

These four models were well accepted, as Scott was a pioneer kit boat builder up in Canada and there was a surge in home boat building back in those years. After looking at some of the ads and photos shown in this section, a person will have to admit the Scott boats looked as nice as most factory-built boats did from that same period. Later on, most kit boats were all planked with marine plywood and their design and style became more boxy and less sleek. In late 1932 a new 10-foot Dink rowboat was also added to the line. This kit sold for only $65 at that time.

By 1933 Scott announced that all Scott boats built at the factory in Toronto were water tested before delivery. Bert Hawker, famous Canadian designer, drew up all the plans for each model. Dave Fettes, formerly of Ditchburn and later, FettHall, was in charge of construction activities.[5] A new 17-foot split-cockpit runabout, the Allouette was being offered for the first time. Scott boats enjoyed increased business, even though both Canada and the United States were suffering through the Depression. The following models were offered for 1933:

Ranger...
beautiful
30 M.P.H.
mahogany
runabout
for $1,895

What a boat to drive over the sparkling waves! One glance at the illustration quickly exemplifies the beauty, contour, and dignity of this true — performing Hawker designed 20-foot V-bottom mahogany runabout. Carrying 9 people with ease, this ultra smart craft solicits admiration with its rich blue upholstery, wonderful equipment and finish. What more could be desired for wonderful boating.

Buy a SCOTT Motorboat
This Year! . . . Enjoy
the boating pleasures you've always wanted
at reasonable outlay.

Gadabout
Very smart 5 seater mahogany V-bottom runabout, 17-feet long, 5-foot 4-inch beam, with beautiful lines, equipment and dashing performance that will quickly win your desire to own this speedy Scott Motorboat. Quality from stem to stern in construction and finish for only $1290.

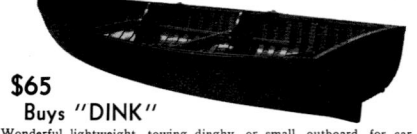

$65
Buys "DINK"
Wonderful lightweight towing dinghy, or small outboard, for car roof transportation. The ideal small boat for many uses. 10-feet 6 inches long with a splendid 4-foot beam, Dink is seaworthy and very wide. Carries 4 persons and is fitted with seats, flooring, deep keel and 2 bottom rubbing strips. Just the roomy small boat you need for easy rowing or the smallest outboard motors.

Write for interesting catalogue, describing our complete line of outboards and motorboats in detail, or visit our factory and see for yourself.

The J. C. SCOTT CO., LIMITED
90 - 108 RIVER STREET - - TORONTO, CANADA

Scott Boats ad from June 1932.

Ranger 95	20' x 6'	Runabout	Farr	95 h.p.	36 m.p.h.	$1,895.00
Ranger 85	20' x 6'	Runabout	Chrysler	85 h.p.	35 m.p.h.	$1,845.00
Ranger 72	20' x 6'	Runabout	Buchanan	72 h.p.	30 m.p.h.	$1,625.00
Ranger 58	20' x 6'	Runabout	Chrysler	72 h.p.	25 m.p.h.	$1,390.00
Gadabout 58	17' x 5'4"	Runabout	Chrysler	58 h.p.	32 m.p.h.	$1,125.00
Gadabout 45	17' x 5'4"	Runabout	Chrysler	45 h.p.	27 m.p.h.	$1,085.00
Sinbad 45	17' x 6'5"	Utility	Chrysler	45 h.p.	25 m.p.h.	$1,025.00
Sinbad 32	17' x 6'5"	Utility	Gray	32 h.p.	21 m.p.h.	$1,000.00
Hornet 45	14' x 5'	Hydroplane	Buchanan	45 h.p.	40 m.p.h.	$1,395.00
Hornet 55	14' x 5'	Hydroplane	Gray	55 h.p.	40 m.p.h.	$1,480.00
Hornet 57	14' x 5'	Hydroplane	Universal	57 h.p.	42 m.p.h.	$1,690.00

[5]"Scott Introduces Economy Runabout at Low Selling Price," *Power Boating* (Feb. '33), p. 14.

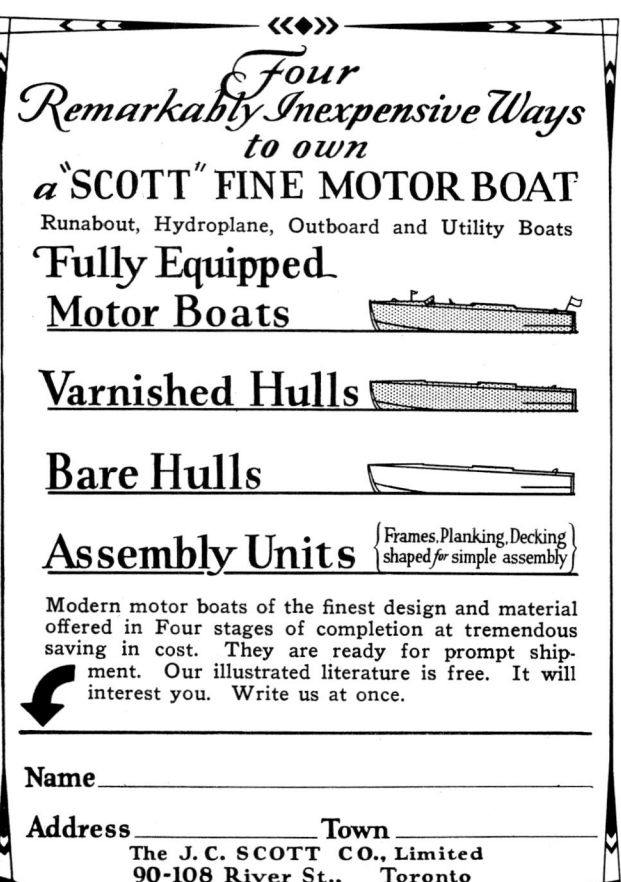

Scott Boat ad from April 1932.

Your Boat for 1933!
A SCOTT BOAT

Designed and Engineered by
BERT HAWKER!

Authoritively designed—unusually sturdy construction—selected materials—water tested—PROVEN. These are facts that will mean ultimate satisfaction to you in the ownership of a SCOTT BOAT. True performing, sane, seaworthy and beautifully finished, Scott Boats will give many years pleasure. What is more, you can buy a Scott Boat in any stage of construction you desire.

1. Assembly Units   3. Varnished Hulls
2. Bare Hulls   4. Fully Equipped with Motor.

Write at once for our illustrated catalogue.

Name ....
Address ....
Town ....

The J. C. SCOTT CO., LIMITED
90 - 108 RIVER STREET   --   TORONTO, CANADA

Scott Boat ad from September 1932.

Pictured above is the 20-foot, Hawker designed, vee-bottom runabout hull sold in known-down frames, or in completed hulls by the J. C. Scott Company of Toronto.

ALOUETTE $1090
Wonderful V Bottom Family Runabout   *fully equipped*

FEATURES

V-Bottom for safety stability and speed.
17-6 x 5-9 beam.
Actual 26 M.P.H. with 45 H.P. motor.
Low operating cost.
Unusual roominess—7 passengers.
Beautiful finish and appearance.
Solid mahogany decking. Smooth-skin cedar planking; oak framework.
Scott special upholstery.
Safety drag-link steering —auto type.

• Do Not MISS . . .
Another Summer's Boating Pleasures

With many expensive boat features, Alouette is a beautifully made, low-priced family motor-boat carrying up to 7 passengers. Generous 5' 9" beam gives unusual stability, safety and seaworthiness. Proven performance, economical operation . . . built for long service with outstanding V-Bottom design.

25% Payment NOW Insures Delivery in JUNE

$1090. Standard model complete, 45 H.P. 26 M.P.H., all accessories, upholstery, lights, fittings.
$740. Economy model, 18 M.P.H.
$340. Varnished Hull, ready for motor and equipment.
$175. Complete Assembly Units.
Sales Tax Extra.

The J. C. SCOTT CO., Limited
90-108 River St., TORONTO

Many other Inboard and Outboard Models

J. C. Scott Boat Co. ad from May 1933.

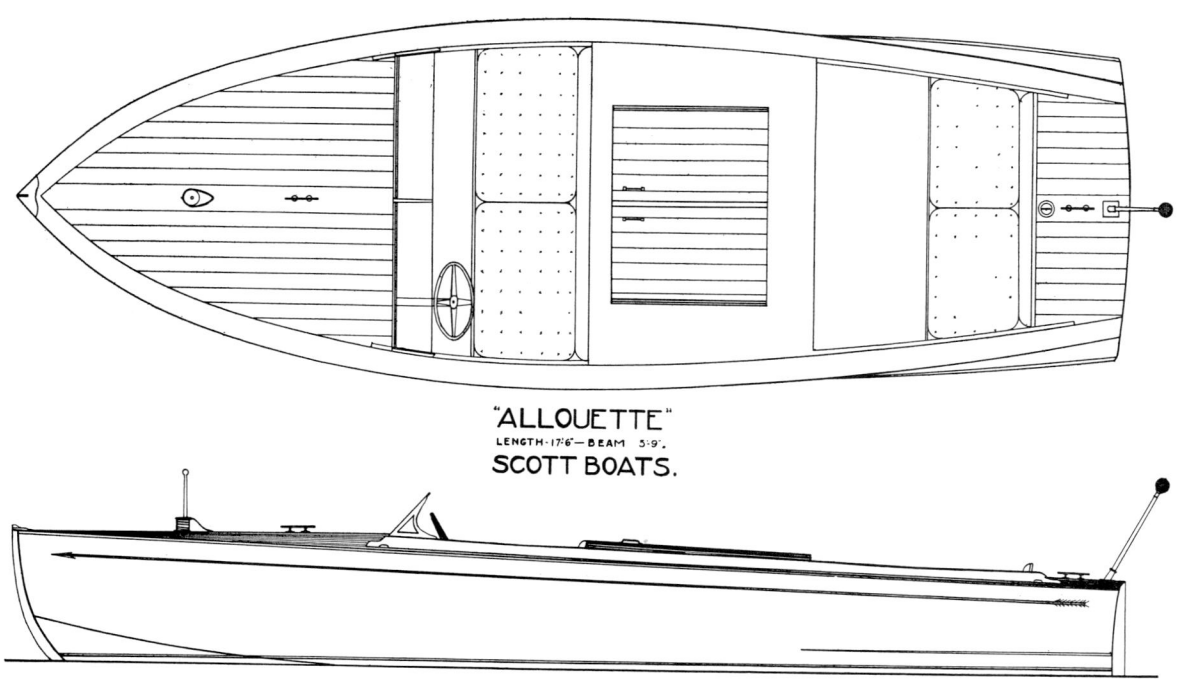

"ALLOUETTE"
LENGTH-17'6"—BEAM 5'9"
SCOTT BOATS.

Scott Introduce Economy Runabout Selling At Low Price

Y showing constantly an extensive display of their full line of inboard and outboard runabouts, the J. C. Scott Company's River Street plant in Toronto is a popular visiting place for motor boat owners and prospective owners.

A ready welcome is given all, whether you are a prospective buyer or not, and by numerous talks with these enthusiasts the company has been able to gather valuable information which has enabled them to give careful consideration to what is desired in the runabout field today.

As a result of this consideration they are offering in their line for 1933 an economy runabout, "Allouette" which has been designed and built from the viewpoints of the many enthusiasts who have visited their plant in the past months.

Price was the main item to be considered when "Allouette" was introduced. To bring this boat within the range of hundreds of boat buyers, expensive fittings and gadgets which were but flashy imports and of no useful value have been dispensed with. In length "Allouette" measures 17 ft. 6 in. and has a beam measurement of 5 ft. 9 in. Construction is oak frames with cedar planking and mahogany deck. It is of smooth skin construction. Seating is provided for six passengers and speed with a 24 H.P. motor is expected to be at least 18 miles an hour; with a 45 H.P. motor, speed is 25 miles an hour.

This model is available in any stage of construction up to the completed boat with motor installed. By buying the hull without motor and installing a used marine engine, an enthusiast with but a few hundred dollars to spend can enjoy the pleasures of boating at minimum expenditure. The price, however, for the complete boat with motor installed is so attractive that but few would care to do the extra work entailed of installing their own motor.

During the summer Scott Boats were all fully tested. A complete listing of these models is given in the Buyer's Guide Section and no further mention of details is required here.

Many of these models are Hawker-designed and have been tested by Bert Hawker to his own satisfaction before they were offered to the public.

Mr. David Fettes, well-known in the boat building industry by his former connections with Ditchburn Boats and Fetthall Boats, is in charge of the building activities of the J. C. Scott Company. The company building Scott Boats are widely known in the woodworking industry where for many years they have been the leading firm doing the finer woodworking required in the building of expensive homes and office buildings.

Below: Scott 17 foot Hawker designed runabout.
Right: Scott "Sinbad" model, a utility runabout.

Scott Boats ad, February 1933.

• SCOTT BOATS ROLL CALL •

RANGER • Beautiful 20 foot 8-9 passenger mahogany runabout, 32 M.P.H., $1695.00.

GADABOUT • 17 x 5-4 Sport runabout, 5 passenger, 25-35 M.P.H. $1225.00 to $1450.00.

ALOUETTE • Seven passenger smart family runabout 17-6 long, very steady $740.00 to $1090.00.

SINBAD • Knockabout—fast rough water boat 17-4 x 6-5, 18 to 25 M.P.H. $775.00 to $1125.00. ... ...

HORNET • 14 x 5-0 Inboard Hydroplane, Hawker design, 38 to 42 M.P.H. $1335.00 to $1690.00.

SNIPE • Sturdy seaworthy sailboat 15-6 x 5-0 completely rigged, $295.00.

PLAYBOY • Sport mahogany outboard 16 x 4-4 smart and fast, $290.00.

SCOUT • Family outboard, round bottom cedar, sturdily built, $110.00.

DINK • Canvas covered dinghy; towing or car top, 10-6 x 4-0 beam, 70 pounds, $65.00.

SALES TAX EXTRA

NEW
IMP
10-0 x 4-0 SEA FLEA

Latest girder type sea-flea, 10-0 x 4-0 for class A motor or 8 to 10 H.P. Our interlocking unit construction makes this the easiest building sea-flea.

Built-up frames and all materials machined to shape, including screws and fastenings —

$48

• Except last two items, all models are fine V-bottom designs and can be obtained in "Assembly Units" for quick and accurate building; varnished or bare hull ready for motor and equipment; or fully equipped with a motor to suit your requirements.

NAME ....

STREET ....

• TOWN .... PROV. ....
PB15

THE J. C. SCOTT CO. Limited
90-108 RIVER STREET, TORONTO

Scott Boats ad from July 1933.

Now's the Time . . .
To Buy Scott Boat Units

ASSEMBLE this popular "Alouette" model during winter; Owners are enthusiastic. Complete units cost but **$175.**

The units reach you ready to commence assembly. Necessary instructions, frame units, shaped planking, bolts and screws are all included. Above is shown a typical example of the beauty and quality of Scott Boats.

$48. Buys all the woodwork machined and prepared for a new girder type sea-flea for 7 to 10 H.P. motors. A boat that any young enthusiast will be proud to drive.

$374. Buys the complete assembly units of an exceedingly high class mahogany runabout, seating 8-9 persons. With an 85 H.P. motor this boat gives wonderful performance and our tests show 35 m.p.h.

WRITE AT ONCE

Other interesting models are shown in our literature which is yours for the asking.

The J. C. SCOTT CO., Limited
108 RIVER ST. - TORONTO, CANADA

SCOTT MOTORBOATS

Scott Boat Co. ad from September 1933.

SCOTT BOATS · for 1933

GADABOUT • Dashing gaily over the water at 32 M.P.H. in this brilliant 5 pass., 17 footer is always thrilling. A smart Mahogany boat of unusual safety.

Wonderful Motorboats for Every Purpose — a revelation in Speed .... Safety .... Performance and Price!

• Fully proven 1933 Motorboats. Bringing you variety, the finest in design and execution. Give Scott Boats careful consideration for the better you know them the more you like them!

SCOTT BOATS Made in Canada

GADABOUT • and her designer — Bert Hawker, on Lake Muskoka.

SINBAD • Tripping Georgian Bay at 25 M.P.H. Unique fast V-bottom rough-water boat of many uses. 17'-4" x 6'-5" beam. Very steady, dry, serviceable and low-priced.

COMING! "ALLOUETTE"!!
A new V-bottom Runabout. As low as $795.00
Smooth skin, smart, seaworthy and speedy.

PLAYBOY • Sport outboard, 4 pass., Mahogany runabout. True V-bottom—25 M.P.H., with 16 H.P. motor.

RANGER • Travelling 35 M.P.H., with a 1933 Chrysler Crown motor. An 8-9 passenger runabout of striking beauty, style, and perfection in performance—at $1,895.00.

The J. C. SCOTT CO. LTD. — 90-108 RIVER ST., TORONTO

HORNET • A 14 ft. inboard Hydroplane doing 42 M.P.H.

WRITE for Illustrated CATALOG and prices

Name..................
Address..................
Town.............Prov..........

All models available in any stage of construction.

Scott Boats ad from February 1933.

The next full page ad shown will give you an idea of what many of the 1933 Scotts looked like.

The last year I was able to find anything about Scott Boats was for the year 1935. In that year several new models were added. They are listed below:

Dart—15'6" x 5'3" Family runabout, Gray 32 h.p., 25 m.p.h., $660.00
Pilot—18' x 6' Round bilge runabout, Kermath V-8, 37 m.p.h., $1,395.00

YOUR BOAT FOR 1934
Should be underway before long

A visit to our factory would convince you of the superior quality of Scott Boats. Our sheet of Action Pictures is next best. Write for your copy and a price list. An outline of the service you desire will enable us to make helpful suggestions.

BUILD A SCOTT BOAT

Up to date designs—Smart appearance. Sturdy construction—Proven performance. Unusual stability and safety. Most attractive prices for quality boats.

Write Without Delay

THE J. C. SCOTT CO. LIMITED
90-108 RIVER STREET - 17 - TORONTO, CANADA

1934 Scott Boats ad.

DART 15-6x5-3

WITH 4 CYL. GRAY MARINE MOTOR—BUILT IN REVERSE

ONLY $660.
A COMPLETE INBOARD MOTOR BOAT READY TO RUN

- CONVENIENT • SAFE •
- DEPENDABLE •

ENJOY BIG BOAT PERFORMANCE....
....AT SMALL BOAT EXPENSE

A SPECIAL FOLDER AWAITS YOUR REQUEST

SALES and SERVICE
Gordon Boat Works, Bobcaygeon
Huntsville Boat Works, Huntsville
Vincent Robinson, Port Sandfield

10 OTHER MODELS.
PROMPT DELIVERIES.

WRITE TODAY

The J. C. SCOTT CO.
Established 1879 Limited
108 RIVER ST. TORONTO

Scott Motor Boats ad from August 1934.

All other models previously listed for 1933-34 were also offered in 1935. I was unable to determine exactly when Scott Boats stopped production but I am quite sure it was about 1936. So often the amount of information I can obtain on firms is much less than I would wish, but often after readers see what I do have they will write or call with additional history, photos, etc., and that material can go into future books. I wonder if any Scott runabouts, outboard or inboard, still exist? There probably is a good chance that some are around, though their owners may be unaware of their true identity.

Now, on to George Vandenbossche Boats, Inc. in Wallaceburg, Ontario.

GEORGE VANDENBOSSCHE BOATS INC. "VAN-CRAFT"

Our final Canadian builder to be reviewed in *Volume V* is the George Vandenbossche Boat Company., Inc. of Wallaceburg, Ontario. A big thank you to our Canadian researcher, boat owner and good friend, Alan Mann, who has discovered yet another what we might call regional inboard builder. Van-Craft probably are unfamiliar to most of you as it was to me. Their history, though not very long, is interesting, and the two photos Alan has included along with the story give us an idea of just what some of their boats used to look like. Let's start our review of Van-Craft now.

A smaller independent boat building firm flourished in Wallaceburg, Ontario, following World War II. George Vandenbossche, a native of Holland, came to Ontario in the mid-1930s and began a boat repair business near Dresden, ten miles east of Wallaceburg. He then moved to northern Ontario and joined the staff of the Greavette Boat Works at Gravenhurst, Ontario, where he shared in the production of those beautiful Muskoka Lakes runabouts that soon became motorboat classics.

In 1938 the new Mac-Craft Corporation was established in Wallaceburg and George Vandenbossche accepted the opportunity to join the new company as a marine carpenter. When the firm moved to Sarnia in 1941 he decided to remain in Wallaceburg and carried on with marine repairs until the end of the war.

After the cessation of hostilities, restrictions on purchase of gasoline, oil and related marine supplies were eased. Being in the center of such a vast network of marine waterways, the Wallaceburg area once again buzzed with activity as its reputation of a recreational mecca once more surfaced. George Vandenbossche

VAN-CRAFT
WALLACEBURG — ONTARIO

Custom Built Motorboats & Cruisers

GEORGE VANDENBOSSCHE - *prop.*

realized the unlimited potential and established his own boat building firm, George Vandenbossche Boats Inc. Wood was still king and it was a few years before plastic boats made inroads in the area.

The adjoining waters of nearby Lake St. Clair were reputed to be among the best hunting and fishing areas in North America. Vandenbossche realized this ready market and began production of duck boats, many of which are still in use more than four decades later. As well, the firm produced 16' and 18' outboard hulls of lap strap design with a small forward deck.

The firm's main production number, however was the 20' runabout, which was marketed in the area under the Van-Craft label. Somewhat similar in appearance to the Mac-Craft runabout produced in Wallaceburg a few years earlier, the marked difference was the fact that Van-Craft out sides were painted a gleaming white. Along with rich red mahogany topsides contrasted with white-leaded deck seams, the Vandenbossche-produced craft became very popular. The craft would seat a maximum of six passengers comfortable with a narrow mid deck separating the forward cockpit from the passenger's compartment. Completed bare hull sold for $925. Either Chrysler or Gray engines were installed according to the customer's preference, as well as individual tastes in the hardware and accessory line.

Side view of a 20-foot Van-Craft runabout, once built in Wallaceburg, Ontario, Canada.

Deck hardware was produced locally by the Wallaceburg Brass Company, using the dies from the former Mac-Craft line of fittings.

The company branched out, added additional staff, and produced custom-built cruisers. A former Wallaceburg realtor revealed that his 26' cabin cruiser built by George Vandenbossche Boats was every bit compatible with the local waterways as were similar models built by the giants of the industry such as Chris-Craft and Matthews.

Gradually, as happened to other smaller "wood" builders, the gradual popularity of plastic hulls and more powerful outboard engines, less orders came the way of Vandenbossche's firm. To diversify, he opened up a Kaiser-Fraser auto dealership in the front portion of his boat building operation but kept his hand in his "first love" by continuing with repairs and the occasional custom-built contract. Several decades later many of the craft produced by George Vandenbossche Boats were still in everyday use, a testimony to a highly skilled craftsman.

In the late 1950s Vandenbossche moved to Windsor, Ontario, where he kept his hand in the boat repair business. He continued dabbling in the craft he loved dearly with his final project, a cement hull vessel, involving him right up to the time of his passing. George Vandenbossche died in Windsor, Ontario, in December of 1983 at the age of 80.

Well, from Van-Craft boats we shall now move on to Chapter III, new Material that Applies to *Volume I*. Hope you find material on boats that interest you.

Head-on view of 20-foot Van-Craft runabout. Built after World War II and sold for $925.00.

The final photo shown here really was a bit of modern Canadian Marine history. My dear friend, J. Darragh M. Elliot of Don Mills, Ont. provided me this photo I am including here. The caption will identify everyone. Darragh's own Chris-Craft Riviera 18' - 1950 model tows the famous Miss Canada out on the course at the 1980 Buffalo, N.Y. Antique Boat Show.

Seated in *Miss Maydell* from left to right, front seat: **J. Darragh, M. Elliott—Owner, President Toronto Chapter A.C.B.S., James C. Potter—National Director A.C.B.S.**
Rear seat from left to right: **Douglas Van Patten—Marine Designer of *Miss Canada III* Van Patten Jr.**
Rear deck: **Sidney Herwig—Member Manotick Chapter A.C.B.S.**
Seated in *Miss Canada III* from left to right: **Bill's mechanic "Pete", Bill Morgan—Owner, National Director A.C.B.S.**

CHAPTER III
Material Applying to Volume I

It is again my pleasure to share with you some newly unearthed material concerning firms covered in the original *Volume I* over seven years ago. As in past volumes I shall follow the same sequence of firms as they appeared in that first book, right through to the end. There are a few firms that I have no new information on, and I will mention that fact when it occurs throughout this chapter.

As you will remember, Chris-Craft was our first firm back in *Volume I*. First of all I wish to announce to everyone the formation of the official Chris-Craft Historical Society. At the time of this writing the official announcement has not yet been made, but if you would please send me a stamped, self-addressed envelope, I will be more than happy to send you an application blank. A lot of exciting things are being planned for this club, and I am sure before very long it will be one of the most active and well organized groups in the hobby. I am also honored and excited to be named one of the national board of directors of the new club. When you see the list of directors you will realize the great amount of authorities in antique wooden boats that they have gathered to help you, the members, with all facets of boat restoration and ownership. Not only Chris-Craft owners, but all wooden inboard speedboat owners of all makes and varieties should take note of this new group. You will hear lots of good things coming out of the new Chris-Craft Historical Society.

Now to get started looking at new Chris-Craft material. I wish to first thank F. Todd Warner of Classic Runabout Corporation of America for loaning me many

1921 - 26' Chris-Craft 8-passenger runabout. She sold then for $4,450.00.

of his bound volumes of *Rudder & Yachting* magazines from which some of the material used in this book has come. In reviewing the "Chris" material in *Volume III* I note there that photos, ads, etc., from prior to 1926 were hard to come by. Well, since then I have found material to fill a lot of the gaps we missed in those early years at Chris-Craft.

The oldest Chris-Craft photo of an actual runabout I have unearthed so far is shown here. The year is 1921 and the runabout was a new 26-foot Chris-Smith 8-passenger Express runabout. It came with a Hall-Scott engine with a guaranteed speed of 33 m.p.h. It was planked with mahogany outside and butternut wood on the interior areas. Price for that "Chris" back in 1921 was a staggering $4,450 complete. The dealer who displayed this craft as well as Hacker-Craft back then in

1922 or 1923 27' Chris-Craft Smith runabout owned by Martin Tuckett and restored by E. J. Mertaugh Boat Works, Hessel, Mich.

Detroit, Michigan, was Central Marine Service Corporation.

Probably one of the oldest Chris-Crafts still in use is shown next. The *Queen*, as it is known up around Hessel, Michigan, is owned by Martin Tuckett of Rockford, Illinois. It was built in either 1922 or '23 (no one knows exactly), but it is 27 feet long and is in use every season, not just a pampered "show boat" like many others. I just thought you would enjoy a photo of such an historic boat that has been redone and is enjoyed so much by its proud owner and family.

From the mill room each part of the boat is sorted in racks in the mill stock room. The correct number of pieces for each successive operation are carried to the production lines by truckers

The next operation shows the diagonal bottom planking being laid and the canvas inner lining being glue fastened to this planking preparatory to the second layer of planking being fastened

This is the start of the Cadet production line, showing the boat in frame with the chine about to be attached. Note that two boats are started at the same time and when framed are moved to the center where side planking is fastened on

Next, I am reproducing an article entitled, "How Boats are Built in Algonac." Some of you may have seen this, while others I am sure will find it new and very informative on the Chris-Craft boats from that era.

From here on we shall look mostly at old ads. I have tried to rearrange them in the order they appeared during a particular year. We shall begin with 1925. Though small in size, these ads show us some of the first Chris-Crafts that were built on a larger scale than earlier ones. Price had dropped to $3,200 each. Note the old oblong glass windshield with the center dividing, upright piece. After 1926 that was dropped so that the

View of the Chris-Craft plant in 1926-27. Note old autos on the lot.

Screw fastening the outer planking to the frames by Black and Decker electric screw drivers

After planking the green bottom paint is applied

With the forward decking, hatch coamings and covering boards fastened in place and being scraped and sanded

After varnishing the Cadets are moved to another room where the Chrysler Imperial motors are installed. Here the metal trim is attached and the upholstering supplied

Cleaning seams of sawdust and shavings by vacuum cleaners and filling the wood

Ready for loading on a freight car

THE Chris-Craft embraces every virtue of the ideal speed craft. It is comfortable—economical—and speedy. It is beautifully built—luxuriously fitted—travels 35 M.P.H. You will take pride in its ownership and thrill at its performance.

$3200. at Algonac, Mich.

Chris Smith & Sons Boat Co.
Algonac, Michigan

CHRIS-CRAFT
RUNABOUTS

Small 1925 Chris-Craft ad.

No Boat Can Give You More

More thrill in performance; more pride in ownership of a beautiful boat; more comfort; more speed; more economy. Owners possess a runabout with every essential of the ideal speed craft,—a boat that attracts envious attention anywhere. This beautifully built, luxurious runabout provides thrills with safety. The price, $3200 complete at Algonac is a remarkable value, explained by building as a standardized model.

Chris Smith & Sons Boat Co.
Algonac, Michigan, U. S. A.

CHRIS-CRAFT
RUNABOUTS

CHRIS-CRAFT
RUNABOUTS

Step into a Chris-Craft. Just ask for power. You'll get it. More power! See how quickly Chris-Craft responds. Day or night under any condition Chris-Craft answers a demand for power.

Beauty of design, luxurious fittings, dependability and a guaranteed 35 M. P. H. speed are features of CHRIS-CRAFT ownership that provide new thrills and matchless pleasures for lovers of Water Sports.

CHRIS-CRAFT standardization makes possible immediate delivery from stock.

Price $3200

CHRIS SMITH & SONS BOAT COMPANY
Algonac, Michigan
"Builders of the World's Fastest Boats."

When writing advertisers—Just say POWER BOATING

1925 ad.

windshield was one solid piece of glass, unobstructed by that center piece of frame. The glass was narrower, too, with the bottom of the wooden windshield frame that runs across the top of the deck being raised to take up some of the space of the formerly rather high all glass windshields as shown on the 1925 ads.

For 1926, there are nine very interesting full-page ads shown. You will note that a single 26-foot runabout was offered, though either a 100 h.p. or 150 h.p. Kermath engine was offered for power. Prices in '26 were $3,500 for the 100 h.p. runabout or $4,000 for the 150 h.p. model.

In 1926 Chris-Craft also built some fireproof on-water storage sheds at their Algonac, Michigan, location. Four sheds were being built, two for storage of customer boats where they could be hoisted from the water and blocked up for winter; in the summer they could "reside" right in their slip, always ready for use but safe from the elements. Two additional sheds were built for storage of new Chris-Crafts awaiting delivery to customers. This method of storage allowed for a good inventory of completed Chris-Crafts ready for immediate delivery. A photo here shows one of the metal sheds plumb full of

1925 Chris-Craft ad.

Wrought By Men Skilled in the Art of Boat Building and Design

The Chris Smith organization still holds the record of having produced the world's fastest speed boats. More, they have turned this hard won experience to practical account. For three years past, Chris Smith & Sons have been building a beautiful standardized Chris-Craft mahogany runabout. Today this boat is unequalled anywhere for price—performance and appearance.

The Chris-Craft possesses all the qualities for an ideal runabout. It offers abundant power and speed; it combines rare riding comfort with an unequalled sense of security. Extreme ease of handling is one of the inbuilt features to make the twenty-six-foot Chris-Craft the perfect family runabout. A specially designed marine motor gives a new meaning to runabout values.

The smart appearance of the Chris-Craft finds favor in every one's eyes. The boat is marked for its trimness. Every line bespeaks well conceived design. Its highly finished mahogany decks and glistening hull mark the Chris-Craft as the perfect product of the boat builder's art.

$3500—f. o. b. Algonac

CHRIS SMITH & SONS BOAT CO.
ALGONAC   Largest Builders of Fast Runabouts   MICHIGAN

When a New Record was Established by the Kermath Chris-Craft

The 26-foot Chris-Craft is all mahogany with rubbed finish. Bottom is screw-fastened and double-planked for strength, sides single-planked battened seam construction. Windshield heavily reinforced and full tilting. Lifting rings fore and aft. Power is the Kermath 150-H. P. six-cylinder valve-in-head marine motor. Speeds, 38 to 40 miles per hour. Salt water equipt throughout.

POSSIBLY the greatest endorsement ever accorded any runabout was received by Chris-Craft during the week of the National Motor Boat Show. Boats of all makes, all sizes, all prices were on display. Buyers were offered an unusual opportunity to make comparisons and the result of their choice is significant. Twenty-eight bona fide orders [with deposits] were placed for Chris-Craft, making this all mahogany boat the outstanding "buy" in the field of fine runabouts.

Chris Smith & Sons Boat Co.
ALGONAC, MICHIGAN

$3500 f.o.b. Algonac

LARGEST BUILDERS OF FAST RUNABOUTS

The Chris-Craft Runabout

The Chris-craft 26-foot runabout

Classification—Double cockpit runabout.
Length—26 ft., beam 6 ft. 8 in., draft 22 in.
Builder—Chris Smith & Sons Boat Co.
Price—$3500, f.o.b. Algonac Mich., complete with 6-cylinder, 150-horsepower Kermath marine engine.
Other Models—Furnished with the same hull but powered with an 8-cylinder, V type engine at $2875, or with a 6-cylinder 100-horsepower Kermath at $3290.

PARTICULARS

The hull has keel, stem and chine of selected oak with planking of mahogany throughout. The bottom planking is double with canvas, laid in white lead, between the two layers. The side planking is with batten seam construction.

Equipment—includes two large fuel tanks securely fastened under the stern deck. These tanks are filled through filler caps located on the stern deck and instantly accessible without disturbing or interfering with passengers or guests. The six-passenger forward cockpit is protected by a ventilating windshield manufactured in the Smith plant especially for this boat. Fittings include electric running lights of a special type combined with forward flag pole socket and mooring post, electric engine room lights, combination flag pole and stern light, forward flag pole, boat hook, paddle, four fenders, anchor and line, cotton mooring lines, seven life preservers, fire extinguisher, electric horn, name and government registration numbers in gold leaf on either side. Chris-craft were the first standardized boats to be equipped with hoisting rings forward and aft. These are of immense advantage to owners who keep their craft in boathouses when they wish to hoist them out of the water for storage or inspection.

The upholstering of Chris-craft is done in the Smith shops. The materials used have been thoroughly tried out and are of the very best quality. All upholstering may be readily removed for cleaning. Strut, rudder and propeller are of manganese bronze of the highest possible quality. The deck hardware, fender streaks and cutwaters are of bronze, nickeled and polished. Steering gear and controls of automobile type. Steering wheel and all instruments mounted on the forward bulkhead of the forward cockpit so that the operator has complete control of the boat at all times. Instruments include oil pressure gage, tachometer and electric ammeter. Reverse gear lever is close at the operators hand to control the neutral, forward and backward running of the boat.

Engine—the regular power plant is the new 6-cylinder 150-horsepower Kermath marine engine which gives a speed of from 36-40 miles per hour. For those who do not require as much speed the boat may be powered with the smaller 6-cylinder Kermath of 100-horsepower or may be obtained, at a still lower price, with the 8-cylinder V-type Curtiss which was formerly the standardized power plant and which will furnish speeds up to 32 miles per hour.

These boats are equipped for either fresh or salt water and are ideal for general runabout use either in open or protected waters. The forward cockpit seats six persons and the rear cockpit four, so that a total of ten persons may be carried if desired.

Unexcelled for Performance

CHRIS-CRAFT will impress you with its unmatched performance—once you have taken the wheel. As one who may never have driven a runabout before, you will marvel at its ease of handling, its driving simplicity. As an experienced driver you will immediately sense the superiority of Chris-Craft action; its flashing acceleration and fleetness, its superb buoyancy and sensitiveness to control. This brilliant performance of Chris-Craft can be attributed only to the outstanding experiences gained in a lifetime spent building every type of boat from the light duck skiff to the world's fastest racing boats.

Chris Smith & Sons Boat Co.
ALGONAC, MICHIGAN

Send for this handsomely illustrated catalog on Chris-Craft runabouts. It will be mailed to you on request

Chris-Craft

1926 ads.

1926 Chris-Craft ads.

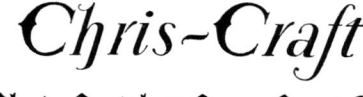

Another 1926 Chris-Craft ad

Take delivery of your new Chris-Craft in Florida during the winter of 1926!

A More Impressive Standard of Excellence

MANY of the wealthiest men in this country have discriminated in favor of Chris-Craft. They selected Chris-Craft above all others for very definite reasons. Chris-Craft assures absolutely reliable engine performance, a perfect obedience to throttle and wheel, a beauty and luxuriousness of appearance tempered by judicious design and a speed of 40 miles an hour. With these attributes, Chris-Craft imposes an almost irresistible obligation to buy. The new model now available for immediate delivery has set a new and more impressive standard of superiority and excellence.

Inspect the Chris-Craft on display in our New York Show Rooms, 393 Seventh Avenue, opposite the Pennsylvania station.

Chris-Craft
Chris Smith & Sons Boat Co.
ALGONAC,   MICHIGAN

1926

1926 Chris-Craft on parade.

26-foot Chris-Craft runabouts just waiting for new homes. Racing, inboard style, was still in its infancy back in 1926, but nonetheless often as part of Gold Cup Races, pleasure boats would get in there and run also. The next view shows nine Chris-Crafts of varying ages running almost neck and neck down the straightaway. Can't tell you who won, though. Sorry!

Little seems to have surfaced concerning the very unique Yacht Tenders which Chris-Craft started promoting in 1927. In that year an ad mentioned a 22-foot as well as a longer 26-foot model available from $7,000 to $7,500 with the 150 h.p. Kermath. Nine passengers could ride in style and safety aboard the Yacht Tenders. Also in 1927 the smaller 22-foot Cadet was

New 1926 boats in the storage shed ready for immediate delivery.

available. The next ad shows both the Cadet and the original 26-footer. The unique thing about this ad is that it shows the optional folding top for the Cadet as well as the then new seating arrangement for the 26-foot mahogany Chris-Craft runabout. The remaining ads for 1927 show Chris-Crafts from that year in various poses. Chris-Crafts fared very well in 1927, race-wise, winning the Boston Regatta held June 17, 1927, winning both heats in the 22-foot inboard class.

1928 was a super year, sale-wise, for Chris-Craft. Their sales for the first five months of 1928 were 25 percent greater than for all of 1927. That year models from 22 feet through 30 feet were offered. Some of the newest models for '28 were a 26-foot split-cockpit mahogany Sport Hydroplane. All mahogany 26-foot and 30-foot sedan roofed 3-cockpit runabouts made their debut that year as well. The most expensive Chris-Craft for 1928 was the 30-foot Custom Commuter which could seat 14 people in total, and was powered by a 200 h.p. Chris-Craft engine. Its price tag in 1928 was $9,750. It is interesting to see how firms like Chris-Craft expanded their model selections more and more each year.

The year 1929, though beginning during the Great Depression, saw Chris-Craft offering their first 38-foot V-bottom Commuter cruiser that reached top speeds of 30 m.p.h. and sold for a cool $15,000. Chris-Craft had

A very rare ad for 1927 describing both fast yacht tenders offered by Chris Smith & Sons Boat Co.

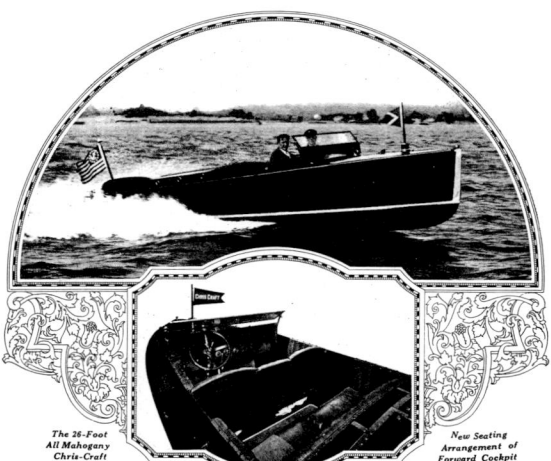

Great 2 page 1927 Chris-Craft ad. Note interior view and folding top shown.

72

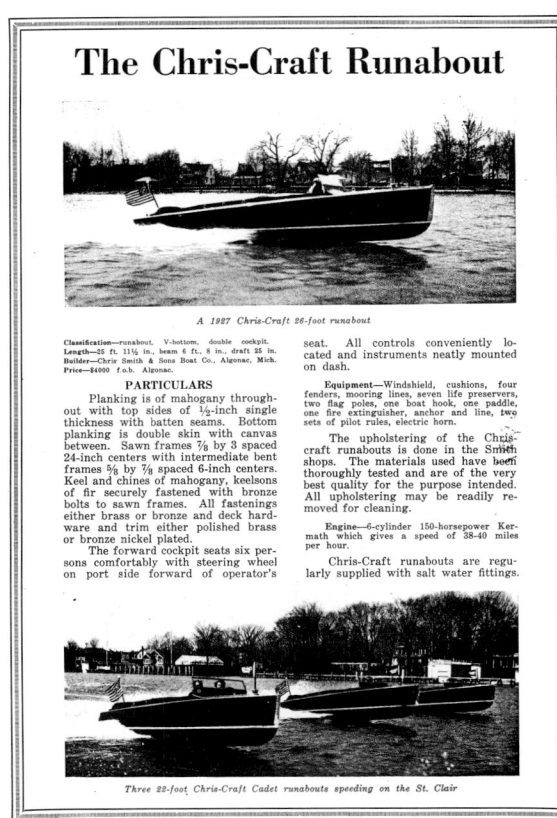

More information on the 1927 Chris-Craft runabouts!

June 1, 1927 saw Chris-Craft still promoting their 26' runabout at the same price as 1926, $4,000.

Even in 1927 Chris-Craft's won their fair share of races!

Another late summer 1927 ad for the 26-foot Chris-Craft runabout.

THE WORLD'S LARGEST BUILDERS OF ALL MAHOGANY RUNABOUTS

Chris-Craft

WHEN YOU respond to the irresistible charm of Florida ... When a luxurious Chris-Craft with its inviting freedom of action is yours ... Then you will truly mark this winter the most glorious one in all your experience.

Direct Factory Branches:
153 West 31st Street at 7th Avenue, New York City
3107 East Jefferson Avenue, Detroit

$2395 $ to 7500

Chris Smith & Sons Boat Co.
ALGONAC, MICHIGAN

SOME VALUABLE DISTRIBUTOR TERRITORIES AVAILABLE

In Dec. 1927 suggestions were made to own a new Chris-Craft in Florida!

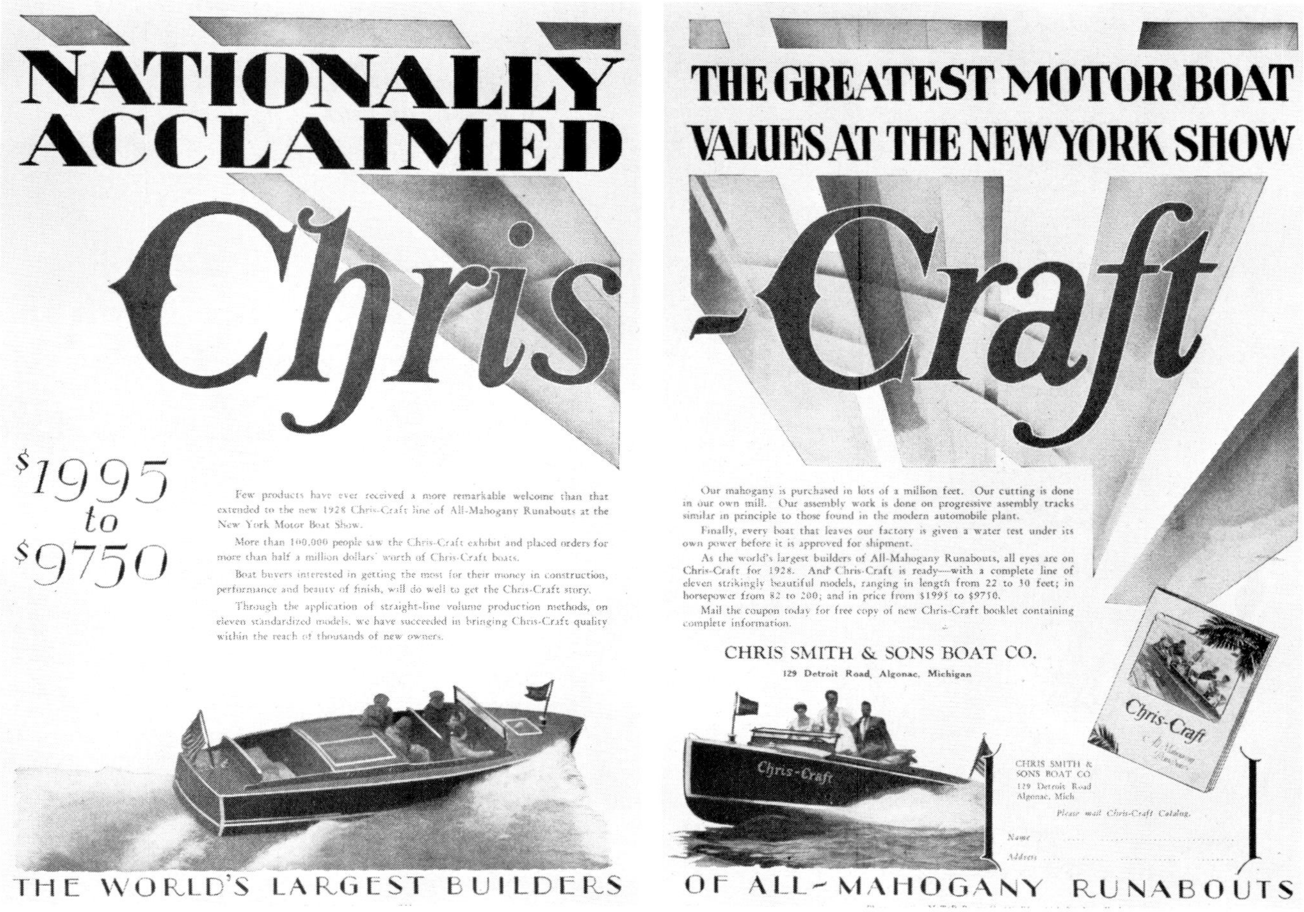

Another two page Chris-Craft ad for 1928.

A 1928 model Sedan type Chris-Craft.

# of Course You Want a full Season's Use!

Buy Your Chris-Craft NOW and make sure of it—

Once again, spring is here with its age old invitation to get outdoors—to shake off the shackles of winter—to open up the summer cottage—fish, play golf—go boating, camping, picnicking, swimming and aqua-planing.

Get your Chris-Craft now and enjoy a full season's use. Spend your leisure summer hours on the water. Enjoy the new water born freedom which only a Chris-Craft can give you.

See the new Chris-Craft line at your nearest dealer's. Ask him to give you and your family a demonstration ride. Note the increased power, speed, seating comfort and refinement of finish provided in the new 1928 models.

As the world's largest builders of all-mahogany runabouts, we are producing this year the greatest runabout values ever offered the boating public. Volume production and standardization have made Chris-Craft leadership more pronounced than ever.

Eleven Models—Including Two New Sedans

You may select the Chris-Craft best suited to your individual needs from a complete line of eleven models, ranging in length from 22 to 30 feet, in seating capacity from 8 to 14 passengers, in speed from 30 to 45 miles an hour, and in price from $2235 to $9750.

Included in the line are two new sedan models with permanent, custom built cabins as illustrated on opposite page.

Many new dealers have been appointed recently, thus making inspection and demonstration still more convenient. If there is no Chris-Craft dealer in your city, mail the coupon or write us and we will give you the name of one nearby.

Order now to insure delivery. Even with our tremendous capacity, we are unable to accumulate stocks for future delivery. See your dealer without delay.

CHRIS SMITH & SONS BOAT CO.
386 Detroit Road · · Algonac, Michigan

Chris-Craft

THE WORLD'S LARGEST BUILDERS OF ALL-MAHOGANY RUNABOUTS

11 Models $2235 to $9750

By 1928, Chris-Craft offered 11 different models, the 2 Sedans were beauties!

Chris-Craft Sales Records~

11 Models $2235 to $9750

WORLD'S LARGEST BUILDERS OF ALL-MAHOGANY

Smashes All

Deliveries and Unfilled Orders Greater Than Ever Before in the History of The Company

Day after day...week after week...month after month...Chris-Craft continues on its record-breaking wave of popularity! As the world's largest builders of all-mahogany motor boats, Chris-Craft is setting a terrific pace. Sales for the first five months of this year are 25% greater than for all of 1927.

It's a Chris-Craft year! Standardization and volume production have done the same thing to motor boat values that they did to automobile values. Values are higher than ever before. Prices are lower. No one any longer need deny himself the enjoyment of a Chris-Craft! Hundreds have bought and more are buying every day!

Even with a 24-hour schedule, the 56-acre Chris-Craft factory is unable to keep up with the demand.

Order your Chris-Craft now if you want early delivery. Eleven magnificent models await your inspection. There's a dealer near you to give you a Chris-Craft ride. Mail the coupon for his name if you do not know him.

CHRIS SMITH & SONS BOAT CO.
387 DETROIT ROAD · · ALGONAC, MICHIGAN

$2235 to $9750   22 to 30 Feet—30 to 45 Miles an Hour—82 to 200 Horsepower.

Chris-Craft

MOTOR BOATS

1928

1928 saw Chris-Craft offer a new 1-year deferred payment plan.

Chris-Crafts won about 7 races in 1928.

Chris-Craft ads 11 models, $2,235 to $9,750 with lengths from 22' to 30'.

A new 1928 Monnier Bros. & Co. boat "elevator."

Excellent 1928 photo showing close-ups of the Sedan cabins available then on the 24' and 26' Chris-Craft runabout. Roofs made by Kercheval Upholstering Co. of Detroit.

Even Commercial Credit Co. promoted Chris-Craft sales for 1928-28.

A fine 1929 Chris-Craft ad. Wish I had a copy of that catalog, don't you?

A neat 1929 Chris-Craft ad.

Excellent close-up of Chris-Craft yacht tender from about 1930.

pulled in their horns by 1930 and did a lot less advertising than in earlier days. I did find a few more photos of a couple of Chris-Craft Yacht Tenders still being made then on special order. The 38-foot Commuter cruiser had been slightly restyled by '30, sporting that convertible-type top located over the driver's station aft as shown.

By 1931 Chris-Craft was doing well enough to plan the construction of an all new administration building and

Two of the popular Chris-Craft yacht tenders built by Chris Smith & Sons Boat Co. The year was 1930.

Chris-Craft

The handsome 1930 38-foot commuter built by Chris Smith & Sons Boat Co., Algonac, Mich.

The Finest Tops That Can Be Made ✒ *for the finest boats that can be built*

Both Cruiser and Runabout Styles

KROH TOPS are standard equipment on—Chris-Craft, Gar Wood, Dodge, Hacker, Dart, Lyon-Tuttle, Corsair, Robinson. See them at the Show.

Made of Fade Proof Burbank Cloth and tailored like a glove. All Hardware is Rust Proof.

Write for Illustrated Booklet, on Tops and Cushions.

C. Z. KROH MANUFACTURING CO.
1922 Linwood Ave.,   Toledo, Ohio

C.Z. Kron made the finest tops used on the old "Woodies" back about 1930.

Artist's sketch of new Chris-Craft administration building and showroom to be built starting in late 1931.

Another fine 1931 Chris-Craft ad.

Scenes at the Taxi dock at Michigan Avenue Bridge, Chicago, one of the main stations of the Chris-Craft Water Transit Company. Here thousands have found the motorboat taxis a cheap, convenient, comfortable and pleasant way of getting quickly to their destinations. On the upper picture, left to right: The Wrigley Building, the Medinah Temple and the Tribune Tower.

showroom there at Algonac. A sketch of that building is shown here. Honest to goodness cabin cruisers came on the scene by 1931 at Chris-Craft, too. In that year, cabin cruisers in lengths of 31 feet and 36 feet were offered in five different cabin designs. An all varnished 34-foot Custom Commuter as well as a much larger 48-foot Custom Yacht was also added. That 48-footer priced out at $35,000 ready for the water. The rest of this section on Chris-Craft covers ads and photos from the years 1931 through 1955. I think they are all self-explanatory.

It has been fun to discuss with you this latest bit of newly found Chris-Craft material. Without further ado we shall now move right on to our next builder, Hacker Craft of Mr. Clemens, Michigan.

The 1931 Chris-Craft runabout was the hit of the Paris Boat Show!

A beautiful 48' Chris-Craft custom yacht built for O.M. Reif of Pittsburgh, Pa. Top speed was 30 m.p.h. with (2) 250 h.p. Chris-Craft engines — 1931.

Beautiful 1931 - 22' Chris-Craft Model 202 owned by George Sills of Peterborough, Ont. Canada. Photographed in 1980.

Turning the first shovel of earth for the new Chris-Craft office building. Left to right: Harsen Smith, Assistant to the President; Jay W. Smith, President; Chris Smith, Chairman of the Board, and Bernard Smith, Vice-President in charge of production.

A fleet of the new Chris-Craft "Level Riding" 1932 runabouts.

A nice little 16' - 1935 Chris-Craft runabout that sold for just $945.

A custom 1935 - 30' cruiser built for F. W. Hurlburt of Green Bay, Wis.

Unique aerial view ad of Chris-Craft factory in 1938.

1938 Chris-Craft ad.

1939 - 19' Chris-Craft. Note the single hatch cover.

Beautifully restored 1948 - 20' Chris-Craft custom runabout. Winner of "The Real Runabouts Award" at 1982 L.O.L. Antique Boat Show in Minnesota.

It won't be long before this "Red and Whiter" slides over the edge and into the water for 1940!

1940 ad.

1942 ad.

Larger Chris-Craft military boats — 1942.

Chris-Craft October 1942 ad.

July 1943

Futuristic 1942 Chris-Craft ad showing things to come.

1950 Chris-Craft ad showing the new outboard line.

1955 Chris-Craft ad.

HACKER CRAFT BOAT COMPANY

Hacker Craft inboards continue to enjoy nationwide interest as perhaps the ultimate runabout that collectors everywhere are seeking. I am surprised no one has started a Hacker owners' group or club. Probably since there are not as many Hackers as say Chris-Craft, Century or others, not enough people are available to make it viable. I have a rather interesting (though smaller than I would wish) new supply of Hacker materials to share with you here. First of all, I discovered an old November 1920 Hacker Craft ad that showed four "High-Class, Hight-Speed Pleasure Craft" built by the firm back then. Two of the boats shown are 35-foot runabouts while the larger two are 40-footers: one an express cruiser, the other a Commuter model. Without knowing what year those four Hackers were built, I myself would have thought they came from the late 1920's, not 1920 itself.

1920 - 40' Liberty powered Hacker-Craft express cruiser. Powered by Liberty engine with top speed of 39 m.p.h.

"Fastest displacement runabout in the world." "Sure Cure," a 35-foot 7 passenger beauty from 1920!

40-foot 1920 Hacker-Craft commuter powered by (2) LM 6 Hall-Scott engines. Top speed, 36 m.p.h.

"Snapshot" a speedy 1920 35-foot 7 passenger runabout powered by GR 6 sterling engine. Top speed was 39 m.p.h.

A beautiful early 1920's era 35-foot Hacker runabout powered by a Strasburg Wilson 450 h.p. Liberty engine.

The next photo of interest is a much smaller runabout, one with painted sides and just 21 feet long. This Hacker made quite a hit at the 1921 Detroit Boat Show. It was powered by a small Kermath and sold by Central Marine Service Corporation of Detroit, Michigan. Incidently, that same firm, Central Marine Service, also displayed the 26-foot 8-passenger Chris-Smith runabout shown earlier in the Chris-Craft section. By the way, if the Hacker-Craft history is a little blurry, may I suggest you take your *Volume I* and turn to page 26, running through page 35.

The next two ads are from 1922 and 1923, and give you some idea of what types of boats they were building back in those days. By 1923, Hacker Boat Company had moved up to Mt. Clemens, Michigan, where they remained in business until the firm finally ceased boat building many years later. Next are four Hacker Craft ads from 1926. The two new models for that year were the 22-foot Baby Dolphin with 2 seats aft and a small cockpit forward of the engine. Later in 1926 the old Baby Dolphin was redesigned with the more conventional split-cockpit arrangement with the engine mounted amidships and an early V-style windshield installed up front. I must include at this point a current photo of a restored 1926 35-foot Hacker runabout that once was owned by President Roosevelt. When new, it was powered by an 800 h.p. V-12 Packard engine. The boat was owned by Harper's Marine Restorations of

1921 Hacker-Craft 21-foot runabout powered by small Kermath. Top speed, 20 m.p.h. sold for $1,975.00 complete.

HACKER-CRAFT
AMERICA'S FINEST RUNABOUTS
PROPERLY DESIGNED   HONESTLY BUILT

Ask Any Owner

26-Foot Special Runabout

We can still make good delivery on a few of these special mahogany runabouts. They are completely equipped in every respect. Powered with a model D Scripps motor, speed from 23 to 25 miles. With 100 H.P. Hall-Scott, speed 30 to 33 miles. A better outfit could not be had at any price. Full particulars will be sent upon request.

Special Outfits

We are prepared to figure with you on any kind of a high-class runabout, sedan or limousine proposition. Speed guaranteed, and Hacker-standard quality. Prints, specifications and price upon knowing your requirements. Satisfaction guaranteed.

Hacker Plans

Send for the new Hacker book of plans before deciding on your next boat. Brimful of up-to-date high-class designs.

HACKER BOAT COMPANY
1525 CRANE AVENUE   DETROIT, MICHIGAN

Arrangement has been made with Fellows & Stewart, of Wilmington, Calif., to build 26-foot Standardized Boat in California.

1922 Hacker ad.

Hacker Craft

WOODFISH, Owned by Mr. Edsel Ford, FASTEST DISPLACEMENT RUNABOUT IN THE WHOLE WORLD

WE ARE now in position to build a number of Runabouts for 1923, and will be glad to figure on that SWEEPSTAKES, GOLD-CUP, CLASS-BOAT, or SPECIAL BOAT. WE build only the highest class, and DESIGN, WORKMANSHIP, & Maximum results are absolutely assured.

MODEL—23.

Get full particulars on this new HIGH GRADE, HUSKY, DOUBLE COCKPIT Mahogany Runabout, before placing your order for 1923. The greatest value in such combination ever offered to date. Will seat six or eight comfortably. Controls from forward cockpit. Will take you anywhere. Powered with 50 H. P. Marine Motor, speed 20-24 miles. Electric starter and lighting. Windshield, and completely equipped. Must be seen to be appreciated.

Price complete F. O. B. Factory $2750.00

ALSO POWERED WITH PACKARD Single Six Motor. Price upon request. Twelve of these boats will be available for FLORIDA deliveries.

We have for immediate delivery a few of our 21 foot, and 26 foot standard outfits, with speeds of from 18 to 25 miles. Also, a few good used Hackercraft boats.

HACKER BOAT COMPANY
1525 CRANE AVE.   DETROIT, MICH.

SEND FOR THE HACKER BOOK OF PLANS
WE ARE PREPARED TO FURNISH PLANS FOR ANY TYPE OF RUNABOUT, DAY CRUISERS, AND REGULAR CRUISERS TO YOUR ORDER, UP TO 125 FOOT, and solicit correspondence.

By 1923 Hacker-Craft runabout could really move out!

Raja—A 1925 handsome 26-foot runabout owned by R. B. Pettit of Cleveland. Powered with a high speed Kermath 6-cylinder engine, this handsome craft makes better than 30 m.p.h. It was built by the Hacker Boat Co.

Showing the New 22-foot Baby Dolphin Runabout

Two New Models for 1926—The Dolphin and Baby Dolphin Runabouts

A Faster 26-foot Dolphin

The 26-foot standard Dolphin in the new model is virtually the same as the previous one with the exception of several changes in hull lines that have given these runabouts an additional 2½ miles of speed. Nickel metal supplants the brass trim and gives the Dolphin an added air of beauty and refinement. Guaranteed speeds of more than 30 miles per hour with a standard six-cylinder marine motor go with every boat sold.

"Spend your play hours on the water in a Dolphin"

The new 22-foot runabout built by the Hacker organization and to be known as the Baby Dolphin has been designed to meet a very definite need. It is almost a duplicate in appearance of the refined 26-foot Dolphin with its smart lines and general effect. It is extremely staunch, is salt water equipped throughout and is ideal as a yacht tender or for small bodies of water. Equipped with either the Scripps F-4 or Scripps F-6 it attains speeds of 25-35 miles per hour, depending on the size power plant used.

You will find this roomy seven-passenger runabout ideal for any use and extremely economical to purchase and operate.

HACKER and FERMANN
INCORPORATED
DISTRIBUTORS
Sixty-three hundred E. Jefferson
DETROIT

"Baby Dolphin" in Foreground; Dolphin Behind

"Baby Dolphin"—A Show Hit

At three national boat shows—New York, Detroit, Baltimore—the "Baby Dolphin", newest product of Hackercraft, scored a decided hit.

Boat lovers and yachtsmen frankly expressed surprise over its refinements, seaworthiness and, particularly, its price. The "Dolphin" too, proved a popular exhibit, with its greater power and speed.

Both Dolphins are built of Honduras mahogany with double planked bottoms, full length engine timbers, copper and brass fastenings—salt water equipped.

1926 Prices

BABY DOLPHIN
21' 10" x 5' 10", Double Cockpit, Aft Control, 7 Pass., Speeds 23 to 37 mi., Motor Equipment as follows:

Continental-Van Blerck No. 250	$2475
Scripps F-4 Marine	2595
Scripps F-6 Marine	2995
Scripps F-6 Junior Gold Cup	3095

DOLPHIN
25' 10" x 6' 6", Double Cockpit, Forward Control, 10 Pass., Speeds 30 to 38 Mi., Motor Equipment as Follows:

Scripps F-6 Marine	$3900
Scripps F-6 Junior Gold Cup	3975
Scripps G-6 Marine	4625

You will want your boat without fail when spring arrives, so order it early to insure delivery in ample time.

New Agency Connections
Announced for the Benefit of Boat Buyers in neighboring localities.

NEW ENGLAND STATES—
Walter E. Moreton Corp.
1045 Commonwealth Avenue, Boston

MARYLAND—
Fred'k Read Strow
308 E. Lombard St., Baltimore, Md.

NEW YORK AND ENVIRONS—
Belle Isle Boat & Eng. Co.
Suite 1210, 393 Seventh Ave., New York, N. Y.

MIAMI, FLA.—
Clement Amory
118 North Bay Shore Drive

HACKER and FERMANN
INCORPORATED
DISTRIBUTORS
Sixty-three Hundred E. Jefferson
DETROIT

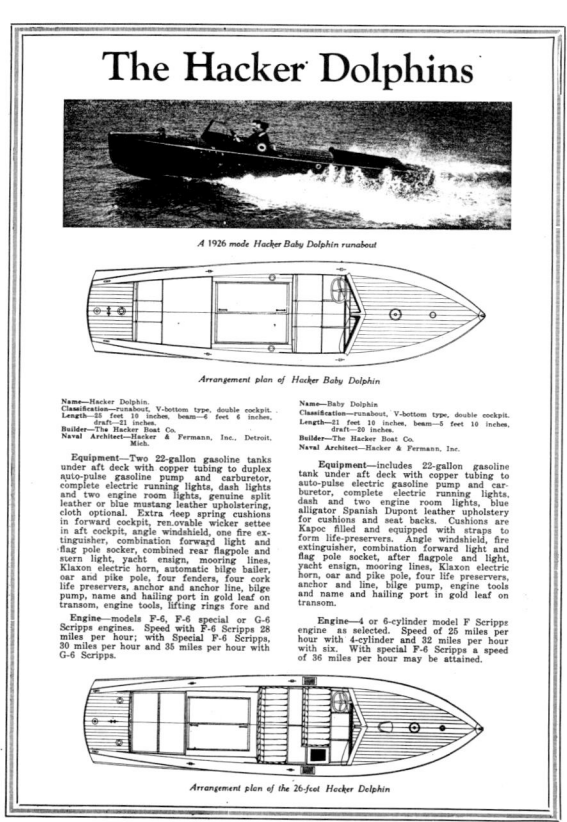

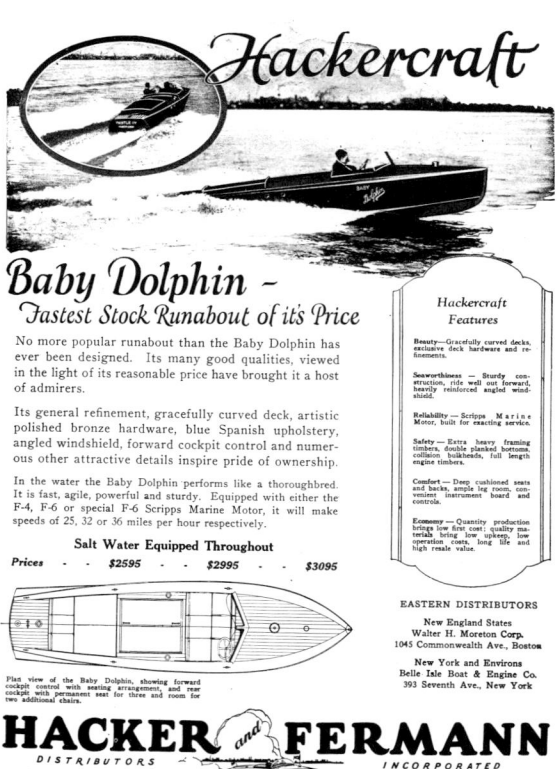

1926 ads.

1926 - 35' Hacker runabout once owned by President Roosevelt. It had an 800 h.p. V-12 Packard.

1927 Hacker ad.

For 1927 Hacker-Craft offered the Dolphin & Dolphin Deluxe.

This 1927 29-foot Hacker runabout was built for E. M. Payne of Winnipeg. She has a five passenger cockpit forward and carries three in the stern. With an F-6 Scripps engine she has been able to do a consistent thirty miles.

HACKERCRAFT
Husky - Fast - Safe - Sure

"OH BOY"—28-foot DOLPHIN DE LUXE, powered with Sterling Petrel motor (optional equipment), does better than 40 miles per hour. It is the first of our Southern Shipments. Duplicates of "OH BOY" are now ready for immediate delivery. The **added length** of this De Luxe model adds materially to comfort in a delightfully different way. Personal demonstration will prove this quickly to you. There is no finer or faster boat on the market under $10,000. The price, fully equipped, is $4,950.

The DOLPHIN

Has all the qualifications of the De Luxe model in a smaller boat. All the luxury. All the comfort. And that seaworthiness which makes it the best performing boat under 28 feet ever built. Speed close to 34 miles per hour. Price, fully equipped, $3,450. We will gladly arrange a personal demonstration at your convenience. Get behind the wheel and drive a Hackercraft yourself. That is the best proof.

HACKER BOAT CO.
MT. CLEMENS, MICHIGAN

Distributors:

Belle Isle Boat & Engine Co.
Detroit, Mich.

Chicago Motor Boat Mart
Chicago, Ill.

Walter H. Moreton Corp.
Boston, Mass.

John Wanamaker Stores
New York City

1928 - 28' Dolphin Deluxe.

Hackercraft
For 1929

Ten Outstanding Refinements and Improvements

AGAIN for 1929 Hackercraft will set new and higher standards of excellence in runabout design and construction, supplemented by surpassing beauty of line and finish. The creative art of John L. Hacker, internationally accepted as the world's foremost designer of fast pleasure boats, has attained new heights, and only in Hackercraft is available such blending of beauty in contour and efficiency in running lines.

Accurate woodworking machinery and the latest factory equipment open up the fullest possibilities for economical production. There are, however, time established standards of hand craftsmanship zealously retained in the Hacker shop practice because they can not be dispensed with except at a sacrifice of lasting qualities and staunchness. In the selection of materials is held equally important with inspired design and meticulous workmanship.

While it is only natural that Hacker prices must be slightly higher than those of competing boats, the almost negligible difference in price is more than compensated for in greater intrinsic value. A production program that warrants every practical manufacturing economy insure honest value giving.

1929 production is already under way on three standardized runabout classes, a 24, 26, and 29 foot in both open and Sedan types. A fine product has been made even better through the addition of ten outstanding refinements and improvements.

Inspection and demonstration can be arranged for at the factory or through the following distributors: Howard W. Lyon, Inc., 532 Lexington Ave., New York City; Walter H. Moreton Corporation, 1043 Commonwealth Avenue, Boston, Massachusetts; George L. Cropper, 2306 E. 71st Street, Chicago, Illinois; B. H. Hebgen, 326 Market Street, San Francisco, California; W. L. Hughes, 3213 Fairmount Blvd., Cleveland, Ohio; and Henry Farnsworth, West Palm Beach, Florida.

DEALERS: *Applications from new territories are now being considered.*

HACKER BOAT COMPANY
MOUNT CLEMENS   (Suburb of Detroit)   MICHIGAN

Getting ready for 1929. A 1928 Hacker ad.

Hackercraft

Hackercraft

29-ft. Dolphin
Eleven Passengers
40-42 Miles per Hour
Sterling Petrel Engine
$4,950
f.o.b. Mt. Clemens

Dolphins Are Bigger—Faster—Safer—Roomier—Easier Riding—Better Built

IT doesn't take five years, five months or even five days to show the superiority of Hacker Dolphins over other boats in their class. Five minutes' observation of their action under actual service conditions will prove it, if you are experienced in the fine points of speed boat performance and construction. Here is quality that can't be mistaken, efficiency that can't be faked, controllability and seaworthiness that has never been equalled.

John L. Hacker, the most successful speed boat designer of the day, has combined in the Dolphins the best features, discovered and developed in building hundreds of famous racers and fine custom boats. And at every point he has employed in the Dolphins the very best available, the most expensive materials, the strongest and most durable construction. Hacker Dolphins cost more to build and are worth more.

Hacker Dolphins have everything! Speed—riding comfort—seaworthiness—beautiful lines—exquisite finish—silent dependable power plants—roomy cockpits—deep spring cushions—remarkable responsiveness to throttle and wheel. They are easily America's finest runabouts.

Compared with other boats in the $4,000 to $5,000 class—

Bigger
29 ft. long, 7 ft. beam.
Far more seaworthy than other boats only 10% shorter.

Faster
40-42 miles per hour cruising speed easily maintained by its powerful Sterling motor.

Safer
Safer in rough water due to its liberal size, staunch construction and its dependable power plant.

Roomier
Ample seating for eleven passengers without crowding, and room for extra chairs. Forward cockpit over 9 ft. long, seats eight or more. After cockpit seats three.

Easier Riding
Doesn't pitch or pound. Skims over the top of the water, planes almost level, and rises and settles bodily when speeding up or slowing down.

Better Built
Nothing but the best in materials and workmanship. Selected Honduras mahogany—not African or Philippine. Heavy oak frames—not scrap mahogany. Solid nickel alloy hardware—not nickel-plated. Bronze screw fastening—not brass. Double planked bottom, bronze screwed and plugged. New Hacker design adjustable windshield with Triplex non-shatterable glass. Aeroplane type cockpits without coaming give improved appearance and perfectly streamlined decks. Interiors of cockpits fully lined with Spanish leather. Patented Erico self-aligning shaft log with inside stuffing box. Shortest length of exposed propeller shaft under boat—less than 30 inches in 29-ft. Dolphins; less than 26 inches in 26-ft. Dolphins. Goodrich Cutless rubber strut bearing. Yale lock on engine compartment.

Four Models—$2975 to $5850

29-ft. Dolphin, eleven passengers..........$4,950	26-ft. Dolphin, Jr., nine passengers..........$4,275
29-ft. Dolphin Sedan, ten passengers..........$5,850	24-ft. Baby Dolphin, nine passengers..........$2,975

Prices quoted f.o.b. Mt. Clemens, Mich.

Don't miss an opportunity to ride in a Hacker Dolphin. Demonstrations arranged by appointment. Complete data mailed on request.

HACKER BOAT COMPANY, MT. CLEMENS, MICH.

Distributors:

HOWARD W. LYON, INC.
Hotel Barclay
532 Lexington Ave. (at 49th St.)
NEW YORK

BELLE ISLE BOAT & ENGINE CO.
9662 E. Jefferson Ave.
DETROIT

WALTER H. MORETON CORPORATION
1043 Commonwealth Ave.
BOSTON

Dolphin Sedan Is the Ideal All-Weather Runabout

29-ft. Dolphin Sedan
Ten Passengers
40-42 Miles per Hour
Sterling Petrel Engine
$5,850
f.o.b. Mt. Clemens

26-ft. Dolphin, Jr.
Nine Passengers
40-42 Miles per Hour
200 H.P. Scripps Engine
$4,275
f.o.b. Mt. Clemens

Hackers race across this 1928 ad.

29-ft. Dolphin
Eleven Passengers
Sterling Petrel Engine
40-42 Miles per Hour
$4950 f.o.b. plant

Hackercraft Dolphins Are America's Finest Runabouts

THE 1928 Hackercraft Dolphin models are the finest standardized runabouts ever produced by this or any other company. This broad statement is warranted by tangible qualities of appearance, performance, equipment, construction and finish,—qualities which can be checked and verified by inspection, comparison and demonstration.

Dolphin quality is the result of a deliberate policy of building better, faster, safer, sturdier, more durable and more seaworthy boats, regardless of cost. And no other designer is so well fitted to carry out such a policy, for John Hacker's reputation is based on not merely one or even a score of successful racers, but upon literally hundreds of fine boats he has designed and built during the past 35 years.

A Hacker Dolphin is an investment for a lifetime of service. With reasonable care, any Dolphin will look and run like new five or even ten years from now. Surely Hackercraft quality is worth more than the little extra that it costs.

29-ft. Dolphin Sedan
Ten Passengers
40-42 Miles per Hour
$5850 f.o.b. plant

Dolphin Sedan *for* All-Weather Service

THE Dolphin Sedan is an enclosed runabout of the latest type, a boat combining the fleetness and easy handling of a fast runabout with the complete weather protection and comfort of a large cruiser. You can use this boat for more miles and more days of the year than any other type of craft you could own.

The ventilating windshield and sliding glass windows insure full ventilation when desired. Within a few seconds you can convert the sedan into a storm-tight, water-proof cabin, without leaving your seat or even slowing down. The windshield is raised and lowered from the driver's seat by a Packard type control. The powerful electric search-light on the forward deck is also controlled and directed from the dash.

The exceptionally large forward cockpit of the 29-ft. Dolphin makes it more roomy and practical as a Sedan than any other standard runabout model now on the market. This cockpit measures nine feet long by five feet four inches wide, inside dimensions. The sedan seats seven inside, with room for extra chairs, and three additional in the after cockpit.

Hacker Dolphins from $2975 to $5850

29 ft. Dolphin, eleven passengers..........$4,950	29 ft. Dolphin Sedan, ten passengers..........$5,850
26 ft. Dolphin, Jr., nine passengers..........$4,275	24 ft. Baby Dolphin, nine passengers..........$2,975

Prices quoted f.o.b. factory

Write today for complete details. Or better yet, examine the boats themselves and arrange with our nearest distributor for a demonstration.

HACKER BOAT COMPANY, MT. CLEMENS, MICH.

Distributors:

HOWARD W. LYON, INC.
HOTEL BARCLAY
532 Lexington Ave. (at 49th St.)
NEW YORK

BELLE ISLE BOAT & ENGINE CO.
9662 E. Jefferson Ave.
DETROIT

WALTER H. MORETON CORP.
1043 Commonwealth Ave.
BOSTON

26-ft. Dolphin Jr.
Nine Passengers
Scripps H-6 Engine
40-42 Miles per Hour
$4275 f.o.b. plant

1928 Hacker ad.

Meredith, New Hampshire. For 1928 Hacker offered the same 22-foot Baby Dolphin runabout, along with the 26-foot Standard Dolphin. Prices for that year were as follows: 22-foot Baby Dolphin, $2,500 to $3095. The larger 26-foot Standard Dolphin sold for $3,900 up to $4,625.

In 1928 Hacker Craft offered four models in total. There was the 24-foot Baby Dolphin, the 26-foot Dolphin Jr., the 29-foot Dolphin, and finally the new 29-foot Dolphin sedan, a 10-passenger runabout. With 1929 in poorer times Hacker, like all other boat builders, began to cut back. For that year only three models were built. The same three lengths—24', 26', and 29'—were offered, little changed from 1928.

I shall list for your review some of the firms selling Hacker Craft for 1929. The list is longer than I myself would have thought.

Howard W. Lyon, Inc. - New York, NY
Walter H. Moreton Corp. - Boston, Mass.
George L. Cropper - Chicago, Ill.
B. H. Hebgen - San Francisco, Calif.
W. L. Hughes - Cleveland, Ohio
Henery Farnsworth - West Palm Beach, Fl.

The conclusion of the material on Hacker Crafts runs from 1931 through the 1950s. It has been a pleasure sharing this new Hacker Craft material with you. By the way, Chapter IX will cover the *new* Hacker Craft runabouts turned out by our old friend, Bill Morgan, the "dean" of Hacker authorities in every way. I think you will greatly enjoy the material on Bill's new boats; there you can have the best of the old with the technology of today, and the prices are not that bad either.

Our next firm we shall look at is Century Boat Company, builders of Thoroughbred boats.

Over the transom of a 1929 Hacker.

1929 Hacker-Craft Gold Cup winner.

1931 - 22½ Hacker-Craft 3 cockpit runabout. A 6 cylinder 75 h.p. Chrysler provides the power.

1931 - 28' Hacker-Craft runabout powered by Kermath Sea-Wolf 22 h.p.

King of Siam's special 38' custom sedan Hacker-Craft commuter.

1932 - 14' single step Hacker-Craft hydroplane powered by a Universal Blue-Jacket 40 h.p. engine.

1931 view of the new Lake of the Ozarks novel boat house which lifts itself, including the boat, out of the water at the touch of a button.

The latest 1931 type Hacker designed 125 cubic inch class hydroplane built by the Hacker Boat Co.

1931 - 40' Lockpat II.

El Lagarto was a very successful racer — 1931.

Original factory photo of the Helen-A, 1936 - 33' Hacker-Craft runabout, powered by a 750 h.p. Capital engine. Photo from Gordon Fairbanks collection.

CENTURY BOAT COMPANY OF MANISTEE, MICHIGAN

I am pleased to tell you that interest in wooden Century Boats has grown greatly since *Volume III* was written. The Century Boat Club, now in its fourth year, has a membership nearing 1,150. As with all the other antique boat clubs, this one also suffers from some membership turnover, but all in all it has done much better than any of us ever imagined. Currently, the Club's *Quarterly* magazine runs about 20 to 22 pages per edition. If you would like a sample copy of the Newsletter and a membership application, please send a self-addressed business size envelope with 37¢ postage to the following address:

Mrs. Barb Sima, Sec.
CENTURY BOAT CLUB
20 W. 309 Frontage Rd.
Lemont, IL 60439

I don't wish to bore you, but I now finally have my own inboard, a 1964 15' Resorter with 160 h.p. Interceptor, and as of this writing it is being converted over from a utility to a custom split-cockpit runabout. Will have more about that later.

The rest of this report will be broken down into sections. The first one will consist of 8 photos, most of which have appeared in the Century *Quarterly* magazine over the last four years in a column which we call

22' Hacker-Craft runabout.

19½' Hacker-Craft owned by D. S. Anspach, M.D., Snow Farm, E. Montpelier, Vt.

A custom built Hacker-Craft runabout located in Canada.

Father B. R. Hubbard off the northwest coast of Alaska in 1939. His Century 20' sport utility was powered by a Gray Phantom six-103 motor.

A Century Sea Maid being trailed from the factory in Michigan to Columbus, Ohio to the dealership of W. C. Kennedy & Son. Trailers like this were rare in 1939.

1940 view of Tippicanoe Boat display at Outdoor Show in South Bend, Ind.

New showrooms constructed at Fall River, Mass. by the Capt. Joseph O'Connell Co. in 1954. This firm sold many Centurys over the years.

A portion of Kinn Motors Marine in Oconomowoc, Wis. The year was 1955.

1931 Barrel-Boat Race being refereed by two fellows in a Thunderbolt two seat racer.

1938 display of Chiott & Son Boat Co. as shown at the Vermont Sportsmen's Show held in Burlington, Vt. This firm sold Centurys in large numbers!

New Century Sedan Being Delivered by Elmer Schneider of St. Louis, Mo.

Elmer Schneider, head of Schneider Sales & Service, Inc., 4919 South Kingshighway, St. Louis, Mo., recently made a trip with his service truck to the Century Boat Co., Manistee, Mich.

Upon his return to St. Louis Mr. Schneider brought a deluxe 20-foot Century Sedan with a Gray Phantom six-103 h.p. marine engine driving direct to a Michigan Aquamaster high efficiency propeller 12 x 12. This unit is capable of a speed of 34 m.p.h. 1941.

"Centurys in the News." They start in 1932, showing the Century Boat Company display at the Chicago Boat Show. The other 7 depict some showrooms and famous boats. Perhaps the best photo in this first section is the view taken during the South Bend Outdoor Show in 1940, featuring the Century and Wolverine boats then sold by Tippicanoe Boat Company of Leesburg, Indiana.

Moving on, the rest of this material covers Century Boats in general from 1932 up to 1963. Perhaps the most unique Century ever built was the 1932 Sea King 93. It was 22 feet long and equipped with a beautiful "torpedo" stern, and was 6'10" wide. The hull was planked all in Peruvian mahogany on the deck, with the hull sides painted black with white waterline and bright red bottom paint. This beauty was powered by a 93 h.p. Gray Phantom engine and was to sell for $2,185—no cheap price for 1932. So far we have not learned of one of those Sea King runabouts still in existence and we seriously doubt if any are still around, much less in good shape. There is a good chance that not even one of these boats were ever made, though that earlier photo showing the Centurys on display in 1932 in Chicago says a Sea King 93 is in the background. 1932 was such a poor year for boat builders and dealers that I really doubt if very many of this expensive Century was ever built or sold.

1932
Century's runabout exhibit, with the "Sea Maid 65" in the foreground and the "Sea King" bow-on in the left center.

Century's 1932 Sea King.

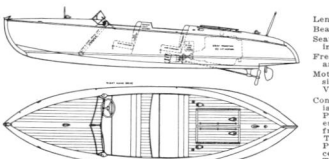

1932 Century Boatgram announcing the new 22' Sea King runabout.

A "Thunderbolt" streaks down the course to victory.

The next four views show the famous Thunderbolt 2-seat runabout in various activities. Interest in these boats runs very high, and I am proud to announce that Chuck Miklos of Pittsburgh, Pennsylvania, has found one of the speedsters and is currently restoring it back to its former glory. Century Club member Jim Johnson of Illinois is seriously considering building a replica of a Thunderbolt very soon. Century in the year 1939 began offering smaller, less deluxe utility crafts ranging in size from 15 feet through 20 feet in length. The 15-foot model was basically the same as the 15-foot outboard and featured the round bilge design feature. Two sedan utilities were offered in 1939: an 18' and 20' version were available.

The Century sedan utility craft first was introduced in 1939, replacing the line of wooden pleasure class sail-

Century Thunderbolt doubling as the net line for a hot game of tennis during the summer of 1931.

1939 - 15' Century utility with 45 h.p. Sea Mate sold for from $565 to $585 each. New round bilge model.

1939 - 16' utility with 45 at 75 h.p. Gray engines. "A high class boat at a medium price."

1939 - 18' utility with engines from 75 to 103 h.p. "The Aristocrat of service models."

The New THUNDERBOLT by CENTURY

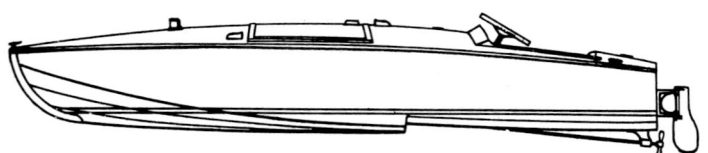

Speed 45 m.p.h.
Gray "Blue Streak"
63 h.p. Racing Motor

$1,075
F. O. B. Manistee

14 feet long
54 inches beam

$600 Without Motor

With the CENTURY Air-cushion Bottom (Patents Pending)

The Inboard Racing Field is Dominated by CENTURY Boats, Just as CENTURY Hydroplanes Dominate Outboard Racing

We, at CENTURY, are pardonably proud of the 1932 THUNDERBOLT, the logical and proven choice for 125 cu. in. class racing, for it has winning speed, structural quality and strength for long life, and sales possibilities which appear unbounded.

The whole world knows and acknowledges CENTURY leadership in the outboard racing field; leadership that is a matter of cold, immutable record established in National Championship competition and in thousands of races the world over.

The consummate designing skill which developed CENTURY'S outboard racing fleet has scored again with the new CENTURY inboard racers. The new THUNDERBOLT will actually develop 45 miles per hour with the Gray 63 h. p. Blue Streak racing motor, miles per hour faster than competition. The performance qualities which made it the outstanding sensation of 1931 power racing have been improved. We suggest, advisedly, that no other racing creation on the market can even approach the high characteristics of the new THUNDERBOLT.

Difficulty experienced in 1931 with the rudder-strut arrangement has been eliminated with the new stream-lined underwater parts of the new model. The rudder bearing has been displaced by a perfected strut and Goodrich Cutless rubber bearing ahead of the propeller. The rudder has been improved to give maximum positive control at all times.

The addition of heavy hogging stringers to add longitudinal strength, and of a new type of under-deck construction to add lateral strength and provide against deck warping are features which will be of interest to all dealers and their boat-buying prospects. The THUNDERBOLT has been "dressed up" to present an even more striking appearance than the previous model. And the 1932 model, with greater speed and improved performance, more strength and striking beauty, has been reduced more than two hundred dollars in price as compared to last year's THUNDERBOLT.

The THUNDERBOLT is very economical to operate; it is the safest racing craft ever manufactured; it has a dual purpose in that it may be used for class racing or for high speed pleasure boating; it has the already tremendously famous air-cushion bottom; and it now sells at a price well within the reach of thousands of sport-loving Americans. It is a profit boat for the dealer, for a present sales field, an established market.

The THUNDERBOLT hull without motor, shaft and propeller, is now available at $600.00 list price, subject to contract discount. There is a real sales field for this hull. Many owners of 125 cu. in. or 151 cu. in. motors will buy it and install their own motors. It has sufficient strength and correct design to handle even more powerful motors. At the price quoted above, upholstery, steerer, rudder, fittings and other items of equipment are included.

THUNDERBOLT SPECIFICATIONS

Length—14 feet.

Beam—54 inches.

Freeboard—Bow 16 inches; amidship 16 inches, stern 12 inches.

Motor—Gray Blue Streak, 125 cu. in. racing special, four cylinder, four cycle, 63 h. p., complete with electric starter and generator, oversize reverse gear and all necessary equipment, mounted amidship and driving direct.

Speed—45 m. p. h.

Seating—two, in single aft cockpit.

Constructed entirely of selected highest quality Philippine mahogany, CENTURY processed to impregnate each plank against moisture absorption, finished natural with Valspar. Air-cushion bottom (patents pending). Racing green bottom paint. Bottom double copper riveted, sides and deck brass screw fastened.

Deck hardware and fittings highly polished, durable white metal, salt water corrosion resisting.

White metal cutwater; combination bow plate and cleat; forward mooring cleat; bowlight and bow flag pole; four ventilators; two hatch handles; gas tank filler plate and cap; two stern cleats; stern flag pole, light and socket; brass rub rails. CENTURY pennant; white metal fender rails; brass rub rails, and fin.

Ross special steerer, cam and lever, with direct, positive outboard rudder control; special upholstery of Russialoid, cushion Kapok filled, spring back, red and black; 13-gallon gas tank; CENTURY instrument panel with ammeter, oil pressure guage, tachometer, choke control, light and ignition switch; self-aligning shaft-log; ⅞ in. Monel shaft; CENTURY strut with Goodrich Cutless rubber bearing; CENTURY type propeller; Manganese Bronze rudder and brackets; lifting cables fore and aft; CENTURY type self-bailer, full automatic and fool proof; two rubber step pads.

Keel—forward, 1⅝ in. x 3½ in., aft, 1¼ in. x 3½ in.; frames, ⅝ in. x 2½ in.; chines, ¾ in. x 2 in.; planking—bottom, ⅜ in., sides, 5-16 in., deck ¼ in.; battens, ½ in. x 1⅜ in.; transom ¾ in. solid. Planking set in Dolphinite.

"Race with CENTURY—The Choice of Champions—And Ride to Victory"

CENTURY THUNDERBOLTS Placed First and Second in the 133-mile Albany-N. Y. Marathon—1931

CENTURY BOATS, Inc.   ::   ::   Manistee, Michigan

1932 Century Thunderbolt ad.

1939 - 18' sedan with power from 75 h.p. through 140 h.p. A great rough water boat priced from $1,395 to $1,845.00.

1939 - 20' Sedan utility, a beautiful hard-top model. Had power up to 140 h.p. with lots of extras available.

boats the firm had been building I am sure there are a few of the sedans around, but we have yet to have one register with the Century Club.

In 1940 Century issued a beautiful catalog, so here we share with you a selection of models from that year. Not a whole lot had been changed, but still I think a quick photo review of Centurys from 1940 wll be interesting. Probably the most rare model shown here is the 20-foot 3-cockpit runabout. Though short, the boat could seat 10 people, as shown, in relative comfort. One of our Century Boat Club members has one of these 3-seaters and is now in the process of restoring it. The next photo shows a Century 17' Deluxe runabout sporting a then all new wraparound Plexiglass windshield. It was 1955 when Chris-Craft first used that type of windshield.

I am not sure just how many Century boats were

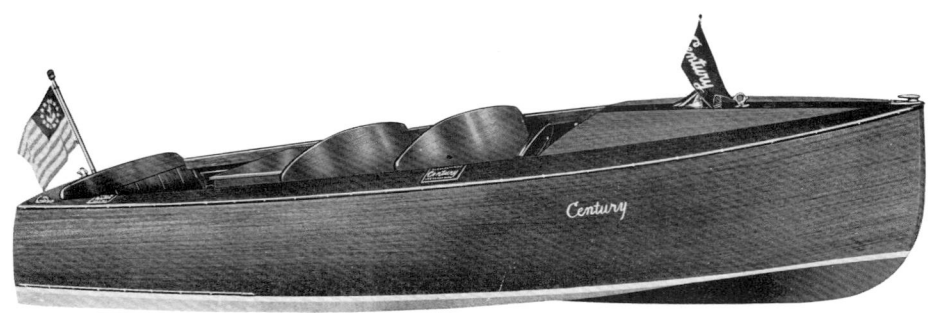
1939 - 20' 3 seat utility. "A big boat for utility jobs."

1940 - 16' Sea Maid runabout powered by a 62 h.p. engine.

1940 - 17' Deluxe utility.

All aboard for fun in a 1940 - 18½' DeLuxe utility.

A less deluxe 1940 - 20' Century utility.

Excellent view of 1940 - 18½' sport utility.

1940 - 18½' Sedan utility powered by a 90 h.p. Gray.

Close-up stern view of 20' Sedan utility with engines up to 103 h.p.

The sleek, streamlined Model 54 - 17' Sea Maid runabout. Note wrap around windshield for 1940.

made in 1942, but recently I had the use of two flyers from that year that showed three different runabouts and utilities built in that year. My own favorite was the 17' Sea Maid twin-cockpit model. The rest of this section will be all photos running up as far as 1963.

Hope you have enjoyed the Century material, and if you are interested in joining the Century Boat Club be sure to write Mrs. Sima for your sample issue and application form.

Our next stop will be Dee-Wite Boat Company, one of my all-time favorite builders, especially their beautiful Lodge "Torpedo"-styled runabouts.

1940 split-cockpit 17' runabout powered by a 90 h.p. Gray.

1940 Sea Maid Model A91 - 18½' with engines to 140 h.p.

1940 - 20' - 3-cockpit Century runabout.

1941 - 17' Century DeLuxe runabout equipped with plexiglass sprayshield.

1942 - 17' utility. These boats were nicely finished with dark red marine naugahyde upholstery.

A rare view of one of the last 1942 - 17' Sea Maid runabouts ever built before the start of WW II.

1942 Century runabout.

Tippicanoe Boat Co., Leesburg, Ind. trailer with two new Centurys just back from the factory in late 1940's.

November 1943 ad.

A "Bevy of beauties" pose aboard a new Century Sea Maid thirty years ago. Photo courtesy of Tippicanoe Boat Co. of Indiana.

1947 ad.

Century G-M, Harold V. Bright and Buel B. Nave, sales director, inspect a 1950 - 20' Century Resorter ordered by Count Maximillen Pulaski of Cannes and Paris. This boat was to be used for water skiing.

1950 - 20' Century Sea Maid equipped with optional top.

1951 ad.

sea maid 20

The Queen of the Century Fleet — an all African-mahogany speed boat that's right in every detail. Speeds up to 44 m.p.h.

"You need CENTURY plus values to help you beat competition"

Roland B. Mueller and his brother operate the INLAND MARINE CORPORATION in Minneapolis, Minnesota and have been exclusive Century Dealers since 1941.

"It takes the plus values in a product to stay out front in a highly competitive market. That's why I sell Century Boats year after year successfully. I find that Century's extras — the mirror finish, the wide choice of engines, the fine materials and the excellent taste in fittings and appointments — outweigh any other advantage my competition may have. You just can't beat true value when it comes to building customer confidence. That's one thing that builds your volume and profits and helps you stay in business year in and year out.

D. B. Mueller, President

THESE SALES ADVANTAGES WILL HELP YOU STAY AHEAD OF COMPETITION

1. A complete line of beautiful, expensively built outboard and inboard boats.
2. A thoroughly pleased, happy and enthusiastic group of Century owners to help you sell new prospects.
3. National advertising and Dealer Helps to back your selling.

To complete our present fine Dealer organization, some Century Dealerships are still available. Write Sales Manager, Century Boat Co., Manistee, Michigan.

the thoroughbred of boats

Century

CENTURY BOAT CO., Box 425, Manistee, Mich.

1951 ad.

Inside of 1950 Century cover.

Front cover of 1953 Century catalog.

Close-up of Century single-plank batten-seam construction.

1953 Century Sea Maid 18 and 20.

1953 Century Viking 19.

1953 Century Resorter 16.

1953 Resorter 18 and 20.

1953 Century Viking 19.

1953 Century Resorter 18 and 20.

1953 Century Sea Maid 18 and 20.

First 1957 Raven built by Century. Owned by Bob J. Loop of Kingsville, Ont. Canada.

1963 Coronado 21' - 325 Crusader V-8. Custom equipped and owned by L. R. Hardy of Dayton, Ohio.

1959 experimental Century Coronado "Show Boat."

DEE WITE—"THE TORPEDO FLEET"

I have come up with some new material concerning Dee Wite boats. Just to show you how rare Dee-Wite inboards and outboards really are, a quick glance through the 1983 Antique & Classic Boat Society, Inc. Directory shows only four of that brand of inboard listed. Of course, there are others around, as I myself have seen at least two others. One is located at Sierra Boat Company on Lake Tahoe while the other "lives" in northern Iowa, tucked away and waiting for a complete restoration to be done very soon.

Joseph B. Lodge

In September, 1931, Joseph B. Lodge, photo shown here, announced plans to completely reorganize both Dee-Wite, Inc. and Lodge Motors. Lodge acted as president of both firms and announced to the public that John E. Clifford would join the new operation as vice president and director of sales, advertising and service.[1] Clifford had been very active in the marine industry through the years and was most excited about his new position at Dee-Wite. Lodge announced that shipments to dealers of new Dee-Wite boats during July of '31 were the highest ever with the exception of May, 1930. In August, 1931, the following inventory was all that remained at the Detroit, Michigan, plant: no cabin cruisers left, with 17 runabouts in various stages of completion making up the firm's entire remaining inventory.[2]

In *Volume II*, page 119, I made mention of the trip undertaken by two brave young ladies attempting to pilot several new 22-foot twin-cockpit runabouts from Detroit, Michigan, to St. Louis, Missouri. Shortly after that, Joseph Lodge decided to really give his crafts a test by starting at Detroit, Michigan, going east and eventually arriving in New York City, then working their way down the Eastern seaboard, across to the Gulf, and then up the "Mighty Mississippi," finally ending at St. Louis. Rather than telling you more about this exciting endurance run for boats, women, and yes, four men drivers where water and weather conditions called for it, I shall tell you what magazine the complete story appears in so you can go to the library and read it yourself: *Power Boating*, February, 1931, pages 25-29. The entire trip took 248 hours and 2 minutes for the 4,430 mile trip. The trip was a success in every way. Five excellent photos are shown at this time which will show you those two 22-foot Dee-Wites during various stages of the trip.

The endurance party. Left to right: Carl Mehrer, Miss Peggy Radcliffe, Ralph Hulton, L. F. Rogers, Miss Maude Hughes and Jack Prosser.

The first overnight stop was at the Cleveland Yacht club at Rocky River, O., after the run from Detroit.

Miss Maude Hughes and Miss Peggy Radcliffe and the boat which they piloted from New York City to Miami.

---

[1] "Runabouts Tame Lake, Ocean and River," *Power Boating* (February '31), p. 29.

[2] "Dee Wite & Lodge Motors Plan Expansion," *Motorboat* (September '31), p. 51.

On the way up the Mississippi River. One of the boats speeding along the Arkansas shore of the river.

The new Dee-Wite Model 3 is 16 feet long and powered with a 4-cylinder motor.

Taking on gas at a refueling barge on the Mississippi River at Natchez, Miss.

Model 9 of the new Dee-Wite line is a snappy, roomy craft on a length of 19' and powered with a six-cylinder motor.

The rest of this section of Dee-Wite basically consists of photos I have gathered that show these boats in use back over 50 years ago. The first is a view of what I am told is a 1930 Dee-Wite Custom Commuter still powered by her original V-12 Scripps engine. The cabin and flying bridge have been remodeled and modernized over the years, but this has to be one rare boat. The next four photos are of 1930 Dee-Wite inboards demonstrating their riding and operating capabilities for the camera. I think the 19-foot split-cockpit runabout is probably the rarest one shown in that section of photos.

The 19-foot Dee-Wite powered with a 4-cylinder motor is said to develop speeds up to 28 miles per hour.

Dee-Wite 1930 custom commuter, remodeled has original V-12 Scripps engine.

A speed of 32 m.p.h. is claimed for this 19-foot Dee-Wite. It is powered with a six-cylinder motor.

Fleet of five Dee-Wite runabouts which served as officials' boats during the American Legion regatta Sept. 21 on the Detroit River. These same boats served in a similar capacity during the Harmsworth races.

What will DEE WITE do in 1932?

Q. Is Dee Wite prepared to dominate its market in 1932?

A. Most emphatically, yes! Never before has any manufacturer in the boating industry been in a more favorable position, from the engineering, manufacturing and sales standpoint.

Q. Will Dee Wite offer complete model coverage?
A. Yes.
Q. Will they have models in the $1,000 class?
A. Yes.
Q. Will they have models in the $1,500 class?
A. Yes.
Q. Will they have models in the $2,000 class?
A. Yes.
Q. Will they have models in the $3,000—$4,000 class?
A. Yes.
Q. Will they have models in the $5,000—$10,000 class?
A. Yes.

Q. Will they have boats beyond this price classification?
A. Yes. Models ranging in price up to $60,000.
Q. Will they have custom-built models?
A. Yes, in several different price groups.
Q. Will they have anything new in hull and deck lines?
A. Yes, again. Before the season is over, several refreshingly new departures will have set an advanced style in boat design.
Q. Will the Dee Wite merchant make money?
A. Yes.
Q. Will Dee Wite owners receive greater values?
A. Yes, outstanding values, reflecting fully the economies of lower material and production costs, plus unique manufacturing advantages.
Q. Will Dee Wite exhibit at the New York Boat Show?
A. Yes.

Those interested further in the Dee Wite 1932 program are invited to visit the Dee Wite plant or write for additional information.

DEE WITE, INC. DETROIT, MICHIGAN
Manufacturers of Mahogany Runabouts, Cruisers, and Custom-Built Boats

Watch for the DEE WITE Announcement NEXT MONTH

Ad for Dee Wite explaining their intentions for 1932.

Dee-Wite, 22-foot runabout used by Pittsburgh police for patrolling Monongahela River.

The remainder of photos are from late 1931 through 1933. The only one that is probably not self-explanatory is the nice shot showing the Dee-Wite, Inc. display at the 1933 Chicago Power Boat Show. My favorite is the Model 651 28-foot 10-passenger Torpedo runabout shown to the far left of the photo.

I am happy to report that Al and Brett Schinnerer are now the proud owners of the *Miss Dee-Wite II* shown on page 123 and 124 of *Volume III*. The fellows, who are very active in the manufacture of marine hardware for the antique and classic boats as well as selling and buying boats, tell me the old racer needs lots of "T.L.C." before it ever runs again. Brett tells me they found it out in California where some years back it was used as a lowly fishing boat. The owner had sawed off the torpedo stern and built a conventional square transom on it. The fellows plan down the road to restore this old racer and maybe, if we are lucky, we will have a photo or two of it in *Volume VI* or *VII*.

The final firm we shall review in this first section is Gar Wood—The Commodore's Fleet.

1933 - 22' DeLuxe runabout by Dee-Wite powered by a 135 h.p. Lodge engine.

Dee-Wite Inc., had a particularly fine display at the recent Chicago Power Boat Show. Left to right: The model 651 Lodge 28-foot 10-passenger runabout; the model 600 six-passenger 17-footer; the model 606 six-passenger 19-footer; model 625 eight-passenger 19-footer; model 627 eight-passenger 22-footer and the well-known Dee-Wite 24-foot popular priced cruiser.

GAR WOOD— THE COMMODORE'S FLEET

Interest in the beautiful boats built by the firm of Gar Wood just continues to grow all the time. A big part of this new interest definitely has to be attributed to the Gar Wood Society headed by Tony Mollica, a good friend and fellow wooden boat buff. Tony and the members of the Gar Wood Society have over the last few years strived diligently to reproduce for members of that club authentic refinishing supplies such as varnishes, stains, paints, brushes, and many other needed items that are so hard to find today. In a recent telephone conversation with Tony he told me the club is going along nicely and he hopes to soon start publishing more of the Gar Wood Society. News-letters that everyone enjoyed so much in past years. Gar Wood material is not the easiest thing to find, but I feel fortunate to have unearthed some very interesting old photos and ads to share with you here.

The first ad shows a pictorial history of Gar Wood boats that dated way back to the year 1898. This

In 1922 Gar Wood's Baby Gar runabout was guaranteed to go 50 m.p.h. with a 450 h.p. Liberty Marine motor.

1923 Baby Gar ad.

The world's speediest standardized runabout in 1925 was Gar Wood's Baby Gar.

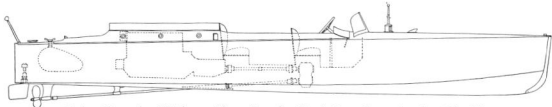

1926 Gar Wood ad explaining the advantages of a gear box.

Coming!

(next issue)

a **GarWood** Announcement

$3,500
$4,000
$6,000
$9,800
$11,800

that will Startle the Boating World

1898 The "Ark," Gar Wood's first boat. Speed 6 miles per hour with a 3-H.P. single-cylinder Truscott motor.

1912 "Little Leading Lady," Gar Wood's first winner. A single-step hydroplane that made 30 miles an hour with its 6-cylinder Emerson 2-cycle motor. The hull cost $40.

1915 "Miss Detroit" first won the coveted Gold Cup for Gar Wood in 1915. Other Gar Wood boats won this event every year from 1917 to 1921 when the rules were changed to limit the power.

1920 The first of the Miss America which brought the Harmsworth International Trophy from England to America, emblematic of the world's championship in boat racing. Speed 76.915 miles per hour with two 450-H.P. Libertys. Also won the Gold Cup in 1920 and 1921.

1921 "Miss America II," the fastest boat in the world, official speed 80.567 miles per hour. Four Liberty engines. Successfully defended the Harmsworth International Trophy in 1921.

1921 "Gar Jr.," the 50-ft. express cruiser that beat the express train schedule from Miami, Florida, to New York, making 1217 miles through the open ocean in 47½ hours. Speed 36.6 miles per hour. Two 450-H.P. Gar Wood Liberty Marine Engines.

1923 "Cigarette," a Gar Wood built 70-ft. cruiser, the fastest boat of its size ever built. 50 miles an hour with five Gar Wood Liberty engines totalling 2210 H.P.

1925 "Baby Gar IV," the boat that beat the crack Twentieth Century Limited from Albany to New York, making 137 miles in two hours and fifty minutes. This run attracted greater public attention than any other motor boat achievement.

1926 "Miss America V," successful defender of the Harmsworth International Trophy in 1926, made a 3-mile lap in 72.702 miles per hour, a world's record for speed in competition. Maximum speed never officially timed.

1927 And what is coming for 1927, after this long string of Gar Wood achievements? Only a few of the high spots are shown on these pages. Next month Gar Wood's latest will be unmasked. It is decidedly worth waiting for!

Gar Wood was preparing the boating world for 1927 in this December 1926 ad.

complete 2-page ad was run in boating magazines here in the U.S. back in December, 1926 to announce exciting plans for the 1927 Gar Woods. A little later in this section we shall see just what exciting 1927 models were offered for that year that "would startle the boating world." First, though, I have a very old 1922 Gar Wood ad to share with you. In '22 a 33-foot "Baby Gar" sold for $7,250 to $8,250, depending on horsepower selected. 1923 saw another ad where the same basic boat was offered, still powered by either a 300 h.p. Fiat-type engine or the massive 450 h.p. Liberty marine engine.

The next five old ads run from late 1923 up through October, 1926. If you recall, Howard W. Lyon started out as exclusive distributor for Gar Wood not only here in this nation, but also in England. Howard Lyon did an excellent job as Gar Wood distributor in the years just prior to forming his own runabout building firm, Sea Lyon, which we have reviewed in *Volume II*. I noted with interest that Minneapolis, Minnesota had a Gar Wood dealer located at 528 University Avenue, S.E. in 1927.

For 1927 Gar Wood offered three different inboard runabouts. The queen of the fleet that season had to be the 33-foot Baby Gar runabout. This beauty was the largest and fastest stock runabout then on the market. The middle-size Gar Wood was the Baby Gar 28-foot followed by a new Baby Gar Jr. 26-footer. Various old photos and ads pertaining to the 1927 Gar Woods are shown here for your review. The Baby Gar Jr. 26-foot runabout was equipped with a single front cockpit with a large open rear cockpit that had a front facing rear seat, plus room for two wicker chairs.

F. Todd Warner, collector-dealer from Mound, Minnesota, owns a 1927 33' Baby Gar that originally operated on Lake Geneva, Wisconsin, being part of a fine old estate. This boat had been stored for many years, and following a complete refurbishing it appeared in the 1981 Land-O-Lakes Chapter of the Antique & Classic Boat Show held on Lake Minnetonka, just west of Minneapolis, Minnesota. There are three photos showing this beautiful boat at this point. I was most fortunate in being able to have a ride in the *Phoenix*, as it is now called, during that weekend. I must relate the

Gar Wood sets a New World's Record in 1926.

The Baby Gar was doing good in Europe too in 1926.

For Boating Post Graduates

If you have passed through the various stages of boating experience and are ready for the last word in performance, speed and reliability

Get a *BABY GAR*

The final development of Gar Wood's 12 years' experience.

Immediate Delivery Now

For Demonstration Communicate With

HOWARD W. LYON
EXCLUSIVE DISTRIBUTOR
Gotham National Bank Building
1819 Broadway, New York City
Telephone: Columbus 1212

Built by
GAR WOOD, Inc., Detroit, Mich.

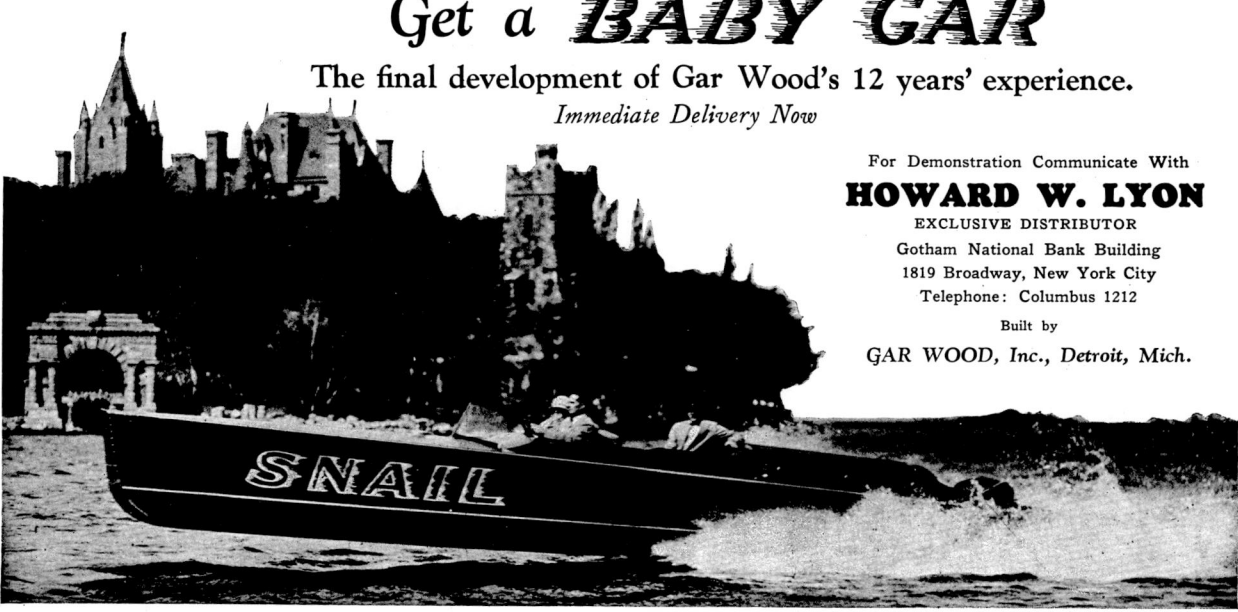

1926 Baby Gar ad.

On These Five Points

you must judge a boat—

1. Seaworthiness
2. Safety
3. Comfort
4. Quietness
5. Durability

OF course thrilling Speed is obviously an outstanding feature of any boat built by Gar Wood. And you will find that all Baby Gar runabouts excel in each of these other important boat qualities, too.
A ride in a Baby Gar will convince you. Seeing the boat is only half the story. You must ride in it, drive it yourself, and try it in a real sea.

Don't postpone your investigation if you want early season delivery. Visit any of our showrooms and make an appointment for a demonstration. Write today for catalog.

HOWARD W. LYON
INCORPORATED
PERMANENT EXHIBIT AND SHOWROOMS
HOTEL BARCLAY 538 Lexington Avenue NEW YORK
(at 49th St.)
Telephone: Vanderbilt 4445

Seven Models
30 to 55 miles per Hour
$3500 to $11800

Also on Exhibition at—
London: 12 Regent St.   San Francisco: 3075—17th St.
Boston: 316 North Beacon St.   Los Angeles: 1210 Mateo St.
Detroit: 415 Connecticut Ave. Seattle: 2319 Fifth Ave.
Chicago: 301 West 37th St.   Minneapolis: 528 University Ave. S.E.

The Baby Gar for 1927.

1927 ad.

A 1927 Gar Wood ad featuring the 33' Baby Gar, the 28' Baby Gar-28 and introducing the new Baby Gar Jr. - 26' runabout.

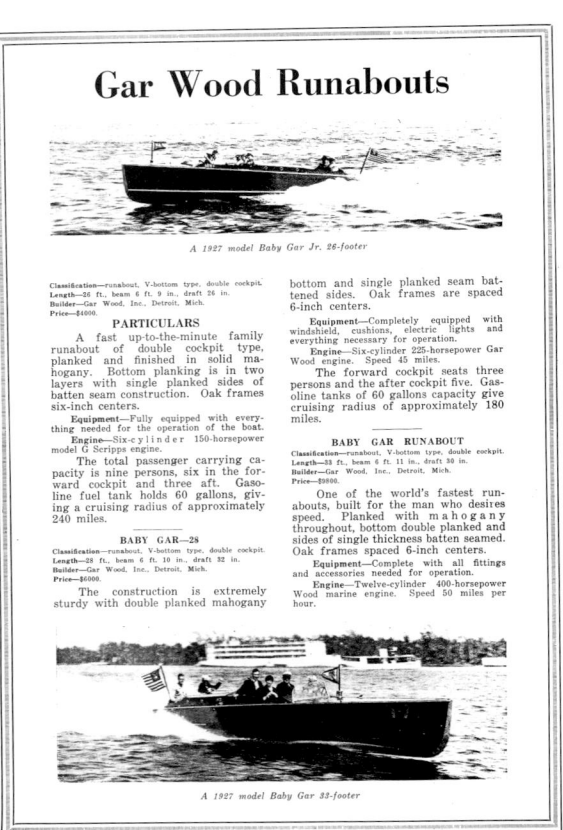

Gar Woods 1927 Baby Gar Jr. and Baby Gar.

1927 - 26' Baby Gar Jr. runabouts with 100 h.p. Scripps-6. This beauty sold for $3,500, f.o.b. Detroit, Mich.

1927 - 26' Baby Gar Jr. power either 100 h.p. or 150 h.p. Prices ranged from $3,500 to $4,000 each.

1927 - 28' Baby Gar runabout powered by a 225 h.p. Garwood engine.

1927 - 28' Baby Gar runabout.

The Smartest of All Fast Runabouts
BABY GAR JR.

IN the whole boating field, including both standardized and custom built craft, there are no popular priced or high priced runabouts quite so perfect in design, construction, finish and equipment as the seven models of Baby Gar Runabouts. Ranging in speed from 30 to 55 miles an hour, and in price from $3500 to $11,800, you'll find the touch of the master builder and designer in every one of these boats.

Gar Wood served his boat apprenticeship in preparing racing boats for his personal use—boats that not only would and did beat the best productions of all other builders, but that established many records never equalled for speed or endurance. He did all his experimenting at his own expense, and more than a million dollars' worth of it, at that. The Baby Gar models he builds for you now are fully developed types, brought up to their present standard of perfection by many years of refinement.

If you are undecided about what type of boat to buy, a ride in a Baby Gar Runabout will help you to settle the problem.

26-ft. Baby Gar Jr.	Sedan	Baby Gar-28	33-ft. Baby Gar-
30-32 miles per hour, $3500	$4100	45 miles per hour	50 miles per hour, $9800
38-40 miles per hour, $4000	$4600	$6000	55 miles per hour, $11800

All prices F. O. B. Detroit

Write today for the Baby Gar catalog. Or make an appointment at our nearest showroom for demonstration. For early delivery, we advise telegraph or long distance telephone.

HOWARD W. LYON
INCORPORATED

HOTEL BARCLAY   532 Lexington Avenue (at 49th Street)   **NEW YORK, N.Y.**
Telephone: Vanderbilt 4445

Also on exhibition at all of the following branches:
London: 12 Regent St.   Chicago: 301 West 37th St.   Boston: 316 North Beacon St.   Detroit: 415 Connecticut Av.
San Francisco: 3075 17th St.   Los Angeles: 1218 Mateo St.   Seattle: 2318 Fifth Av.   Minneapolis: 528 University Av. S.E.

Baby Gar Jr. Sedan, the all-weather runabout. $4100-$4600. (Patents Applied For)

The smartest of all fast runabouts for 1927, the Baby Gar Jr.

Launching of "Phoenix," 1927 - 33' Baby Gar runabout 520 h.p. owned by F. Todd Warner, Mound, Minn.

Todd Warner's Gar Wood "Baby Gar" 1927 - 33' runabout. 520 h.p.

following story, as wooden boat owners should really find it of interest.

Todd invited myself and perhaps seven others or so to take a short spin the the *Phoenix* on Sunday morning during the Minnetonka Show, and we were all excited to have a chance to ride in such a beautiful boat. When we pulled away from the slip a fellow with a "glass" Wellcraft or Thunderbird or some such similar modern Deep "V" I.O. smiled at us as he idled alongside until he was out far enough from the docks, when he suddenly hit the throttle and roared off down the lake. He looked back and smirked, probably thinking that skinny old wood "canoe" was only a slow launch. Boy, was the man in for a surprise! Shortly after that, Todd put the "peddle to the metal" so to speak, and we were off like a flash. Those two big Chevy V-8s roared to life, and before we knew it we passed that joker in the I.O. like he was sitting still. He pulled over in a hurry, slowing down to a crawl with his tongue hanging out, unable to believe a boat with so many passengers could pass his modern boat with so much ease.

All of you who know me realize I am no mechanic, but I do have to tell you about the power plants in that Baby Gar. Todd Warner, along with the mechanical genius Keith Katcher, formerly of Lake Minnetonka, perfected a system by which two Chevrolet V-8 engines were run in tandem, one in front of the other, connected to only one shaft and prop. It took a lot of adjustment to get this unusual power system to work, but the fellows worked it out. By the way, the 33-foot Baby Gar planes very flatly over the water; it does not rear up out of the water like some big runabouts but seems to just slide up and out of the water onto a quick plane before you know it.

Crowds eye the "Phoenix" at the 1981 Land O'Lakes Antique Boat Show, Excelsior, Minn. A 1927 - 33' Gar Wood beauty.

The salt water proof closed body on the Baby Gars makes a most comfortable boat.

The Baby Gar runabout which is owned by President Machado and Dr. Miguel de Cespedes, of Cuba.

The Fastest St. Lawrence River Runabout
Snail—owned by Edward J. Noble of New York and Alexandria Bay, a Baby Gar runabout capable of 55 m.p.h.

a symphony
-- of design and motion!

THE fine skill of the same boat designers, motor experts and craftsmen, who have produced Gar Wood's best and fastest boats—a knowledge gained from thirty years of effort and study, together with a million dollars for development, all contribute to the background of this symphony of design and motion—Baby Gar "28" and Baby Gar "33" for 1928.

Vivid colors, sedan top, especially designed heavily plated hardware and an interior finish unsurpassed by the finest custom body shops, set a new standard of runabout building. And you get all of this, at a cost no greater than for other boats of the same size and speed.

Baby Gar "28"

The trim graceful lines of the Baby Gar "28" furnish a pleasing relief from the conventional stock runabout design. All hull planking and decks are of finest matched African mahogany, and the boat is finished in four rich and harmonious color combinations.

Specifications: Length 28', beam 7'2". Powered with a 200 h. p. Model H. SCRIPPS Marine Engine. Speed 38 to 40 miles per hour. Completely equipped and fitted for salt water throughout—Open Runabout, $4500. Sedan Runabout, $5100. F. O. B. Detroit, Michigan.

New Baby Gar "33"

Back of this boat is a history of races won and records created which entitles it to be placed in a class by itself in the runabout world.

Specifications: Length 33', beam 6'10". The Baby Gar "33" is powered by the famous Gar Wood Twelve which is furnished in two models. A 400 h. p. 12 cylinder V-type Marine Engine, speed 48 to 50 M. P. H., price $9800, and a 500 h. p. 12 cylinder V-type Marine Engine, speed 53 to 55 M. P. H. Price $11,800. F. O. B. Detroit, Michigan.

GAR WOOD INCORPORATED, 415 Connecticut Avenue, Detroit

Some excellent dealer territory still available

1928 Gar Wood ad.

A limousine top for the Baby Gar was introduced in 1928.

The FAVORITE at the Regattas

Either drifting along in the wake of the college crews, or dashing over the course in a speed boat race—Baby Gar is the favorite.

Wonderful is the sensation of riding in a Baby Gar, for the level planing position of this boat makes it easy riding and dry even at high speeds over rough water. So little effort is required to control and steer, that boating enthusiasts of long experience tell us Baby Gars have given them a new appreciation of runabout performance.

Baby Gar 28 (Illustrated)

Baby Gar lends color to any event—she is more than just a fine mahogany speed boat. In a choice of four color combinations—with distinctive trim lines and glistening chromium plated lamps and hardware—with deep leather upholstery and sedan top—Baby Gar is different where difference counts.

New Baby Gar 33

This new Baby Gar has all of the speed, stamina and endurance for which Baby Gars have always been famous. And now in addition this *aristocrat of runabouts* has added greater

Illustrated Baby Gar 28 Sedan in a choice of natural mahogany finish or three striking color combinations $5100. Open Runabout $4500 also in a choice of four color combinations.

Conveniently divided front seats

seaworthiness, beauty and comfort, making it more truly than ever the "Highest Class Runabout in the World".

Though powered with the Gar Wood Miss America V-type motor, Baby Gar 33 is not a race boat but a safe, dependable runabout with thrilling speed. (53-55 M.P.H. $11,800. 48-50 M.P.H. $9800.)

Your Baby Gar 28 is Ready

Baby Gar distributors and dealers are now ready to show and demonstrate this beautiful distinctive boat creation. If not conveniently located to a Baby Gar distributor write for descriptive literature and the address of the nearest dealer.

GAR WOOD Inc., DETROIT, MICHIGAN

In NEW YORK — Wood Hydraulic Hoist & Body Co. Office, 1457 Broadway, Showroom Vernon Ave. and Broadway, Long Island City.
In CHICAGO — Wood Hydraulic Hoist & Body Co. 301 W. 37th Street. Also on Display Motor Boat Mart.
In BOSTON — Horace P. Hill, 882 Commonwealth Ave. W. F. Sauters, Leader Building
In SAN FRANCISCO — Wood Hydraulic Hoist & Body Co. 17th and Folsom Streets.
In CLEVELAND —

BABY GAR
THE ARISTOCRAT OF MOTOR BOATS

Advertisement featuring the Baby Gar 28 and the new Baby Gar 33.

BABY GAR
...adds a new thrill to motor boating

No matter what your experience with fast runabout performance—if you have yet to ride in a Baby Gar, there is a new and lasting thrill to add to your motor boat enjoyment.

Irresistible is the sensation of riding in a Baby Gar for it rides, drives and maneuvers with the ease and comfort of the most luxurious closed automobile and besides Baby Gar drivers feel no fear for rough water as the level planing position of this boat makes her easy riding and dry even at high speeds.

Any Baby Gar distributor or dealer is ready to add this new and lasting thrill to your motor boat experience.

GAR WOOD INC.
Detroit   Michigan

In New York   In Boston
1457 Broadway   882 Commonwealth Ave.
In Chicago   In Cleveland
301 W. 37th Street 816 Leader Building
In San Francisco   In Detroit
17th and Folsom Streets Jefferson at Chene

Baby Gar 28 Sedan (Illustrated) - $5100
Baby Gar 28 Open Runabout - $4500
Speed 38-40 M.P.H.

Baby Gar 33 - $9800
Speed 48-50 M.P.H.

Baby Gar 33 - $11,800
Speed 53-55 M.P.H.

1928 Baby Gar ad.

GAR WOOD
has taken the bumps out of fast boating

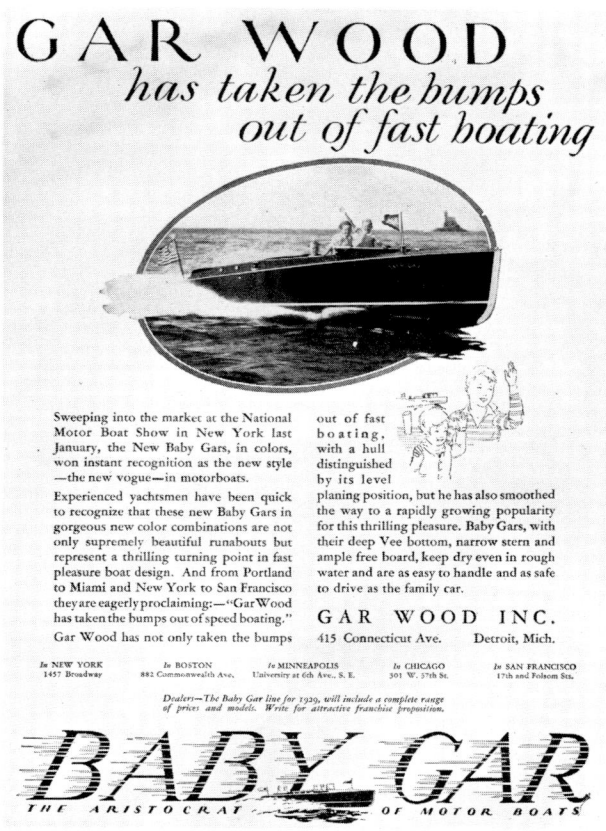

Sweeping into the market at the National Motor Boat Show in New York last January, the New Baby Gars, in colors, won instant recognition as the new style—the new vogue—in motorboats.

Experienced yachtsmen have been quick to recognize that these new Baby Gars in gorgeous new color combinations are not only supremely beautiful runabouts but represent a thrilling turning point in fast pleasure boat design. And from Portland to Miami and New York to San Francisco they are eagerly proclaiming:—"GarWood has taken the bumps out of speed boating."

Gar Wood has not only taken the bumps out of fast boating, with a hull distinguished by its level planing position, but he has also smoothed the way to a rapidly growing popularity for this thrilling pleasure. Baby Gars, with their deep Vee bottom, narrow stern and ample free board, keep dry even in rough water and are as easy to handle and as safe to drive as the family car.

GAR WOOD INC.
415 Connecticut Ave.   Detroit, Mich.

In NEW YORK   In BOSTON   In MINNEAPOLIS   In CHICAGO   In SAN FRANCISCO
1457 Broadway   882 Commonwealth Ave. University at 6th Ave., S. E. 301 W. 37th St. 17th and Folsom Sts.

Dealers—The Baby Gar line for 1929, will include a complete range of prices and models. Write for attractive franchise propositions.

BABY GAR
THE ARISTOCRAT OF MOTOR BOATS

Advertising the smooth ride of the 1928 Baby Gar.

Numerous and varied old Gar Wood ads make up the next portion of this section. World War II saw Gar Wood building numerous war craft as did Chris-Craft, Hacker and most others. A reader, Monty Watson of South Carolina, wrote me a nice letter back in 1980 telling about time he spent in World War II when he was a crash boat operator in the Army Air Corp stationed at the Crash Boat Station, Myrtle Beach Air Base in South Carolina. The first two views shows a 42-foot Chris-Craft cabin boat that was powered by twin Hall-Scott power plants. Monty also enclosed two views of what he believed were Hacker Craft Target Boats stationed at his base during World War II. The final photo shows a closeup of a Gar Wood utility that Watson used during his stint in the service there in South Carolina over 40 years ago. Not only were crash boats built by Gar Wood, but such nonglamorous vessels as tug personnel boats were also turned out back in the early 1940s. Several more of those bygone models are shown here.

There is but one ad I have to show for the year 1946. It was a preview of new utility models to be offered in 1947, all designed by Norman Bel Geddes. Hope you enjoy seeing those rather unique looking utility craft. As we all know, Gar Wood ceased to operate some time later, leaving a void that was slow in being filled by other wooden boat builders at that time.

If you are interested in Gar Woods I recommend that you join The Gar Wood Society as it is a very worthwhile organization to belong to (no need to own a Gar Wood to belong).

From major speedboat builders covered in *Volume I*, we shall now move on to three regional builders, namely Hafer Craft of Iowa, Curly Craft of Detroit, Michigan, and finally, Ramaley Boat Works of Minnesota. Each firm will be reviewed in the order just listed. I am very sorry that I have unearthed no new material on Sunflower Boat Works of Wisconsin, so they will be left out of *Volume V*. Maybe something more interesting will come up and I can "squeeze" it into *Volume VI*.

As stated above, we shall begin this section of Chapter III with a look at Hafer Boat Company which used to operate out of Spirit Lake in northwest Iowa.

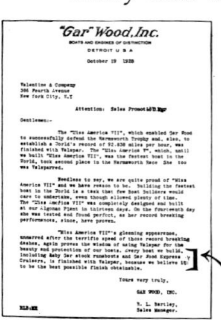

In 1929 all Gar Woods were finished with Valspar.

The new 1929 Baby Gar "30", 120 h.p. 30-32 m.p.h. for $2,950.

Illustration at top of page shows the 33' fast runabout, one of the new Gar Wood models for 1930. Center view is a closeup of the 28' Gar Wood runabout. Lower view is a profile of the same craft.

1931 Dealer's demonstration boat used in Venezuela.

Gar Wood dealer ad from 1938 issue of *Boating Industry,* a trade journal.

Miss America's four Packard engines totalling 6,400 h.p. were too much for the tiny British challenger.

Delhomme Boat Co. in Texas in 1938. Note Gar Wood sedan in foreground.

A large Gar Wood cruiser front and center at Delhomme Boat Co. of Houston, Texas in 1938.

An Important GAR WOOD MESSAGE

EVERYTHING YOU WANT AND NEED IN A BOAT FRANCHISE

98 New Models—40 runabouts—58 utilities, open and cabin. Every one completely redesigned.

55 Exclusive Models offered by no other boat manufacturer. All fresh, new "in demand" merchandise. "America's Smartest Boats" for America's Smartest Marine Merchants. 12 Motor Options.

NOW you can give your customers Gar Wood quality, style, superior finish and performance... and make bigger profits at the same time... through a new and more liberal schedule of discounts.

Don't guess at how good the new 1939 Gar Wood franchise really is. Find out for yourself! Write or wire for the facts today! All inquiries confidential. Several very desirable territories are still open.

Gar Wood has everything you want and need for a successful and prosperous 1939. More advanced styling! Every model completely redesigned! More horsepower! More usable floor space! More selling help and advertising! All with attractive new low prices!

Write or wire for complete details today.

BIGGER and Better Advertising Campaign and Finer Sales Literature—all designed to produce more inquiries and sales.

LARGER Discounts with Extra Discounts for Dollar Volume and Early Shipments.

NEW Low Retail Prices. Reductions as Great as 10%. Prices start at **$1295**

Gar Wood Builds Better Boats

GAR WOOD INDUSTRIES, INC.   **BOAT DIVISION**   **961 RIVER ROAD, MARYSVILLE, MICH.**
LARGEST EXCLUSIVE MANUFACTURERS OF RUNABOUTS AND UTILITIES IN THE WORLD
Write Gar Wood and Please Mention THE BOATING INDUSTRY.

A *Boating Industry* ad for Gar Wood in January 1939.

New transom and stern lines add new smartness to Gar Wood 1939 boats.

1939

Among recent Gar Wood sales to individuals of prominence in the boating world is the sale of a Gar Wood 24-foot Streamline cabin utility to Mr. W. K. Vanderbilt, owner of the yacht ALVA, on which the new Gar Wood will be used as Mr. and Mrs. Vanderbilt's personal boat while at anchor. Mr. Vanderbilt captains his own boat while at sea, and enjoys the rare distinction of possessing an unlimited Master's License.

42' Chris-Craft rescue cruiser used in South Carolina by Army Air Corp.

On patrol aboard 42' Chris-Craft cabin boat off South Carolina coast.

Hacker-Craft WW II target boats at Myrtle Beach Air Base in South Carolina.

Continued on page 149.

1931 or 32 Gar Wood 33' runabout lopes across Lake Tahoe, CA. Powered by a V-12 Curtis Conqueror and a top speed of near 50 m.p.h. It is owned by B. C. Wheeler of Courtland, CA.

ANTIQUE BOAT SHOWS

1. 1983 "Real Runabouts" Invitational Antique and Classic Boat Show, Albert Lea, Minnesota.

2. Clayton Shipyard Museum Boat Show, July 22, 1978 at Clayton, New York.

3. Con Course de' Elegance at Lake Tahoe in 1982.

4. 1978 Land-O-Lakes Antique and Classic Boat Show, Mound, Minnesota.

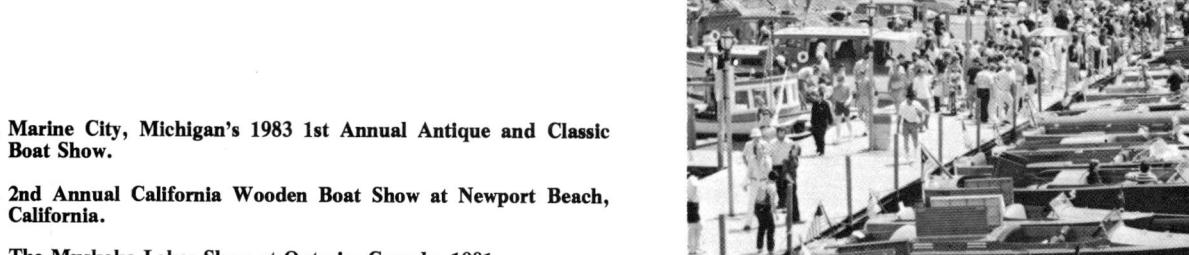

5. Marine City, Michigan's 1983 1st Annual Antique and Classic Boat Show.

6. 2nd Annual California Wooden Boat Show at Newport Beach, California.

7. The Muskoka Lakes Show at Ontario, Canada, 1981.

8. 1983 Lake Winnipisauke Boat Show, Wiers Beach, New Hampshire.

CANADIAN INBOARD SPEEDBOATS

9. Minett-Shields Racer.

10. Christopher Hawleys' 1948 Seabird 18'.

11. Minett-Shields two-seat runabout from 1934.

12. 1921 21' Ditchburn Launch.

13. A Greavette at the Lake Muskoka Boat Show, 1981.

14. 1966 24' Greavette runabout with a 350 h.p. Crusader engine.

CANADIAN INBOARD SPEEDBOATS
(Continued)

15. 1955 29' Greavette Cruiser.
16. Minett-Shields 1936 Hydroplane built to Ventnor Boat Co. specifications.
17. 1956 27' Shepherd owned by Don Jones.
18. 1946 18' Mac-Craft utility owned by Brad and Steve Randall.

A GALLERY OF MODERN WOODEN CHRIS-CRAFTS

19. 1963 18' Chris-Craft Holiday.

20. 1964 18' Chris-Craft Super Sport owned by Ken Garlick.

21. 1965 17' Chris-Craft Custom ski boat owned by Ken Garlick.

22. 1968 17' Chris-Craft Grand Prix owned by Paul Hoyt.

23. 1968 20' Chris-Craft Grand Prix owned by John Routh.

ITALIAN WOODEN BOATS

24. A portion of the massive Riva Service Center in Monaco on the Riviera in the early 1980's.

25. 1958 26' Riva Tritone powered by two 250 h.p. Chrysler engines.

26. 1930-35 Baglietti runabout.

27. Rio utility from the early 1960's.

THE GREAT NORTH AMERICAN INBOARD RUNABOUTS

28. 1983 20' Marinacci "Torpedo" runabout.
29. 1935 15½' Chris-Craft Model 63 utility.
30. 1978 20½' Philbrick runabout powered by a 250 h.p. Chrysler.
31. 1935 36' Hutchison 36' sedan from Lake Tahoe, California.

32. 1948 21'8" Stan-Craft Torpedo powered by a 115 h.p. Chrysler. Owned by Chad and Frank Thomas.

33. 1981 21' Ace Speed Boat Co. runabout.

34. 1920 23' Dingle sedan owned by Tom Coen.

35. 1938 29' Chris-Craft Sportsman owned by Richard Sligh.

36. 1950 18' Century Sea Maid.

37. 1946 18' Vanguard "Hydro-Wagon."

38. The author's 1964 15' Century Resorter powered by a 160 h.p. Interceptor V-8.

39. Jim Johnson's 1955 18' Century Arabian powered by a 135 h.p. Gray engine.

40. The "Rocket" docked at Curly Lewis Boat Lines pier at Clear Lake, Iowa in the early 1940's.

41. SAMAR V, a 1947 17' Chris-Craft Deluxe runabout owned by the author's father from 1961 through 1964 at Albert Lea, Minnesota.

42. 1937 22' Chris-Craft sedan owned by Jim Potter.

43. 1924 23' Dodge Watercar powered by a Ford 100 h.p. engine owned by Syd Herwig.

44. 1928 Laker 26' owned by Charles L. Harper.

45. 1930 27' Fitzgerald and Lee fishing boat owned by Alan C. Ray.

46. 1948 19' Truscott runabout.

47. 1978 19' Mayea-Craft two-seat custom runabout with 351 Ford V-8.

Standard Morehouse Boat Company's 18'6" cedar hull utility.

1962 21' Century Coronado special built blue and white show boat.

1937 22' LaCaille runabout with 85 h.p. engine.

1948 48' runabout, "Pardon Me," by Hutchinson Boat Works.

McKee Nunnally's 1947 19' Chris-Craft Racing Runabout.

1930 30' Hacker Craft powered by a Kermath 225 h.p. six cylinder. Owned by Bill Morgan.

1930 26' Chris-Craft runabout with a 225 h.p. Scripps engine. Owner, Pete Henkel.

1929 26' Hacker Craft runabout.

1929 32' Dingle powered by a Chrysler 350 h.p. engine.

Continued from page 132.

The target boat beached between runs.

Close-up of WW II Gar Wood "crash boat" utility model.

Shown above are two photographs of the 24-foot Navy Plane Personnel boats that have been built at the Marysville plant of Gar Wood Industries.

Gar wood building tow boats for U.S. Army.

The post-war Gar Woods are shown in this 1946 ad.

149

HAFER BOAT COMPANY OF SPIRIT LAKE, IOWA

Glenn Hafer, congenial former owner of Hafer Boat Company, is alive and well, living in the home he and his wife built 20 years ago. Though Mrs. Hafer is no longer living, Glenn keeps very busy every day walking, I believe, four to six miles each and every day all year long. Though getting up in years, Glenn still has a twinkle in his eyes when you talk wooden boats to him. The last time I stopped to see him was the summer of 1983 when I brought my new 1964 15-foot Century Resorter home from Okoboji. Glenn walked all around the trailer, giving the boat a real "once over." When he was done he said, "They really knew how to build wood boats at Century." Maybe he just said that for my benefit, I am not sure. Anyhow, I felt good because Glenn does know a lot about wooden boats and boat building. He probably has forgotten more about wooden boats than most of us will ever know, including this writer.

Glenn Hafer, enjoying the First Annual Iowa Great Lakes Chapter of ACBS Boat Show in August of 1982.

"Kansas Wind" a well restored 1950's era Hafer runabout.

The first picture shown here was taken by me in August, 1982 at the First Annual Lake Okoboji Boat Show. Though only 22 boats took part, it was a great start and the 1983 version was much larger and better. Some time back I convinced Glenn to allow me to reproduce some old photos from his personal family album. All the material from here on, unless otherwise noted, is from Glenn's own collection. The first five views are from the period starting about 1915 through 1920. Glenn can't pinpoint it any closer than that after all those years. Anyway, they are excellent views of big runabouts (or should I say launches) built by his dad, John Hafer. I never expected to find photos of such good quality from way back then.

1915-20 - 30' Hafer 150 h.p. Sterling engine.

1915-20 - 30' Hafer 150 h.p. Sterling.

The next boat shown attracted a lot of attention when it appeared back on page 61 of *Volume I*. The 1938 19' Hafer runabout with the Mercury V-8 was an instant hit. It seems this boat was delivered to Wyoming rather than Montana as mentioned in *Volume I*, but nonetheless Glenn loaned me a few photos he himself took of the launching of that boat in Sheridan, Wyoming. It looks like Glenn used the firm's pickup truck to tow the 19-footer out to Sheridan. The trip was uneventful, and all went well. I often wonder if that old beauty is still "hiding" in some old barn out that way someplace.

Hafer built hundreds of rowboats over the years, as did the old Wilson Boat Works also located on Lake Okoboji. Anyhow, not many of those old rowboats still exist, but at the 1982 Lake Okoboji Boat Show one of those old rowboats, all restored of course, did make an appearance. That photo appears here. It was painted all white on the outside, dark green inside, and it had a

1915-20 - 30' Hafer 150 h.p. Sterling.

1915-20 - 32' Hafer 225 h.p. Sterling.

"Eagle #1"
32' Hafer 300 h.p. Fiat engine speed boat ride runabout.

1938 - 19' Hafer Mercury V-8 powered runabout on trial run at Spirit Lake, Iowa before delivery to Wyoming.

Close-up view of front cockpit of 1938 - 19' Hafer-Craft runabout.

Unloading boat at Sheridan, Wyoming.

On Lake DeSmet in Wyoming.

19' Mercury.

Finely restored Hafer rowboat - year of boat uncertain.

August 27, 1951
Dr. Ted Myers at Lake Okoboji, Iowa - 14' Hafer-Craft.

varnished transom. Glenn loved seeing the old rowboat, but let the owner know they never varnished any transoms on rowboats all the years he built Hafer Craft rowboats. The owner was said to have been planning to quickly "redo" the transom properly in white paint soon after that show. My good friend Dr. Ted Myers of Albert Lea owned a 14-foot Hafer split-cockpit runabout back when he was a kid spending summers with his folks at Lake Okoboji. Their boat is shown here, and was painted all red with varnished decks. The year was 1951.

I wish here to include a photo of a rare, probably the last remaining Hafer outboard runabout. In 1936 Harold

1936 - 16' Hafer-Craft outboard runabout in excellent condition owned by the family of the late Harold Sorenson of Estherville, Iowa.

Mike Martin's fully restored Hafer-Craft runabout. The year is unknown. Note the "sling-style" trailer from the 1950's.

Mike Martin of Ankeny, Iowa restored this Hafer to perfect condition.

Crowding around the Hafer Craft at Lake Okoboji, Iowa.

A Hafer pulling an Aquaplane past Arnold's Park on Lake Okoboji, Iowa.

Francis Flyer II, 14' Hafer 1955 utility, being restored by Steve Kennedy of Spirit Lake, Iowa in 1982.

A favorite method of mooring boats here in the Midwest on a boat lift. Both boats shown are owned by Steve Kennedy of Spirit Lake, Iowa.

Sorenson of Estherville, Iowa commissioned Glenn to build him a family outboard runabout. Well, because of the good construction that went into that boat and the fine care Harold always gave it, the boat is still in use to this day. Harold passed away this past fall; he is missed by all his many friends and family. Harold received an award at the first year's show at Okoboji, The Longest Wedding between Skipper and Boat." You could tell he and his family were just so thrilled to get the plaque. By the way, Harold's family is keeping their cabin and the ol' Hafer runabout as sort of a shrine to Mr. Sorenson's memory. I believe Harold always kept that 1936 Hafer in a boat house on a marine railway, safe from harm.

The remaining seven photos show various restored small Hafer Craft inboards, all located in Iowa. Last time I talked with Glenn he was all excited because one of the nearby community colleges had purchased his old marina site and were going to revitalize it to use as a place to teach outboard motor repair and related marine activities to interested students. I told Glenn he and I would have to check it out as soon as it opens. On that upbeat note concerning Glenn Hafer and the old Hafer Boat Company, we shall close this section. Our next stop is a brief one: Curly Boat Company formerly of Detroit, Michigan.

CURLY CRAFT BOAT COMPANY OF DETROIT, MICHIGAN

Since *Volume I* was written, back in 1977, I have beem attempting to obtain more material on firms covered in that book. So far the firm of Curly Craft has eluded me.

Recently, two members of the Century Boat Club have sent me a photo of their nice little 1957 14-foot Curly Craft utility powered by a 45 h.p. Gray. Gloria and Norm Nichols are proud of that little inboard shown here. Gloria did all the restoration work herself, including the paint, varnish and upholstery. Any other readers still

1957 - 14' Curly-Craft utility 45 h.p. Gray owned by Gloria Nichols of W. Bloomfield, Mich.

The initial twin-six Van-Blerck installation.

have a "Curly" inboard in good shape like this one? If so, send me a photo and a short article about it, and we will try to use it in future books, articles or columns down the road. From this perhaps the shortest review in Chapter III, we shall now move on to Ramaley Boat Works of Minnesota.

RAMALEY BOAT WORKS

One of my favorite "home state" boat builders is the Ramaley Boat Works, formerly of White Bear Lake and Wayzata, Minnesota. Since the writing of *Volume III* I have found a few additional items on Ramaley boats. On page 66 of *Volume I* I mentioned a 44-foot monster Ramaley which was built back in 1916. Since then I have been fortunate to find the article mentioned in *Volume I* which told about that boat. Forty-four m.p.h. was fast back in 1916, just as it is today.

The next Ramaley I have to show you was built in the summer of 1926. If you remember, it looks a little like the Zephyr, another big Ramaley we discussed in *Volume I*. The 1926 Ramaley runabout was 26 feet long, 7 feet 6 inches wide, and sped along at 40 m.p.h. with a 6-cylinder 150 h.p. Scripps engine. The boat was custom built for C. A. Velle of Minneapolis, Minnesota. Those early Ramaley inboards never seemed to have

Mouser II is a finely built double-planked runabout which takes her medicine in rough water without the slightest complaint.

A 44-footer owned by Senator George F. Harding, Jr., which tears through the sometimes placid waters of Lake Michigan at a speed greater than 44 m.p.h.

The Ramaley Boat Co. of Wayzata produces this type of runabout as a standardized craft. She is 26 feet long, 7 feet 6 inches wide and runs at 40 miles an hour with her model G-6 150 h.p. Scripps.

At 42 m.p.h. on Lake Minnetonka! *Red Oaks II,* a 30-footer, with 200 h.p. Hall-Scott engine, owned by T. B. Janney, of Minneapolis, which do not have to take the wash of anything on the lake.

This fast 26-foot runabout is a standardized product of the Ramaley Boat Co., Wayzata, Minn. Powered with model G-6 Scripps, it has a speed of 40 m.p.h.

windshields. Guess Jean Ramaley must have felt that the wind deflector mounted on the deck took care of wind in the passengers' faces, who knows for sure? Ramaley seemed to build more painted inboards than varnished ones. The last two shown are from 1922 and 1927. Even by 1927 Ramaley still did not use windshields like most other builders were doing by then.

We shall now move on to a firm still building fine wooden inboards to this day: Streblow Boat Company of Kenosha, Wisconsin. Streblow is basically a custom builder.

STREBLOW BOAT COMPANY OF KENOSHA, WISCONSIN

One firm which is still very active in the building of "Real Runabouts" of wood is the Streblow Boat Company of Kenosha, Wisconsin. Streblow appeared back in *Volume I* (Chapter IV) as the first custom builder. Since that time, Larry and Randy Streblow have been as busy as ever, still building their beautiful all mahogany inboards. The 23-foot open utility with sun lounge area aft of the engine box is the firm's best seller. Randy dug through his library of photos and slides to send me the following items. Last year the fellows built 12 inboards and still have a waiting list of over a year and half for boats already sold.

1983 saw Streblow setting up a new dealer in Waynesville, North Carolina, to cover Florida and the Carolinas. Having displayed two inboards in the 1983 Miami International Boat Show last February, the fellows sold both boats right at the show. Randy and his dad tell me they could sell more boats if they wanted, but their wish is to keep the firm small, thus allowing them to put their "all" into each boat to make it as perfect for its new owner as possible—a good policy, if you ask me.

1955 - 22' Streblow operated on Lake Geneva, Wis.

Randy sent me a photo of a 1955 22-foot Streblow that is still in use on Lake Geneva, Wisconsin, each season. From the back that style of Streblow looks like a Canadian Shepherd from the same era. Another Wisconsin Streblow, also still in use, is the 1958 17' Streblow utility shown here. This boat had only 76 actual hours of use when its owner, Loren Anderson of Minocqua, sent me the two photos. Note the unusual rear-facing seat near the engine box, or should I say, on top of it?

One of the very few Streblow three-cockpit runabouts ever made is shown next. The *El Do VIII* was built in 1969 and is 23 feet in length. The boat is still in use and the owners just love it. The upholstery was turquoise with white trim. The following nine photos show you Streblows going back from 1977 up through 1982. You will note little change in the boats through that 5-year period, and I can tell you the 1984 models are still pretty much the same style. If you have something going well, why change it?

1969 - 23' Streblow 3-cockpit runabout.

Mint 1958 - 17' Streblow, #1702 just 76 hours! Owned by Loren R. Anderson of Minouqua, Wis.

1969 - 23' Streblow

1977 - 23' Streblow and factory.

1958 - 17' Streblow utility owned by Loren R. Anderson.

1980 - 26' Streblow

1981 - 23' Streblow.

Two 1981 Streblows race across Lake Geneva, Wis.

1982 - 23' Streblow straight drive, Chrysler powered.

1981 - 23' Streblow Chrysler powered runabout.

Interior close-up of 1982 Streblow 23' runabout.

1981 - 26' Streblow utility, one of the firm's most popular models.

1982 - 23' Streblow.

If you are interested in learning more about Streblow, I recommend you send a stamped, self-addressed envelope to Streblow Boat Company, 2317 Springbrook Road, Kenosha, Wisconsin 53140, and they will mail back to you a copy of their first color brochure.

Our next firm is another custom builder, a favorite of mine and I am sure yours too. Hutchinson Boat Works is still in operation on the St. Lawrence River at Alexandria Bay, New York. The Hutchinson launch with sedan roof is about as good as they come.

HUTCHINSON BOAT WORKS OF ALEXANDRIA BAY, NEW YORK

I put out a plea for material on Hutchinson launches, particularly the sedan variety, and did get some help in that vein from two good friends, Riggs Smith and Ray Rogers of Rogers Marina of Alexandria Bay, New York. Both of these fellows dug into their files to share excellent material with us here. I will try to lay the photos out in the order of their age, starting with the oldest first.

Hutchinson runabouts closely resembled Hacker Crafts. At one time I guess there was some talk concerning possible litigation pending between both firms, but nothing ever happened as far as I could find out. The very first photo is a 1940-41 view of the Hutchinson Boat Works from the water. A lot has changed around there since then. One of the hits at the 8th Annual Lake Minnetonka Antique & Classic Boat Rendezvous was the 1915 30-foot launch, *Frolic*. This very beautiful boat swept several awards and actually was the first Hutchinson ever seen out here in our part of the world. Quite a few people mentioned they would never have known what a Hutchinson launch was except for having seen it in one of my books. While running at full speed, this launch sliced through the water at a very nice pace, throwing much less wake than most launches do. Doctor Dick Clark and his wife Jane can be very proud of their beautiful as well as rare Hutchinson. Three different photos will give you a good idea why the *Frolic* was so popular here in our midwest shows.

1913 - 30' Hutchinson, owned by Dr. Clark of Oshkosh, Wis. 1982 view.

1915 - 30' Hutchinson.

1941 view of Hutchinson's Boat Works in Alexandria Bay, N.Y.

The bulk of the rest of the photos are from Riggs Smith and Ray Rogers and the captions pretty well tell the story. Hutchinson runabouts and launches have always been a favorite of mine, and I hope they are of yours too. *Wooden Boat Magazine* a year or so back did an excellent 2-part article on boats built along the St. Lawrence River where most of these beauties still reside.

I have tried to gather at least a partial list of Hutchinson inboards, and I shall list them here even though I know there many more of them still around. It is at least a start at trying to catalog these rare and beautiful boats.

Ray Rogers at Hutchinson Boat Works casting off lines for Mrs. George Pullman (Pullman car).

1915 Hutchinson 40' launch, *"Wild Goose."*

"V.I.T." custom Hutchinson Sedan.

1927 - 30' Hutchinson runabout *"Surprise"* 200 h.p. Chrysler V-8 owned by Bob L. Wagner of Michigan.

"Red Cloud" Sedan
1922 - 30' Hutchinson

Hutchinson Sedan — #2 of two.

Hutchinson Sedan
Early 1930 era
Powered by 155 h.p. Nordberg 2 to 1 reduction gear - still in operation.

26' Hutchinson at Club Island, Alexandria Bay. Photo taken approximately 1950.

Hutchinson Sedan now powered by old Chy. Hemy still in operation - hauled 11/81 out of water for winter.

22' Hutchinson runabout.

36' Hutchinson *"Columbia"* completely restored and now residing at Sierra Boat Co. on Lake Tahoe, Calif.

HUTCHINSON BOAT LISTING

Name	Year	Length
Surprise	1927	30 foot
Curlina	1937	32 foot
Lazy Lady	1927	32 foot
Alexandria	1939	28 foot
The Queen	1920	28 foot
Columbia	1935	35 foot
Wild Goose	1915	40 foot
TomBoy	1937	26 foot
Sunlight	1938	21 foot
Missue	1939	20 foot
Fiji	1936	26 foot
JIM-JAM	1940	26 foot
His Own	1926	36 foot
Monitor	1916	38 foot
ACS	1931	35 foot
Wildu	1939	26 foot
Char Mar	1939	25 foot
Puddle Jumper	1940	22 foot
Nokomis	1948	26 foot
Phoenix	1930	26 foot
Express	1940	36 foot
Rum Runner	1926	26 foot
Sophisticated Lady	1929	24½ foot
Nancy Lou	1939	28 foot
no name	1940	22 foot
Pardon Me*	1947	47½ feet
Bonnie	1936	25 foot
G.L.R.	1928	40 foot
Cahoret II	1938	28 foot
Little Totem	1937	22 foot
Virtous Partner	1937	26 foot
Poisson	1928	22 foot
Voyager	1940	22 foot
Sunlight	1938	21 foot
Idyllocks	1926	30 foot
Kit	1930	26 foot
Old Mole	1934	28 foot
Lotus	1937	25 foot
Cossack	1930	24 foot
CDS	1917	30 foot
Water Waif	1939	21 foot
Hustle	1939	28 foot
Red Cloud	1922	36 foot
DAR	1960	22 foot
Missy II	1946	23 foot
Claire II	1917	35 foot
Yardarm	1947	27 foot
T. Stage's Coach	1938	26 foot
Swift Water	1938	26 foot
Beverly C	1940	26 foot
Her Mink	1947	22 foot

*Pardon Me, later called Lock Pat III, will be featured in a "One-of-a-Kind" review in Volume VI.

Hutchinson Launch

"Lazy Lady"
Hutchinson runabout with Lycoming engine. All the hardware is gold plated. The owner is N. D. Arnot, manufacturer of deck chairs for ocean passenger ships. It was restored in approximately 1962 at Rogers Marina, Inc. The driver is Fred Barker of Alexandria Bay, spad mechanic, Hall Scott expert and Hispano and Liberty expert.

"Lazy Lady"
Hutchinson runabout No. 2 of two. The owner is N. D. Arnot of Baltimore, Maryland. Ray Rogers is in the boiler room.

1937 - 22' Hutchinson lapstrake utility launch.

"Vagabond King"
Hutchinson runabout of the early 1930 era. Sister to *"Lazy Lady"*. The owner is N. D. Arnot of Baltimore, manufacturer of deck chairs for ocean going ships.

1938 - 26' Hutchinson runabout *"Virtuos Partner"*.

Ray Rogers with Hutchinson fishing boat approximately 1940.

1939 - 22' Hutchinson.

Ray Rogers with new Hutchinson built twin engine Sedan in the late 1940 era.

22' Hutchinson built approximately 1960. One of the last built by Hutchinson. 1981 - Boat to be refinished. My Boat - DAR.

"O. G." a Hutchinson runabout after running about! Owned by Rand McNally of Rand McNally maps. Picture is taken at Ray Rogers new marina that was acquired after leaving Hutchinson Boat Works, approximately 1950.

There is supposed to be a Hutchinson Boat Owners Club, but so far I have heard nothing from them. Here is the fellow's address if you wish more information: Wally Young, 516 Prospect Avenue, Syracuse, New York 12208.

Since I have no new material on either Dingle Boat Works or Fitzgerald & Lee, we shall move on to "Speedboat Builders in Canada," starting with an old favorite, Greavette.

SPEEDBOAT BUILDERS IN CANADA

This forth section of Chapter III will deal with Canadian inboard speedboat builders that we looked at back in *Volume I*. Our first firm we shall review briefly is Greavette Boat Company of Gravenhurst, Ontario, Canada.

GREAVETTE BOAT COMPANY

I mentioned in *Volume III* that originally the boat firm started by Tom Greavette was for a short while known as the Rainbow Craft Boat Company, but in early 1931 the name was changed to Greavette Boat Company to prevent a problem arising for Greavette with another boat builder whose name was very similar to Rainbow Craft.

The first photo I have to share was sent to me quite a while back, and if I am not mistaken the *Lady Elgin* is probably one of the oldest Greavette launches still in existence. I have no notion whether or not this old beauty is still in use, but I hope so. Perhaps one of you readers will let me know if the *Lady* is still in use or has disappeared all together.

By January of 1931, Greavette Boats Ltd. of Gravenhurst decided to switch from more or less a custom builder to one who built on an assembly line basis like Chris-Craft was doing here in the U.S. The first two ads here

WATERWAYS ARE SPORTWAYS

THE year 1931 brings a new departure in the building of watercraft in Canada . . . With the organization of Greavette Boats Limited and the erection and equipment of a new factory, sports boats will henceforth be produced combining the quality of the finest custom-built craft with the economies of modern efficiency methods . . . Designed from the boards of the leading naval architects, and built for use in either salt or fresh water, each boat will be thoroughly tested for speed, dependability, comfort and refinement. And when you purchase a Greavette Boat, you do so with the assurance of a continuous, nation-wide service unsurpassed anywhere in America.

Greavette Boats Limited

GRAVENHURST  **ONTARIO**

Specifications

At Left Model 26 — Runabout—Length 26'; Beam 6' 8"; Draft 24"; Seating capacity 10; Speed 45; Planking, mahogany.

At Right Model 22 — Runabout—Length 22½'; Beam 6' 1"; Draft 22"; Seating capacity 8; Speed 37; Planking, mahogany.

Below Model 18 — Runabout—Length 18½'; Beam 5' 6"; Draft 18"; Seating capacity 6; Speed 33; Planking, mahogany.

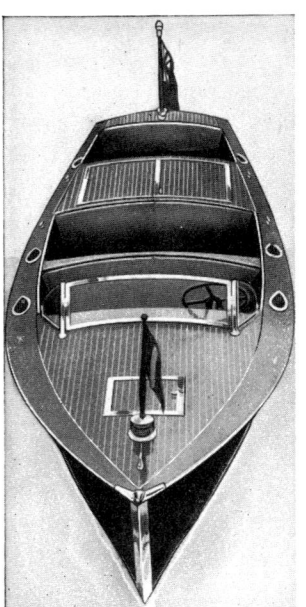

1931 Greavette ad.

"Lady Elgin" **Greavette Launch.**

show just what models were being offered for 1931. Don't you agree that these boats are "dead ringers" for Dart runabouts built here in this nation? I tried to find some material concerning whether or not Greavette and Dart had some sort of building arrangement where Greavette built Darts in Canada, using the Greavette name on them. By June 1931, Greavette was up to four different models, ranging in size from the 17-foot Sunflash up through the big, 26-foot Comet "45" which is shown with the identical photo that Dart used in their ads here. In fact, I recall a man from Canada calling me about, I believe, a 26-foot three-cockpit runabout that he was told was a Greavette but looked just like a Dart, even down to having Dart step pads. At the time I was stumped, as until recently I had seen only one photo of the very early Greavettes.

I wish I had the following material when that man called. All I could tell him was that maybe the boat was a Dart and was sold by Greavette in Canada, or perhaps a previous owner just did not know what kind of boat he had and just called it a Greavette. Anyway, two 1931 ads should be of interest.

By the spring of 1932, Greavette had opened a new Toronto showroom in the Prince George Hotel and another showroom at Montreal. You will note that five models were available for 1932. The next ad I have was from December 1933, and described the 18-foot mahogany runabout the firm was building for both pleasure and racing. If you will recall, Minett and Minett-Shields also built quite a number of the sleek

Greavettes 1931 line, the Ensign "33" 18½', the Comet "45" 26', the Mohawk "37" 23' and the Sunflash "25" 17' runabouts.

165

Announcing NEW SHOWROOMS

THE COMET "45"—26-foot; 10 passengers; 45 m.p.h. Engines; Kermath 225 h.p.; Scripps 200 h.p.; Chrysler Imperial 125 h.p. Prices $4,400 to $4,800.

THE MOHAWK "37"—23-foot; 9 passengers; 37 m.p.h. Engines; Chrysler Imperial 125 h.p.; Scripps 134 h.p.; Chrysler Crown 85 h.p. Prices $2,900 to $3,200.

THE ROAMER "33"—18½ foot; 6 passengers forward; 33 m.p.h. Engines; Chrysler Crown 85 h.p.; Chrysler Regal 56 h.p.; Farr 45 h.p. Prices $1,800 to $2,050.

THE ENSIGN "33"—18½ foot; 6 passengers; 33 m.p.h. Engines; Chrysler Crown 85 h.p.; Chrysler Regal 56 h.p.; Farr 45 h.p.; Prices $1,750 to $1,995.

THE CADET "25"—18-foot; 6 passengers; 25 m.p.h. Engines; Farr 4-cylinder 45 h.p. Price $1200. The ideal low-price family runabout.

All prices f.o.b. factory, Gravenhurst, Ont., taxes extra.

TORONTO
Prince George Hotel

MONTREAL
1626 St. Catherine St. W.

This is good news for water sportsmen who live in or around Toronto or Montreal. Now, you can inspect the new Greavette runabouts at your leasure, with courteous factory-trained attendants at your service. See the brilliant new Greavette "Cadet" runabout—the popular new "Roamer"—the "Ensign"—and Greavette's de luxe runabouts, the "Comet" and the "Mohawk". And remember, if you do not see exactly the runabout you want, Greavette will build one for you to your own individual specifications at a very moderate price. Please accept our invitation to visit these new showrooms as soon as you can. If it is not convenient, write to Gravenhurst for complete catalogue and the name of your nearest Greavette dealer.

GREAVETTE BOATS
GRAVENHURST — ONTARIO

1932 Greavette ad featuring the new Roamer "33" and Cadet "25" runabouts.

GREAVETTE Leads
In Custom Boat Building

A GREAVETTE custom-built boat means extra comfort—absolute safety—improved performance—economy in cost and operation . . . for every custom-built boat produced by Greavette is designed and supervised by that master of designers—John L. Hacker. The illustration below is a typical example of the custom-built quality craft developed by the Greavette organiza-

Order Your Boat Now!

tion . . . an 18-foot mahogany sport runabout of finest construction powered with a 6-cylinder motor and with a guaranteed speed of 40 honest miles per hour—unbelievably smooth and soft-riding . . . now can be built for YOU, with choice of finish and seating arrangement, at a cost under $2000!

1933 WINNER:
100 H.P. Class—Muskoka Regatta.
100 H.P. Class—Bala Regatta.
Free for all—Orillia Regatta.

OWNER:
Mr. Harold Wilson,
Ingersoll, Ont.

GREAVETTE BOATS LIMITED, Gravenhurst, Ontario

1933 Greavette ad.

2-passenger rear-driven runabouts. In fact, elsewhere in this book and in *Volume VI* you will see photos of other such fine boats. The next rare ad shows three Greavettes from 1935. The Greavette Flash evolved from the boat we saw in the 1933 ad shown just prior to this one. The Greavette Fury was a 225 cubic inch class designed for all out racing. The boat shown in the ad was similar to F-29 *Little Miss Canada* shown on page 84 in *Volume I*. The Greavette Custom 23-footer is my favorite of the three shown. Note the very unusual transom design on this model. A hidden rear seat is located under the hatch just aft of the engine hatch. The outboard mounted rudder was quite unique as well. Have any of you ever seen a Custom 23 from 1935? With all the photos, slides, etc. that people are kind enough to send me, I have yet to see one of these boats. If you happen to have one identical to the one shown in the above ad, and if it is in excellent condition, send me a photo of it and I will use it in *Volume VI*, okay?

The next ad was from 1950. None of the Streamliners and Sheerliners are shown here. Most of us probably for-

got Greavette ever made any other type of boats, but this ad should change that idea. I was unaware that Greavette made sailboats, but evidently back in 1950 they did turn out numbers of the 12-foot National Dinghy class, didn't they?

The final Greavette photo shows a nice 17-foot Sunflash utility owned by Brock Park of Canada from 1962 through 1972. The boat was originally built in 1957. By the way, Brock says he wished he still owned it today. In Chapter V of this book two Greavette inboards shall be looked at in more detail in the "One-of-a-Kind" section.

The next firm we will review is Shepherd Boats Ltd. of Niagara-On-The-Lake, Ontario, Canada. I was very fortunate to have been the guest of honor at the First Annual Toronto Canada Antique Boat Show held back in 1981. At that show a fine variety of nicely restored Shepherds were on display. Though I still cannot really pinpoint exactly the early history of Shepherd, I have come up with some more ads, old photos, etc. Let's move on to Shepherd right now.

Custom Built By Greavette

GREAVETTE FLASH

GREAVETTE FURY

GREAVETTE CUSTOM 23-FOOTER

FOR 1935 Greavette brings to you a line of speedy, safe, beautiful, custom built runabouts incorporating many worthwhile features to improve your boating pleasures. And most important . . . the Greavette 1935 runabouts bring you a new conception of softer riding throughout their speed range.

GREAVETTE FLASH . . . A fast, sports 18-foot runabout, the Greavette Flash seats five. A feature is the cleverly arranged forward cockpit which can be opened or closed at will like the rumble seat of an automobile. Closed, the cockpit hatch matches the decking. Beautiful, like all Greavette boats, and a remarkable level-riding, smooth, quiet running boat.

GREAVETTE FURY . . . The famous Little Miss Canada III, 225 cubic inch class design is added to the custom built line of Greavette boats for 1935 as the GREAVETTE FURY. The performance of this world champion racing craft is proof enough that this model is designed to win races. But not only in racing ability do they excel, for these racing craft carry the mark of Greavette quality—now considered to be the utmost obtainable in pleasure craft.

GREAVETTE CUSTOM 23-FOOTER . . . At last, a positive non-pounding, fast runabout. The Greavette 23 foot runabout shown, as well as the larger 26 foot runabout, have the riding qualities of a round bottom runabout and the speed of a vee bottom. Clever designing brings this great advancement in pleasure boat performance. These Greavette runabouts are round bottom forward and a special design of vee bottom aft, with a wave collector incorporated in the chine, assuring dryness at all speeds. Speedy, safe, beautiful runabouts.

GREAVETTE BOATS LIMITED — GRAVENHURST

The 1935 Greavette Flash 18' with hatched over front seat. The Fury racing runabout and the Custom 23'.

You CAN Afford To Own A Greavette

COMPARE the PRICE!

COMPARE the QUALITY!

for quality it's always GREAVETTE

← **$2990.** and up, sales tax paid, is the low prevailing price of the Greavette "20" series runabouts. Here is the greatest value in a 20-foot boat that you can get anywhere, and besides it carries the Greavette name of custom built quality.

$600. → taxes paid
A 12-ft. National Dinghy designed by Canada's famous dinghy sailor and designer, Charles Bourke. Costs only $600. tax paid when built by Greavette. Used by leading Canadian yacht clubs and acclaimed by Canada's top ranking dinghy sailors.

The famous Greavette "15" is an outstanding buy at $1642. up to $1850., **$1642.** (depending on engine), all taxes paid, to give you speeds up to 32 m.p.h. Top seller in the runabout field this season.

← **$762.** The greatest little motor boat afloat is the Greavette-built Dispro, with its famous disappearing propeller device. Costs only $762. tax paid. There are more Dispro boats in operation today than any other inboard boat.

Descriptive literature available for all models, including the custom built Streamliners and Sheerliners and Greavette cruisers.

GREAVETTE BOATS LTD.
Gravenhurst, Ontario

In 1950 you could own a Greavette for only $600.

1957 - 17' Sunflash with Buchanan 100 h.p. owned by Brock Park. 1962-72.

SHEPHERD BOATS, LTD. OF CANADA

Interest in Shepherds of nearly every age keeps increasing each year. Here in Minnesota you see a few of the Shepherd boats, but I think back East, in the area around New York, there appear to be a lot more. In Canada they are really starting to show up at the boat shows in large numbers. As I mentioned earlier, on my visit to the First Annual Toronto Canada In-Water Antique Boat Show I was really pleased with the good variety of Shepherds taking part in the show.

The oldest ad I have found to date on this firm is shown here. The 1949 Canadian National Exhibition used the two inboards shown to tow Florida water skiers who entertained at that annual summer event. The best thing about this photo is that for once a person can see what the hull side decals reading "Shepherd" actually looked like. For you owners of a Shepherd looking for replacement decals, I am pleased to advise you that in Chapter VIII of this book, listed under "Decals and Nameplates," a source is listed for both dash and hull side Shepherd decals once again.

Recently I obtained a Shepherd catalog that I believe is for 1954. The photos are blown up pretty large here so that you can get a much better look at what these boats were supposed to look like. For 1954 Shepherd offered the small 18-foot utility, an 18-foot V-drive runabout, a 22-foot utility, plus a 22-foot runabout and a 24-foot utility now shown, plus the 27-foot Express cruiser. The final three photos show more views of 1956 Shepherds. Little was changed from 1954 except hull sides had a two-tone design on the models that year, and King Planks and Covering Boards were blonde.

That's all I have for you on Shepherd. The rest of this section will deal with a firm only mentioned in Volume I, Peterborough Canoe Co., Ltd. of Peterborough, Canada. Interestingly enough, the other firms mentioned in the Canadian section of Volume I are covered in later editions, so Peterborough will be the only remaining firm we shall review here.

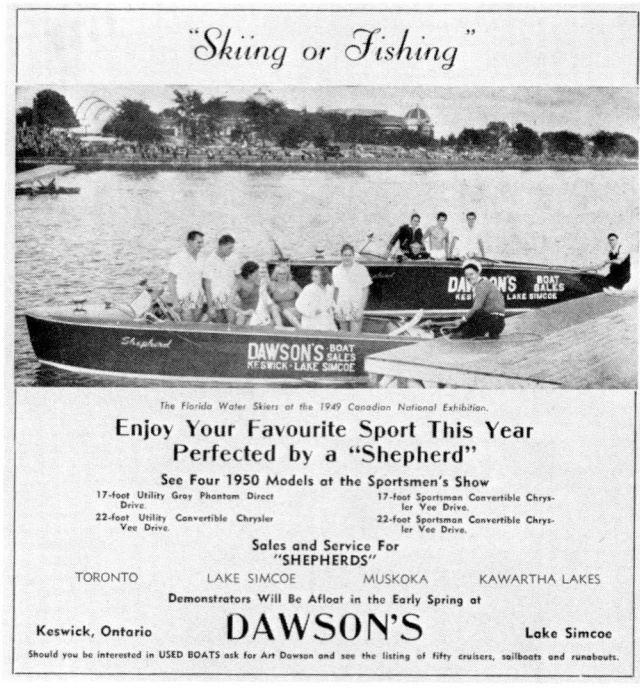

1950 Dawson ad for Shepherd.

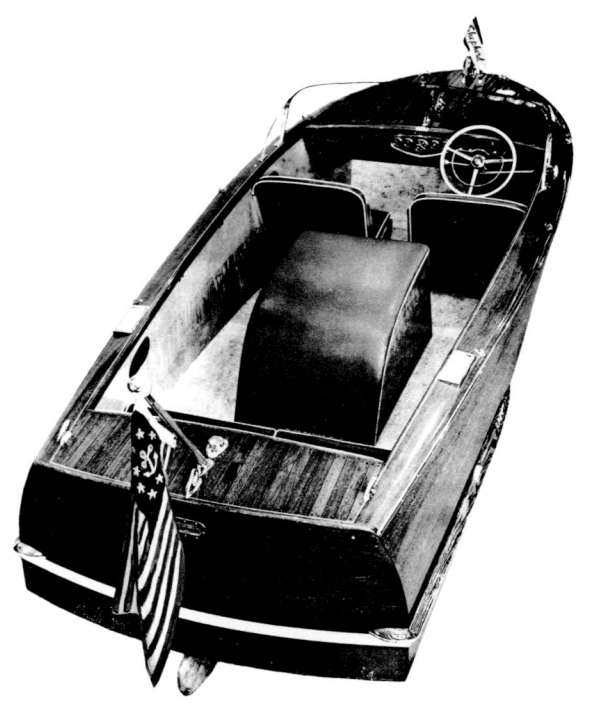

1954 18' Shepherd Utility
Power options range to 200 h.p. with speeds to 41 m.p.h. The cleanly designed, graceful hull is typical of all Shepherd Boats as is the generous free board to insure dry riding in choppy waters.

1954 Shepherd "V" drive runabout 18'.

22' Shepherd, top speed was up to 41 m.p.h.

22' Shepherd with convertible top.

27' Shepherd Express Cruiser.

Three 1954 Shepherds run in perfect formation for the camera.

1956 - 27' V-drive Express Cruiser.

Shepherds luxurious 27' twin screw **Express Cruiser.**

Shepherds 24' V-drive runabout for 1956.

1956 Shepherd 22' direct drive utility.

PETERBOROUGH CANOE COMPANY LTD

The Peterborough Canoe Company was incorporated in 1892 by a Col. Rogers,[3] built out of a former canoe company that had been destroyed by fire. The new firm was one of the pioneers in building and selling the new, all wood planked canoes. As canoeing grew in importance, canoes eventually were covered on the outside by canvas and paint. This practice kept maintenance down as well as made the canoe more impervious to damage while in use. Peterborough Canoe Company finally closed down in 1961, fatality of the Recession and the switch from wood to "glass" and aluminum boats and canoes.

Back in the 1930s Peterborough branched out into outboard runabouts, racers and inboard launches. Peterborough was never well known for their runabouts as, I believe, they were a lot like Fay & Bowen, who kept building slower speed launches instead of runabouts until other builders had taken away most of their old customers. The following eight ads show you the range of Peterborough inboards from 1930 through 1932. You will note that the last ad, one from 1932, even shows a

[3] *The Real Runabouts, Volume IV*, p. 350.

Peterborough 24' Auto-Craft 1930 ad.

Peterborough Sea-Hawk 1930 - 17' runabout.

1929 Peterborough runabout ad.

1931 ad for 18' split-cockpit "Sea Hawk."

THE NEW SIX PASSENGER RUNABOUT for 1931
19′ x 5′
TWENTY MILES PER HOUR

Smooth Performance
Smart Appearance
Luxurious Comfort
Ease of Control

This Peterborough Six Passenger Runabout — distinctive in design and staunch in construction—strikes a new note in 1931 watercraft. Her sweeping lines, graceful flare forward and trim stern show thoroughbred stamina and speed. Her performance will impress and delight you.

Write for further information. The price will prove particularly interesting.

SPECIFICATIONS

Finish — Natural mahogany throughout.

Motor — 4 cylinder, 4 cycle, Buchanan Bulldog Continental Red Seal, with electric starter, generator and reverse gear.

Drag link steering wheel

Kapoc life preserver cushions

Pyrene fire extinguisher

and complete equipment throughout.

PETERBOROUGH BOATS
"FOR OVER FIFTY YEARS - BUILT RIGHT"

The Peterborough Canoe Co. Limited   -   Peterborough

1931 ad by Peterborough Canoe Company featuring their new six passenger 19' runabout.

PETERBOROUGH
BOATS
"FOR OVER FIFTY YEARS - BUILT RIGHT"

Announcing for 1932

The most complete line of Watercraft offered in our 53 years of boat building experience

5 Inboard Motor Boats

In sizes from 18' to 20'
including

"The TRAVELLER"

a neat, fully equipped 9-passenger boat at $775 and up according to motor equipment.

Outboard Boats

Including 3 new designs

The "VIKING"   The "SPEEDSTER" and The "FISHERMAN"

All remarkable Values.

The CRUSADER
A six-passenger 20-mile an hour, round bilge runabout in mahogany.

The SEA HAWK
An 18' speedy "V" bottom runabout in mahogany—a fine boat in both performance and appearance.

The FRONTENAC CRUISER
A 24' cruiser with complete equipment.

Investigate the Peterborough line before buying.

It Will Pay.

Quality Products at Popular Prices

Send for 1932 Catalogue

•

Tell us the type of boat you are interested in.

The 18' "TRAVELLER"
Level Riding, Roomy, Seaworthy and equipped for comfort.

The Peterborough Canoe Co., Limited
306 WATER STREET « » « » « » **PETERBOROUGH**

Canadian Power Boating ad, April 1932.

1931 ad.

1932 ad for 19' Crusader runabout.

cabin cruiser, plus the firm built three new outboards for that season and five different inboard motorboats.

Sorry that I did not find more on this famous Canadian builder, but maybe this mention will bring in further information and photos for future editions.

We now shall cross the Atlantic Ocean and zero in on two of our old favorites, Riva and Rio, both builders of fine wooden inboards.

RIVA BOAT COMPANY OF SARNICO, ITALY

I have been fortunate in finding some new additional facts and photos of the beautiful Riva wooden inboards to share with you. I have seen some very old Riva photos from back in the 1930s, but they were not clear enough to reproduce here. The first photo I do have shows a 1946 7.5 metre Tourism model Riva runabout. I have always wondered what the older Rivas have looked like, haven't you? Well, to me they look very graceful for that period, comparable to American-built inboards at that same time.

Riva wooden inboards are becoming more common here in the U.S. and Canada as time goes by. Lake Tahoe, California, has a number of finely restored Rivas plying that waterway, thanks for the most part to Dick Clarke of Sierra Boat Company who, over the last few years, has purchased Riva inboards from European dealers, had them shipped back to Tahoe, and run through his shops where they are completely restored from stem to stern, inside and out. I can personally tell

1946, 7.50 Metre Tourism model RIVA runabout.

George Bucci's 1960 RIVA 26' tri-tone, all restored and in constant use near Mobile, Ala.

The *Il Capo* a RIVA tri-tone shows the streamlined design that makes RIVA tops with wood inboard boat buffs.

Twin Chryslers aboard George Bucci's RIVA tri-tone.

The beautiful RIVA Aquarama is seen at the 1984 Genoa, Italy Boat & Yacht Show.

you that those Rivas are as good as new or, in some cases, probably even better.

There are several people I must thank here for providing material on Rivas for this edition. Jay Black of Des Moines, Iowa, had his son stop and photograph the Riva Service Center in Monaco a year ago. In the full-color section of this book you will see a shot showing a whole dock of Rivas uncovered, tied to the pier, stern first, all ready for a day's fun on the Mediterranian. Thanks, Jay; that photo is great!

The other man I wish to thank is Randy Leathers of Hillsborough, California. Randy owns a beautiful 1964 Riva Super Florida utility which he keeps on Lake Tahoe, California. Randy was fortunate to have attended the Genoa Italy International Yacht & Boat Show, purported to be the largest "new" type boat show in the world. Leathers advised that there were three huge

Randy Leather's beautiful 1964 super Florida RIVA utility shown on beautiful Lake Tahoe, Cal.

Close-up view cockpit area in new RIVA Aquarama runabout.

Queen of the runabouts is the Italian RIVA. the 21' Ariston is equipped with a 175 h.p. Chris-Craft engine which gives 42 m.p.h. 1960 view.

The hit of the Genoa, Italy Boat & Yacht Show — The RIVA Aquarama. Photos by Randy Leathers.

RIVA wood and fiberglass boats at rest in St. Tropaz, France Harbor.

Nautica Maglietta was created in 1961 in the very heart of Naples in Southern Italy. This nautical base is for pleasure craft up to 20 tons.

1970's era view of beautiful RIVA Aquarama under full power.

buildings full of boats, plus a large outdoor display area as well. Riva displayed many of their large fiberglass boats, plus one new Aquarama Special which, when he was there in the fall of 1983, was selling for 200,000,000 lira or $133,000 plus shipping. The cooperative salesman stationed at the Riva display was quick to tell Randy that there shortly would be another price increase, so if he was interested, he better buy right then. Fortunately Randy had his trusty wide angle lense camera along and got the next three photos of that beautiful Riva on display at the Genoa show. Since these photos are not in color, I shall describe the colors of the boat to you. The bottom was painted all white with a light blue or turquoise-colored waterline, followed by a white and turquoise interior. The newer Rivas now have the split bucket front seats, which are shown in more detail here.

I always wondered how many Aquarama Rivas were made over the years, haven't you? Take a guess. They have made the Aquarama runabout since 1961. I thought maybe a couple hundred, tops; boy, was I wrong! Get this: since 1961 no less than 700 of those beautiful, big, plus Aquaramas have rolled out of the Riva plant in Sarnico. On this interesting note I shall close this section on Riva, and we shall now move on to Rio, another popular though less known wooden inboard runabout from Sarnico, Italy.

NAUTICA RIO OF SARNICO, ITALY

I really have unearthed no new history on Rio Boats of Italy, but the firm was kind enough to send me more photos of some of their boats built back in the 1950s and 60s. Where possible, dates and model names are given. Otherwise we had to guess on a few of them. I am sure you will enjoy them nonetheless. You will note that several of the inboards show a wooden trim or extension type device sticking off the transoms of some of the boats shown. I am not sure if that is just decoration or has a purpose of some kind. I think more than likely it served some purpose but I have been unable to find out what it was.

The first photo in this section deserves mention. The 1960 18' Rio utility shown on the trailer belongs to a dear friend of mine, Juan Muchuca of Malaga, Spain. Juan owns and operates a shipyard in Malaga and restored that Rio back to new condition himself. Juan is very interested in antique powerboats as well as old outboard motors and boats. I was thrilled on Christmas Eve Day,

1960 - 18' Rio utility restored and owned by my dear friend, Juan Machuca, of Malaga, Spain.

RIO factory photo from 1960's. Location and model of boat unknown.

Cruising around aboard a 1960's era RIO somewhere in Europe.

Close-up of the interior of a "ROLLS-RIO" runabout.

The RIVA Espera twin cock-pit forward runabout. Early 60's vintage.

Another RIO runabout speeds by the photographer.

"The only way to fly," on a wooden RIO runabout!

A RIO Espera T.A., model runabout. Note padded lounge area atop engine compartment.

The RIO Colorado, largest RIO ever built. Note the unusual wood overhang or trim beyond transom. This beauty made in late 1950's to early 60's.

1983 to receive a phone call from Juan wishing me a Merry Christmas. To remind you of the great contrast in weather between Minnesota and Spain, Juan said it was 71 degrees above zero there, while here we had a severe blizzard with windchills of 85 degrees below zero.

Enough for the weather reports. Enjoy the rest of the Rio photos, and with this I shall conclude Chapter III, "Material Applying to *Volume I.*" In *Volume VI* we shall include new material that applies to *Volumes II* and *III*.

Chapter IV will cover all the remaining Chris-Craft wooden inboard runabouts and utilities built in the years from 1961 through 1968-69. Along with showing each boat and its vital statistics, it will show you production figures for each model. You will be surprised at how few boats were made in certain models during those years. Now, on to "Antiques of Tomorrow—The last of the Wooden Chris-Craft Speedboats."

CHAPTER IV
A Collector's Guide to Classic Chris-Craft Speedboats 1961 through 1968

Response to the appearance of all the Chris-Craft speedboats from 1950 to 1960 has convinced me to go ahead and show the remainder of all wooden Chris-Craft speedboats here in Chapter IV. Many readers and callers are continually seeking material about the newer wooden Chris-Crafts, so we shall include each model in this chapter. As you all know, by 1961 Chris-Craft and all other wooden boat builders of note appeared to be losing the race for sales with fiberglass and aluminum boats. Chris-Craft trimmed back their offerings, streamlined models offered, and attempted to cut down the annual maintenance connected with wood boat ownership in those years. We are quick today to find fault with some of the rather gaudy paint and varnish jobs, tail fins and other gimmicky things used back then. But, remember, those items were right in step with the auto industry of the same period and it seems America and the world liked what they saw. Let's move on here and look at each year in some detail to see what Chris-Craft actually did offer at that time. Remember, the classics of today will be our antiques of tomorrow. Myself, I have become quite attached to the newer inboards, now owning a 1965 model Century. I find they have some unique advantages no older inboard could ever offer. The choice is entirely up to you as to what period or style of boat you like. Correct? The first year we shall look at is 1961.

In 1961 Chris-Craft issued a super, full-color 35-page catalog. A number of old familiar models were dropped for 1961. I shall list the models no longer produced at this point: 17' Sportsman utility, also the 21' Continental was redesigned with no large, white tail fins and sloping rear deck. The biggest change finish-wise in 1961 was the change over from red/white interiors to more colorful metallic green, gold and white.

Following is a list of all five models offered by Chris-Craft, speedboat-wise, in 1961. As in *Volume III*, I will list as much pertinent material on each boat as I can find.

Four our of five of the 1961 C-C inboard speedboats parade by in formation for the cameras.

1961 17' ski-boat powered by a 185 h.p. engine. A great ski boat and all-around performer!

1961 MODELS

MODEL	LENGTH	ENGINE OPTIONS	COLOR COMBINATION	UPHOLSTERY
Ski Boat—17-CUA Hull series #001-280	17'	100 h.p. six or 185 h.p. V-8	Varnished hull, deck and transom; blonde king plank.	Metallic green, gold and white
Continental—19-CUA Hull series #001-180	19'	Chris-Craft V-8 power options	Varnished hull, deck and transom; blonde king plank, white fins, aft	Metallic green, gold and white
Capri—19-CRB Hull series #001-060	19'	100 h.p. six or 185 h.p. V-8	Varnished hull, decks and transom; blonde king plank, white fins, aft	Metallic green, gold and white
Continental—21-CUA Hull series #001-095	21'	Up to 275 h.p.	Varnished hull and decks; blonde king plank; white fins, aft	Metallic green, gold and white
Sportsman (Figures not available)	24'	Single or twins up to 370 h.p.	Varnished hull and decks; blonde king plank; white fins aft	Metallic green, gold and white

1961 19' Continental utility, lengthened by one foot for 1961 and given a whole new look.

1961 19' Capri, the last all wood runabout built by Chris-Craft in those times.

The 1961 24' C-C Sportsman offered over 50 sq. feet of cockpit space, a favorite with both fishermen and cruising fans.

1961 21' Continental with optional "T" top. Speeds were estimated to reach 42 m.p.h. with 275 h.p. V-8 engine.

The year 1962 found a completely new Chris-Craft catalog being issued—32 pages in full color. Some changes from 1961 to 1962 included the following: the 19' Capri runabout was dropped, along with the 19' Continental. The last large Sportsman also disappeared that year, never to appear back in the line again. The 21' Continental was dropped by Chris-Craft and replaced by a new 23-foot Holiday.

Big changes in 1962 were basically the addition of the 18', 20' and 23' Holiday series. As you know, the Holiday series appeared first back in 1950 and lasted until 1958 when they too were replaced in the line by the more deluxe Continental series. 1962 also saw the end, for the most part, of all varnished decks. To help cut down maintenance, fore and side decks were covered with white vinyl, as were the floors. King planks on the larger runabouts were still varnished. White fins appeared for the first time in 1962. These fins, though mostly for decoration, doubled as spray rails and rub rails along the hull side.

For 1962, quite a lot of changes again occurred in models of speedboats offered by Chris-Craft. Models dropped from the 1961 line included a 17' Ski Boat, 19' Continental, 19' Capri runabout, 21' Continental, and 24' Sportsman. In fact, everything that was built and sold for the 1961 model year "bit the dust" for 1962. An old familiar model name, Holiday appeared in 1962, as only four actual inboard speedboats were built. No longer did Chris-Craft offer a true varnished runabout like the Capri, as all 1962 models were utility types in the strict sense of the word. We shall now look at each of the four 1962 Chris-Crafts in detail.

1962 MODELS

MODEL	LENGTH	ENGINE OPTIONS	COLOR COMBINATION	UPHOLSTERY
Ski Boat—16-CUA Hull series #011-300	16'	185 h.p. V-8	Varnished hull sides and transom; white vinyl decks, black bottom, and white waterline	Black and gold with white trim
Holiday—18-CUA Hull series #001-170	18'	185 h.p. V-8	Varnished hull sides and transom; white vinyl decks, interior trim and flooring; black bottom with white waterline	Black, gold and white
Holiday—20-CUA Hull series #001-170	20'	185 h.p. V-8 or 275 h.p. V-8	Varnished hull sides and transom; white vinyl decks, interior trim and flooring; black bottom with white waterline	Black, gold and white
Holiday—23-CUA Hull series #001-040	23'	185 h.p. V-8 or 275 h.p. V-8	Varnished hull sides and transom; white vinyl decks, interior trim and flooring; black bottom with white waterline	Black, gold and white

New model in 1962, the 16' ski-boat. Featured first vinyl decks.

1962 18' Holiday, an all new model. Top speed with a 183 h.p. V-8 was estimated at 40 m.p.h.!

For the year 1963, Chris-Craft offered another large full-color catalog. Models not reappearing for 1963 included the 16' Ski Boat, and the 23-foot Holiday. A new model for '63 was the 17' Ski Boat, along with the 20' Caravelle. Let's now look at the five inboard speedboats built that year.

Popular with skiing crowd was the sleek 20' Holiday for 1962. 47 m.p.h. was possible with the large 275 h.p. V-8.

This sleek new 1963 17' custom ski-boat came in 2 versions, fancy and plain. Powered by 185 h.p. V-8 Chris engine.

"**Queen**" of the Chris-Craft speedboats was the 1962 23' Holiday, an optional fiberglass "T" top was available at extra cost.

1963 16' C-C Ski-Jet, top speed of 43 m.p.h. trailerable and great ski boat.

Unchanged for 1963, the 18' Holiday was always a popular model. The Holiday seated 5 in comfort.

An all new model in 1963, The 20' Caravelle was a beamy, high- freeboard boat ideal for all general boating activities.

The raked bow of the 1963 20' Holiday made her look like she was flying while tied to the pier. Top speed was said to be 47 m.p.h.

1963 MODELS

MODEL	LENGTH	ENGINE OPTIONS	COLOR COMBINATION	UPHOLSTERY
Ski Boat (jet)—CUA-J Hull series 251-297	16'	185 h.p. V-8 C-C and Beuhler pump	Varnished hull sides and transom; white vinyl decks, flooring and paneling; black bottom with white waterline	Black and gold
Custom Ski Boat and 17-CUD Standard model (2) Hull series #001-160	17'	185 h.p. C-C V-8	All white vinyl decks; varnished hull sides and transom; black bottom with white waterline	Bright red and white
Holiday—18CUB Hull series #001-110	18'	185 h.p. C-C V-8	All white decks; varnished king plank; hull sides and transom; black bottom with white waterline	Black and gold
Holiday—20-CUB Hull series #001-080	20'	185 h.p. or 275 h.p. C-C V-8 engines	All white vinyl decks; varnished king plank, hull sides and transom; black bottom with white waterline	Black and gold
Caravelle—20-CUC Hull series #001-080	20'	185 h.p. or 275 h.p. C-C V-8 engines	All white vinyl decks, interior panels and flooring; varnished covering boards, hull sides and transom; wide, white waterline with black bottom	Bright red and white

For some odd reason, the Chris-Craft catalog I have for 1964 was a black and white version, though I am somewhat sure they published a full-color edition as well. I am sure at least a hundred readers or more will advise me I am correct. I would love to obtain a full-color 1964 "Chris" catalog if someone out there has a spare one to dispose of. Anyhow, let's now move on to the '64 C-C "fleet" of speedboats and see what changes took place from 1963.

Two models disappeared in 1964. One was the 16' Ski Jet utility that was thought to be the newest rage when it came out the year before. Lack of seating, poor maneuverability at slow speed, and other problems with Jet inboards brought production of that model to a quick halt. The other model dropped was what today would probably be considered a rare boat, the 20' Caravelle utility. I was fortunate enough to see one of these boats last year, and found it a very attractive-looking model, especially on large lakes and rivers.

Now for the model lineup itself for 1964. I must mention, too, that for 1964 a popular series of what could be called "high performance" inboard utilities were first introduced. The Super Sports, as they were to be known, came in four lengths: 17', 18', 20' and 21' versions. Today Super Sport models appear to be much in demand. (A good friend of mine here in Albert Lea, Minnesota, just picked up a 17' Super Sport and hopes to have it all restored by next summer.)

The catalog is done in black and white, and on most of the models it is not listed as to upholstery colors, but after studying the photos used in 1964 edition, I think they were shot in 1963. The reason I say that is that the models used appear to be the same, with the same clothes and skis as shown in the earlier edition. The only thing that appears to be different is that the photos used were shot, in most cases, from the other side. You be the judge; therefore, I am not sure what the true interior colors actually were. I do know for sure, the Super Sports all had white and light blue interiors. On the other four models I am not one hundred percent positive. By the way, a new 21-foot Continental was added to the line in '64. It appeared to be little changed in dimensions or design over the former 21' Caravelle.

Without further ado, then, here is the complete listing of 1964 Chris-Craft utility inboard speedboats.

1964 MODELS

MODEL	LENGTH	ENGINE OPTIONS	COLOR COMBINATION	UPHOLSTERY
Custom Ski Boat—17-CUE Hull series #001-090	17'	185 h.p. V-8	Varnished hull sides and transom; white vinyl decks, dash, and interior panels; copper bottom with wide, white waterline	Turquoise metallic with white interior
Holiday—18-CUC Hull series #001-035	18'	185 h.p. V-8	Varnished hull sides and transom; white vinyl decks, dash, floor covering and interior panels; copper bottom with white waterline	Turquoise metallic with white interior
Holiday—20-CUD Hull series #001-010	20'	185 h.p. V-8	Varnished hull sides and transom; white vinyl decks, dash, floor and interior panels; copper bottom with white waterline	Turquoise metallic with white interior
Continental—21-CUB Hull series #001-040	21'	185 h.p. V-8	Varnished hull sides and transom; white vinyl decks, dash and interior panels; copper bottom with white waterline	Turquoise metallic with white interior
Super Sport—17-CUF Hull series #001-110	17'	210 h.p. V-8 275 h.p. V-8	Varnished hull sides and transom; white painted upper hull sides; white vinyl decks, interior panels, etc.; copper bottom with white waterline	Turquoise metallic with white interior
Super Sport—18-CUD Hull series #001-065	18'	210 h.p. V-8	Varnished hull sides and transom; white painted upper hull sides; white vinyl decks, interior panels, etc.; copper bottom with white waterline	Turquoise metallic with white interior
Super Sport—20-CUE Hull series #001-050	20'	210 h.p. or 275 h.p. V-8 engines	Varnished hull sides and transom; white painted upper hull sides; white vinyl decks, interior panels, etc.; copper bottom with white waterline	Turquoise metallic with white interior
Super Sport—21-CUC Hull series #001-040	21'	210 h.p. or 275 h.p. V-8	Varnished hull sides and transom; white painted upper hull sides; white vinyl decks, floor, interior panels, etc.; copper bottom with white waterline	Turquoise metallic with white interior

1964 17' custom ski boat—a 6-seater, both fast and luxurious.

The luxury appointed 1964 18' Holiday powered by a 185 h.p. Chris-Craft V-8.

An old favorite, the 1964 20' Holiday Chris-Craft utility. This boat could reach close to 40 m.p.h.

A new model in 1964, the 21' Continental was a beamy, high free board family go-getter.

Skiing was great with the 1965, '66 and '67 17' C-C custom ski boat with 185 h.p. V-8 engine.

The 17' Super Sport C-C for 1965, '66, and '67, seating for 5 in comfort with twin bucket seats up front for driver and co-pilot.

1965, '66, '67 18' Super Sport, seating for 5, speeds to 41 m.p.h. with a 210 h.p. V-8.

Starting with the years 1965, 1966 and 1967, the very same color photos appeared in the Chris-Craft catalogs for each year. Therefore, that leads me to believe that all inboard utilities for those years were basically the same. Different interior colors were possibly used, but I have been unable to determine that fact for sure. Therefore, the next listing shall cover all three years rather than repeating everything over three times. Changes saw dropping the 18' Holiday as well as the 20' Holiday and the 21' Continental. 1965 saw the production of the four Super Sports, plus the 17' Custom Ski Boat. Here is the breakdown for 1965, '66 and '67.

1965, '66 and '67 MODELS

MODEL	LENGTH	ENGINE OPTIONS	COLOR COMBINATION	UPHOLSTERY
Custom Ski Boat—17-CUG 1965—hull series #001-60 1966—hull series #2001-2050 1967—hull series #3001-3040	17'	185 h.p. V-8	Varnished golden walnut stain transom and hull sides; white vinyl deck, interior panels, floor, etc.; copper bottom with wide, white waterline	Turquoise and white (Same interior colors all three years)
Super Sport—18-CUH 1965—hull series #001-080 1966—hull series #2001-2050 1967—hull series #3001-3040	17'	210 h.p. V-8	Varnished golden walnut stain transom and hull sides; white vinyl decks, interior panels, floor, etc. copper bottom with white and black waterline	Turquoise and white (Same interior colors all three years)

1965, '66 and '67 MODELS

MODEL	LENGTH	ENGINE OPTIONS	COLOR COMBINATION	UPHOLSTERY
Super Sport—18-CUF 1965—hull series #001-070 1966—hull series #2001-2040 1967—hull series #3001-3030	18'	185 h.p. or 210 h.p. V-8 engines	Varnished transom and hull sides; white vinyl deck, interior panels, floor, etc.; copper bottom with etc. copper bottom with wide, white white waterline	Turquoise and white (Same interior colors all three years)
Super Sport—20-CUF 1965—hull series #001-040 1966—hull series #2001-2035 1967—hull series #3001-3015	20'	210 h.p. or 275 h.p. V-8 engines	Varnished hull sides and transom; vinyl white decks, interior, etc.; copper bottom with wide, black and white waterline	Turquoise and white (Same interior colors all three years)
Super Sport—21-CUD 1965—hull series #001-040 1966—hull series #2001-2025 1967—hull series #3001-3020	21'	210 h.p. or 275 h.p. V-8 engines	Varnished hull sides and transom; vinyl white decks, interior, etc.; copper bottom with wide, black and white waterline	Turquoise and white (Same interior colors all three years)

Top speeds of 45 m.p.h. were obtainable in the 1965, '66, and '67 20' Super Sport with a 300 h.p. engine.

Queen of the C-C speedboats in 1965, '67, and 68, the 21' Super Sport with 300 h.p. engine. It could hit 44 m.p.h.

A sleek 17' 1968 C-C Grand Prix—quite a rare and beautiful 43 m.p.h. speedster.

The new 1968 17' SS 283 ski boat. Vinyl decks and floor cut down upkeep.

Last big 20' C-C, the Grand Prix, sported white bottom and black waterline.

1968 MODELS

MODEL	LENGTH	ENGINE OPTIONS	COLOR COMBINATION	UPHOLSTERY
Ski Boat—17-CUI Hull series #001-010	17'			Tempra-ginger
Grand Prix—17-CUJ Hull series #001-050	17'	210 h.p. V-8	Mahogany varnished decks, hull sides and transom; white bottom with black waterline and blonde king plank	Tan naugahyde
SS 283 (Statistics not available)	17'	283 cu. inch V-8	Varnished hull sides and transom; silver vinyl decks; white bottom with black waterline	Rust and silver
Grand Prix—20-CUG Hull series #001-035	20'	210 h.p. or 300 h.p. V-8 engines	Varnished hull sides, transom, and decks; white bottom with black waterline; tan carpet floor	Tan naugahyde

In 1968-69 Chris-Craft offered only three wooden inboard speedboats. I have done some indepth research concerning whether any 1969 C-C wood inboards were built, and as best I can determine, any boats sold in that model year had to be carry-over stock from '68, not actually 1969 models as such. The three speedboats of wood offered in 1968 were all new in every sense of the word. In fact, I have grown to feel that both the 17' and 20' Grand Prix will someday down road really end up as valuable classics. I love their almost stark, uncluttered lines—quite a change from earlier years. Elsewhere in this book you will see colored photos of both a 17' and 20' Grand Prix. I think you will have to agree that these two boats were real knockouts.

Well, here are the specifications on the final three wooden Chris-Craft utility inboards—an end of an era.

Well, everyone, that winds up my review of the Chris-Craft classic speedboats from 1961 through 1968. Hope you have enjoyed it. If you own a "Chris" from this period, take good care of it as it will be the antique "woody" down the road.

A special "thank you" here to my good friend, Joe Morrison at Chris-Craft in Algonac, Michigan, for providing many of the upholstery colors used by "Chris." Joe also was kind enough to include the hull-series number for each model shown. You owners of those more current Chris-Crafts now can see how many hulls of your specific models were ever built—Thanks Joe!

CHAPTER V
One-Of-A-Kind Real Runabouts

All of us, at one time or another, have dreamed of owning one of the rare, giant runabouts such as *Lockpat II* or *Lockpat III*, etc. Correct? Well, the chances of that occurring are very, very slim at best. Anyhow, I felt it would be great fun to review in this Volume V of *The Real Runabouts* a varied selection of rare or one-of-a-kind speedboats. In the following pages I hope you will enjoy special boats that any one of us would be proud to own.

I am not going to review the following boats in order of their size or importance, but rather, mix them up and start out with a boat that has been recently restored by a good pal of mine, Dale Tassell, from Mt. Dora, Florida. Many of you may recognize Dale as he is the fellow who, almost single-handedly, puts on the antique boat show each spring on Lake Monroe that is the Southern states' premiere event for antique and classic woodies—but that's a whole other story.

Chris-Craft Antique Boat Club officials announced some time ago that only 70 Model 65 Utility inboards were ever built, with just 30 of those ever being sold. The remainder were scrapped and destroyed. *Era Past*, Dale's little gem, was sold originally in May, 1935, by Stearns Marine Company of Boston, Massachusetts, to R. J. Putnam of Hanover, New Hampshire. Total cost of the rig, including freight and transportation insurance, totaled just $406.50. The Putnam family used their Chris-Craft for many years on Lake Murray in Vermont for surfboarding, fishing and joyrides. After the owner died, the ol' "Chris" languished away many years in a storage shed owned then by the original owner's son who did not use the boat. In fact, it had not been in use since 1957 when John DeSousa, then of Friendship, Maine, bought the boat with plans to restore and use it. John's plans did not come to fruition, so in November, 1981, Dale Tassell purchased the little

About to go for a cruise in perhaps the last tiller-steered C-C utility in existence.

Era Past—just prior to starting restoration!

Dale is the proud owner of perhaps the only remaining 1935 15½ foot Chris-Craft Utility model #65 that sold for $495.00 new back at that time. This starkly equipped little beauty was the only model Chris-Craft ever offered equipped with the over-the-stern operated tiller steering device. Some specifications on Dale's boat are the following:

LENGTH	BEAM	DEPTH	SPEED	MOTOR
15'6''	5'5''	For'd 25''	25 m.p.h.	Gray
H.P.	WEIGHT	FINISH		WOOD
32	344 lbs.	Varnish		Philippine mahogany

Chris-Craft utility and over the next year and a half he completely rebuilt the hull as well as the engine, which was a very scarce model Gray that the engine builder himself did not even have records on its manufacture. Today, Dale has a beautiful and rare example of one of Chris-Craft's earliest attempts at offering a boat that the general public could afford back in the dark Depression era long ago. Dale advises me his plans are to tour the country with *Era Past*, displaying her at as many antique boat shows as he is able to attend. Maybe you already have met Dale and his *Era Past*; if not, you have a real treat ahead of you, that's for sure.

Real one-of-a-kind Chris-Craft if ever there was one! In use on Lake Sanford in Florida, owned by Dale Tassell.

1935 15½ C-C Model 6J utility restored and owned by Dale Tassell of Florida.

1946 Pedal-boat built for Gary Smith by his father, George Smith.

We shall now move on to another one-of-a-kind speedboat that I hope you will also enjoy. Our second boat is, strictly speaking, not really a boat, but a peddle car. What is a peddle car doing in this book? Well, George Smith many years ago built his son Gary a toy any of us would love to own.

First off, I wish to thank George B. Smith, one of Chris Smith's grandsons of the Chris-Craft family, for providing material concerning the next boat to appear in Chapter V. Technically, it is really a peddle car, but Mr. Smith took it apart almost 40 years ago and rebuilt it for his young son, Gary. Back in 1946, George bought Gary a peddle car when he was just three years old. Smith, not being satisfied with his son just having a little peddle car like the neighbor kids, decided to make Gary a sleek little wooden Chris-Craft runabout, and that's just what he did.

George used 1/8" plywood for the hull sides and Philippine mahogany on the decks and transom. All deck hardware, including windshield brackets, were specially designed and cast at Chris-Craft for this marvelous little boat. In the year 1967, the little Chris-Craft was given to its third owner, young Gary Smith, Jr., George's grandson. Recently the boat has come full circle, back into the possession of George Smith, its builder. The runabout recently was refinished and looks as good as new. Steve Northious of Grand Craft tells me that Chris Smith also built a boat-style peddle car for his son, but he did one better than George since the hull of his boat was all stained and varnished mahogany, just like the real thing. I had hoped to obtain photos of that boat also, but I was unable to do so. There are a number of interesting photos at this point showing the *Gary*. Since they are not in color, here is the color scheme that was used:

Bottom—red
Hull sides—blue
Water line—white
Decks & Transom—varnished mahogany
Steering wheel—red
Flag poles—bleached mahogany

Thanks, George Smith, for sharing the interesting material on *Gary*. Few, if any, of us would ever have seen your son and grandson's cute little rig had you not been so kind as to share it with us; thank you very much, Boy, wish I would have had a little boat like that when I was a kid. Would probably keep it in my office if I had it now, wouldn't you? From peddle boats, our next stop in Chapter V will see us reviewing an unusual craft. Chris Smith, brother of George, also built a beautiful little boat for his children, and we will look at it next.

1951 CHRIS-SMITH BOAT CRIB

Chris Smith, grandson of Christopher Columbus Smith, dropped me a line sometime back, including with his interesting letter a black and white photo of a very unique Chris-Craft boat.

Back in the year 1951 Chris built for his newly-born daughter one of the most unique baby cribs ever built. The photo shown here will give you a good view of the bed which was built by Chris to resemble the lines of a Chris-Craft Holiday Utility. Under the front hatch, which lifts up, there is plenty of space for the storage of fresh diapers, baby powder, etc. The boat rests on its own wooden cradle just high enough off the floor to keep younger brothers and sisters from bothering the new arrivals.

Chris tells me that the boat crib is now in use in Utah for his fourth granddaughter, and is as good as the day he built it. Smith says the crib is a testimony to the dura-

Red, white and blue beauty—a Chris-Craft in every sense!

Bow-on view of 1946 C-C toy runabout *Gary*.

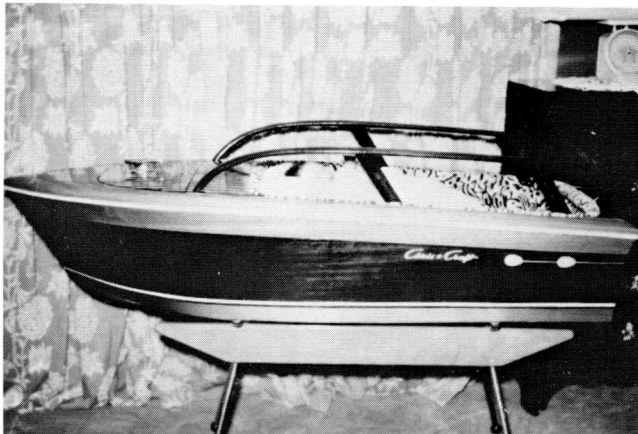

A beautiful all mahogany Chris-Craft crib built by Christopher J. Smith, grandson of Chris Smith back in 1951 and still in use!

bility of wooden boats and he only hopes it will be around for many years to come to cradle further Smiths.

Thanks, Chris, for sharing this unique piece of Smith family "boating" with the readers of *The Real Runabouts*.

From our review of three Chris-Crafts of all lengths and varieties, the fourth in our "parade" of one-of-a-kind inboards will be the only Greavette Cruiser ever built. The *Jay W II* is really a beauty.

1955 29-FOOT GREAVETTE DAY CRUISER

On page 155 of Volume IV there was a small photo of a very unique and very rare 29-foot Greavette cruiser. Since that book was written I was able to get in contact with the owner of that beauty and here is his story.

J. H. Wallace of Canada, present owner of *Jay W II*, advises me that the boat was designed back in 1954 by John Hacker and built by Greavette Boat Company. Construction time took almost a year, so it was the spring of 1955 when the cruiser was finally launched. Mr. Wallace purchased the *Jay W II* in 1970 and had Greavette Boat Company totally restore her in 1971.

The power plant is a 450 h.p. Chrysler Imperial engine, mounted backwards in the boat, connected through a "V" drive to a stainless steel shaft to which is attached a 27" x 18" bronze propeller. The top R.P.M. reached to date was 4400, though general cruising speed is in the 3000 to 3300 range.

Two 30-gallon fuel tanks, along with the engine, are mounted under a teak deck. As you enter the boat over the rear deck you go down three steps into the broadloomed salon which contains a built-in chesterfield, two chairs, a table, a built-in bar, six roll-up picture windows, and storage lockers. Forward of this is the captain's seat and a two-passenger seat on the other side. Forward of all this is a bunk with two portholes and a lift-up hatch. The boat is totally constructed of mahogany throughout. As you all know, I love the streamlined design of all Greavette boats, whatever the size, and I am so pleased that Mr. Wallace was kind enough to submit material on the *Jay W II* for inclusion in this book. The *Jay W II* really is a true one-of-a-kind watercraft one that any of us would be happy and proud to own and operate.

Our next boat started life originally as a PT boat; yes, you are reading this correctly, a PT boat! Though the review is brief, this boat has to be the largest *Real Runabout* ever built!

Front portion of cabin on *Jay W. II*. Bunks located under front deck.

The *Jay W. II* under full power as she crosses her home waters in Ontario, Canada—*only* Greavette cruiser ever built.

Looking aft in main cabin of 1955 29' Greavette cruiser. Note steps for movement up and out onto aft teak deck.

Jay W. II idles along for the camera. Owned by J. H. Wallace of Canada.

"SUPER SPEEDBOAT SEATED 125 PASSENGERS"

A lot of you East Coast readers may remember the famous "Flying Pony" speedboat that used to be operated by a famous seafood restaurant 30 years ago. If not, look at p. 178 in Volume II. I now have found two photos that show what has to be the ultimate inboard speedboat. This "beast" was a converted PT boat that could seat 125 passengers and travel up to 90 m.p.h. with power provided by three big Packard engines.

Boy, a boat like this one would really be something to see and have a ride in, wouldn't it? Looks like it sports varnished decks and painted sides, correct?

If this boat is still in existence, much less in use, I would be very much surprised. If you know anything more about this "giant," won't you please drop me a line so that I can share the news with my readers?

I guarantee our sixth boat to be examined was built by a firm few of us will recognize the name of, but still it is a fine looking split-cockpit inboard runabout.

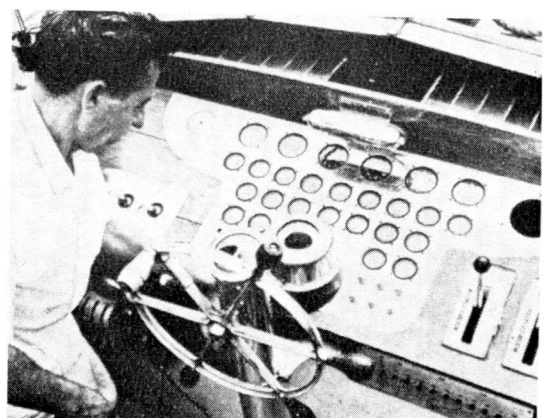

Three full sets of controls and gauges for massive 125-passenger Super speedboat.

About to shove off with a load of paying guests on a converted Tri-engine P.T. boat.

1934 19' PHELPS & CORNELL RUNABOUT OWNED BY THE FAMOUS MARINE HISTORIAN, COLLECTOR RIGGS SMITH OF ENDICOTT, NEW YORK

A very good friend of mine, Riggs Smith of New York, sent me an interesting report written by him about his smart 19-foot Phelps & Cornell runabout. Talking about one-of-a-kind, the *Comet III* really fits into this category. As far as Riggs knows, his runabout is the only one built by this firm that still is in existence.

First, a short look at the history of Phelps & Cornell as relayed to me by Riggs. The Cornell and Phelps families were the best of friends. Phelps was a "jack of all trades," being able to build about anything he put his mind to. A good example was a full size steam shovel he built totally himself that was still in use a few years ago, after over 40 years of hard use. Phelps, the other partner, was a Ford man. Feeling their engines were best, he installed Fords of varying sizes in all the boats they built. Unless the owner provided a special engine of his own, Fords were standard fair. Relatives of Mr. Cornell, one of the two founders, was unable to verify how many boats were built by the firm over the years.

Riggs felt, since restoring his runabout, that he knows Phelps had to be a real craftsman by the detail of workmanship evident throughout the boat. The bulk of the hardware used on the runabout was custom-built and much heavier than it would have had to be. Smith feels that is probably why the boat lasted so many years

19' Phelps-Cornell runabout, Gray 4-cylinder, 70 h.p., *Comet III*. Riggs Smith, owner, and family aboard at the Clayton, New York, Antique Boat Show, 1976.

through a rather rough and hectic life.

The Phelps & Cornell runabout was never as fast as Chris-Crafts and Gar Woods of the same era, but just the same ran well and was a safe, family boat in all weather as well as water conditions. The bow is almost perpendicular to the waterline stripe. Riggs Smith feels that design is "New York State," typical of the 1920s and '30s. Such other firms as Fay-Bowen, Albany Boat Company, and Fitzgerald & Lee, plus Hutchinson, used the same basic lines.

The original owner told Riggs Smith's dad that the boat was built from "Richardson plans," but that statement was never proven and seems quite unlikely. Little more is known of this builder, though Mercier Marine, formerly located in Clayton, New York, used to sell engine parts, hardware, props, shafts, etc. to Phelps & Cornell back in the 1930s. Before I forget, Phelps & Cornell boats were built in Endicott, New York, as well as Henderson Harbor, New York.

The *Comet III* goes back a long way in the Smith family. It seems that shortly after the conclusion of World War II, Riggs' dad told his kids they would buy an inboard runabout from monies the kids earned during the war selling eggs and caring for the family's chickens, etc. After looking at quite a few disappointing craft, Mr. Smith, an eye doctor, answered an ad for a boat for sale in Henderson Harbor, New York. After a 5-hour drive up there, Mr. Smith and the children bought the boat from its original owner, a Mr. Schofield. Part of the agreement was that Schofield would deliver the boat down to the Smith cottage on the St. Lawrence River in the spring. So in the spring Schofield launched the runabout and proceeded to drive it about 50 miles across the eastern end of Lake Ontario, down past Cape Vincent and Clayton, to Fishers Landing where a local marina operator gave him specific directions to the Smith cottage. For the next 10 years the *Comet III* was used frequently, the family enjoying their "Real Runabout" immensely. While Riggs was in service in 1955, his dad wrote the bad news that the *Comet III* had sunk in her slip. Though the boat was raised from her watery grave, the engine was never drained and was totally junk by the following spring after a disastrous winter of freezing did its "thing" to the original Ford V-8!

For the next 10 years the ol' runabout continued to deteriorate in the boat house with Mr. Smith completely losing interest in the boat, while Riggs Smith was busy making a name for himself in the field of outboard boat racing and antique motor collecting. About that time one of Riggs' brothers decided he would take the old Phelps & Cornell runabout and restore it for his family boat.

First of all, he towed the runabout to his home in Pennsylvania where he stripped the decks and followed that with several coats of varnish. The hull sides and the rest of the boat were left untouched as he was unable to find a suitable high performance auto engine to install in the boat. Luckily, Riggs remembered the old family runabout, and in 1971 he "bought-out" his dad and brother, and *Comet III* was his, free and clear. Until 1973 Riggs scoured the nation looking for hardware and missing parts for his soon-to-be beauty of a runabout. Since the old engine now was no good for anything other than anchor, Riggs eventually settled on a 1954-56 era 70 h.p. Gray. Though not an engine in mint condition, it did a good job up to the 1977 season when it had a rod let go. By then Riggs had obtained a fine 75 h.p. Gray that just fit into the engine compartment and which gave about equal performance to the 85 h.p Ford V-8 that originally powered the boat. The new Gray weighs 200 pounds less than the Ford did and also burns less gasoline.

Well, my hat goes off to Riggs for sharing this exciting story of his *Comet III*. Though I have never met Riggs in person, we have conversed many times by mail and phone the last few years. Very active in The Antique Outboard Motor Club, Riggs keeps me on my toes as I am publisher of the Club's fine quarterly magazine. If you ever are on the St. Lawrence River and see a 19-foot split-cockpit runabout cruise by named *Comet III*, you know you are seeing a very rare and unique watercraft.

Coincidently, our seventh boat also is called *Comet*, the *Miss Comet*, to be exact. This twin-cockpit runabout originally resided in Michigan but currently calls Sierra Boat Company, Lake Tahoe, California, home.

1949 23.5-FOOT *MISS COMET* CUSTOM INBOARD RUNABOUT

I can recall seeing on occasion, some years back, a small postage-stamp size "For Sale" ad describing a very unique round-sterned inboard that was really sharp-looking. When the idea came to me to include a chapter in this book on one-of-a-kind inboards, *Miss Comet* seemed like a likely candidate.

First of all, the boat has a most unique and interesting history, some of which I share with you now. She was originally designed by Naval Architect Monty O'Shea, who earlier had designed the Dodge yacht *Delphine*. A Mr. Ocha built the boat in his Detroit, Michigan, shop, beginning in 1945 with completion in 1949. The boat is built totally of laminated solid Honduras mahogany with canvas in between layers. Right now, considering her age and lack of use, the boat is as tight as she ever was.

The dashboard of this sleek beauty is one solid 4 x 8 piece of solid mahogany. She is equipped with a 2-step planing hull with stainless steel covering the aft hull bottom. Power is supplied by two Chrysler Hemi engines developing over 350 h.p. each. Other unique features of each engine include (four) 2-barrel carburetors, oversized pistons, high lift cam, Mallory duel-point ignition, adjustable electric fuel pumps, specially designed intake manifold, aluminum manifolds, and cylinder heads. In earlier days the boat could reach speeds of just over 80 m.p.h. Today, due to some changes in hull design, top speed is estimated to be about 70 m.p.h. at sea level.

The boat was owned for many years by a marina operator, Al D'Eath, now deceased, of Harsens Island, Michigan. The current owner is Dick Clarke of Sierra Boat Company, Lake Tahoe, California. Dick, to date, has not yet been able to run the *Comet* through his myriad of restoration shops, but when he does, look out. You are going to see a really great twin-cockpit runabout like nothing else you might see anywhere.

While attending the 1983 Concourse de 'lgance at Lake Tahoe, I caught a glimpse of *Miss Comet* stored at

1949 23'5" custom runabout built in Detroit, Michigan.

Sierra Boat Company. Even though she needs to be refurbished, she has a look of class and custom style about her. Dick says the original engines were built by Danny Foster, Gold Cup racer in 1948. Under Lake Tahoe's thin air, Dick figures his little *Miss Comet* should still reach top speeds of at least 45 m.p.h., which isn't bad.

The first photo shows *Miss Comet* resting on her cradle while she was still in Michigan. Her cockpit is a little narrow compared to regular runabouts of the same length, but then *Miss Comet* is no regular runabout, is she? The second photo reveals the twin engine hatches raised, revealing the "twin" Chrysler Hemis that reside inside. Those "mills" look "lean and mean," I think. Instrumentation on the dash looks pretty impressive as well. Perhaps the least attractive photo of the *Miss Comet* is the one showing you her rounded transom. This runabout has her rudder mounted up under the front deck for better, safer steering and handling in rough water and/or at top speed.

All in all, the *Miss Comet* is a true one-of-a-kind; a boat any of us would be proud to "tool" up into the dock of a local posh watering hole some hot, sunny July

Close-up view of round transom on *Miss Comet*. Rudder is mounted forward under front deck.

Cozy front seat of twin engine 1949 23'5" custom runabout, *Miss Comet*.

Huge power plants, 700 h.p. total, push Comet at almost 80 m.p.h.

Sunday, wouldn't we? When Dick Clarke, Tony Brown, Pat Bagan and the "crew" of Sierra restore this 23-plus foot speedster, she will be another "jewel" on that jewel of a lake, Lake Tahoe.

From sleek, speedy runabouts, the next boat we shall review finds Lake Michigan just her "cup of tea"—*The Cart* is a rare 1938 29-foot Chris-Craft sportsman.

1938 CHRIS-CRAFT 29-FOOT SPORTSMAN

Richard Sligh of Holland, Michigan, sent me material concerning his very rare 1938 Chris-Craft Sportsman just a little too late to appear in Volume III. Therefore,

I advised Dick that *The Cart* would appear in Volume V in the One-of-a-Kind chapter, so here goes.

Dimensions on *The Cart* are as follows:[1]

1938 Chris-Craft 29-foot Sportsman
Length—29'
Beam—8' 6"
Draft—2' 6"
Weight, dry—6,000 pounds
Power—Twin Chris-Craft "M" 320 cu. inch.
130 h.p. @ 3200 r.p.m.
Name, *The Cart* (condensed from cartographer-chartmaker, hence explorer)

Dick Sligh advises me that three boats were built for a customer in Wisconsin. George Smith, grandson of the founder of Chris-Craft, said he remembers when the three boats went through the Algonac, Michigan, plant. *The Cart* was traced back through four previous owners to the original owner, Jim Kimberly of Kimberly-Clark Corporation, who reportedly ordered all three. It is very possible that more 29-foot Sportsmans were built later, as the first three were very well received. Of the first three, one and two had twin "m" and the third had a single Scripps V-12. *The Cart* is number 2.

Sligh found *The Cart* in Algoma, Wisconsin, in July, 1975, in fair condition, floating and running. The next four years were spent in storage as courage was necessary to undertake the restoration project. Finally in 1980 work began. Dick pulled the engines, removed all hardware, turned the boat bottom up, and work commenced. Thirteen months later results of all the labor could be seen. The restoration consisted of a new transom, new flooring, new upholstery, some new planking, new engine hatches, some new hardware, re-chroming the old hardware, installation of some new instruments (heat gauges, engine hours, gas low meter, sun log, electronic compass, depth finder, fuel gauge, bilge pump, radio and clock). In addition, the engines needed a valve job, thrust bearings and oil seals, vacuum cylinders rebuilt, and new exhaust elbows.

The boat was originally equipped with a system for shifting that I had not seen before, Dick advised. Eight-inch diameter air cylinders are used for moving the shift lever at the engine. Chrome levers at the helm activate the cylinders which operate on engine vacuum. The shift speed is nearly as fast as manual shifts. The boat was also equipped with a mechanical engine syncronizer. With the syncronizer engaged, the port throttle only is used. The starboard engine r.p.m. was mechanically matched to the port engine r.p.m. February, 1983, at the time of construction, a CO_2 system was installed with discharge nozzles located in the engine, battery and gas tank areas.

---
[1] Letter, Richard Sligh, 2/21/83

1938 29' C-C Sportsman, powered by twin "M" engines.

The Cart, **1938 C-C 29' Sportsman owned by Richard Sligh.**

The boat will reach speeds of close to 36 m.p.h. but most cruising is done at 25 m.p.h. At that speed it consumes 10 to 12 gallons per hour depending on the load. During the summer of 1982, Sligh crossed Lake Michigan four times as well as cruising the Mackinac Straits and Lake Charlevoix. Under the foredeck is room for a head and considerable storage space. Although there are no bunks, we do "camp" on the boat for periods of four to six days at a time, said Sligh.

The chrome bars that travel aft from the windshield support a navy top. Side curtains and stern curtains were also made to offer protection for passengers and the boat.

Thanks, Dick Sligh, for sharing the above information as well as fine photos on your beloved *Cart*. She is truly a beauty, a boat you and yours can be most proud of.

Though Higgins inboards were never really considered one-of-a-kind, today a Higgins 19-foot runabout is a rare sight. Our next boat we shall look at is just such a boat.

1947 19-FOOT DELUXE HIGGINS RUNABOUT

In most cases, we think one-of-a-kind runabouts always have to be the sleek, slinky, varnished types, about 40 feet long and "decked out" like a show girl. Correct? Well, some time back a fellow from Hoquiam, Washington, Gil Stork, sent me color photos and information on not one, but two beautiful Higgins inboards.

Gil's 1954 17-foot Higgins utility, though beautifully restored, would not be considered by most of us as a one-of-a-kind inboard speedboat, but Gil does own what I am sure is a rare Higgins, that being a beautiful 1947 19-foot Deluxe Higgins runabout. Stork has been kind enough to send some history along with the photos shown in this article on his fine Higgins runabout, *Whangdoodle*.

"The 19-foot Deluxe runabout was purchased new in 1947, from a marina in Olympia, Washington, by a Hoquiam businessman. In 1952 it was sold to the sons of my father's business partner," Gil reported. "They had a summer home on Mason Lake that my family would use for two weeks each summer. I'm 34 years old, so I sort of grew up with this boat," Gil stork advised me. "I can still remember the thrill when I was a young boy and my father would let me sit on his lap and steer the *Whangdoodle*.

"In 1964 my father bought his partner out and we no longer used the summer home. I pretty much forgot about the old Higgins until 1970. I heard from the owner's nephew that the old boat was for sale. Remembering how it used to look, I decided to drive to the lake and check it out. What a shock! It's hard to explain how it looked, but to say it was rough would be an understatement, the results of numerous sinkings, etc.

"Anyway, to the astonishment of my friends and family, I bought it. Then, not knowing exactly what to do with it, I decided to check with a local boat shop as to the best method to use in restoration. The shop owner took one look at it and suggested fire would probably be the best (sounds familiar doesn't it?). His second suggestion was to use the West Epoxy System."

This excellent Epoxy incapitulation process seals the wood inside and out without the use of fiberglass mat.

"The clear finished deck you see in the photos is not original, but I think you'll agree it is better looking than red paint. The engine is not original, being a Chris-Craft Chevrolet 283, and reaches speeds to 50 m.p.h. The boat is much more useable now for water sports than she originally was equipped."

That about does it for Gil Stork's beautiful Higgins. I have only one thing to add to Gil's fine report. I have not seen a 19-foot Higgins runabout back here in this area for many years. In fact, when there were many Higgins inboards still on Clear Lake, Iowa, I don't recall seeing any that looked as nice as the *Whangdoodle*. In closing, Gil says he saw one other 19-foot Higgins runabout, and that was out at good ol' Sierra Boat Company on Lake Tahoe in California. When I was there in July of 1983, I only saw one Higgins, if I remember correctly, and that was a utility model from the middle 1950s and not a true runabout.

I hope you enjoyed reading and seeing photos of the above runabout. Gil reports that interest in the great Northwest concerning inboard wood speedboats is on the increase. Everyone will probably agree with Gil's remark about increased interest in wooden boats of all types. Even here where I live in southern Minnesota, our little 4 mile shoreline, Fountain Lake, now boats over 10 wooden inboards, where years ago never more than one or two ever appeared.

The last true Greavette Streamliner, built back in 1965, will be our next subject. Greavette built mahogany inboards later then 1965, but no other Streamliners after that year.

Beautiful fully restored 19' 1947 Deluxe Higgins runabout, owned by Gil Stork, Hoquiam, Washington.

1965 24-FOOT GREAVETTE STREAMLINER RUNABOUT

Mention the name "Greavette" and the thoughts of sleek Streamliner or Sheerliner runabouts come to mind. I am very pleased to be including in this Chapter of One-of-a-Kind runabouts a report on the last Greavette Streamliner inboard to be built.

Overall view of Ernie Waddell and his wife aboard his beautiful 1965 24' Greavette runabout.

The proud owner of this boat is Ernie Waddell of Windsor, Ontario, Canada. All photos shown here were taken by the owner in July, 1982. I shall relay Ernie's material to you which he provided about the boat.

The Greavette Streamliner was built during the winter of 1965 up at the firm's Gravenhurst, Ontario factory and delivered during the spring of 1966.[2] Ernie tells me she was the last Streamliner constructed, as the man who specialized in building those beautiful boats passed away shortly after the Waddell boat was completed. He was in his seventies when he died.

The boat is powered by a 350 h.p. Crusader engine and is equipped with a 55-channel Ship to Shore radio. An AM-FM radio with an 8-track tape deck is built right in. The instrument panel is an exact copy of a dashboard from the 1962 Ford Thunderbird that Ernie owned. The interior seating is also a copy of the 1962 Thunderbird. There is an excellent photo shown here that gives you a fine view of the interior and dashboard just mentioned in this report. Upholstery color is bright white with gold and brown flooring. If you recall, most of the other Streamliner Greavettes we have seen in Volumes I, II, and III were of the larger, longer three-cockpit models. Therefore, the boat we are reviewing here would be a very rare model for sure.

To the starboard side of the rear seat, the locker has a bar complete with bottle holders and chrome glasses. The port side locker is used for storage of dock lines, etc. In the engine compartment there are holders for spare gas container, shaft, propeller and spare rudder strut, and a shelf for a rubber raft. Talk about being complete!

Thanks, Ernie Waddell, for sharing the material just discussed, along with the fine photos of your beautiful 1965 24-foot Greavette Streamliner runabout. I am sure every one or all of us would be proud to own your excellent craft.

I wish to include a "Laker" in this chapter also. "Lakers" were the "bridge" between the displacement slow speed launch and the high speed runabouts. The following "Laker" is probably one of the finest still in use.

---

[2]Letters, Ernie Waddell, 10/9/80 and 9/10/82, Windsor, Ontario, Canada.

Custom 1962 Ford Thunderbird interior installed in 1965 24' Greavette Streamliner.

Bow-on view of the famous cigar-shaped Greavette Streamliner.

Last Streamliner built, 1965 24' Greavette 3& h.p. Crusader.

"THE MERRY GO ROUND"

Our next one-of-a-kind boat to be reviewed is a Laker. Lakers were boats built during the period just prior to the evolution of the true runabout. They really were not a slow speed, neither were they a high speed powerboat. Lakers were found mostly in the East, but similar style inboards were also built here in the Midwest, though here they most often were called launches.

I feel *The Merry Go Round* deserves a place in this chapter as it is among some of the finest Lakers you could ever hope to see. Charles and Jane Harper of Meredith, New Hampshire, are the proud owners and restorers of this beautiful craft. The Harpers have provided me with the following fine history of their boat, along with the excellent photos shown throughout this section.

The Merry Go Round was designed and built in 1928 for Harry Richardson of Meredith, New Hampshire, in Camden, Maine. When the 26-foot Laker was completed, the hull was shipped to Brown's Boat Basin in Meredith where a new Kermath engine was installed. Mr. Richardson used the boat until the middle 1940s when he sold it to Roger Clapp, also of Meredith, who owned it until 1970. It spent the next 10 years at the Maine Maritime Museum and the Museum of Transportation in Boston.

Thanks to the efforts of Robert Valpey, Charlie Harper and his wife Jane were able to acquire *The Merry Go Round*. It is now totally restored and back on Lake Winnipesaukee, New Hampshire. Its color scheme is as follows: varnished decks, white hull sides, red bottom, and black waterline. Her canopy roof is bright blue and white with small black stripes—a real colorful, yet tastefully appointed and finished Laker.

The Harpers restored their Laker during the summer of 1980 and won first place in the Laker class in both the

A beautiful Laker at rest on Lake Winnipisaukee, New Hampshire.

Note the fine riding angle of this 1928 26' Laker.

26-inch model of the *Merry-Go-Round*, towed by model of a 1930 Packard Speedster made by Charles Harper, Box 5, Meredith, New Hampshire 03253.

1928 26' Laker built in Camden, Maine. Engine mounted ahead of rear cockpit amidships.

1981 and 1982 Lake Winnipisaukee, New Hampshire boat shows.

The hull is planked totally of hard pine with a mahogany deck. Power is provided by a 135 h.p. 6-cylinder Scripps engine. She will cruise at a top speed of 30 m.p.h., quite fast for the average Laker, which normally are a slower type craft than that.

In the process of restoring *The Merry Go Round*, a 1928 penny was found in the bilge of the boat. It is now imbedded in the dashboard as the year the penny and the boat were made, and Charlie Harper was born.

The Harpers use their boat every summer; in fact, they estimate they travel at least 300 miles aboard that beautiful craft each season. There is one photo I must describe to you in more detail: note the exotic car hooked up to the Harpers' Laker. Fooled you! That's not the real thing, but a beautiful model. The model is a 26-inch beauty built by Charlie, along with the trailer and a 1930 Packard Speedster model as well. That model rig is certainly one of the finest I have ever seen, especially having a trailer and car in the correct scale to go with it. A tip of the captain's hat to Charles Harper for *The Merry Go Round*—both large and small.

Our next to the last boat we shall review here is one, if it was still in existence, that would rank right up there with *Lockpat II, Lockpat III, Thunderballs,* and other beauties. Some of you may remember the *Typhoon* from the late 1920s, a boat once owned by Edsel Ford.

1928 40-FOOT CUSTOM RUNABOUT, *THE TYPHOON*

One of the first runabouts ever built was the *Typhoon*. It was built in 1928 originally for Edsel Ford by the Nevins Ship Yard, City Island, New York, at a cost of over $70,000. You readers who have back issues of an old *Antique Boating* magazine will recall two articles they did on tracking down this beautiful boat.

Back when I was in high school, about 1958 or so, I wrote to George Babcock, the last owner of *Typhoon*, and he was so nice to write me a letter about his boat. He also sent me an autographed picture of him sitting at the controls. As you will read in the following report, the boat met a cruel end—such a shame, as today with the interest in antique inboard speedboats growing all the time, the *Typhoon* would have enjoyed great prominence everywhere.

A special thanks goes to Mike Martin of Ankeny, Iowa. Mike used to be a crew member on the *Typhoon*. He called me several years ago and asked if I would like to have material from his personal collection to use in a

The Puritan "TYPHOON"

SPECIFICATIONS

Length: 40 feet

Beam: 7 feet 8½ inches

Weight: 14,000 pounds

Engine: V-12 Packard Marine 4-M-2500, W-14

Horsepower: 1500 hp at 2500 rpm

Shaft: 1¾" diameter Monel

Propeller: 24 x 36 Nibral

Speed: Estimated in excess of 70 knots

HISTORY

The TYPHOON was built in 1928 for Mr. Edsel Ford of the Ford Motor Company, Detroit, Michigan. Her designer was Mr. George W. Crouch and the TYPHOON was built by H. B. Nevin, City Island, New York. The TYPHOON'S original power plant was a 600 hp, 12 cylinder Wright "Typhoon" engine.

The boat has had several owners through the years. When discovered by Puritan early this year the TYPHOON was in poor condition and virtually abandoned. A complete overhaul was begun in May and the TYPHOON is now in perfect condition.

Specification sheet on *TYPHOON*

future book. You can bet I jumped at the chance, so you shall now read his report, first hand, along with excellent photos, plus several things I gathered on her myself. I rank the *Typhoon* right up there with *Lockpat II and III* myself. How do you feel about it? Incidentally, Mike Martin is quite an experienced boat restoration man himself. Elsewhere in this book you will see several photos of a beautiful split-cockpit Hafer Craft runabout that he rebuilt about three years ago.

Now, without further ado, let's take a look at the boat that Edsel Ford often called his all-time favorite, the *Typhoon*.

BIG WIND FROM THE PAST

The discovery and resurrection of the *Typhoon,* one of the world's most unusual boats.

The *Typhoon* represents an era in boating that can never again return. Built during the Golden Age of the late 1920s, the *Typhoon* recalls a day when boating was done in the grand manner—a time when pleasure boating was attainable by only the wealthy, and completely beyond the reach of the average man. This was a time when boating was all romance and glamour with no commercial undertones, before it became the business that it is today.

George W. Crouch, a renowned naval architect at the time, designed the *Typhoon* specifically for Edsel Ford of the Ford Motor Company. The boat was built in 1928 by the Henry B. Nevins Ship Yard, City Island, New York, at a reported cost of more than $70,000. To duplicate the *Typhoon* today would require an expenditure exceeding $100,000.

The design of the *Typhoon* was unique in 1928 and it remains unique today. The 40-foot runabout has a beam of only 7 feet 8½ inches, and is pointed at both bow and stern. There are three seats, each with its own windshield, two forward and one aft of the engine. Constructed of solid mahogany and oak, the *Typhoon*'s sleek, almost awesome, lines are indeed something to behold.

Mr. Ford used the *Typhoon* on the Detroit River to commute between his home and the Ford Motor Company. At this time the boat was powered by a 600 h.p., 12-cylinder Wright Typhoon aircraft engine, originally intended for use on a dirigible. Undoubtedly Mr. Ford's travel to and from work was impressive.

It is understood that doctors advised Mr. Ford that the *Typhoon* was not conducive to his continued good health, so the September, 1934, issue of *Motor Boating* magazine carried a half-page ad offering the *Typhoon* for sale. The boat had several owners in and around Chicago and Detroit up until World War II. The *Typhoon* sat out the war years in storage.

After the war, in 1946, the *Typhoon* was completely rebuilt by the Emancipator Boat Company in Miami, Florida. During the late '40s and early '50s its power plant was changed, and at one point an Allison aircraft engine with a marine conversion unit was installed.

Due to the difficulty of obtaining 100 octane gasoline at that time, and the intricacies of the Allison engine, one of its well-known owners, Dr. Paul Lenz, decided to again change the boat's engine. He replaced the Allison with a V-12 Hall-Scott Defender engine that developed 650 h.p. at 2200 r.p.m. and weighed an incredible 4,300 pounds.

FOR SALE

High Speed, Heavy Duty, Open Runabout, Perfect Condition

Length O. A.—39′ 10½″   Beam—7′ 8½″

Designed by Geo. W. Crouch   Built by Henry B. Nevins in 1928

Power—600 H.P. 12-cyl. Wright Typhoon

Location—Detroit, Michigan

ADDRESS OWNER, EDSEL FORD, FORD MOTOR CO., DETROIT

For Sale Or Trade...

45′ HACKER DESIGNED CUSTOM RUNABOUT

Top Speed 73 MPH

44′10″ LOA x 40′ LWL x 9′8½″ Beam x 3′6″ Draft

This is the most beautiful speedboat in the world. Hull built in 1939 for Edsel Ford, Jr., not completed until 1948 by Emancipator Boat Co., Miami Beach, Fla. at cost of $55,000. All natural finished Honduras mahogany hull, copper riveted. Three cockpits, foam rubber seats, cockpit padding.

New Hall-Scott Defender, 630 HP, installed fall 1950. Speed with present engine 50 MPH cruising, to top of 58; with Allison: 60-70, top of 73 MPH. New spare Vimalert Allison V1710 which has never been in boat.

Equipment: 70-watt Fisher ship-to-shore telephone; radio direction finder, Groco electric toilet, 150# CO2 system piped to all bilges, air horns, built-in Monel refrigerator—and every other conceivable piece of equipment.

Owner will consider direct sale or trade for 40-50′ cruiser of comparable value.

Baudhuin Yacht Harbor

ALL MARINE SERVICES

Phone 61 & 675

STURGEON BAY, WIS.

Feb '51 ad advertising *Typhoon* for sale.

Pilot's view of *Typhoon* in use. Note flotilla of small boats following behind.

Full blast down the Ohio River aboard the *Typhoon*.

The "test crew" pose for photo near the torpedo-sterned *Typhoon*. Note "step" built into the bottom near stern.

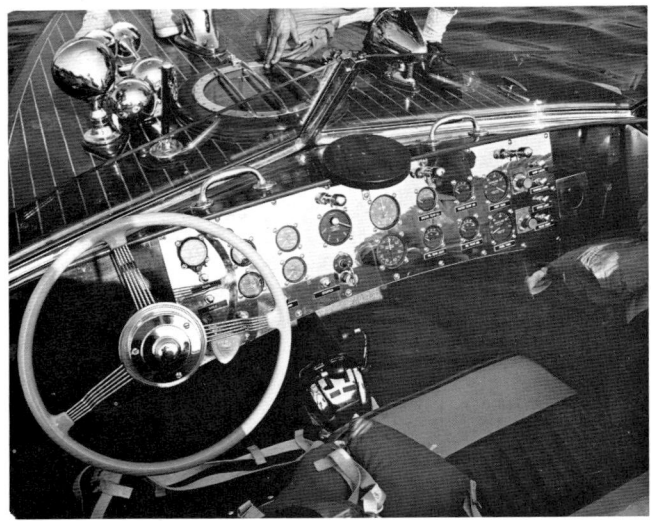

What a dashboard, just like a 747! Lots of deck hardware too.

Another of the *Typhoon*'s owners was Joseph VanBlerck, Jr., famous boat and unlimited hydroplane racer, who also installed the custom engine manifold systems on both the Allison and Hall-Scott engines.

The *Typhoon* has spent very little of its 34-year life in the water. George Babcock of Puritan Cordage Mills discovered the boat late in 1961 at Henry C. Grebe and Company, Chicago, where it had been in storage since 1956. He decided to once again bring the boat back to life. The *Typhoon* was shipped to Louisville, Kentucky and its restoration was begun early that year.

A thorough inspection revealed that the *Typhoon*'s hull planking and construction were still sound even though the boat's electrical systems, accessories and finish had deteriorated badly and would have to be replaced. The Hall-Scott engine virtually collapsed after running about 15 minutes, and had to be replaced. The *Typhoon* was blocked up and the job of bringing it back to a usable boat was begun.

The Hall-Scott engine was replaced by a V-12 Packard W-14, 2500 cubic inch marine engine. This particular engine was brand new although it was built in 1945 for use in U.S. motor torpedo boats. Each PT boat used three of these engines to provide its spectacular speed and performance. The super-charged engine develops 1500 h.p. at 2500 r.p.m. and is one of the finest engines of any type ever designed and built as a power unit for marine or other use. Each of these Packard engines cost the U.S. government $19,000 in 1945. To duplicate the engine today is economically impossible.

The *Typhoon* is now in absolutely perfect condition, inside and out. Many well-known marine industry names are aboard: Perkins hardware, Dupont paint and varnish, Kidde fire extinguisher, Peters and Russell bilge pump, and Kuhls caulking compounds are just a few. The boat has a completely new instrument panel, electrical system and a customized actuating system for the reverse gear, a refinement beyond the imagination of the *Typhoon*'s earlier owners.

It is estimated that the *Typhoon*'s top speed is over 70 m.p.h. At that speed the boat's engine will consume about 125 gallons of fuel per hour. The *Typhoon* carries 240 gallons of 100 octane gasoline (which must be used to develop top engine efficiency) in two tanks holding 120 gallons each.

What's in store for the *Typhoon*? Present plans call for it to be shown at various regattas, boat races and other water shows. It will also be exhibited at boat shows around the country. The boat's unusual design

The beautiful *Typhoon* rests on her cradle after a trial run in 1962.

Almost lost in the "fleet" of spectator boats, the *Typhoon* enjoys the "ohs" and "ahs" of many folk on the Ohio River.

and appearance will be of interest to all boating enthusiasts, and it is hoped that the *Typhoon* will recall, and retain, some of the glamour in boating.

The optimistic plans of George Babcock were dashed when, in the fall of 1965 the beautifully restored *Typhoon* went up in flames at her new home in Seattle, Washington. George had moved there in 1963, becoming part owner in the then flourishing Bryant Marina. While stored for the winter in one of the firm's many storage sheds, a careless yard employee evidently flicked a burning cigarette on the *Typhoon*'s canvas cover, and in just a matter of minutes that beautiful runabout and everything else in the shed burned to the ground. Only a smoldering pile of ash and twisted metal remained of the boat. A sad end to a boat that today would be drawing huge crowds wherever she would be displayed.

Another shot of the crew discussing their favorite runabout, *Typhoon*.

Our final boat we shall review is one that was built here in the midwest and still cruises Lake Geneva, Wisconsin, every summer.

"THUMPIN' AGAIN"
1962 26-FOOT BUDYCH-HACKER
CUSTOM UTILITY

Lake Geneva, Wisconsin, has remained a hot bed of wooden boat activity all these years. Though many fiberglass boats dot the lake each season, a nice variety of wooden boats still call "Geneva" home.

Back in 1980, Jerry B. Polek sent me material concerning an unusual inboard that he owned and was very proud of. I saved the material as *Volume III* was complete and I thought, if things went well, I someday would do another book. Well, here we are, and this following boat deserves very much to be included in this One-of-a-Kind Chapter of *Volume V*.

Back when Gage Marine of Williams Bay, Wisconsin, was still busy building wooden runabouts and utilities, their head craftsman at that time was young Bill Budych. Bill decided at that time to build his own personal 26-foot inboard while building another the same size for Gage. It took over 4 years for Bill to complete his unique utility. Bill named his completed inboard *Thumper*. Bill ran and enjoyed the craft for 4 seasons when he finally sold her to raise money to buy a home that he needed. The new owner was George Getz who owned an estate on Lake Geneva and was also related to the Wrigley chewing gum family. George kept the boat in excellent condition and used her sparingly over the next 5 years. Getz had the name *Thumper* removed and then called it *The Olive A*, after his wife, though he never actually had the name painted on the boat's transom.

In 1971 George sold his estate and made plans to move to Arizona. George had always been a "boat nut" over the years and was very fussy about what happened to boats he had owned when it came time to sell them. After all, George Getz manufactured and sold the Globe Master Craft inboards, which were built near Lake Geneva back in the very early 1950s or so. Jerry Polek's next door neighbor, Larry Larkin also a "boat nut," advised George Getz that Jerry would be an excellent owner for *The Olive A*. After one meeting with George Getz, an agreed upon and very reasonable price for the boat was arrived at. On July 2, 1971, Jerry's dream came true when he took delivery on his beloved new boat.

Jerry soon renamed the boat *Thumpin' Again*, as a throwback to her original name. The boat is powered by twin 225 h.p. Graymarine Fireball V-8 engines connected to Warner Velvet-glide gears and a single-pole Morse throttle-gear shift controls. When Polek purchased the boat she had only been run 201.5 hours since construction. In 1980, 413 hours of pleasure had been received from the use of this very beautiful boat. You

1962 26' Budych-Hacker custom utility.

Twin 225 h.p. Gray Fireball V-8s power the *Thumpin' Again*.

will note the seating configuration is modeled closely to that of a 26-foot Chris-Craft Continental built about that same time and in most cases powered with twin engines. Jerry tells me there are still two 26-foot Continentals on Lake Geneva even now. Bill had an upholstered panel made which slips in between the engines to give a large sunning lounge. All of the upholstery on the boat is still original and was custom-built for the boat, not merely the standard interior material used by Gage Marine.

For dramatic effect, Bill used a full range of double instruments instead of the normal double-use gauges. Because there is one 55-gallon fuel tank, Bill still used double fuel gauges to keep symmetry of the instrument panel. As a bit of fun he had a switch installed under the driver's seat which controls the dummy fuel gauge and he could regulate its reading in the event he wished to "run out of gas" on a moonlit evening on Lake Geneva. As an additional romantic idea, Bill padded and paneled the under-bow area into what he called the "playpen." You can see that he was a bit of a devilish fellow. In addition to the name *Thumper* he had two rabbits painted alongside the name.

He had an AM radio and a small DC converter to power AC equipment up to 250 watts. He had engine starting crossovers to allow both engines to be started off one battery in case the other failed, and a device to charge one battery using the power from both engines.

If you will notice the next photo, along the white slash there is a nameplate. The plate states "Hacker." Bill took the standard Gage-Hacker nameplate and removed the "Gage" portion. He felt since he built the boat on his own time and did much of the customizing himself, it was not really a Gage-Hacker. Jerry Polek tells me that there was a bit of a problem over the logo used back in 1962, but nothing ever came of it. Over the years the relationship between Gage Marine and Bill Budych has remained good. The boat actually is titled and insured as a Budych-Hacker custom.

Sideview of 26' custom-built utility on Lake Geneva, Wisconsin. Owned by Jerry B. Polek since 1971.

In closing, Jerry Polek informs me that Bill Budych, as of this writing, is still around Lake Geneva and does all of the engine work and layups for *Thumpin' Again*.

I hope you enjoyed reading about this truly unique "woody" that still is in use here in the midwest every year. I can't recommend to you enough to visit Lake Geneva, Wisconsin, if ever you are in this part of America. You will be amazed at the number of beautiful old wooden boats—from canoes to stately launches—that grace that beautiful lake. Two of my biggest and oldest dealers for all my products, namely, Gage Marine and Fontana Marine Service, both operate on those waters along with several other firms who "care and feed" our favorite wooden boats.

This concludes Chapter V. I am happy to advise you that other one-of-a-kind inboard speedboats will appear in *Volume VI*!

We now shall move on to Chapter VI.

Many readers continually write and call concerning various problems they encounter with their inboards. I am pleased to share with you in Chapter VI a whole gammet of various technical articles for your benefit. If you are like me, we all can use all the help we can get when it comes to our boats!

CHAPTER VI
Little Things You May Not Know About Concerning Your "Real Runabout"

Remember back to when you bought your first inboard? If it was in the last 10 years, chances are better than not that if you bought her from a new boat dealer, he probably knew less about its "mysterious" traits than you did. Back in those days, dealers could hardly give wooden boats away, much less sell them for any profit. Now, since you are maybe on your second, third, fifth, whatever "woody," you may have learned much of the following information "the hard way."

Over the last 8 years I have probably received more phone calls and letters from runabout and utility owners about the following subjects then anything else. If you are an old "pro" at wood inboards, you may wish to pass over this. If you are new to our sport, I hope you will find much of the following a big help. I shall preface each portion with a little first hand information, while relying on the "meat" of the subject coming from old owner's manuals which are very hard to come by these days.

If you happen to own a brand new inboard or have just repowered your old rig, we first must be concerned with BREAKING IN A NEW ENGINE. The main suggestion I can give you is to follow exactly whatever instructions the engine manual tells you about "break in." The following subjects can be applied to almost any inboard engine. Good luck, and follow all instructions to the "T" and you will have years of trouble-free and glorious boating ahead.

BREAKING IN A NEW ENGINE

The first few hours of operation have a great deal to do with the successful performance of an engine. Engines properly broken in will give much longer satisfactory service.

The instructions given in the *Engine's Operator's Manual* should be followed completely.

WATCH THE INSTRUMENTS

Many repair bills and inconveniences may be avoided if you will get the habit of looking at the instruments frequently, especially when first starting the engine. They are there for your protection and if you will watch them you will be able to detect anything wrong long before a great amount of damage has been done.

Oil Pressure Gauge

This gauge may be considered one of the most important instruments. There is very little that can happen to the engine without a timely forecast from the pressure gauge. The maximum pressure is controlled by an adjustable valve on the oil pump which has been properly set at the factory. Observe what it is when the boat is new and if at any time a radical departure from the normal reading is observed, consult your dealer or a good mechanic at once. The minimum pressure at idling speed should be not less then 3 pounds.

Fluctuation of oil pressure may be caused by characteristics of the lubricating oil. Further information on this may be found in the next section under "Lubrication."

Ammeter

This instrument is for the purpose of indicating the amount of current being produced by the generator and the amount being consumed by the electrical system. The normal charging rate will vary, depending on the engine model. We suggest you observe the maximum rate without any lights or electrical equipment turned on and if at any time this rate is not maintained, consult a mechanic. The ability of the generator to maintain the battery depends on the ratio of the current generated and the rate of consumption by the electrical units.

Tachometer

This instrument is for the purpose of indicating the revolutions per minute of the engine. It has nothing to do with the speed of the boat because of the factor of slippage at the propeller wheel. This slippage will vary with the type of boat, load carried, and condition of boat bottom. For further information on this subject refer to the section on "Loss of Revolutions" and "Propeller Selection."

Temperature Gauge

This gauge is not standard on all boats. It is very limited in its importance because of the fact that the true indication of the engine temperature is the ratio of temperature rise. In a radiator type of water system, as in an automobile, the water enters the engine at approximately 120° and comes at approximately 160° at top speed or a rise of 40°. In a boat where the fresh water enters the engine at 60° it would come out at 120°, which is about the normal reading on a marine engine. On engines equipped with a Chris-Craft thermostatic temperature gauge, the reading would be 140° to 150°.

Special Instruments

Special instruments, such as battery indicators, hour meters, and fume detectors, may be installed at the request of the purchaser and are not guaranteed by the factory as they are usually guaranteed by their respective manufacturers.

Fuel System

The fuel lines are provided with two shutoff valves, one at the tank so that the line may be disconnected for cleaning. Also one at the carburetor for convenience in removing the carburetor for cleaning.

The fuel tank has an anti-siphon jet inside the tank. The purpose of this jet is to break the vacuum whenever the engines are stopped, thereby preventing the syphoning of the fuel in the event the carburetor leaks or a line is disconnected.

LUBRICATION OF YOUR ENGINE

An inboard engine, unlike the bulk of all outboard engines, requires adding oil into the engine itself, rather than mixing it in the gas as you do with your outboard motor. I am told by all my friends in the boat business that an inboard owner should carry at least one quart, or maybe two, aboard your runabout or utility for adding to the engine when it is needed. Many of you may already know that on a lot of Chris-Craft runabouts, down in the engine compartment there is that little box built-in, just large enough for a small tool box plus one quart of oil in its original container. My dad was always a sticker for having the can of oil along in the boat, always ready whenever we needed to add it. Another good habit is to regularly check the oil level in the engine. In the utility type inboards, like my Century, there is no room under the engine box for tools or a container of oil. However, I solved that problem by carrying the can of oil wrapped safely in a piece of cloth, high and dry under the rear seat frame, along with my hand tools, also wrapped for protection and easily accessible when I need them.

The rest of this short section on lubrication comes from a Chris-Craft owner's manual. Remember, it is just as bad to have too much oil in your engine as not enough.

LUBRICATION

Detailed lubrication instructions, as well as recommendations for breaking in the engine, will be found in the *Engine Operator's Manual*.

We are, of course, primarily interested in seeing that every Chris-Craft is serviced with oil of good character and quality because the use of such oil means not only dollars in the owner's pocket, but smooth engine operation, freedom from trouble, and maximum engine performance. A marine engine works at maximum capacity 90% of its lifetime, whereas in an automobile the engine rarely, if ever, works at its maximum more than 10% or 15% of its lifetime. Hence the demands on the oil are far greater in a marine engine.

We recommend the use of a detergent oil with additives. A straight mineral oil of high quality may be used but we want to caution you that the two types should never be mixed. To do so may cause the formation of sludge. Always replenish with the same make and type of oil that is in the crankcase. If it is necessary to change the make of oil, always drain the crankcase and make a complete change.

The oil in the engines of new boats shipped from the Chris-Craft factories is SAE #20 *Havoline* motor oil. It should be changed after ten to fifteen hours running to SAE #30 motor oil. See the *Engine Operator's Manual* on changing oil.

The extra gallon of *Havoline* oil on the boat is furnished with the compliments of the Texaco Company. If used for replenishment, be sure to replace it for it is advisable to have an extra gallon of oil aboard the boat for emergency purposes.

REDUCTION IN SPEED & WHY THIS OCCURS

If you are like most of us, you feel your inboards never reach the speeds and/or r.p.m.s listed for your boat-engine combination in the catalog for that year. Well, my own boat runs about 500 r.p.m.s slower than it is supposed to, but I am not worried. All of the following subjects discussed can "shave" a few precious revolutions away, and when they are all taken as one, that in most cases is why our boats may not be running up to par as we would like them to.

One example of loss of revolutions is weather. The summer of 1983 here in Minnesota was hot and dry almost every day. In fact, our lake dropped almost 2 feet in depth from its high point in June. Every time I drove my Century, even with just myself aboard, she only would top out about 4,300 r.p.m.s. If I had one person or five in the boat, it was always about the same. Since my boat was kept off the water and on a lift when not in use, I knew that "water-weight gain" was not the problem. It just so happened that the night I took her out of the water it was a rather cool evening, only about 70 degrees or so. When I headed up the lake towards the launching ramp, I opened that 165 Interceptor wide open and she bounced right up to 4,600 r.p.m.s. That was the fastest my boat ran all year. That's a good example of how, when it is cooler and less hot and humid, boats run at their very best. If your rig is not running at what you think it should, why not check out some of the following things to see if they might be the cause of your problems?

LOSS OF REVOLUTIONS

The catalog or advertised speed of a boat is the average speed attained at the factory over a certified course, under favorable conditions with a new boat and is not guaranteed.

A normal loss of speed is expected after the boat has been in the water for a while, but the total loss of speed depends on the circumstances under which the boat is used.

That this loss may be kept to a minimum, the following contributing factors must be given consideration.

Atmospheric Conditions

It is not generally known that an engine will develop more horse power in the early spring and late fall than it will during the middle of the summer. Our laboratory tests have shown this variation to be from five to ten percent.

Therefore, it is reasonable to assume that this loss of power will be reflected in loss of boat speed during the summer when both the air and cooling water is very warm. This loss must be taken into consideration when comparing the speed of a boat that is tested at the factory at Algonac, Michigan, and shipped into southern territory.

Normal Absorption of Water

After the boat is in the water for a few weeks, considerable water will be absorbed into the hull that will increase the weight of the boat as much as 10 percent of its total weight.

This condition is unavoidable, but it can be kept to a minimum by keeping the boat bottom free from marine growth, and the bilge pumped dry. Also the entire boat must be kept well protected from the weather with paint and varnish.

Personal Equipment and Extra Accessories

This is a loss of speed that is many times overlooked by the boat owner. It is easy to observe the loss of speed when several passengers are aboard the boat, but sometimes the owner will load the boat down with supplies, personal equipment and many accessories without taking into consideration the effect on the performance of the boat.

Marine Growth and Moss

If the boat speed is to be maintained, it is necessary to keep the bottom free from marine growth and moss. For more detailed information, we refer you to the subject of "Care of the Boat Bottom."

Water in the Bilge

This is more or less dependent on the condition under which the boat is used. When driving in a heavy sea, considerable water may come in over the deck into the stern cockpit; also on boats moored in open water, rain may enter the cockpit, as not all boats have cockpit scuppers. A barrel of water weighs over 400 pounds; therefore, keep the bilge pumped dry.

Damaged Under-Water Equipment

Elsewhere in this book we have pointed out the loss of speed and vibration that can result from a damaged wheel, shaft or strut. We refer you particularly to the subjects of "Propeller Selection" and "Shaft Alignment."

Engine Efficiency

It must be remembered that to maintain maximum speed, the engine must maintain its maximum power. With normal care and proper lubrication with the right kind of oil, the engine should require very little attention. Let us point out to you again that the engine is the *heart* of the boat, and the performance and pleasure you get out of the boat is dependent on the care you give the engine. To neglect it leads only to disappointment and expense.

Space will not permit a detailed account due to the many different models of engines, but let us refer you to the *Engine Operator's Manual*. In general, ordinary maintenance consists of proper lubrication as previously mentioned, as well as valve tappet adjustment, seasonal valve grinding, clean gasoline lines and carburetor, periodic adjustment and cleaning of the spark plugs, distributor points and spark timing.

Effect of Altitude on R.P.M.

Loss of boat speed may result from the effects of altitude. It is customary to reduce the pitch of the propeller to compensate for this loss of horsepower. The higher the altitude, the less density the air has and to maintain the proper fuel-to-air ratio a leaner mixture is required. On fixed jet carburetors a smaller size jet may be recommended. On carburetors having a main jet adjustment, this correction can be made without change in the carburetor jets.

ENGINE ROOM VENTILATION

When laying up the boat for any period of time over an hour or two, always *open the engine hatches*. If your engine is in a box with a cover, take the cover off. Leave the boat in this condition until after you start it again and get it out of the boathouse or slip. Then you may close the hatch covers or replace the box cover. This is a safeguard against the possibility of fumes accumulating which may cause fire.

CARE OF THE BOTTOM OF YOUR BOAT

Wooden boat owners probably worry more about the bottom of their boat then any other part of her. If your boat is moored permanently in the water, the bottom must be in excellent shape or your beauty may slip to the bottom some night when you least expect it to. The use of anti-fouling paints vary nationwide. In this modern day and age, numerous brands, types and styles of anti-fouling paints are made for both fresh and salt waters. Years ago if you wanted anti-fouling paint, you probably used copper, copper-bronze, or maybe a few other shades, and that was about all. Now, you have almost a rainbow of colors to choose from, though most of us still like the bright red, green or copper, as our bottom paint color.

Those of us who keep our boats suspended out of the water normally should not have to repaint the bottom of their boat each year, unless the color fades or weathers, as it sometimes will. If you keep your craft in the water, be it fresh or salt, you can figure that the bottom must be painted just as a part of annual maintenance, and that's all there is to it.

Take care of your boat's bottom and it will take care of you.

Anti-Fouling Bottom Paint

An *anti-fouling* or *copper bottom* paint is a type of bottom paint that will remain soft and has incorporated in its formula a poison, the purpose of which is to kill barnacles and marine growth found in salt water. The soft properties of the paint allow this dead substance to be scrubbed from the boat bottom by the action of the boat going through the water.

Every manufacturer has his own formula and it is necessary to change the formula for different parts of the country; thus, a paint that is satisfactory in one locality may not be suitable in another. It is therefore important that you select your paint with care, using the recommendations of other experienced boatmen in your locality. It must be emphasized, however, that any copper paint is not necessarily a good copper paint. It is not a question of copper content alone but one of formula that affords the anti-fouling and protection qualities. A sheet of pure copper suspended in salt water will accumulate barnacles and growths.

It is impossible to tell how often it may be necessary to repaint the boat bottom. A boat which is used quite often will not require the attention that one does which is used only occasionally. In warm southern waters, the accumulation of moss and marine growth will be much faster.

At least once during the season the boat should be pulled out of the water and scrubbed and repainted if necessary. Under adverse conditions it may be required oftener if a great loss of boat speed is experienced. Not every time the bottom is scrubbed does it need to be repainted.

All Chris-Craft Cruisers have double planked construction and do not require caulking. Inspect the bottom carefully for damaged planks and if the boat has been out of the water for some time, the outer planking may dry out so that the seams may be slightly open. Do not fill these seams but paint the boat as usual and after the boat is put into the water again the planks will expand to their normal position.

After the bottom is perfectly dry, sand and scrape it thoroughly and repaint with a good quality anti-fouling bottom paint. Do not use a priming coat of red lead and linseed oil; in fact, do not use any kind of a linseed oil paint on any part of the boat under the water. Marine growths thrive on it.

Use the same bottom paint for all the coats to be applied. In applying anti-fouling paint, be particularly careful to keep it thoroughly stirred in the can. This type of paint separates quite rapidly. Use a good long bristle brush. Allow the first coat to dry thoroughly before the second coat is put on. The last coat should not be applied until the boat is practically ready to be launched. The paint then should only be allowed to dry for five or six hours if possible, but not over 24 hours at the maximum. In other words, the boat should be put in the water while the paint is still soft for the reasons as explained in the earlier part of this chapter.

On many Chris-Craft Runabouts and Sportsmen a hard racing type of paint is used because in this type of boat maximum speed is sometimes desired. Keep the boat out of water when not being used by suspending it on chain falls or a boat hoist. If the boat must be left in the water all of the time, in salt water it is recommended that the bottom be repainted with a good quality anti-fouling soft copper paint. A copper (poison) bottom paint is not necessary in fresh water.

The most important part of the care to be given a boat is to keep the boat well protected from the elements by plenty of paint and varnish. During the time the boat is not in use, the cabin should be well ventilated because if the cabins are closed up tightly for a week or more at a time they will become very damp and cause abnormal swelling of the locker doors and drawers, as well as the danger of mildewing the equipment. The doors and drawers are originally fit loose enough to allow for normal expansion but it may under some conditions be necessary to dress them down still more after the boat has been in service for some time.

To insure maximum performance and speed in a Runabout or Sportsman, it is advisable that when not in use, the boat be raised clear of the water to avoid becoming water-logged. However, this procedure is not essential except when maximum peformance is desired. It is preferable of course, that a boat be kept under cover in a boat house provided with a well and with two chain falls or a hoist.

When mooring an open boat exposed to the elements, it is advisable to protect the boat with a suitable canvas cover. The cover should be provided with vent holes to prevent an accumulation of dampness that will cause abnormal swelling of the wood and hard starting of the engine. On boats having a large cockpit, a support or ridge pole must be provided to keep water from pocketing in the cover.

RECONDITIONING WOODEN BOTTOMS
by Paul A. Miklos

In a recent reply from Mr. Sima regarding a letter I wrote mentioning my disagreement to Mr. Johnson's advocation of hard gluing and fiberglassing wooden boat bottoms, he suggested that I write on traditional refinishing of bottoms.

First off, I would like to state my reasons for objecting to Mr. Johnson's technique. As he states, the process is very hard, virtually impossible for one who has no previous experience. Fiberglassing totally destroys the originality of a wooden boat. And this whole process is not necessarily going to be a cure-all. If, in the case of leaking, due to deteriorated inner structure, the fiberglass, no matter how well applied, is going to fail. Finally, because of the normal expansion and contraction of wood, planks may bulge and buckle because of the hard seams. When built, Century spaced bottom planks about 3/32" exactly because of this action. They filled the seams with an elastic compound to compensate for this swelling and shrinking.

So to refinish a bottom in original fashion I would suggest first, if feasible, remove the engine and turn the hull over. This makes the job much easier and gives a much better job. When turned over you should only support from the stringers, never the decks. If turning is impractical, it is best to expose as much bottom area as possible. To do this, remove the trailer or cradle and support with the three 35-gallon barrels (safety lines should be secured overhead), one under the stem and one under each corner of the transom. Here again is the messy part: remove the old finish either by the paint remover method or carefully cut with medium-coarse abrasive paper (60 grit) on a feather-edged grinder, removing as little wood as possible. (Respiratory protection should be worn and the grinder should only be used on the bottom.) At this point you should clean the seams of hard dried paint and old caulking. Now sand fine with 100 to 120 paper to obtain a smooth surface. After it has been sufficiently sanded, the bottom should be primed with a clear sealer, then wet sand with 220 grit to remove the raised grain. It is now ready for the first coat. A hard racing copper-bronze is what we use here, but an anti-fouling is advisable for salt water uses. (Green bottoms were prevalent prior to WW II and a charcoal gray was used in 1967 and 68.) After the first coat, it is ready to be caulked. I recommend using Boatlife Life Caulk in the gun-type tubes as it is easy to apply, extremely durable, and never hardens. Any comparable Thyicol-based caulk is acceptable. Be careful to avoid leaving excess caulk around the seams. Now touch sand excess and remaining rough spots, then apply second coat in the same manner. Two may be enough, if not put on a third coat the same as the previous two.

As in fiberglassing, this is quite an involved process and only advisable for a show condition boat or one that leaks heavily. Any bad planks should be removed and all frames should be closely examined, especially where they meet at the chines and the notorious lower transom frame. Two of the major problems are bad frame joints moving, causing the bottom to shift, splitting the first plank off the chine longitudinally (usually even with the length of the engine), and the other one is the planks across the transom dropping because the lower frame has rotted or delaminated. Remedies for these two problems is only by replacement. For a simple case of a good boat for common use in good to fair condition, I recommend simply scraping and going over with a wire brush, spot priming, recaulking the seams and one or two good coats of bottom paint. In order to avoid a build-up of paint you should be wise about painting. Seasonal painting is not always necessary, depending mainly on time in the water and the amount of use. Be careful not to over care for your boat.

In closing I would again like to state that I am not criticizing Mr. Johnson's process. I am sure he does an excellent job, but for normal boaters, this would be quite hard. Myself, if I can go through all the other troubles of a wooden boat, I can surely maintain the bottom in its original state.

Thanks, Paul, for sharing your fine article on bottom refinishing. The Miklos men, Chuck, Paul and Frank are all three "Century Experts," and I am sure they would be glad to help with questions especially concerning Century. The article on hard-glueing your boat's bottom will be a little later in this chapter.

CARE OF VARNISHED SURFACES

That shiny varnish that we are all so proud of when we show and use our inboards does require care to keep it looking good. If you don't like to wipe and clean the varnished surfaces of a wooden boat, then you probably better sell her and buy a "plastic" boat.

Myself, I try to chamois off my boat's decks, hull sides and transom once it is up in the lift, prior to putting on the mooring cover. That cover, by the way, hangs down not to the waterline, but to the chine, where hull side and bottom meet. That way, sun has no chance to either shine on the varnish directly or to also reflect up off the water and hit the unprotected sides a second time. If you don't believe me, just check around your lake and take a close look at those varnished inboards that have mooring covers that only hang down maybe a foot or so on all sides. The varnish will look okay from a distance, but when you get close you will see how dull it gets. My boat will be able to go through next season as she shines just like when I brought her home last spring.

Besides wiping it carefully with a good chamois skin, I also use cold, clean tap water on my chamois. Out at Lake Tahoe, the fellows at Sierra Boat Company do the same thing, so if it is good enough for that huge operation, who am I to do any different? This year I also, once a week, rubbed down the hullsides and transom of my Century with lemon oil. I think the time I spent was well worth it as the wood retained such a fine gloss all year. I was advised by Tony Brown of Sierra Boat Company to do this, and I am glad I did. This fall I gave the whole varnished hull and transom a complete rubdown with lemon oil when I put her away and I am sure it will keep the wood from drying out a lot over the winter ahead.

CARE OF VARNISHED SURFACES

There is no definite length of time that the varnished finish of a boat will last as this is dependent entirely upon the conditions under which the boat is being used. The deteriorating effect of salt water is well known, but we also want to caution you that the ultra-violet rays of direct sunlight will break down the finish as fast or even faster.

You will usually find that the finish will stand up in direct proportion to the time that the boat is exposed to the sun; therefore, it is highly recommended that you endeavor to have a protected place to keep your boat when it is not being used.

Watch the finish of the boat. When it starts to get dull, have a light coat of varnish added rather than wait until the finish has broken through the surface, exposing the bare wood because it will then be necessary to remove all the old varnish and refinish from the wood up.

Do not varnish over varnish that has been waxed without thoroughly washing with a suitable solvent. *This is imperative!*

Any condition that will cause excessive expansion of the wood in a boat will affect the finished surface because it will break the film of varnish at the seams, allowing water to get into the wood. Dark streaks at the butt joints or around the wood bungs are usually caused by a breakdown of the varnish film.

CARE OF STUFFING BOXES

All of last summer my boat had a troublesome, annoying small leak. Since I kept the boat out of the water when not in use, I oftentimes would crank it up off the water, but never could I see any water dripping out. I am quite sure we soaked it up plenty before it was launched, but still it had that continual small leaking all the time. Having talked to Glenn Hafer, former owner of Hafer Craft Boat Company, he said to check the stuffing box. Well, here was something I had never really thought about, but it did make sense. My boat had been "For Sale" two seasons before I bought her, and evidently the braided, waxed hemp wrapped around in the stuffing box needed replacement or tightening. Glenn suggested that I try tightening the packing nut before I do any more. Luckily, that's all my boat needed as she is no longer leaking, much to my pleasure. This whole, rather confusing piece of marine hardware is discussed and shown in this article. If you have a problem, check with your inboard dealer or another wood boat owner who has gone through the same experience as you.

Closely akin to stuffing box care comes shaft alignment. This subject is often overlooked in the haste to get "Ol' Betsy" over the side for the season. Read this review closely and then do what it tells you to, and the chances of serious damage to engine and/or shaft and other underwater gear should be avoided.

CARE OF STUFFING BOXES

It is advisable from time to time to inspect the stuffing boxes, both the propeller shaft stuffing box and the rudder stuffing box.

The propeller shaft stuffing box is fastened to the bronze shaft log by a flexible hose which allow a misalignment up to .010" without excessive wearing of the stuffing box packing. The stuffing box is packed with braided waxed hemp packing, or ordinary candle wicking greased with water pump grease will answer the purpose.

Should it be found that the propeller shaft stuffing box is leaking slightly, this does not indicate that the stuffing box needs repacking. It is only necessary to loosen the stuffing box locknut and tighten up the packing nut. Should the stuffing box still show signs of leakage after some use of the boat, it is then suggested that you entirely unscrew the stuffing box packing nut, replacing all old packing.

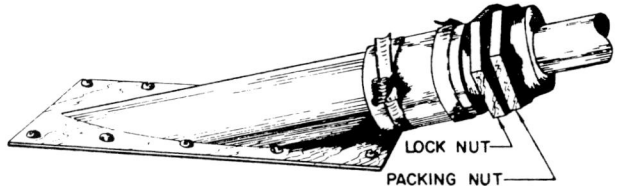

SHAFT LOG AND STUFFING BOX

After the old packing is removed, new packing should be wound around the shaft in separate rings. Enough rings should be put on to nearly fill the stuffing box packing nut. The ends of each ring should touch and the joints should be staggered. The stuffing box packing nut is then moved toward the stuffing box over the packing and screwed on the stuffing box gland. Do not tighten the packing nut too tight as the shaft may be scored. Tighten it just enough to stop any leaking. Be sure to tighten the locknut well. The necessity of frequent tightening indicates either a scored shaft, bent shaft, or engine out of alignment.

Should the propeller shaft stuffing box still show signs of leaking, after all the precautions have been taken, it is then suggested that you go to see your nearest Chris-Craft dealer and ask him to investigate the trouble because the possibility exists that the log may not be properly lined up, the original factory alignment having been affected by the expansion of the wood.

SHAFT ALIGNMENT

Before the boat leaves the factory the propeller shaft is checked for alignment but after the boat has been in the water for a few days, or while in transit, the expansion of the wood in the hull will affect this alignment and it is very important that this adjustment be rechecked.

If the propeller shaft stuffing box requires frequent tightening to keep it from leaking, a bent shaft may be the trouble or the shaft is not in line with engine. Check the alignment by removing the bolts from the shaft coupling just aft of the reverse gear (see illustration).

On all of the Chris-Craft engines there are wedges under the motor legs to facilitate this adjustment. On engines not so equipped, adjustment may be made by using shims under the legs or by cutting down the motor support timbers as required.

Remember it is impossible to properly line up a bent shaft. If you line it up in one position, by turning the shaft only half a turn it will again be out. A straight shaft properly lined up will require very little attention and will add many hours to the life of the strut bushing. Many cases of excess vibration and loss of revolutions are found to be due to an improperly aligned shaft.

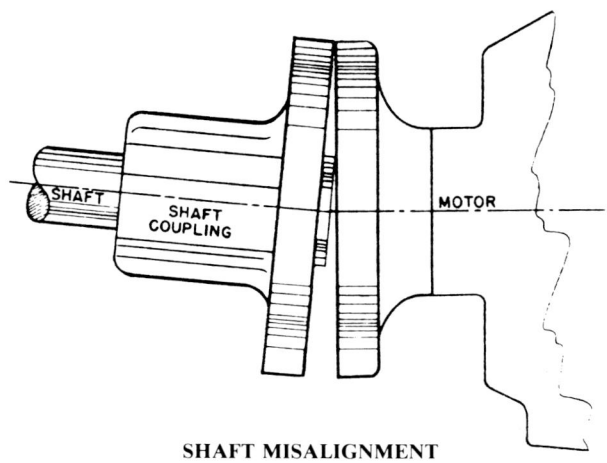

SHAFT MISALIGNMENT

Above figure is exaggerated for emphasis, but a slight misalignment will cause loss of power, excessive wear, noise and vibration. When checking parallel faces, use a feeler gauge, or piece of shim stock, not more than .003 of an inch thickness. When coupling faces are brought together by hand—not bolted—the .003 feeler should be tightly gripped at all points around the edges of the couplings. Alignment must be correct when couplings are viewed from the side as well as when seen from the top.

It is necessary to lift lightly on the shaft and coupling to compensate for the weight of these two items, but be very careful that only the weight is lifted and the shaft is not sprung.

INSTALLING A PROPELLER WHEEL

Be sure the bore of the wheel is free from dirt and corrosion and the tapered end of the shaft is clean and smooth. The keyway in the wheel and shaft must be free from burrs that will prevent the wheel from seating tightly on the shaft.

Put the wheel on the shaft first and make sure the keyway in the shaft and wheel are lined up. Note that one end of the key is rounded. This end of the key should be inserted first with the rounded end toward the shaft (see illustration).

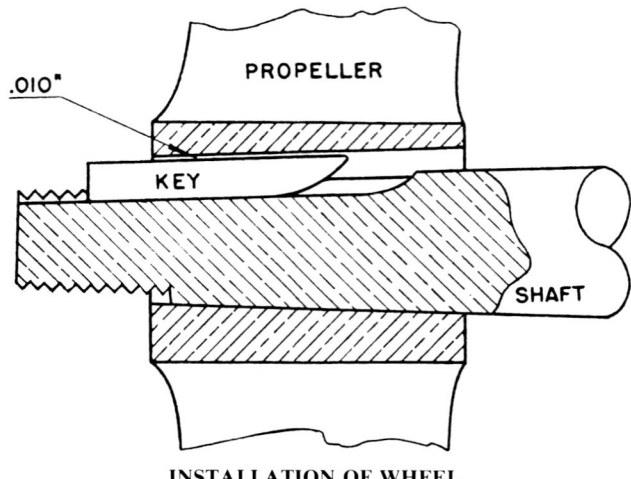

INSTALLATION OF WHEEL

The key should fit snugly at the sides but must not bind at the top. There should be at least .010" clearance as shown in the sketch. If the key fits too tightly at this point and is driven in by force, the wheel will be pulled off center and will be out of balance. Many cases of vibration are traced to this cause.

WATERPROOFING HULLS
by Lance E. Johnson

"HARD GLUEING"

I have never been satisfied with old mahogany inboard hulls that have to be soaked before they can be used, and then carry water inboard throughout the season. Every inboard I have worked on has had the hulls completely waterproofed to keep them light and maintenance free.

There are two steps to this process: (1) hard glueing all seams, and (2) fiberglassing from waterline on down.

Neither of these processes are easy or cheap. If you want to save money and do a cheap job, then don't read any further. On the other hand, if you really want a first class job, do not plan to cut corners, substitute materials or hurry through the job. Patience will pay off if you really want your boat to retain its value and appreciate.

Another word of caution: unless you have good to excellent ability to work with your hands and use tools, I don't recommend you begin a job of this magnitude.

This paper will deal with waterproofing only from the waterline on down. However, *all* seams should be hard-glued with the method I will now outline.

The first step is a messy one. All the finish—yes, those thirty layers of paint—must come off to the bare wood. This will require about two gallons of paint remover for the average runabout. After the boat has had the engine removed and been turned over, remove the spray rail if you have one. If you don't plan to do anything with the sides of the hull, mask off with paper and tape half way up on the spray rail. Pour remover over hull working, only in three square foot sections. Spread it around so it stands up about ¼" thick. Then quickly cover this area with wet rags or wet newspaper. This will prevent the remover from drying out. After about twenty minutes, remove rags and scrape loose paint with a broad knife. Apply three or more applications if necessary.

The next step is to belt sand the bottom with 100 grit resin bond belts. Move the sander on a 10 degree angle but move back and forth with the grain. This will prevent the sander from digging in and leaving divits. Then take a block ¾" x 3" x 9" and wrap a sheet of 100 grit paper, aluminum oxide breaking the edges as it goes around the block. Sand with vigor with the grain with one hand and hold a 200 watt globe light with the other, shining it across the hull to create shadows. This will tell you where to sand to reshape the hull. Don't think you can leave the hull rough from belt sanding and go directly to the fiberglassing process. Your divits and gouges will stick out like a sore thumb through your glassing job. You will have to sand more by hand on the rounded edges and bow.

As the boat loses its bottom finish, you will notice large cracks in all the seams from dry-out. It is necessary to have the wood absolutely dry before new material can be applied.

After you have finished with the sanding and your arms are so sore they feel like they will fall off, you now can begin sawing out the seams. Take your portable electric hand saw and insert a carbide blade. Free hand saw each seam, just barely touching the wood on both sides of the seam. Set your blade so it will cut only two-thirds of the thickness of the plank. Go over all your seams visually to make sure there are no spots with caulking still in. *All* seams must be open to bare wood on both sides, no exceptions. Plan to hit some screws in this process.

At this point you are ready for the taping. Using ¾" masking tape, tape each seam on each side so only the bare groove is exposed. This has two purposes: first, to keep the run over glue from getting on the hull where it is not needed; secondly, it will be less glue to sand down later. After about one to two hours, depending on drying conditions, the tape can be removed. If you wait until the glue sets, you will not be able to remove the tape.

The glue you will use is made by the Co-Polymer Chemical Company of Livonia, Michigan. Ask for number EA-2043 epoxy adhesive. It is very expensive but well worth it. A boat of say 18 feet in length will require about eight quarts to do the bottom only. The glue comes in clear and white. The white is best for hard glueing because it is more liquid and can be applied with a caulking gun, the type that does not use cartridges (hand-loading). You mix equal parts of each part A and part B and it is ready to use immediately. Since it is very slow to set, you need not be in a hurry to use it. It is good usually for an hour after mixing. Load your caulking gun with freshly mixed adhesive and squeeze out into the seams. Adjust your flow so that it will stand up higher than the seam so that you can sand it down flush later. For cleanup, use lacquer thinner. It may be necessary to apply two coats to the vertical portions of the hull as well as the bow since it will run down and partly out of the seam. This adhesive can also be applied with a broad knife, but it takes much longer and is more messy. After 48 hours you can take your belt sander and sand each seam down flush with the hull. Go very carefully as the glue will sand down quickly and you don't want to spoil your hand-sanding job! After you have sanded all the seams flush, you will notice some air holes from the bubbles. These can easily be refilled with fiberglass putty. If they are large, then you had better mix up some more adhesive and fill them in.

You are now ready to begin fiberglassing.

"FIBERGLASSING YOUR INBOARD"

Assuming that you have sanded the wood to the bare hull and have removed all traces of paint, you are then ready to fiberglass. There are two basic types of cloth: plain cloth and roving. Roving is the heavy cloth that looks like the material used on wicker furniture. What we are using is the regular cloth. I will leave it up to you whether or not to use one or two layers. If your hull was in bad shape, then I would suggest two layers.

The first step is the sizing. Mix up your resin and add about 20 percent acetone in order to thin out mixture. Then you can add the acid catalyst, using 11 cc's per quart mixed. Using a wide brush or roller, cover the whole bottom to be glassed with resin. (Be sure you have masked off the portion you don't want glassed or you will have a messy cleanup later.) Be sure to smooth out the coating and don't allow sags or bare spots to appear. After the coating has completely set up, you are ready for the cloth application. (If you find that you have spots that don't seem to get dry, it could be that you have not mixed the acid well enough.) The warmer the room, the faster the resin will set up.

Now take your fresh batch of resin and after catalyzing it, apply it to the hull as heavy as possible. Then take your cloth, and with the help of a friend, lift it over the hull and lay it down. Now comes the messy part. You must move around the boat and stretch it away from the hull in order to reduce air bubbles. Keep pulling on it until the resin begins to set up. There will be some bubbles that simply will not pull out. Then take a sharp knife and make a small slit a half inch to one inch in length to bleed out the air bubble. Don't be concerned about the slit. Your glass job will not be affected because of it. Your cloth very likely will not cover the entire bottom. Just wait until the resin has dried and apply the next half (or quarter) on the exposed bottom and overlap about three inches onto the old layer. After this has dried, apply two more heavy coats of resin, allowing them to dry completely between coats. As you brush on resin, keep one thing in mind: if you get sloppy with your brush work and allow sags to appear, you will have much work ahead of you in sanding out those sags later! If you apply two coats of cloth, be sure to sand out the overlap seam from the first layer.

After the second coat of resin, begin sanding the bottom to make it smooth. The end result should be that your bottom is as smooth as if it were just painted. There should be no sags or divits. Now apply two more coats, sanding between coats with 60 grit paper or slightly finer. Use high grade aluminum oxide paper with the stiff backing and wrap it around a ¾" block of wood measuring 3" x 9", breaking the edges so it won't slip on the block. After your final coat of resin you should have a smooth job provided you have sanded it well between previous coats.

For your color coats, use only epoxy paint. Plan on at least three coats since epoxy has some transparent qualities and it doesn't cover as well as conventional paint. Again, sand between coats of paint but with 100 grit or slightly finer sandpaper and tack rag between coats. Good luck!

"HARD GLUEING"

The two-part series on the hard-glueing of hulls was meant to be a brief, yet comprehensive paper on this subject. After submitting these reports I have talked with a few boat restorers who have used our system with tremendous success.

One boat enthusiast called me one evening and told me that everything went well with his hard-glueing except one item: he noticed that the glue line on his transom was quite noticeable. Not being able to see his project, I advised him to do the following to disguise the glue line: take masking tape and tape off the seam just as was done just before applying the epoxy adhesive. Then take the mahogany stain and paint the seam with a brush, using the stain as paint and not wiping it, and allowing it to dry. Then remove the tape and apply two or three coats of varnish, preceded by the sealer coat. Then take very fine wet or dry sandpaper, about 400 grit, mix with water and sand out the ridge left by the tape. Then tack rag and apply several more coats of varnish. This should mostly disguise the glue seam which some may find objectable, especially if the finish is light colored. Using the EA—20-42 which is clear, your seam will look greenish brown after staining over it with the stain-filler mixture.

Now some tips for future care. If properly cared for, your hull will never need soaking or patching again. The hull becomes one solid piece of wood. This means you must never use a plastic full-deck cover on your boat as it does not breathe and moisture will build up inside the boat. Never allow water to stand in the hull if you have had rain, leaking stuffing boxes, leaking water from cooling system, or splash-in water. When you are through for the day, get every drop of water out of the boat. I have 2 one-inch diameter Moeler drain plugs in the transom where the transom meets the bottom so as to drain out both sides of the keelson. I bushed the holes with brass tubing and glued the bushing in the epoxy. If your engine leaks oil, you can have more serious problems as the water will not wash out the oil when the hull is being drained. If you have oil spillage, wipe it out with paper towels and paint thinner or degreaser. Prolonged oil film in the boat could loosen your fiberglass job; or, if you didn't fiberglass, the screw filler will pop out when the hull is under pressure from the boat moving through the water at high speeds. Then your screws will allow water to seep in.

GROUTING
by J. Carl Hamblin
courtesy of Carl Hamblin,
Shepherd inboard expert.

After trying many types of solutions advertised and recommended for grouting and deck seams or grooves in the restoration of runabouts, etc., and after talking to many others, plus reading many different recommended procedures for this operation, I have found this procedure to be the easiest and most satisfying, especially for do it yourselfers!

1. Get a supply of three to five tubes of Masonite white caulking compound (or brown where needed) and a caulking gun.
2. Get one or two large packages of cellulose flat block type sponges from any supermarket. I used 8 sponges on a 22-foot boat because as they are used, small particles tend to fall off so I throw them away and start a new one.
3. Clean and tack decks thoroughly.
4. Put sponge in bucket of water, ready to use.
5. Apply grouting from gun ½ the length of one groove.
6. Lightly wring out sponge and wipe excess grouting from groove, flush with surface.
7. Do the same for rest of groove, cleaning off all excess grout.
8. Keeping finger wet, and using an even pressure, run down groove with finger to make concave groove, forcing out the excess.
9. Clean off this excess grouting again with sponge.
10. Any boo-boos at this stage may be lifted out with a pen knife and regrouted, using a wet finger to blend in, before a film of any setting up takes place.
11. Do one groove at a time, till satisfied.
12. After all grooves are done, let set overnite, followed by successive varnish coats.

Varnish darkens the best of any white grouting material, so if white seams are desired, purchase a striping tool with various size wheels, and using a fine enamel deck paint, apply the white striping.

This grouting, applied properly, will last as long as any other and will save hours of labor and untold headaches.

Also, for an amatuer or do it yourself refinisher, I would highly recommend using Interlux #99 varnish that is especially formulated for use in Florida type climates, where it tends to set varnish up faster.

This #99 holds a wet edge longer than others, and gives an amateur more time to brush it in from succeeding sections before it sets up and leaves excessive brush marks in overlaps.

This is an exceptionally high gloss varnish with built-in U/W restrainers.

Passing this along, just to help others who may have been really frustrated trying other products and methods.

RESTORING INSTRUMENT FACES
by Lance E. Johnson

Probably the most difficult part of restoring faces of old instruments is getting them apart! Many types are crimped together so some meticulous work with a knife and very thin screwdriver are in order. After the instrument is apart, you will notice dust and possibly some corrosion due to condensation.

While working with the face, be extremely careful around the needle as a slight nudge can break it.

The face will have to be drawn on another piece of paper, mapping out the dial to scale. Your measurements will have to be very precise, as a slight mistake in spacing out the letters and numbers will stick out like a sore thumb. After you have done this, you then measure the exact height of the letters and numbers within

1/64th of an inch. To obtain new letters and numbers, contact your local drafting supply store and ask for transfer letters (the type used by draftsmen and architects to give a very professional look to their blueprints). Before placing your order, be sure you have enough zeros, as these are the most called for number on your instrument face. Bring your instrument to the store if you can for matching letter styles.

The next step is to refinish the background of the face. Most old instruments were black. Use a spray paint of high quality in a semi-gloss finish. Do not use a flat paint such as primers as the face will catch dust and oil from your fingers and then it is there to stay. A gloss finish will not match what was on the face before. Don't bother to mask off your needle. You can touch up the needle with white gloss enamel with a tiny brush just before re-assembling your instrument.

Allow your paint to dry overnight even if it is the "fast dry" type. If you do not, your transfer letters will not stick. Your new transfer letters are mounted on a clear vinyl backing with the letters and numbers being quite close together. It may be necessary to make cuts in your letter card to get your letter close enough on the face. The letters are laid on the face and rubbed with a pencil from the back. The letter then leaves the vinyl and sticks to your instrument face with its own adhesive. Don't worry if you make a mistake. The letter can be easily lifted off and another put in its place. If your old instrument had raised letters, your job of finding the spot for the new letters will be easier. The raised letters will stand up through your new black paint job in relief.

In conclusion, some letter or number types will not be available. Then you just select the closest style available.

STEERING WHEELS USED ON VARIOUS CENTURY INBOARD SPEEDBOATS FROM 1954 THROUGH 1977

Compiled by Carl J. Kofron,
Century Boat Club Member

Late 1940's through 1954	1937-38 Buick Banjo Wheel
1955-58 Century	1953-55 Lincoln
1959-64 Century	1956-57 Lincoln

Some late '64s had Marine Destroyer Wheels.

1965-68 Century	1964 Ford Galaxie
1969-75 Century	1966 Plymouth Barracuda Sport Wheel

Some 1975s had the Speed Shop Accessory Wheels.

1976-77 Century	Speed Shop (Grant)

CARE & FEEDING OF VACUUM-TYPE AUTOMATIC BAILER

This type of bailer is used only on Runabouts, Sportsmen and light Cruisers having sufficient speed to develop enough vacuum to make it function. The only care or attention it needs is to keep it from becoming clogged. Should the boat not readily expel the bilge water while running at speeds above 15 miles per hour, it is likely that something may have obstructed the automatic bailer. To clean it, loosen the hose clamp at "B" (see cut) and remove the tube. Push a wire through the hose into the hull fitting to be sure it does not have an obstruction.

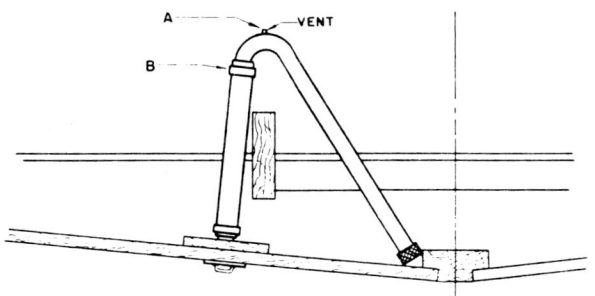

AUTOMATIC BAILER (VACUUM TYPE)

Jet "A" at the top of the tube is to prevent water from siphoning back into the boat and *it is important that this jet be kept open*. This type of bailer would not be practical to use without this vent, which because of its small size does not affect the performance of the bailer.

For large cruisers and other boats too slow for the vacuum type automatic bailer, an electric automatic or manual pump may be installed. Since these units are special equipment, their care and attention would depend upon the make and type used. We refer you to the instructions furnished with the unit.

WINTER STORAGE OF THE WOODEN RUNABOUT AND/OR UTILITY

Probably more damage can be done to your prized wooden runabout or utility from carelessly storing her for the off-season. Many folks wait until the last minute, just prior to freeze-up of the waterways, pull out the boat, put it on an old trailer, maybe or maybe not winterize the engine, and tie an old shredded-up tarp over it and let it go. If this sounds like you, and it happens more than you think, you better read this final article over more than once. A little common sense goes a long way here. Take the time to put your boat away well in the fall, and in the spring you won't be facing an avalanche of work to get it back into shape. As you can imagine, most people who own wooden boats today do give them the good care they deserve.

WINTER STORAGE OF THE RUNABOUT OR SPORTSMAN

The original cradle is ideal to use for storing the boat. Be sure that the saddles of the cradle are located on the boat so they will be *directly under a frame, never between frames.*

If the original cradle is not available, the boat may be supported on two or three timbers across the well under the boat at the points shown on the illustration. Next, secure two taper blocks, placing one on the left and one on the right side of the aft supporting timber. To illustrate this more clearly, refer to the sketch. When the boat is supported in this manner you will observe that the forward end is supported by the keel, the stern of the boat is supported at the chine, and is not resting on the keel.

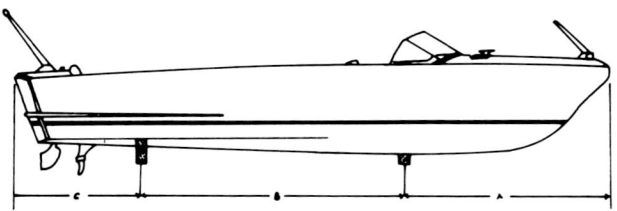

LOCATION OF SUPPORTING TIMBERS

Length of Boat in Ft.	Number of Supports	A	B	C
16	2	5'8''	5'1''	4'9''
17	2	5'4''	7'8''	4'0''
18	2	5'6''	7'5''	5'1''
19	2	5'9''	9'2''	3'5''
21	2	7'¾''	8'5¾''	5'7½''
22	2	7'6''	10'0''	4'6''
24	2	8'0''	10'0''	6'0''
25	2	8'4½''	10'7¼''	6'0''
26	2	8'6''	11'0''	6'6''
27	2	8'0''	12'0''	7'0''
28	2	10'0''	12'1''	5'11''

Space will not permit a complete list of all lengths of boats ever built, but the above general lengths will give you sufficient information. For boat sizes not listed, use nearest approximate locations but be sure that all supporting timbers are placed *directly under a frame, never between frames.*

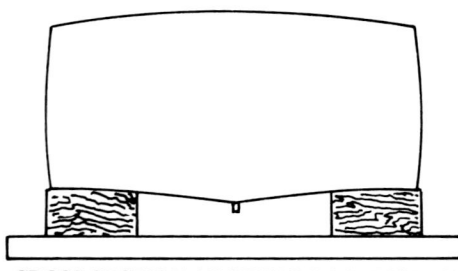

CROSS SECTION SHOWING LOCATION OF CHINE BLOCKS

Clean the Boat Bottom

As soon as the boat is hauled out of the water it is very important that the boat be thoroughly washed and cleaned of all marine growths and barnacles. If this is done when the boat is first taken out of the water while the marine growths and barnacles are soft, they are much more easily cleaned off than if allowed to remain on the boat until they are dry and hard. It is best not to repaint the bottom of the boat until just before the boat is to be launched again, giving the bottom of the boat more time to thoroughly dry out.

Draining the Boat

After the boat is pulled out of the water, the bilge should be thoroughly drained. On most runabouts there is a drain plug provided for this purpose, although there may be some compartments in the bilge that will not drain, depending upon the position of the boat. These should be pumped out and water wiped up with a sponge. The water system should be drained, being sure to drain all water lines and the pumps in both the lavatory and sink. After the water system is drained, a small quantity of heavy oil should be put in the water pumps and the pump worked a few times in order to thoroughly coat the inside of the pump and leather plunger to keep it from drying out and cracking (diaphram-type galley pumps excepted).

Drain all gasoline from the tanks. It is recommended at this time to flush out thoroughly with a quantity of flushing oil or kerosene so that all dirt that may have accumulated in these tanks is removed. Be sure to close all gasoline tank openings to prevent the entrance of dirt and dampness during storage period.

Batteries

Batteries should be removed and stored in a battery service station where they can be periodically charged to keep them from running down during the storage season.

Ventilation

If the boat is stored in a building, a hatch or window should be left open to allow circulation of air throughout the boat to prevent excessive moisture. If the boat is covered with a canvas or cover out-of-doors, it is best that this covering be made over a framework so that there is ample circulation of air around the boat, and some means of ventilation should be provided for. All drawers, clothes lockers, cabinets and doors should be left partially open to allow free circulation of air.

The upholstery should be removed and stored in a safe place where it will not get damp and soiled.

One of the special waterproof cabin ventilators illustrated in the Chris-Craft equipment catalog is highly recommended for boats that do not have them, since they allow free circulation of air in the boat without permitting water to enter.

Protect Chrome Plating

Clean all chrome-plated parts with a good chrome cleaner. Then cover the chrome with a suitable protector of clean lubricant.

I hope this material just discussed has been a help to you. If you have other more specific questions, feel free to contact me or the myriad of dealers and repair shops listed in this book.

The next chapter will discuss speedboat rides and also old time dealer photos.

CHAPTER VII
Speedboat Ride Operations and Old-time Wooden Boat Dealer Showroom Photos

Early 1940's speed boat rides. Boat, *Little Audrey,* taking off from Witke's, Clear Lake, Iowa.

SPEEDBOAT RIDE OPERATIONS

When I was a kid there was something that fascinated me about going down to Clear Lake, Iowa, Lake Okoboji, Iowa, or anywhere else where speedboat ride operations were located. To this day I still don't know what excited me, whether it was all those sleek, "woody" inboards with their exciting names, the drivers in their white coverall suits with a Chesterfield or Pall Mall draping at a rakish angle from their lips, or what. Anyhow, I have felt for a long time that I wanted to discuss this interesting part of "inboarding" with you.

Where to start this whole thing is a bit of a mystery, but since almost every lake, river, or "pond" (as lakes back East are called) once had a speedboat ride operation, we are probably all somewhat familiar with the subject. Do you remember, like I do, walking out on that long, somewhat shaky pier to board a big 3-cockpit

Speedboat ride dock owned by Touristville Boat Company in early 1950's. Downtown Clear Lake, Iowa.

"Chris" or Hacker with a name like *Comet* or *Zephyr* or *Rocket* emblazoned across its "behind" in letters a foot or more high? From the instant the ropes were cast off and your "captain" idled that "beast" out and

Downtown ride-dock of Curly-Lewis with inland Lake Scow sailboats "jockeying" for positions out on the lake. Get a load of the ride prices charged.

away from the dock, a certain magic occurred that seemed to me like no other. It seemed like no time and your annual speedboat ride was over for another summer—once out across the lake, wide open, in a big circle, then back into the dock where the driver pulled up to the boat's assigned slip without even nudging the pier. That was some driver back then.

Probably the major lake resorts were the scene of the greatest activity in speedboat ride operations. I will have to concentrate my material more in the Midwest as that is where I had most of my experience. Jim Irwin and his big fleet of 3-cockpit Chris-Crafts is for certain among the most famous speedboat ride operators.

As all of you must know by this time, Clear Lake, Iowa, is less than 35 miles due south of where we live here in Minnesota. Turning the clock back some 35 years, which would allow for me being just 5 years old, I will try to re-create speedboat rides, Iowa style.

You know as well as I that back in 1947-48, a trip to a neighboring state was something to be looked forward to and planned for, for weeks prior to its happening. The case was the same with our family. As an older kid, I always figured Saturday afternoon was a good day for Dad, Mom, my twin brother Art, our sister and me to go somewhere. With Dad being in the grain elevator business, weekdays were always too busy, but even farmers take Saturday afternoons off during late summer. On the day we would be going down to Clear Lake, all of us would swallow down our lunch in eager anticipation. Dad would listen to Cedric Adams' Noon-time News on WCCO radio. When that was finally over, he usually lit one of his big, black, long cigars and we all piled into the family car. In 1948 there were no interstates, so we had to first drive to Mason City, Iowa, then 12 miles or so straight west to Clear Lake. When we arrived at the lake, car traffic suddenly became much heavier with lots of teenagers and young college kids in evidence everywhere.

Usually our first stop was at Witke's Chris-Craft dealership. This old-time "Chris" dealer was located just north of the downtown area proper in Clear Lake. There are several views shown here—one of the docks from the air, and another with the *Comet* pulling up to unload a boatful of passengers, with the big "A" Class sailing scow also ready to give about 12 paying guests an exciting sailboat ride. This shot is about how I remember Witke's. About 1950 or so they added a big, white, wooden arch right by shore that said "Witke's Speedboat Rides" on one side; as you walked back off the dock after your ride, the other side said "Thank You for Your Patronage," or something to that effect.

As business got better, Witke's added more and more boats to their fleet of passenger boats. The first photo I ever took there myself was in 1955. By then, interest in riding in the old wooden speedboats was fast on the way

About 1940 birds-eye view of Witke's. Surf Ballroom, to right of Witke's, burned down about that time.

About 1940—looking out on the Witke Boat Co. main dock. "Ride Boats" came and went all day long.

I took this view of the Witke Boat Co. docks in 1955. At that time the firm probably was the largest it ever was.

The Comet roars off with another load of paying riders about 1940.

The famous Witke *Comet No. 1* speeds by the docks, off for a fast ride!

17' Chris-Craft "Ride Boat" owned by Witke Boat Co. waiting to head out with another load of passengers.

19' Chris-Craft "Barrel Back" used for over 20 years by Witke's Boat Rides.

Side view of *Peep* ride boat. I never saw this boat myself.

out, but, nonetheless, Witke's still had at least five runabouts and utility inboards, plus their large Chris-Craft cruiser which took guests on a slow and stately sunset cruise around the lake every evening during the summer. The "queen" of the Witke fleet was always the *Comet*. It was a beautiful 3-cockpit "Chris" with twin folddown windshields, and it could really step out, speedwise. I can't remember the original *Comet* very well, as I was still very young when it was in use. However, a smaller 3-cockpit Chris-Craft runabout from about 1940-41 or so replaced it, and they used that boat up into the early 1960s. Other old familiar Witke "ride boats" as they were called included the 25-foot C-C named *Sportsman,* the *Peep,* and the *Jeep* (both smaller twin-cockpit models, both shown here), plus a 22-foot C-C sedan from about 1950 or so. They had other boats before that time, but I was unable to find out much about any of those boats.

Witke's, in conjunction with the speedboat ride operation, also sold minnows, rented rowboats and motors, as well as operated a very fine restaurant and bathing beach. In the summer those folks were busy from dawn to dusk. The firm's tiny showroom was large enough to display not more than one or two small inboards, with the remaining space devoted to a small refinishing shop, plus storage space for *Miss Clear Lake* (the biggest cruiser on the lake), and a few of their ride boats. As boat sales continued to increase, Witke's

View looking east toward Witke docks. Inboard hanging on lift to extreme right is Clear Lake Police boat—early 1950's.

Early morning at Witke's. Looks like the police boat must already be out on rounds?

Spring is here! *Miss Clear Lake* is floated off her cradle into the lake.

Finally free of her cradle and afloat *Miss Clear Lake,* the largest cruiser on Clear Lake, Iowa.

Finally off the cradle and out into Clear Lake for a new year.

eventually sold Evinrude motors and other lines of boats.

Clear Lake used to sport a very nice amusement park, including a large roller coaster and many other thrill rides. Witke's also ran their speedboat rides from there. If I am not mistaken, you could ride a speedboat from the park to their main location across the lake and back, just like taking a bus or a taxi today. On holidays and weekends that park was bumper-to-bumper customers wanting a fast "thrill" ride aboard one of the Witke speedboats.

I wish to thank Don Humburg of Clear Lake, Iowa, who, as a youth, worked for Witke's as a speedboat driver. Don spent an afternoon with me a year or so back and we discussed the "old days" at Clear Lake when speedboat rides were big business. Don tells me that during the winter months he and the other five or six drivers would refinish boats in the Witke shop. With six men working on one boat at a time, about one week was all that was needed to perform a total refinish job from start to finish. The ride boats were also refinished and overhauled during the off season. In the spring the crew at Witke's installed the docks and boat lifts, and got all the boats into the water for another year.

There are some photos here showing the launching of *Miss Clear Lake* out of the shop's back door and into the lake. Getting this big boat in and out of the water each year was a real chore. In 1957 or 1958 I remember being down to Clear Lake with my dad and brother. We

Three young ladies pose aboard the *Comet* before she heads out for a ride.

The *Jeep* awaits her next passengers. This view probably shot on a weekday. Again about 1950 or so.

stopped at Witke's for a few minutes and watched them laboring to get that boat up into the building. The lake was very low that year, and they had a most difficult time, slowly winching the boat up onto its cradle and then pulling the boat up to shore, rolling along on rollers that were positioned under the cradle over which the boat moved. I guess it took several days that year to finally get the big "Chris" cruiser into winter storage.

Don never really told me, but I feel that back in the 1940s and '50s driving a speedboat was sort of an exciting and glamorous type of job, at least in the eyes of the younger generation. There are some photos scattered throughout this report showing young kids and high school and college girls who came to Witke's for speed-boat rides. They may have been attracted to the "he-man" type that drove those boats. After all, the skipper caps they wore, the cigarettes hanging out of their mouths, and their sun-tanned faces made heartthrobs for some.

Another fellow who shared material about the speedboat ride business on Clear Lake is Kenneth R. Anderson. His mother lives here in Albert Lea and she gave him *Volumes I and II* of this series for Christmas, 1982. Ken now lives in Northbrook, Illinois, but during his high school years he worked summers as a "dock boy" at Clear Lake for Witke's. He worked at Bayside Amusement Park dock and over at the main Witke dock in 1942, '43, and '44. Ken sold speedboat rides while his older brother was a driver for Witke's. He advises me that the *Zephyr,* one of my all time favorite speedboats (discussed in detail in *Volume 1*), was towed back to Clear Lake by "Curly" Lewis behind his 1937 or '38 V-16 LaSalle Coupe. Curly often used the LaSalle as a "tractor" at his shop to launch and retrieve boats. Ken Anderson tells me that the story around Clear Lake was that the *Zephyr* originally came from Chicago after a man was killed in the boat following a collision which had a stove in the craft's bow.

If you will recall, we started this report by turning back the clock to the year 1948 and trying to envision what Clear Lake, Iowa, speedboat rides were like in those years. Well, the other firm running such a business on that lake was the Curly Lewis Boat Lines. Ken Anderson's best friend, Roger Johnson, was a "dock boy" for Lewis. Both Witke's and Lewis Lines were in competition each summer for the passenger business on the lake. There was a lot of kidding back and forth between the crews from both operations about who did the most business, had the fastest boats, etc. I will share with you here some of Ken Anderson's memories of Curly Lewis and his boats. The photos throughout this section are of the *Zephyr, Princess, Rocket,* and other boats owned by Lewis and later, after his death, by the Touristville Boat Company of Clear Lake.

Ken told me he used to have a chunk of aluminum piston as well as the top of a valve from the original old Packard Liberty engine that powered the *Zephyr* when Curly first owned her. The *Zephyr* was repowered by a Wright Tornado with a marine conversion by Capitol Gearworks of St. Paul, Minnesota. Anderson remembers watching the first test run of the repowered boat, and how it had to be unceremoniously towed back to the dock as the torque wound the shaft like a rubber band and fractured it. A larger diameter shaft and new prop were feverishly prepared and installed which proved successful. To watch the *Zephyr* blast off was a real thrill. Ken says that Curly would idle out slowly to clear the dock area and then pour the coal to it.

Front seat of Zephyr. **Note the extreme width of the seats.**

The Zephyr **blasts off at the start of her run—about 1940.**

Before I go further, the next photo of the *Zephyr* will illustrate just how that big "beast" looked as it took off. First there would come a great roar, then the stern would all but disappear (note photo) as it created a huge quarter wave. As speed built up it would come back to a more horizontal position. Then at full speed it would skip like a stone . . . shhsh . . . shhsh . . . shhsh at about one-second intervals. I had forgotten that characteristic of the *Zephyr,* but Ken's letter brings it back to mind. It had almost no steering control at speed; it took a country mile to turn it. That characteristic was responsible for an accident one July 4th morning that really hurt Curly and coincided with another piece of bad luck later in the same day.

Anderson thinks it was 1944 but can't remember for certain. Anyhow, July 4th was *the* day of the summer for profit. The rest of the summer paid the overhead, but the 4th was the day to really make the "bread" as they say these days. That morning Curly had taken a load of passengers toward the downtown dock when some fellows anchored out in a fishing boat saw the *Zephyr* bearing down on them. As mentioned earlier, it was next to impossible to turn it at full speed. As the roaring, skipping runabout bore down on the fishermen, they jumped like two frogs out of their craft into the lake just as the *Zephyr* cut right through their boat and, in the process, lost a propeller blade and bent the shaft. The vibration that resulted caused the skeg to also loosen, so the *Zephyr* was put out of commission for the biggest day of the year that season.

Zephyr **and other ride boats docked between cruises. Clear Lake, Iowa—1953.**

A sleek Gar Wood which operated on Clear Lake for years and was owned by Curly Lewis Boat Lines. All railing shown on decks were made by Lewis crews.

Launching the *Rocket* at Clear Lake, Iowa. Spring 1950 or so.

The Rocket between rides, Clear Lake, Iowa. Lewis Boat Lines, early 1950's.

The *Rocket* and *Packard Clipper* race each other for the cameras. My dad's first inboard was the *Clipper*, later called *Baby Rocket* when Dad bought her in 1955.

Here is a rare photo of the *Rocket* pulling 9 water-skiers about 1953 or so.

The Princess excursion boat, Clear Lake, Iowa.

The normal ride on busy days was a five-minute one with long lines of passengers waiting their turn to board the monster speedboat for a fast, cooling trip out across the blue waters of Clear Lake. Curly also had other speedboats, including the *Rocket* and *Packard Clipper*. Both of those boats are shown here in various views.

For excursion rides the *Princess* (also discussed in *Volume I*) was a big moneymaker for Curly. As a child I can remember seeing the *Princess* slip by about sunset creating barely a ripple on the water, with soft music playing over speakers and a large, happy crowd of tourists aboard. Moonlight cruises from the Clear Lake "City Dock" were also big back in those days for the *Princess*.

The *Princess*, though a double-ended launch, was deceptively fast with power provided by a dual ignition Scripps engine of about 120 h.p. One day it was said to have actually passed a Lyman speedboat from Curly's arch rival, Witke's. Needless to say, a lot of good-natured ribbing occurred after that, and Curly said that Witke's was going to use "shingles" on the bottom of their boats from then on to get more speed.

Roger Johnson, Ken's best friend whom we mentioned earlier, lived near Bayside Park and liked inboards. He always hung around Curly's, and later became a "dock boy" and helper. During his career there Roger caused the *Princess* to blow up and sink. On a stormy Sunday back in 1943, the *Princess* was coming into dock, following a cruise with all the canvas side curtains down to keep the passengers dry. After docking it needed to be refueled. Roger proceeded to fill the tank, which had its filler neck several inches below the opening in the deck. Roger carelessly and unwittingly spilled some gas into the bilge. Curly later on went down to start the boat, still with its curtains down; Roger was sitting in the side hatch. Suddenly, bam! Roger was blown onto the dock, and the deckhouse and boat were all ablaze. The fire was put out after a lot of water was poured into the boat but the *Princess* sank. Curly had minor flash burns, Roger was scarred, and the *Princess* was out of commission for the rest of that year. After a long winter of repair it was ready for July 4th, 1944 when the first thing she had to do that day was tow the *Zephyr* home after it cut the rowboat in two. On the

The Princess in her last days, relegated to being a hot dog stand at a local Clear Lake kiddyland.

Princess' first cruise later that day, only 300 feet out from the dock, the Scripps engine that had been scorched in the explosion the year before quit. Now Lewis had his two best moneymakers out of business on the biggest day of the year.

Curly also operated an 18-foot boat I don't remember, but Ken Anderson tells me it, too, was called *Rocket II,* and was powered by a 300 h.p. Hispano engine. It was very fast, but it, too, had no rudder control and you had to slow it down to turn.

When you travel to Clear Lake, Iowa today, everything has changed. Witke's Boat Company was torn down more than five years ago to make way for a condo built on the site. The original restaurant near where the speedboat ride dock was located still stands, though it has been sold and completely restyled. It has a new name, too. Both the Lewis Boat Lines and the Touristville Boat Company, Curly's successors, have all disappeared from the lake, victims of progress.

I am happy to say, though, that interest in wooden boats is returning to Clear Lake. Robert Kent, Kay Holland, Mr. and Mrs. Jay Black, and others have formed a small nucleus of wooden boat owners who are currently organizing a Wooden Boat Owners' Club, with plans for their first boat show set for the summer of 1984. This is what it takes to get interest in "woodies" to increase. I wish the folks down at Clear Lake all the best in forming their club and restoring fine wooden boats to again cruise the beautiful waters of that fine lake.

With this we shall move on to the second portion of this chapter, "Old Time Wooden Boat Dealer Showroom Photos." So many wrote or called, saying they wished to see more of this type of thing, and I have been able to gather quite a few new photos for your review at this time.

OLD-TIME WOODEN BOAT DEALER SHOWROOM PHOTOS

So many readers asked for more old dealer photos in the next inboard book so I really got digging and have come up with some that even the owners of some firms shown may not remember seeing. To keep this as simple as possible, I have divided the photos into four groupings: East, Midwest, South and West. What is so interesting to me is that quite a few of the firms you will now read about and see here are still in business today, and most of them sell my books and posters as well. Many of these views were lensed from old dealer trade magazines, so most of you probably have not seen them.

The first firm I shall mention is good ol' Irwin Marine of Laconia, New Hampshire. This well known giant of the industry was opened first in 1919, and over the years sold Gar Wood, Fay and Bowen, Dodge Hacker Craft, and DeWitte. Currently Irwin enjoys selling both modern and classic antique boats in a good mix, and is one of the top Chris-Craft dealers volume-wise in the whole country. The first three photos were shot in 1950 and appeared along with an interesting article as told by Jim Irwin to a *Boat Industry* reporter. The next photo is taken from the current catalog issued by Irwin describing their entire marine operation. It's a good brochure, one you can obtain at any of the Irwin locations.

Another firm still in business selling "woodies" is Siegenthaler's Boat Service of Utica, New York. The photo was taken in 1940 showing almost eight brand new Chris-Crafts on display, ready for sale and delivery. Brown's Boat Basin that used to be located on Lake Winnipesaukee, New Hampshire, is our next stop. Back in their heyday they sold Gar Wood, Matthews and Richardson cruisers. You Eastern readers will know what happened to this dealer. I think someone told me once that Brown's later became Channel Marine, owned formerly by Vince Callahan.

Over on the St. Lawrence River at Alexandria Bay,

Irwin Marine, 1950

A corner of the showroom at Irwin Marine Showroom in 1950.

On the lake view of Irwin Marine.

WOODEN BOATS
ANTIQUE AND RESTORATION

Being one of Chris-Crafts oldest dealers and also past dealers for Garwood, Fay and Bowen, Dodge, Hacker Craft, and DeWitt, enables Irwin Marine to give the authentic reproduction desired by the customer and for competition.

CARPENTRY · ENGINE RESTORATION · UPHOLSTERY · RECHROMING

Siegenthaher's Utica Auto, Electric & Boat Service showroom, 1940. This firm was still in business in 1982, though under new ownership, located in Utica, New York.

Brown's Boat Basin, Lake Winnipesaukee, New Hampshire—1940.

Launch time at Brown's in the spring of 1938, New Hampshire.

Lakeside view of Shepherd F. Brown Boat Company on Lake Winnipesaukee, New Hampshire in the year 1938. Brown sold Gar Wood, Matthews and Richardson Cruisers.

New York, we have a nice view taken at Roger's Marina, Inc, approximately 1967. A few "woodies" were in the view even then when interest in our favorite kind of boat was on the wane, even on the mighty St. Lawrence. The remaining two views are of undisclosed Eastern marine dealer showrooms in 1938. Hope you enjoyed the "Eastern" views; now we shall head out to

Roger's Marina, Alexandria Bay, New York. Approximately 1967.

Typical 1938 marine dealer located back east. Thoms. T. Parker, Inc., sold Hacker and Evinrude-Elto outboards as well.

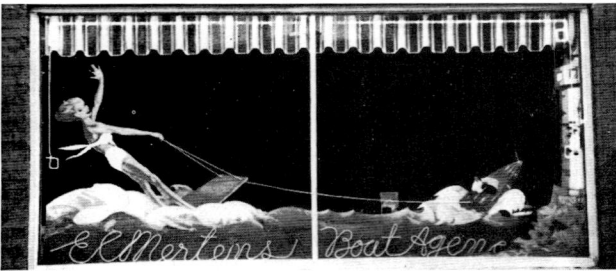

E. C. Mertens Boat Agency

my neck of the woods, the Midwest, and take a look at some of our old dealership photos, etc.

Chicago, Illinois, is a good place to start here in the Midwest, so enjoy the 1933 view taken at Motor Boat & Engine Service Company that was located then on Navy Pier on the city's lake front. I thought the center photo showing some of the many new and used inboards crowded into the showroom made a really fine photograph. A real hotbed of current wooden boat activity is Lake Geneva, Wisconsin, west of Chicago. The next two photos were originally shot in color by my good friend Jim Johnson of Plano, Illinois. Both views were taken in 1981 and show the docks and well maintained building where Jim Humphrey sells, repairs, and stores many of the wooden boats on that beautiful lake.

Overall view of Fontana Marine Service, Fontana, Wisconsin, 1981.

Fontana Marine Service, Fontana, Wisconsin, 1981.

Three views of the Motor Boat & Engine Service Co., Navy Pier, Chicago.

Humphrey has sold Streblow inboards built up in Kenosha, Wisconsin, for many years. Another dealer who is very much into the sale, repair, storage and dockage of wooden boats would be Mineola Marine of Fox Lake, Illinois. The two views shown here were taken during the Century Boat Club Show held there three years ago. By the way, the folks at Mineola have lots of marine hardware as they have operated all salvage work on the "Fox Chain" now for many years. If you are having a hard time finding a particular part, give Mineola Marine a jingle. Their phone number appears in *Volume III,* page 288, top of the page.

Cleveland, Ohio, is represented next by two firms. First, a 1933 view of a Cleveland Yacht & Supply Com-

Mineola Marine

Mineola Marine

Boat Sales, Inc., of Cleveland, Ohio, 1938.

pany, a firm still very much in business to this day. The next view was taken in 1938 of Boat Sales, Inc., the local Hacker Craft runabout and Richardson cruiser dealer for that area. I am not sure if Boat Sales is still in operation, but I rather doubt it. I am sure all you Toledo folks will advise me whether or not the firm still exists after you read this part of Chapter VII.

Gar Wood dealers were fewer in number than say, Chris-Craft or Century, but wherever they were located you saw lots of Gar Wood boats in use. The next photo shows the inside showroom of the Kilpatrick Sales Corporation then located in St. Louis, Missouri. The year: 1939. I bet Tony Mollica and The Gar Wood Society would love to have been around back then. Another marine leader here in the Midwest was, and still is, Tippicano Boat Company of Leesburg, Indiana. Tippicanoe Boat Company sold the heck out of wood Century boats back in the 1940s and '50s. They still are in business, though no longer dealing in wooden boats.

The next midwestern dealer I wish to make mention was Harrison Dudd Chris-Craft of Elkhart, Indiana. I have no idea what happened to the Dudd operation, but from the three photos shown it looks like it was a good

The attractive showrooms of Cleveland Yacht & Supply Co., Cleveland, Ohio in 1933.

Partial display of new and used Gar Wood runabouts and cruisers at the Kilpatrick Sales Corporation of St. Louis, Missouri. Photo taken in 1939.

Showrooms of Tippicanoe Boat Co., Leesburg, Indiana, circa 1947-'48.

Complete showrooms of Tippicanoe Boat Co., selling Century, Wagemaker and other brands, 1949.

A beautiful Chris-Craft dealer in Elkhart, Indiana—1941.

Al Kneith Marina on Alter Road Canal in Detroit, Michigan, 1947-'48.

Refinish shop and storage shed of Kinn Motors Marine in Oconomowoc, Wisconsin, 1955.

one. By the way, the views are shown during the early winter of 1941. The next view, a little small, was taken in 1947 or '48 at the Al Kneith Marina on Alter Road Canal in Detroit, Michigan. You Detroit buffs may remember that one; I am sorry but I can't tell you any more than that about the photo.

Jack Kinn, the congenial owner of Kinn Motors Marina in Oconomowoc, Wisconsin, was written up in the January, 1955, issue of *Boating Industry*. For some reason old Jack doesn't quite look like the "kid" written about in that glowing account of his firm. Don't take offense, Jack, just kidding. Jack Kinn is a walking encyclopedia of wooden boats; if ever you are near Milwaukee, Wisconsin, a stop at his dealership would be a real treat. Jack is also very active in the collection and restoration of antique and classic outboard motors. He has a beautiful display of them in his showroom right alongside the new Johnson motors which he has sold for many years.

Our next stop is little more than 100 miles from my home in Albert Lea, Minnesota. Lake Okoboji over in northwestern Iowa has always been a lake where wooden inboards have been popular. Even when "glass" had all but taken over the boat business, Okoboji appeared to be a sort of holdout, as wooden inboard runabouts and utilities never really lost their appeal there. The first seven photos were all taken about 1950 at Wilson's Boat Works on Lake Okoboji. The first two views show the original wood shop building,

View about 1915 or so on lake side of Wilson Boat House, later Wilson Boat Works of Today.

Covered shed and docks at Wilson Boat Works, Okoboji, Iowa. All have been since torn down. 1950 view.

Marine railway and covered slips at Wilson Boat Works, circa 1950.

Small Century Resorter being hauled out at Wilson's, 1950.

Open slips at Wilsons for runabout docking. This whole section has been completely replaced in the 1970's with covered metal docks.

Russ Young standing on cruiser dock at Wilson Boat Works, summer of 1950.

then painted white with the Chris-Craft name, etc., painted in black. The building is still standing, having been the parts shop and wood refinishing area until the spring of 1984 when a new and larger building was built behind the old building. The covered slips have since been replaced by docks and metal roofs. The third view shows a 16-foot Century Resorter being pulled out on Wilson's marine railway. That same unit is still in use and changed little in the last 34 years or so.

The next view shows the rather strange way Wilson had their slips set up back in the '50s. Some years back Wilson's was sold, and the whole docking system was updated and modernized with nice, neat wood piers with white and blue stripped metal roofs covering them all. My ol' friend from Clear Lake, Iowa, Russell Young, is shown next, standing on the cruiser docks west of the main Wilson buildings in Okoboji. Russ drove speedboats on Clear Lake, Iowa, as well as Okoboji in his younger days. Today Russ is retired from active work in boats, but on occasion does some refinishing of wooden speedboats when time permits.

The final two views were taken looking out on the cruiser slips at Wilsons. Back in the '50s, quite a few

Row of medium-size Chris-Craft cruisers at Wilson Boat Works, Okoboji, Iowa.

Looking south from the shore at Wilson docks for larger cruisers and runabouts.

"Clipper I" speedboat of unknown origin used for speedboat rides at Okoboji in early 1950's.

Fairliner "Torpedo," rare western runabout docked at Gipner Boat Works, Arnold's Park, Iowa. The firm is now known as Okoboji Boats.

A Hafer, Chris-Craft and Globe Master-Craft all docked at Gipner Boat Works, 1950.

small wooden cruisers in the 25- to 29-foot class operated on Lake Okoboji. For some reason, nearly every one of these old beauties are no longer on that lake. The larger speedboat right in the foreground on the right side of the walkway was the *Clipper #1,* a local speedboat ride boat of unknown origin to me. As Wilson sold Chris-Craft, their competition, Gipner's Boat Works, across the highway on the other side of the bay, sold Century. I have two photos here showing a rare Fairliner Torpedo sitting along one of their main piers in front of their marine railway. This firm is now called Okoboji Boats, Incorporated, and the railway and piers are still about the same though they have been made much longer. I purchased my 1964 15-foot Century Resorter from Jim Jensen and the boys (and girls) at Okoboji Boats, and have been very happy with their service and operation. You readers who recall Hafer Crafts will recognize the little split-cockpit runabout shown in the foreground of the next photo. This one was also shot about 1950 at the original Gipner's, now Okoboji Boats. The third boat back in that photo is another rather rare inboard, a 14-foot Globe Master Craft plywood inboard.

The final photo shows a rather unique marina built in the mid-1930s at Decatur, Illinois as a W.P.A. project. It was known as the Municipal Pier and was owned by the City of Decatur. The Schaefer Boat Company originally operated the marina and sold out to W. E. Boyle Boat Company in the early 1950s. Boyle was a Chris-Craft dealer also offering "water taxi" boat rides, sales, service and storage. The original main pier had 32 slips for boats of 30 feet or less. These slips were designed to handle Chris-Crafts and other inboards exclusively. Each of these slips was equipped with electric boat hoists made from the gear boxes of washing machines and coal stokers. The lifts were powered by 1/2 h.p. electric motors and could lift boats weighing 5,000 pounds. The slips were rented on a seasonal basis.

The marina prospered and by the early 1960s 60 new outboard hoists were installed and other services offered. By 1964 the marina was in need of serious piling replacement, and the city felt it too costly to rebuild so it eventually was torn down. Lake Decatur today is heavily silted and in definite need of total dredging. The City of Decatur has opened a new marina, on a much smaller scale, on the sight of the old Boyle Boat Company with newer floating piers. Thanks goes to Jeff Viccone and Mr. Boyle, who wrote the history of his operation there on Lake Decatur. Jeff Viccone is the owner of a beautiful 1955 18-foot Continental and tells me there are still about seven wood inboards on that lake with about another half dozen or so in storage in the area by local citizens. If the lake is dredged deep, as it once was,

Looking out onto the slips and hoists operated by W. E. Boyle Boat Company, Decatur, Illinois, until 1964.

1962 new Boyle Boat Company docks, Decatur, Illinois. Twelve inboards are visible hanging on lifts.

probably the use of wooden inboards would again increase on Decatur Lake. Thanks again, Jeff, for a job well done.

From the Midwest we shall now head down South and view a few dealer shots from that area. As you may or may not be aware, pleasure boating, inboard runabout style, was never as active in the South for several reasons. Lack of natural lakes in many areas and general poverty that existed in some places held pleasure boating down quite a bit. After World War II, with better economic times in the South, plus the building of many large manmade lakes and waterways, helped increase the number of citizens taking part in pleasure boating. The rather humid weather conditions, plus salt water along the seacoasts, also took their toll on mahogany wooden boats of all types. Today though, I think the greatest amount of new growth in wood antique boating is centered all across our southern states from Florida west through Texas. The first photo we shall look at was taken in 1940 at Corpus Christi, Texas. In that year, San Antonio Machine & Supply Company trailered three Chris-Crafts, four Penn Yan outboards, and a big display of Johnson outboard motors 600 miles across Texas, stopping at many communities to display the boats and generate enthusiasm for spring sales, good idea in those days I am sure. The second photo shows the inside of the San Antonio Machine & Supply in the spring of 1939. The showroom was all spruced up for a spring open house when this shot was taken.

Other Texas cities with old-time wooden boat dealers back in the 1930s and '40s have to include Houston, Texas. The first five photos were taken in front of Lechenger Marine Company, exclusive Houston dealers for Chris-Craft, Penn Yan and Johnson motors. Lechenger Marine believed in stocking boats and motors all year around, which was more a novelty back then. I think it is so neat to see photos of these fine old dealerships with no aluminum or fiberglass boats cluttering up any of the photos. Even the large cabin cruisers were able to be well displayed in the showroom of Lechenger Marine. No pillars blocked the view as viewers drove or walked past the store located on the corner of Leland and Fannin streets. The other leading dealer in Houston at that same time was Delhomme Boat Company. This firm sold Gar Wood inboards along with the various other lines of outboard hulls,

San Antonio Machine & Supply 1940 Chris-Craft, Penn Yan and Johnson display at Brownsville, Texas winter Festival.

Displayed in the showroom here are a group of Chris-Craft, Dunphy, Lyman and Penn Yan boats.

1939 showroom of San Antonio Machine & Supply Co., dealers for Chris-Craft, Penn Yan and Johnson.

A beautiful 1940 night-time view of Lechenger Marine Co., of Houston, Texas.

Looking into the showroom from outside, at night. The roll-top door can be seen in the center background.

Twin Chris-Crafts grace the front window of Lechenger Marine in Houston, Texas—1940.

Two Gar Wood sedans grace the floor of Delhomme Boat Company of Houston, Texas—1938.

Front windows of Lechenger Marine Company located in Houston, Texas in April of 1940.

1938 Gar Wood dealer, Boats Inc., of New Orleans, Louisiana, opened their new facilities on the shore of Lake Pontchartrain.

canoes and Evinrude motors. There are some other views of Delhomme Marine shown elsewhere in this book. The photo shown here was from 1938. Owners of the firm advised that every year since 1933 the firm doubled its sales over the previous year.

Another leading marine dealer of the late 1930s was Boats, Inc. of New Orleans, Louisiana, a Gar Wood dealer located on the shores of huge Lake Pontchartrain. The firm also sold Wheeler cabin cruisers plus Penn Yan boats. Eclipse outboard motors, a small, rather unorthodox air-cooled line of engines, were also sold by Boats, Inc. They did most of their business in inboard craft, just as most large dealers did in those days. The bulk of all outboard motors sold back then were of the 10 h.p. and smaller class, so even today some of the firms who started back then never sold outboard motors, just inboards.

Florida always had its share of outstanding pleasure boat dealers. In Miami Beach, Jack Dunn Boat Company, located at 1742 Alton Road, operated a beautiful showroom and service center. The building faced the Dade Canal where boats could be launched directly from the showroom out into the canal which lead direct-

ly into the Bay. The three photos shown were taken during the firm's grand opening in 1938, hence the reason for all the bouquets of flowers sitting throughout the showroom.

The final southern photo I have to show you was taken also in 1938 in the showroom of H. L. Kaylor Company, location of which I believe was in Kentucky

Modern showrooms in Miami Beach, Florida of a leading Chris-craft dealer, Jack Dunn Boat Co., 1938.

Varied display of new 1938 Chris-Crafts on display at Jack Dunn Boat Company in Miami, Florida.

A portion of the, then new, Jack Dunn Chris-Craft showrooms during grand-opening in 1938 located in Miami Beach, Florida.

or Tennessee. The firm sold Chris-Craft, Dunphy, Elto and Evinrude motors. Sorry that I cannot tell you exactly where they were located but I felt the photo just too good a one to leave out.

Our final short stop will be the West Coast of the U.S. The first two photos show the well stocked and neat showroom of John J. Rapp Company located at 123 Second Street in San Francisco. The firm sold not only Chris-Craft, but also fishing boats, outboard runabouts, and canoes. A complete array of Evinrude and Elto outboards can be seen in the showroom windows. October 25, 1929, saw the grand opening of another San Francisco marine dealer, Boardman & Flower Pleasure Boats, dealers for Gar Wood, Penn Yan and Evinrude motors. The photo of the B & F showroom was also taken in 1938. The next single view shows a Chris-Craft dealer from Idaho picking up two new Chris-Crafts at Algonac, Michigan, back in April, 1948. Dealers driving over 2,000 miles to pick up their own boats back then was quite a rarity. Note the old 4-wheel trailer the 25-foot cruiser is riding on—nothing like the modern twin- or triple-axle trailers dealers use in this day and age, is it?

The final identifiable photo here was taken by Tony Brown, good friend and refinishing expert at Sierra Boat Company on beautiful Lake Tahoe, Carnelian Bay, California. I was fortunate this past summer (1983) to visit this "shrine" of wooden boat activity and act as honorary head judge for their beautiful Con curs de elegance Boat Show. This view is looking from the

1938 showroom view of H. Taylor Co., a small 15' Chris-Craft utility shown in foreground. Two Dunphy cedar strip outboards also visible.

John J. Rapp Co., of San Francisco, California about 1938.

Smaller Chris-Crafts and a nice variety of both outboards and inboard engines greeted customers at John C. Rapp Co., in San Francisco, California back in 1938-'39.

J. D. Gardner and son who travelled 2,000 miles from Algonac, Michigan to Salt Lake City, Utah hauling a Chris-Craft 16' racing runabout and a 25' cruiser.

Well-stocked showroom of Boardman and Flower showroom in San Francisco, California, 1938. Both outboard and inboard craft were sold by the firm.

service docks toward the shops and upstairs boat storage areas.

I have been advised by Glen Wilson, one of the leading forces behind wooden boat interest on Tahoe, that he estimates there are close to 1,000 wooden boats of all types from canoes and rowboats through large wooden cabin cruisers on that clear, and beautiful lake. The water there is unbelievable. The boats just seem to sit on top of glass. You can look right under them while they sit at the docks. I recall as we cruised down the lake aboard *Columbia,* a beautiful, old restored Hutchinson sedan driven by Dick Clarke, that I was surprised to be able to see the bottom of the lake so far out from shore.

Service dock of the Sierra Boat Company.

Swan Marine Sales Co., showroom in 1939. Location unknown. Chris-Crafts were main line featured.

When I asked Dick about it, he said, "We're in about 85 feet of water right now." Boy, I was really surprised, as back here in our area few lakes are anywhere near that clear. Anyway, if you ever get anywhere near Lake Tahoe, you make a beeline for "Tahoe" with your camera, lots of film, and time, and you will see more beautiful wooden boats than probably anywhere else in this nation, bar none.

In conclusion, I have one remaining photo that I was unable to determine the location of. The firm was known as Swan Marine, the date was 1938 or '39. My guess it was located back East, but I could be wrong. The thing I like about Swan Marine is how much they went out for really promoting the sale of boats and boating across the front of their store. You couldn't help but know they were in the boat business if you walked or drove by there, night or day.

Well, this closes Chapter VII. I do hope you enjoyed the first section on "Speedboat Rides" as much as I did writing it, and also this second portion which covered lots of old showroom views across the nation. Chapter VIII will cover all new listings for restoration shops, part sources, clubs, magazines, and much more of interest to you wooden boat buffs. None of the following listings have appeared in the other three inboard books, so I am sure there will be some listings here which may be just the ones you have been looking for. I hope so!

CHAPTER VIII
New Listings for Parts, Dealers & Restoration Shops, etc.
(See Volumes I, II, III, and IV for further listings)

OUTBOARD MOTOR PARTS DEALERS

MIGHTY MITE MARINE, INC. (All parts for Mighty Mite outboard engines built since World War II)
2300 8th Street S.W.
Lehigh Acres, FL 33926

INT'L OUTBOARD PARTS (New and used parts for most makes and models of outboard motors)
John C. Renfroe
1310 Beck Avenue
Panama City, FL 32401
(904) 769-7003

BUZZ'S MARINE (Has for sale new and used Scott-Atwater and McCulloch outboard motor parts; list available on request)
c/o Mark
Box 72
Kearney, NE 68847
(308) 234-4576

GJERVOLD MOTOR COMPANY (Possible source for a few antique outboards; in business for over 35 years; contact directly)
A. K. Gjervold
102 University Drive
Fargo, ND 58102
(701) 232-7471

TOMLINSON AUTO & MARINE (Possible source for old Evinrude parts, and limited parts for other outboards too. Check directly)
COMPANY, INC.
Ben L. Tomlinson
Box 597
Eagle River, WI 54521
(715) 479-4471

DOUGLAS PENN (Possible source for sale or trade; many new and used Mercury parts from 1946 through '56 models, including hard to find KG 9 and Quicksilver lower unit parts; contact directly)
12 Cambridge Circle
New Milford, CT 06776

JIM CHOMINSKI (Homelite and Bearcat 55 4-cycle outboard engines, parts and service)
2969 W. Parkway
Algonac, MI 48001
(313) 794-9136

JIM'S OUTBOARDS (Parts for most engines: Evinrude, Johnson, Mercury, Chrysler, Chamion, Oliver, Scott—new, used, reconditioned ignition, water pumps, impellers, rebuilt power heads and lower units)
617 Lakeview Road
Clearwater, FL 33516
(813) 441-4283

ELECTRA MARINE (For sale, Scott and McCulloch outboard motor parts; will ship anywhere; send $1.25 for more details)
610 Merrick Road
Lynnbrook, NY 11563
(516) 599-3003

BELK'S MARINE SUPPLY (Mercury outboard sales and service for 28 years. Large stock of old parts available always)
(215) 532-4344

AMERICAN OUTBOARD
Terry Kilcoyne
3251 Nicollet Avenue S.
Minneapolis, MN 55408
(612) 827-3113

(Specializes in antique outboard parts for most makes and models; 1909-1950, new reproduced decals, parts, books and manuals)

LEE OUTBOARDS
Ole Lee, Jr.
Flathead Lake
Box 86
Somers, MT 59932
(416) 857-3788

(Has many used parts for early outboard motors for sale. Also collects antique outboards himself)

WAUKEGAN MARINE
c/o Gordy Smith
1208 Grand
Waukegan, IL 60085
(312) 336-9400

(Obsolete Johnson, Evinrude and ONC parts back to 1925; all Johnson motor parts books available)

BONFANTI MARINE
P.O. Box 54916
Baton Rouge, LA 70896

(Comprehensive list of OMC outboard, I.O. and Mercruiser parts for sale)

KEN COOK COMPANY
P.O. Box 18636, Dept. RR
Milwaukee, WI 53218

(Offers service literature for 1969 and older Johnson and Evinrude service literature, plus owners manuals, parts catalogs and service manuals)

CROFTON COMPANY
Box 2925
El-Chaon, CA 92021
(714) 440-6621

(Mr. Crofton has parts for Crosley, V-drive, upright outboard, inboard-outboards, "Crosley, Falcon and aerojet")

INBOARD ENGINE, PARTS AND MOTOR MANUAL SOURCES

WASHINGTON MARINA
1302 Maine Avenue S.W.
Washington, DC 20024
(202) 554-0222

(Sells service manuals for most marine engines—OMC, Chrysler, Universal, Chris-Craft, Perkins and Seagull)

MARINE PROPULSION CORP.
2930 S.E. Kensington Street
Stuart, FL 33494
(305) 283-6486

(Offers new water-cooled replacement marine manifolds for some Chris-Craft, Chrysler, Mercruiser and OMC engines. Also engine sales, rebuilt marine reverse gears, conversion kits for auto and marine engines; contact directly for more details)

RED WING MARINE ENGINES
Virgil Mischke
1536 Lincoln Avenue
Red Wing, MN 55066
(612) 388-3045

(Will assist owners of Red Wing motors. He purchased all remaining parts, records, etc., from the firm)

BOATSWAINS LOCKER, INC.
2431 W. Coast Highway
Newport Beach, CA 92663

(Chrysler parts new and used, cylinder heads, cranks, crown block, transmissions, RV 10 Walters Gears. New and used gas and diesel engines)

S & F AUTO ELECTRIC
29335 Harper (at 12 mile road)
St. Clair Shores, MI 48083
(313) 779-2728

(All marine starters, alternators, generators and regulators repaired)

KENT & JOE'S HARBOR SERVICE, INC.
2560 E. 11th Street
Tacoma, WA 98421
Tacoma MA7-3000
Seattle VE8-1003

(Marine specialists, complete repair facilities, engines and installations, stern drives and inboards, engine rebuilding and parts. Service many brands including Mercruiser, Pleasure Craft, Chris-Craft, Chrysler, Crusader and Volvo)

HEADS BY RAY, INC.
2418 Harper
St. Clair Shores, MI 48081
(313) 779-5271

(Complete machine shop services and engine rebuilding. Complete line of parts in stock)

PRECISION MARINE SERVICE
21 St. Jean at the River
Detroit, MI 48214
(313) 821-1358

(The marine engine people now introducing the Crusader V-6 engine)

VACUMATIC
Shelter Island, NY 11964

(32 years in business of replacing faulty Chris-O-Matics and manual gears with reliable automatic controls)

JIM MANDER'S YACHT SHOP INC.
2910 S.W. 28 Lane
Miami, FL 33133
(305) 442-1137

(Used and new engines for sale. Big selection of short blocks and bare blocks in stock; new, used, rebuilt. In stock, new and used Borg Warner velvet drives, reverse gears, all reductions)

MONMOUTH MARINE ENGINES, INC.
536 Union Lane
Brielle, NJ 08730
(201) 528-9290

(Authorized sales, service, parts for Warner, Paragon Transmission new, used, exchange; new, used parts for most engines, complete engine, transmission and water pump rebuilding)

J & B MARINE SALES & SERVICE, INC.
25118 Jefferson Avenue
St. Clair Shores, MI 48081
(313) 776-4220

(We are the largest Chrysler marine dealer in the U.S. We have in stock parts and engines dating back to 1927. These parts are new, refurbished or used. Contact directly)

DAMARK MARINE SPECIALTIES, INC.
29021 Wilson Avenue
Gibralter, MI 48173
(313) 676-2880

(Offers excellent engine repairs; services Chrysler, Harden, Berkeley Jet, Mercruiser, Ford, Volvo. Also, inboard-outboards, jets, plus transmission work and parts)

MARINE MOTOR SALES & SERVICE, INC.
316 Broadway, P.O. Box 1074
Point Pleasant, NJ 08742
(201) 892-1124

(Used marine engines and parts, new-rebuilt Chrysler, Volvo, Gray, Sen-Dure)

CHRIS-CRAFT SERVICE BULLETINS
Bruce Beimers
1735 Lamberton Lake Drive
Grand Rapids, MI 49505

(A complete set of reproduced Chris-Craft service bulletins, 100 in number. Dating from July 21, 1927 through September 5, 1929. A gold mine of needed information. A must for every Chris-Craft owner of that era. $22.50 postpaid)

STAINLESS STEEL "CUTWATERS"
Paul C. Young
4363 Wilshire Boulevard #211
Mound, MN 55364
(612) 472-4348

(Making excellent stainless steel "cutwaters" for all types and sizes of boats. Must have old unit to use as a pattern. Contact for information, prices, etc.)

SERVICE, OWNER & PARTS MANUALS Ken Cook, Co. P.O. Box 18636 Milwaukee, WI 53218	(Have available for sale Johnson, Evinrude and OMC stern drive service literature—1969 and older)
GRAY MARINE ENGINE MANUAL Bob Falcone 2711 James Street Syracuse, NY 13206 (315) 463-9158	(Manuals for all Gray models from 1938 through 1963. Xerographic copy, $20. Send check payable to Bob Falcone)
CHRIS-CRAFT HEAD GASKETS Mike Lynch 18 Hastings Avenue Toronto, Ontario, Canada M4L 2L2	(Chris-Craft 1928 up "new old stock" set of 4 head gaskets for V-8 models A70 225 h.p., A120 275 h.p., A120A 350 h.p.)
BRISTOL SERVICE COMPANY c/o Gary Grown 1314 Conway Avenue Costa Mesa, CA 92626 (714) 892-8541	(Southern California distributor for Gray Marine engines. Carries old parts for all models, engine manuals, plus new engines and "short" blocks available as well. Contact for many other services to antique boats as well)
KOFFEL'S PLACE 4300 Haggerty Road Walled Lake, MI 48088 (313) 363-5239	(Offers all kinds of engine repairs, plus complete transmission repairs and rebuilding. Winterizing and spring preparations, storage, mechanical restorations, custom-fit mooring covers, and much, much more)
APEX GENERATOR, INC. c/o Glenn C. Marchesi 214 Brick Boulevard Brick Town, NJ 08723 (201) 477-1500	(Offers starters, generators, alternator repairs, sales, etc.)
DAVE STOLL'S MARINE CENTER, INC. 2401 E. Anaheim Street Wilmington, CA 90748 (213) 437-0308, 435-7774	(Offers a good selection of obsolete Chrysler engine parts and other items)
G. A. PLUMB Sunrise Avenue Old Saybrook, CT 06475 (203) 388-3541	(Have large library of old engine manuals. Call for a quote; they will make you a page or pages that you need at a reasonable price)
DALE TASSELL Route 1, Box 25H Mt. Dora, FL 32757 (904) 383-6203 evenings and weekends	(Many carburetor parts still available; has copies of parts manuals and operating and service guides. Send number of carburetor along with $3.75 and what it came off. These are ZENITH CARBURETOR PARTS. Dale also has good reproductions of most Chris-Craft engine books and service manuals. Send model number and serial number with $4.75) (Also carries large inventory of hard-to-find Chris-Craft engine parts. Send name and address and he will send a numbered parts list in old Chris-Craft parts numbers)
HANSEN MARINE, INC. Sarasota, FL (813) 365-1770	(Hard-to-find Chris-Craft and Mercruiser inboard parts, instruments, etc. Large stock of older models. Check for more details)
CHARLES F. STOKES, ENTERPRISES 62 Fairfield Drive Coldwater, MI 49036 (517) 278-6300	Back in business with over 45 years of experience. A warehouse full of engine parts for Gray, Buda and others. Also all makes of new, used, rebuilt engines, transmissions, conversion kits and supplies)

CONVERTIBLE TOPS, CANVAS WORK, UPHOLSTERY AND FLOORING

TONY LAURIA
Route 2
Box 253 C
Landenberg, PA 19350
(215) 268-3441

(Offers 1/8" burlap-backed grey, green, black and brown linoleum. Send dimensions and stamped envelope for price and samples)

WALT'S UPHOLSTERY
Blue Hill, ME 04614
(207) 326-8630

(Specializes in boat cushions, seats and interiors)

DESIGN UPHOLSTERY SPECIALISTS
c/o Terry Young, Dept. RR4
4620 Minnehaha Avenue South
Minneapolis, MN 55406
(612) 721-4145

(Does outstanding interior work, upholstering, etc., for boats, planes and cars)

KISSEL CANVAS COMPANY
Route 611
Avon, OH 44011

(Custom boat covers, winter storage covers, custom made, repairs and water proofing)

HOWARD'S FABRICS & FOAM
519 E. Ridge Road
Rochester, NY 14261
(716) 342-9720

(Supplier of Nautolex fabrics, planking, flooring, headlining, cabin tops. Any quantity of foam from 1 yard to full rolls. Adhesive and instructions, etc. Send $2.00 for samples, etc.)

DUANE ASSMANN
The Boat Shop
522 Baker Street
Lake Geneva, WI 53147
(414) 248-3590

1½" sponge rubber half round for edge rolls in 20-foot-plus lengths. Cut to length, call for prices)

FRANK FINLAY
P.O. Box 968
Manchester, CT 06040

(Has for sale linoleum in various colors, 6 feet wide at $20.00 a running foot; ships up to 8 feet via UPS)

FORTIER INDUSTRIES, INC.
259 6th Avenue
P.O. Box 98
Manistee, MI 49660
(616) 723-3765

(Designed and built Century boarding ladders, sliding tops, plus interiors. Still can supply reupholstery kits for nearly every model of Century in correct colors and patterns at fair prices. Contact for more information)

AL PECKENPAUGH
PECKENPAUGH UPHOLSTERY & CANVAS
Main Street
Trumansburg, NY 14886

(Makes boat covers, convertible tops, tonneaus, plus does boat upholstery of all kinds)

WICHTERMANS
P.O. Box K
Excelsior, MN 55331
(612) 474-2273

(Excellent new "do it yourself" 34 page illustrated book on how to custom build your own boat top. 50 illustrations and easy to follow. Other editions to follow including, "Making Your Own Mooring Covers." Send $8.50 for each copy)

PAINT AND VARNISH SUPPLIERS

"Interlux"
International Paint Company
17 Battery Place, North
New York, NY 10004

(Offers broad range of paints and varnishes for every need. Contact for information)

"Regatta"
Regatta Marine Company
(800) 638-1911

(Offers complete line of paints and finishes for wood, fiberglass and aluminum boats)

"Z-Spar"
Koppers Company, Inc.
Dept. 51, 1901 Koppers Building
Pittsburgh, PA 15219

(Offers good selection of marine finishes of all types)

"Epoxycop"
Rule Paint & Chemical, Inc.
Cape Ann Industrial Park
Gloucester, MA 01930
(617) 281-0440

(Offers durable, hard, smooth anti-fouling paint for boats)

"Pettit"
Pettit Paint Company, Inc.
Rockway, NJ 07866
Spring Valley, CA 92077

(Offers broad selection of paints, varnishes, caulks, boot top paints and bottom paints)

"Woolsey"
Woolsey Marine Dept. R-4
1250 Broadway
New York, NY 10001
1 (800) 221-4446

(Offers very large selection of finish products. Write for free 44-page brochure)

"Sunshield"
InterTrade
36 Sir Williams Lane
Toronto (Islington)
Ontario, Canada M9A 1V1
(416) 232-2251

(World's finest clear wood finish. Replaces varnish and does a lot more)

"Bristol Fashion"
Marine Development & Research Corp.
116 Church Street
Freeport, NY 11520

(Manufacturer of high gloss marine varnish; write for 14-page varnish guide, FREE)

"Deks Olje"
The Flood Company
P.O. Box 397
Hudson, OH 44236

(Finish product made under license from Norway, excellent for small craft oars, anything basically made of wood)

"B. L. Norton Boat Shop"
Box 212
Cedarville, MI 49719
(616) 677-1208

(Have for sale "Super Wood Bleach," takes out dirt, stain and discoloration without damage to wood. $26 for 2 gallons plus UPS costs)

"BoatLIFE" Calk
BOATLIFE, INC.
205 Sweethollow Road
Old Bethpage, NY 11804

(Manufacturer of BoatLIFE 2-part life calk. Free care guide available from firm for s.s.a.e.)

INSTRUMENTS AND INSTRUMENT REPAIRS, ETC.

BOB'S SPEEDOMETER
15255 Grand River Road
Detroit, MI 48227
(313) 272-1050

(Speedometers, gauges, dials refinished, silk screens made. Repair and restores dash instruments. Mostly car items, but check with him before you send items. $15 charge for estimate, can be applied towards completed job)

ED HENDEE
Rural Route 3
North Gower, Ontario, Canada K0A 2T0
(613) 489-3189

(Instrument restoration, rebuilding, refacing of old instruments to their original grandeur)

STEERING WHEEL REPAIRS ETC.

BACKWARDS UNLIMITED
c/o Jim Ellis
4143 Gunderson Road N.E.
Poulso, WA 98370
(206) 697-1471

(Has done nothing but steering wheel restoration work since 1975. Takes pride in every job)

BILL PETERS RESTORATIONS
37 DeKiven Court
Brooklyn, NY 11230
(212) 434-7721

(Steering wheel restorations, finest quality, choice of colors, plastic, hard rubber, wood)

ANTIQUE BOAT INSURANCE

HAGERTY INSURANCE AGENCY, INC.
1004 E. 8th Street, Box 87
Traverse City, MI 49684
(616) 941-7477

(Offering insurance for classic and antique boats at competitive rates and a full marine policy)

DON HARTSFIELD & ASSOC., INC.
1852 Washington Avenue
Box 487
Atlanta, GA 30344
(404) 766-0214

(Offers special ski boat insurance available in all 50 states, especially for certified tournament-type ski boats)

LUMBER AND FASTENINGS, ETC.

PAWTUKET PAINT & HARDWARE
2190 Board Street
Cranston, RI 02905
(401) 785-0102

(Hard-to-find bronze fittings, hardware needs and complete paint supplies)

WOOD DIMENSIONS, INC.
12710 Triskett Road
Cleveland, OH 44101
(216) 941-0570

(Boat lumber—teak, Philippine and Honduras mahogany, white and red oak, Sitka spruce, white ash, also other varieties plus plywood and custom machining)

D.R.I. INDUSTRIES
11100 Hampshire Avenue S.
Bloomington, MN 55438

(Producers and suppliers of all types of stainless steel nuts, bolts, screws, washers, cotter pins, etc. Designed for marine use and very excellent in quality. Contact for more information)

JAMESTOWN HARDWARE
28 Narragansett Avenue
Jamestown, RI 02835
(800) 423-0030

(Excellent source for marine hardware and fastenings. Their warehouse is well stocked, their prices are great and you can write for a free catalog too)

TREMONT NAIL COMPANY
Box 111
Wareham, MA 02571
(617) 295-0038

(Exclusive distributor for the entire line of 100% hard drawn copper nails and dished roves. Nails come in sizes from ¾" to 5" and in various thicknesses. This firm offers many other interesting gift and home items too. Send for their catalog)

SKOOKUM FASTENINGS
805 6th Street
Anacortes, WA 98221

(New edge nails for strip-plank builders. Also copper rivets, roves and clench nails)

YANKEE MARINE COMPANY
Rural Route Box 211A
Pittstown, NJ 08667
(201) 228-4982

(Distributor of bronze, brass and stainless fasteners and hardware. Send $2.00 for catalog)

THE TOOL WORKS
76 9th Avenue
New York, NY 10011

(Sells superior quality tools, supplies, etc. for discriminating craftsmen)

CARIBBEAN AMERICAN LUMBER SALES COMPANY
Box 8367
Savannah, GA 31402
(912) 234-3485

(Carries all types of boat building supplies from nails to glues, rollers to bungs, etc. Both retail and wholesale)

CLOTHING, GIFT ITEMS, ETC.

FULL-COLOR BOAT POSTERS
The Real Runabouts
505 Albert Lea Street
Albert Lea, MN 56007
(507) 373-2145

(Offers 4 beautiful 23" by 29" full-color posters on enameled stock. First poster, "The Real Runabouts," shows 53 speedboards in full color. Second poster, "Chris-Craft," shows 49 Chris-Crafts in full color from 1924 through 1965. Both of these are a MUST, great to hang in office or den. $9.65 each plus $1.20 each for postage. Mailed in protective mailing tube by UPS. Dealer inquiries invited. Newest poster, Century Power Boats and Real Runabouts poster #2)

FULL COLOR REAL RUNABOUTS T-SHIRTS
Bob Speltz
505 Albert Lea Street
Albert Lea, MN 56007
(507) 373-2145

(Highest quality crew-neck T-shirts, made from 50% cotton and 50% polyester. Colors available, gold and powder blue. Write for order blank and prices. Dealer inquiries welcome. Please send for new T-shirt catalog, ten all new shirt transfers in black, to choose from)

HOWARD HOELSCHER
4 Pleasant Terrace
Boonton, NJ 07005
(201) 334-9510

(Sells and buys old boat and motor literature as well as other types such as cars, bikes, etc.)

COFFEE CUPS & OLD-FASHIONED GLASSES
Susie & Dave Koffel
Koffel's Place
4300 Haggerty Road
Walled Lake, MI 48088
(313) 363-5239

(Offering generous-size glass coffee mugs as well as clear, old-fashioned glasses sporting a beautiful old 3-cockpit Chris-Craft runabout speeding across with the old logo "Chris-Craft" beneath. Sells for $2.50 each for either style, plus shipping. If you love or own a "woody" you'll want a set of each)

RUNABOUT PLAQUES, MODELS AND ½ MODELS
Bob Davis
1121 Clinton Street
Algonac, MI 48001
(313) 794-7340

(Builds beautiful all wood plaques, half and full models, pen and pencil sets on a custom basis according to your wishes. These models are works of art. Contact Bob for more information)

SPEEDBOAT NOTE PADS
Koffel's Place
(address shown above)

(Beautiful 5½" by 8½" colorful note pad. Each pad sports a fine drawing of either a Chris-Craft, Century, Hacker, Dodge or Gar Wood. Each pad is $1.65 each. Order 1 pad of each kind; they're great!)

1911 FAY & BOWEN CATALOG REPRINT
The Vestal Press
Box 97
320 Jensen Road
Vestal, NY 13850

(A beautiful, authentic reprint, not Xerox, of 1911 Fay & Bowen motor and boat catalog. 50 pages; a must. $6.50 each plus .50 postage)

GAR WOOD FULL-COLOR POSTER
The Gar Wood Society
Box 6003
Teall Station
Syracuse, NY 13217

(Here is your chance to own a beautiful poster of a 1939 Gar Wood catalog cover in full color. 17" by 22", nice for the office, den or bedroom. $8.00 postpaid. Free illustrated folder available)

MARINE WATER COLORS
F. H. Craig
"Shangrilla"
Stoney Lake
Woodview P.O.
Ontario, Canada K0L E30

Will paint your cruiser, runabout or launch for that special place in your den, office, recreation room, cottage or whatever. Please send your crafts and best profile, and directions as to size of finished piece [color keyed if black and white Kodak or Polaroid print]. All photos and materials carefully preserved and returned with estimate of cost or with finished paintings. Average size work is 16" by 18", from $55.00 and up. Shipped to you packaged, postpaid. [I have some of Mr. Craig's works and they are the FINEST available. Great for Christmas or birthday gifts])

CLASSIC BOAT WEAR
1094 Saratoga
E. Boston, MA 02128

(Classic color T-shirts for such makes of boats as Century, Chris-Craft, Gar Wood, Greavette, Hacker, and Riva. $10.00 each, includes shipping. State size: small, medium, large in adult or children's sizes. Colors are black, red, tan or blue. Also offers boat caps, walking shorts, sport shirts. All very nice merchandise)

(T-SHIRTS & HATS)
"T's" 'n Things
c/o R & B Sima
20 W. 309 Frontage Road
Lemont, IL 60439

(Fine selection of boating caps, T-shirts, etc. Write for details. "Century" and "Antique Boating" shirts and hats featured)

T-SHIRTS
Weid 330c
Mead's Mountain
Woodstock, NY 12498

(Custom-designed T-shirt of your boat. Contact for details)

1917 BROOKS BOATS CATALOG
Vestal Press
P.O. Box 97
Vestal, NY 13850

(Excellent reprinting of this 57-page catalog showing boats, hardware, engines and knockdown construction system. A must. 6½" high, 10" wide. $7.50 postpaid in book envelope)

BOOK, "The Steam Launch"
International Marine Publishing Co.
21 Elm Street
Camden, ME 04843

(A must for steamboat buffs, the launch, its history, technology, design and operation. 256 pages with 250 illustrations. Will sell for about $37.00. Published August '82)

BOOK, "Old Marine Engines: The World of the One-Lunger"
International Marine Publishing Co.
(address shown above)

(Brand new book on old inboard engines from mid-1880s through 1950s. All you ever wanted to know about old engines. 224 pages with 60 illustrations, probable price about $23.00)

LAUNCH PLANS FOR SALE
Attention: Boat Lines
Curatorial Department
Mystic Seaport Museum
Mystic, CT 06355

(Plans can be purchased for 5 old launches from 1872 through 1908. All come on 1 or 2 sheets; both lines and construction plans are included, and in some cases the offsets as well. Price is $3.50 per sheet; mailed rolled in a tube costs $1.30 extra. Museum also offers plan sheets in the form of "brown line" art grained permanent prints suitable for framing at $7.00 per sheet)

1901 LOZIER CATALOG
International Marine Publishing Co.
(address shown elsewhere)

(Plans to reprint the 1901 Lozier launch and engine literature the summer of '82. Contact directly for price, etc.)

NEW EASTERN RESTORATION SHOP LISTINGS

BLACK BOTTOM RUNABOUTS,
c/o Pat Carney
Box 1552
Rocky Point, L.I., NY 11778
(516) 744-9944

(Builds beautiful replica mahogany inboards to the standards and styles of the past. Currently offers a 16', 21' and 28' Rumrunner 3-cockpit runabout powered by a modern V-8 engine. Many options available on every model. Contact for brochure and specifications)

KURT MARINE SALES & SERVICE
c/o Roy C. Kurt
Route 3, Intersections 18 & 322
Conneaut Lake, PA 16316
(814) 382-5455

(New Streblow inboard dealer. Also offers storage, repair and refinishing of wooden boats, with an occasional sale of a used wooden boat)

SWIFT CUSTOM BOATS
Rural Route 2
Exter, NY 03833
(603) 772-5557

(Custom wooden boat building, repair, restorations up to 40 feet; 25 years of experience)

R. BIGELOW & COMPANY, INC.
140 MacArthur Boulevard
Bourne, MA 02352
(617) 759-5531 & 4026

(Boat building, brokers, repairs, restorations, storage, supplies. Check to see what types of boats they care for directly)

MID COAST MARINE SERVICES, INC.
Box 103
Bristol, ME 04539
(207) 563-3030

(Restorations, quality repairs and maintenance of fine wooden craft. Quality marine craftsmanship and thoughtful care of your craft)

WOOD BOAT, INC.
55 Day Street
S. Norwalk, CT 06854
(203) 866-5285

(Specializes in repair of damaged boats, rebuilding of tired hulls, restoration of classics. Good reputation, reasonable prices, indoor workshop, outdoor storage, etc.)

KUHN'S MARINE SERVICE, INC.
c/o Chet Kuhn
9276 LeRoy Island Road
Wolcott, NY 14590
(315) 587-9767

(Offers marine repairs, surveying. Specializes in Lyman wood inboard repairs of all types from stem to stern, bridge to keel. Also does engine work, shaft repairs; strives for originality and perfection)

HARPER'S BOAT RESTORATIONS
c/o Jerry Harper
Route 3
Meredith, NH 03253
(603) 279-8841

(Inboard and OMC service and overhauling, wood and fiberglass repairs, repainting, sales, service. Good used wooden boats for sale)

ACE SPEEDBOAT COMPANY
9 Merrill Street
Amesbury, MA 01913
(617) 388-3891

(Builders of classic design power and sail craft. Features a new 21' John Hacker design Gold Cup Racer with 350 cubic inch V-8. Hull built by WEST (tm) system with all custom hardware. The best of old and the new. A real beautiful speedboat)

VINTAGE BOAT COMPANY
c/o Clayton Craig
Box 65
Seaward Mills Road
E. Vasselboro, ME 04935
(207) 923-3164 days
(207) 923-3164 nights

(Located near three Maine lakes, offers antique boat sales, repairs, refinishing, restorations. Also builds whitehall fiberglass rowing boats. Have some old engines, parts and Chris-Craft parts available)

JAY T. SPARROW
P.O. Box 441
Raymond, ME 04071

(A young man who restores only Shepherds for fun and profit)

DONALD W. FARNSWORTH
China, ME 04926
(207) 968-2934

(Restores wooden speedboats as well as launches, canoes, etc.)

EASTERN CLASSICS
c/o Pat Curtin
1156 Union Avenue
Laconia, NH 03246
(603) 528-3411—shop
(603) 279-5595—home

(Offers repairs, dockage, indoor storage, repairs, restorations and other services; some custom building. Contact for more information)

THE BOAT SHOP
c/o Vince Campbell
Booth Road
Trumansburg, NY 14886

(Offers refinishing, reupholstering and lots of other services for wooden boats. Contact for more details)

TURCOTTE BROS. MARINE
7 Southern Drive
Latham, NY 12110
(518) 783-5269

(New firm, owners have over 15 years of experience on caring for wooden boats. Offers complete boat restorations and repairs, plus engine work)

KELLY MARINE SERVICE
c/o Rich Kelly
289 W. Lake Road
Branchport, NY 14418
(315) 595-6688

(Complete restorations, storage, repairs and engine work)

CURTIN MARINA
E. Pearl Street on
   Delaware River
Burlington, NJ
(609) 386-4657

(Boat clinic, offers complete mechanical repair, expert fiberglass repairs and Gel-Coat matching. Also wood and aluminum repairs, upholstering work and accessory sales)

NELSON BOATWORKS
1109 Lakewood Drive
Vienna, VA 22180
(703) 281-3316

(Repairs and rebuilds small craft, also does restoration work in the Chesapeake Bay area)

PROP & SAIL MARINE SERVICE INC.
Route 9
Silver Bay, NY 12874
(518) 543-6411

(Guideboat and small wooden craft repair and restoration, canoe re-canvasing. Lake George region)

CONNEAUT LAKE NAVIGATION
COMPANY
c/o Bud & Betty DeVoge
Conneaut Lake, PA 16316
(814) 382-3255

(Offers sales, service, repairs and restoration work, old parts and factory-trained service department. In business since 1904)

WOOD CANVAS CANOE & DINGHY
RESTORATION
Yacht Finish
(207) 363-5338

(Does everything from basic recanvasing to complete refurbishing)

NEW CANADIAN RESTORATION SHOP LISTINGS

CLIFFE CRAFT LTD.
185 Mill Street
Gananoque, Ontario, Canada

(Wooden boats, specializing in repairs, restorations, rebuilding and refinishing of older wooden boats. Sales, storage, custom-built boats. Over 25 years of experience)

BAYVIEW MARINA
c/o Art Johnson
Stony Lake
Woodview, Ontario
Canada K0L 3E0
(715) 652-8174

(Boat rentals, machine shop, can lift boats to 45 feet in length. Full storage plus boat and motor sales)

MILLER-POTTER BOATWORKS
P.O. Box 56
Manotick, Ontario
Canada K0A 2N0
(613) 692-3455 or 692-4208

(Offers complete restorations, engine work, hull repairs, refinishing, woodworking, recharging, painting and varnishing)

FERGUSON ANTIQUE & CLASSIC
BOAT COMPANY, LTD.
Mike Ferguson
535 Reid Street
Peterborough, Ontario, Canada
(705) 748-2070

(Offers complete restoration and refinishing service. Does excellent work)

THE TORONTO WOODEN BOAT
WORKS, LTD.
224 Yorkland Boulevard
Willowdale, Ontario M2J 1R5
(416) 491-8352
(416) 491-2481 or 82

(Expert construction, restorations and repairs)

NEW MIDWESTERN RESTORATION SHOP LISTINGS

MORIN MAHOGANY MARINE
c/o Douglas Morin
377 State Park Road
Bay City, MI 48706
(517) 686-7353

(Complete boat repairs, wood and glass restoration and services. Limited sales, survey work. Contact directly for more information)

THE REFINISH SHOP
c/o Steve Sudol
95 E. Oak Street
Leland, MI 49654
(616) 256-7201

(Offers both fiberglass and Gel-Coat repairs as well as complete wooden boat repairs, refinishing and restorations)

McCUTCHEON BOAT WORKS
Ferry Avenue
Charlevoix, MI 49720
(616) 547-9714

(In business since 1938, installs engines, does woodworking, restores wooden boats and offers many other services)

ARCADIA MARINE GENERAL
  FIBERGLASS
1st Avenue
Arcadia, MI 49613
(616) 889-4555

(Does fiberglass and wood hull repairs; carries Chris-Craft engine parts)

BOAT BROKERS MARINA
535 Lakeshore Drive
Port Clinton, OH 43452
(419) 734-3545

(Repairs on wood, fiberglass, refinishing, inside storage available; free estimates)

HURON LAGOONS MARINA
Huron, OH 44839
(419) 433-3200

(Complete wood, steel and fiberglass repairs, custom swim platforms and ladders, prop sales, service. Stock mahogany planking, plywood, plus teak planking)

WEST BASIN MARINE
Marilyn & Paul Mallonee
273 Prospect Street
St. Joseph, MI 49085
(616) 983-5432

(Maintenance, refinishing, engine tuneups, repairs, ships store and storage; cater to larger wooden inboard cruisers, some runabouts)

WINDJAMMER MARINA
Oden, MI 49764

(Refinish, repair, store and sell wooden boats)

FOX RIVER VALLEY BOAT CO.
1310 Riverside Drive
McHenry, IL 60050
(815) 385-0454

(Established in the 1930s, offers sales, service, storage and in-out service, paint, etc. Sells art supplies, frames; also generator and starter repairs, sales, etc.)

MARTIN TUCKETT ANTIQUE &
  CLASSIC BOATS
Box 6141
Rockford, IL 61125

(Please contact for services currently offered)

EXCELSIOR BOAT REFINISHERS
Dave Schmitt
Excelsior, MN 55331
(612) 861-4505

(Specializing in complete wood and fiberglass refinishing. Free estimates, some sales and storage also)

MALIBU BEACH YACHT BASIN
Lakeroad 54-49
Osage Beach, MO 65065

(Former Century dealer, sells, restores, docks and offers winter storage)

MACATAWA BAY BOAT WORKS
c/o Steve Northuis
438 W. 21st Street
Holland, MI 49423
(616) 396-5450

(Building 1930 24' 3-cockpit Chris-Craft replica wooden runabouts, plus other models being added. The best of the old tradition coupled with modern methods and power. A beautiful mahogany runabout. Write for folder or see your local dealer)

SUTHERLAND MARINE CO., INC.
Box 2896
Ashtabula, OH 44004

(Offers sales, service, boat refinishing, ship carpentry and storage. Also sells Chris-Craft boats)

KOTOSKI BROTHERS BOAT WORKS
Bald Eagle Indust. Park
5241 130th St. N.
White Bear Lake, MN 55110
(612) 429-8344

(Refinishes and restores wooden cruisers, runabouts, etc. Also can design and build custom cabinetry and appliance installations on your boat. Inboard mechanical work, engine rebuilding and custom upholstery work)

LEIGHTON BOAT HOUSE
252 Portage Lakes Drive
Akron, OH 44319
 (216) 644-2417

(Specializes in wooden boat refinishing and rebuilding, Volvo and OMC outdrive repairs, also offers winter storage)

FOESCH'S MARINE SERVICE
Box 434
Shawano, WI 54166
 (715) 524-4100 or 4433

(Antique inboard boats and antique motors for sale)

DONALD E. FORREST
DBA-Don Forrest, Inc.
303 Cedar Point Roadway
Sandusky, OH 44870

(Can repair any or all Lyman wooden boat parts. Carries the various types of lumber used in Lyman construction. Has available bronze screws and most Lyman hardware)

SLOAN BROS. FIBERGLASS REPAIR
Steve & Mike Sloan
5108 8th Avenue
Marion, IA 52302

(Marine, auto and tub-shower repairs, plus hull restoration and limited wooden boat repairs and refinishing)

STEVE'S MARINE SERVICE
c/o Steve Hahn
2937 Fairchild Avenue
Wayzata, MN 55391
 (612) 475-0243—home
 (612) 534-9388—work

(Marine repair, saw blades sharpened, and snow plowing)

WOOD BOATS EXCLUSIVE
c/o Charles Cassell
115 W. Liberty Street
Hubbard, OH 44425
 (216) 534-9388

(Restorations, refinishing, repairs and sales of wooden boats)

GRAY'S BAY MARINA
Marine Woodworking & Restoration
2831 Highway 101 S.
Wayzata, MN 55391
 (612) 473-2550

(Complete wooden boat restoration, quality woodworking and refinishing)

CLASSIC CRAFT
c/o John Scully
6300 N. Dresden Road
Route 1
Morris, IL 60450
 (815) 942-612

(Offers wooden boat restorations, building and maintenance)

PERLAKY REPAIR & REFINISH
24785 W. Young Road
Millsbury, OH 43447
 (419) 836-8977

(Boat hauling, complete repair or refinish of fiberglass, wood or metal boats, plus complete drive line repair)

BOATS & THINGS
P.O. Box 561
Lake Orion, MI 48035

(Antique and classic boats, engines, engine parts and hardware)

DONALD R. LOGAN,
 WOODWORKING
Box 325
Soudan, MN 55782
 (218) 753-4020

(Antique boat specialists in N.E. Minnesota. Specializing in wooden antique and classic boats, restorations, sales and refinishing)

CEDARHOLM MARINE
c/o Bob Cedarholm
267 Arthur Street
Manistee, MI 49660
 (616) 723-5288

(Dealer for Chrysler engines, Chris-Craft parts, ships locker and marine supplies)

NEW SOUTHERN RESTORATION SHOP LISTINGS

ANTIQUE BOAT SPECIALTIES
c/o Ed Sobko
Box 26005
Birmingham, AL 35226
 (205) 823-6698

(Selection of popular antique and classic boats with refinishing and restoration services available, plus storage covers and old hardware)

SCHERB ENTERPRISES
1654 Baywinds Lane
Sarasota, FL 33581
 (813) 922-3382

(Restorations, boat sales, brokerage, repairs, etc.)

DECKHANDS MARINE
U.S. Highway 98 E.
Fort Walton Beach, FL 32548
 (904) 242-3165

(Rebuilds and repairs wooden sailboats and powerboats. Many other services too)

HUDSON MARINA, INC.
9 Marine Drive
Fort Walton Beach, FL 32548
 (904) 242-3165

(Repairs inboards, outdrives, storage, dockage, repairs, plus sells Chris-Craft boats and other makes as well)

GEORGIA CLASSIC BOATS
c/o Jim Wittenberg
Leisure Cove, Lot 42
Williams Road, Route 3
LaGrange, GA 30240
 (404) 884-1939

(Restorations, repairs, refinishing, boat sales, plus complete service available)

HALL'S BOAT HOUSE
P.O. Box 36
Lakemont, GA 30552
 (404) 782-4981

(Offers excellent restoring and refinishing of classic wooden speedboats, etc.)

COMPLETE WOOD BOAT SERVICE
c/o Jud Laws
Lake Rabun Road
Lakemont, GA 30552
 (404) 947-3411
 (404) 782-5207

(Restorations, repairs, refinishing, and boat sales)

BARLOW MARINE
c/o George Barlow
Box 34
McQueeny, TX 78123
 (512) 557-5000

(Offers full restoration; does many Centurys; good source for parts, etc.)

NEW WESTERN RESTORATION SHOP LISTINGS

FRANK'S BOAT SHOP
Colin, ID 83821
(Offers repair and restoration of wooden inboards near Priest Lake, Idaho. Boat and motor sales as well)

RIO LINDA MARINE ENGINE CO.
6717 26th Street
Rio Linda, CA 95673
(916) 929-1458
(916) 991-5834
(Offers sales of antique runabouts, older engine specialists, boat hauling to 50 feet, bottom painting and surveys, plus brokerage)

WOOD BOAT REPAIR—
WEST COAST
"The Wooden Boat Center"
1300 Culver Boulevard
Maria Del Rey, CA 90291
(Woodworking, repairs, restorations, classes in building small, traditional craft, engines, hardware and wood)

NORTHERN MARINE INDUSTRIES
2400 W. Lake Avenue N.
Seattle, WA 98109
(206) 323-5945
(Offers complete refinishing, repairs, restorations for wood inboards, cruisers, etc. Buys and sells boats, offers dry dock and crane service, does traditional wooden boat work)

BEAR CREEK BOAT WORKS
c/o Greg Smith
Star Route 3
Bear Creek, WA 98528
(206) 275-5191
(Restorations, repairs, new boat construction. Contact for information)

THE DRY DOCK
P.O. Box 567
Kings Beach, CA 95719
(916) 546-7040
(Offers complete restorations. On north shore of Lake Tahoe)

PERFORMANCE MARINE
c/o Joe Galluzzl
8370 Trout Avenue
Kings Beach, CA 95719
(916) 546-7636
(Does engine work, repairs, refinishes and restores inboard speedboats during the winter, and cares for high performance inboards and jets during the summer. Located at Lake Tahoe. Contact directly)

M. R. PRIEST COMPANY
John Sword
515 West Highland
Boise, ID 83706
(Does wooden boat refinishing and restoration work)

McLEANS COMMERCIAL CABINETS
114 E. 40th
Boise, ID 83704
(Does restorations, wooden boat refinishing and repairing of wood)

THE LOST ARK
497 Penninsula Drive
Lake Almanor, CA 96137
(Repairs and refinishes wooden boats, etc. Contact for more information)

WOODEN SHIP BOAT WORKS
Gary Minnis
2421 Front Street
West Sacramento, CA 95961
(916) 371-7447
(Offers restoration work, repairs, refinishing and structural repairs. Also does work on wooden sailboats, cruisers of all sizes)

EMMET R. JONES
30891 Lilac Road
Valley Center, CA 92082
(714) 749-0517
(Boat builder in southern California, also builds some wooden inboard speedboats on special order plus some runabout restoration work as well)

BRISTOL SERVICES COMPANY
c/o Gary Croan
1314 Conway Avenue
Costa Mesa, CA 92626
(714) 892-8541

(Gray engine distributor, parts, magneto. Buy and sell Century, Lyman and Mercury boats. Many other services)

NORTHWEST CLASSIC BOATS
14950 N.E. 95th
Suite 3-C
Redmond, WA 98052
(206) 882-0897

(Restoration, repairs and engine work, boat sales and storage)

PROPS AND PROP REPAIRS

RECORD PROPELLERS
Philip Rolla
cp 224
6903 Lugano, Switzerland

(Designers and producers of record high performance props used by such firms as Riva, Abbate, etc.)

MONTANA PROPELLER REPAIR
c/o Ken Fillbach
2425 Highway 93 South
Kalispell, MT 59901
(406) 755-2021

(Complete repair station, all makes, inboards, outboard and I.O. Also offers pitch changing, cupping, diameter reduction, hub replacement, heliarc welding, skegs and lower units)

PACKING NUT WRENCH
Phun Sales Company
Dept. Rural Route 4
Box 46143
Cleveland, OH 44146

(An 11-inch handle with jaws that open to #3 make this tool a must for all inboard owners. Use for shaft packing, nut tightening and adjusting. U.S. made, machined and plated. $8.95 plus $1.50 shipping)

REPLACEMENT RUBBER PRODUCTS, ETC.

WEFCO RUBBER MFG. CORP.
1655 Euclid Street
Santa Monica, CA 90404
(213) 393-0303

(Makes replacement rubber parts, gunnels, dock bumpers, trim, rollers. Send $1.50 plus stamped, self-addressed envelope for catalog)

METRO MOULDED PARTS
3031 2nd Street N.
Minneapolis, MN 55411
(612) 521-0123

(Mainly offers rubber car parts, but possible source for windshield rubber moldings and other miscellaneous rubber items. Write or call for catalog to use before placing order)

HARDWARE, WINDSHIELD BRACKETS, RUBBER MOLDINGS, ETC.

HARSENS ISLAND MARINA
Pete Henkle
7650 S. Channel
Harsens Island, MI 48028
(313) 748-3600

(Chris-Craft stamped step pad frames as used from 1925-31. Chris-Craft windshield brackets, standard and deluxe, plus miscellaneous other hardware)

CALIFORNIA CLASSIC BOATS
Al & Brett Schinnerer
5581 Ridgebury Drive
Huntington Beach, CA 92649
(714) 846-7454 (evenings or weekends)

(Produce quality authentic reproduction parts for vintage Chris-Craft, Gar Wood, Dodge, Hacker and Sea Lyon. Will do instrument restoration, plus reface and rechrome. Parts catalogs available at $2.00 each)

WINDSHIELD RUBBER
William C. Smith
15 Normandy Parkway
Morristown, NJ 07960
(201) 267-7499

(Windshield rubber for Chris-Craft, Hacker Craft and several others. Used to hold glass against wood decking. $2.50 per foot, prepaid postage C.O.D. Windshield "T" rubber, 1" or ¾", $1.95 per foot, prepaid postage C.O.D.)

WINDSHIELD RUBBER
Jafco Marina
2192 Niagara Street
Buffalo, NY 14207
(716) 876-5944

(Windshield glass black rubber as original standard size for all runabouts with three-piece brackets and glass inserts. $2.50 per foot)

WINDSHIELD BRACKETS
Ross W. Kieffer
(216) 644-9335 (Ohio)

(Offers Chris-Craft brackets, 2 styles, $149.00/set postpaid. Call for more information)

MISCELLANEOUS NEW LISTINGS

ALL POLISHING & PLATING, INC.
Daisson D. Hickel
23 George Street
Newark, NJ 07105
(201) 589-8686

(Chrome, nickel and copper plating. Antique boat, car and motorcycle parts. Specializes in restoration of white [die cast] pieces)

ELEGANT STEAM LAUNCHES
Glyn Lancaster Jones
Bacup Road
Todmorden, Lancaster
England

(Builders of period steam launches and motorboats. Three sizes offered in 16', 20', and 24' versions. The 20' Morven Class is built here in the U.S. for sale from Rhode Island Marine Services, Box 209, Snug Harbor, RI 02880)

THE ADIRONDACK MUSEUM
Blue Mountain Lake, NY 12812
(518) 352-7311 or 7322

(Beautiful museum in the Adirondack Mountains, home of the famous race boat, *Ellagarto,* plus beautiful displays of other pleasure craft, both power and sail. A must stop if you are traveling out East)

GLEN L MARINE DESIGNS
9152 Department WB
Roscrans, CA 90706

(Offers wooden boat plans and kit boats. General catalog is $2.00)

WHEELS, TIRES, HUBS & AXELS
Design Wheel & Hub
2225 Lee Drive
Akron, OH 44306
(216) 773-7873

(12.10 and 8-inch wheels, mounted or unmounted. Top quality tires, fast service, fair prices)

HUTCHINSON BOAT OWNERS
  CLUB
c/o Wally Young
516 Prospect Avenue
Syracuse, NY 12208

CASTINGS FOR SHEPHERD
  V-DRIVE STRUTS
THE BOAT SHOP
Duane Assmann, owner
522 Baker Street
Lake Geneva, WI 53147
(414) 248-3590

(Have available Shepherd V-drive struts for 1¼" shaft, bored and cutless bearing installed. Base to be drilled to fit existing keel holes by purchaser. Price available upon request)

CUSTOM BOAT LETTERING
  SERVICE
Mylitta Bradette
Box 316
Manotick, Ontario, Canada
(613) 692-4135

(Personal design for the lettering of your boat's nameplate, gold leaf—all custom designs)

CENTURY WHITE RUBBER STEP PADS Conrad Adamski c/o Century Boat Company Manistee, MI 49660	(Now available: 3", 4" and 6" white rubber Century step pads. $6.50 each, plus shipping and handling)
MISC. CENTURY HARDWARE Conrad Adamski (same address as above)	(A changing variety of discontinued hardware, windshields, etc.)
POSSIBLE SHEPHERD HARDWARE SOURCE I.T.T. Bryden Division 168 Rexdale Boulevard Rexdale, Ontario M9W 1P6 Canada	(Formerly Brydon Brass Ltd., manufacturers of hardware of Shepherd boats. May have some hardware not listed in their current catalog as it would be obsolete items. Shepherd owners better check this one out)
HERITAGE BOAT CLUB c/o Bob Welther, Secretary 4722 West Berteau Chicago, IL 60641	(A new antique boat club in Chicago, Illinois area. Most of the boats are the larger yacht, cruiser and sailboat varieties)
BOAT TRANSPORTATION VIA WATER Don McIntyre 9507 Edgeley Road Bethesda, MD 20015 (518) 425-9901 July-August	(Retired mechanical engineer will transport and care for your classic power or sailboat as if it were his own. Please contact directly for more details on the service)
CENTURIAN BOATS, INC. 455 Grogen Avenue Merced, CA 95340 (209) 383-1211	(Now offering a custom-built competition tournament inboard ski boat)
HACKER CRAFT BOAT PLANS TEXAS DORY BOAT PLANS Capt. Jim Orrell Box 720 Galveston, TX 77553	(Jim offers plans for old Hacker Craft speedboats, commuters, launches, racers, cruisers, etc. Contact directly for more details. Great for model builders or those restoring or wanting to build an old Hacker from scratch)
MORIN MAHOGANY MARINE 22' Deluxe Triple-Cockpit Runabout Dwight & Doug Morin Bay City, Michigan (517) 684-8025 or 686-7357	(Modern V-bottom with flare forward and tumblehome aft. Philippine mahogany for deck planking, seam batten sides and frames. Bottom would be double marine plywood totaling ⅝" Gougeon's W.E.S.T. system used throughout construction. 250 Mercruiser, 12-volt blower, clear acrylic enamel finish. Contact for delivery date and price)
JOHNSON OUTBOARD MOTOR HISTORY BOOK "The Four Men from Terre Haute" c/o 1,000 Islands Shipyard Museum 750 Mary Street Clayton, NY 13624 (315) 686-4104	(Excellent new hardcover book which covers the story of Johnson Brothers and their various motors, bicycles, inboards, etc. Written by an expert in antique and classic outboards, John Van Vleet. A must for anyone interested in the old outboard engines and their history. $11.95 each, postpaid)
THE MARITIME MUSEUM Wooden Boatbuilding Shop South Haven, MI 49090 (616) 637-8078	(Museum offering courses in wooden boat repair and restoration, plus introduction to small, wooden boat construction)

LA RACCOLTA DELLA Harca Lariana 22010 Pianello del Larino Lago di Como, Italy Telephone 0344-87235	(An association on Lake Como in Northern Italy undertaking the preservation of local boats and boating. Has a large collection of over 150 boats, 40 of which are mahogany inboard runabouts. Has exciting plans for the future. Also, have a good collection of foreign and U.S. outboard motors)
THE TENDER CRAFT BOAT SHOP 67 Mowat Avenue, #031 Toronto, Ontario, Canada (416) 531-2941	(Have expanded their offerings to now include repair work, recanvasing of canoes, structural repairs on other boats, plus the sale of all supplies to build stripper canoes, including strips machined and grooved. Also now sell Kayak kits, Sabot dinghies, etc., plus fasteners of all types and sizes, paints, books, tools, hardware, etc.)
BOOK, "Full Speed Ahead" 2400 Simpson Street Evanston, IL 60201	(A beautiful book by Larry Larkin, second printing, covering the beautiful old launches that once plied Lake Geneva, Wisconsin in huge numbers. This book is a MUST for all antique boat buffs. $12.00, which includes postage)
BOOK "Pleasure Yachts of the Thousand Islands" By Gilbart B. Mercier	(Another very beautiful book every antique boat library should have. Many, many excellent old yacht photos of the "floating palaces" that plied the St. Lawrence River for many years. Order from Shipyard Museum, 750 Mary St., Clayton, NY 13624 at $17.00 tax and postpaid)
SHAW & TENNEY Box 213 20 Water Street Orono, ME 04473 (207) 866-5867	(Traditionally designed paddles and oars handcrafted since 1858. Also offers rowing hardware, canoe accessories, canoe trophies, boat hooks and much, much more)
HACKER CRAFT REPRODUCTIONS Morgan Marine Base Silver Bay, NY 12874 (518) 543-6666	(Builds 26', 28', and 30' Hacker Craft reproductions, plus Hacker restorations. Contact for more details)
JIM VAN VOAST 1810 S.W. 13 Avenue Ft. Lauderdale, FL 33315 (305) 463-9333	(Naval architect and marine engineer (P.E.) specializing in replicas/reproductions of 1850-1920 designs, sail or steam, up to 80 feet)
MODEL SHIP CATALOG James Bliss & Company Route 128 Dedham, MA 02026 (617) 329-2430	(Excellent 98-page catalog, available for $2.00 and covers everything to do with model ship kits, tools, cements, glues, paints and supplies. If you like ship modeling you'll want this fine catalog. In business since 1832)
NAUTICAL ANTIQUES "Nautical Brass Magazine" P.O. Box 744 Montrose, CA 91020	(If you collect any type of nautical antiques, you should receive this magazine. Comes out six times a year and costs $10 per subscription. Covers all types of nautical antiques, has Wanted and For Sale sections, plus good articles on all aspects of the hobby. A very unique publication)
CHRISTMAS LIGHTS & GLASS ORNAMENTS Bob Speltz 505 Albert Lea Street Albert Lea, MN 56007 (507) 373-2145 (collect)	(Collector wishes to buy Sylvania flourescent Christmas tree lights, all types of boxed Christmas tree lights pre-1970, sizes C6, C7½ and C9. Must be in excellent condition. Send list and photo, plus price. Also want old World War II type glass, non-silvered, colored tree ornaments too)
MARINE SURVEYORS Ron Turnow 40 Beverly Road Hillsdale, NJ 07642 (201) 666-7124	(Surveyors of wooden boats)

DECALS, NAMEPLATES, ETC.

RAY BOEDDING
c/o General Marine
239 Horton Street
London, Ontario, Canada N6B 1L1
  (519) 438-8308

(Peterborough hull decals, exact duplicates of the originals, water applied type, $18.00 per pair, includes tax and shipping)

MURRAY WALKER
Rural Route 2
Pefferlaw, Ontario, Canada L0E 1N0
  (705) 437-2068

(Shepherd decals, dash and side varieties)

SMITH ACCESSORIES
(address shown elsewhere)

(Name plate "Dodge Boats" for inside of engine hatch. Brass, red and black, specify engine and hull numbers. $14.50 each plus 75¢ shipping)

MISCELLANEOUS NEW LISTINGS

(Boat and Engine Catalog Sales)
COLUMBIA TRADING COMPANY
2 Rocklyn Drive
Suffren, NY 10901

(Issues complete list of old boat and canoe catalogs as well as engine catalogs. Contact for list. Send s.s.a.e. for current list)

(Wood Stripping Systems)
CLASSIC WOOD
Box B18184
Minneapolis, MN 55418

(Special marine stripping system formulated just for your wooden boats. Contact for more details)

(Parts and Accessories)
CHRIS CRAFT SALES, INC.
Parts and Accessories Division
2001 Pte. Trimble Road
Algonac, MI 48001
  (313) 794-4944

(Chris-Craft owners, this is where you can get help with lots of your C-C supplies and parts needs as well as "lineage" on your Chris)

THE WOODEN BOAT SHOP
8151 Bridgetown Road
Cincinnati, OH 45002
  (513) 941-7281
  (513) 471-7700

(Sales, service and restorations of classic and antique watercraft)

(Gar Wood Sport Shirts)
THE GAR WOOD SOCIETY
P.O. Box 6003
Syracuse, NY 13217

(Beautiful 50% cotton, 50% polyester Champion sports shirts. $12.95 each. Send for order blank and more information)

(Zenith Carburetors)
BARNETT & SMALL, INC.
151 E. Industry Court
Deer Park, NY 11729
  (516) 242-2100

(Brand new Zenith updraft carburetors for Chris-Craft models K, Kr, KS, KL, some Chrysler, Gray, Red Wing and Palmers too. Contact directly for details)

(Autolite Marine Coils)
DAVID FICKEN
Box 1
Babylon, NY 11702
  (516) 587-3332

(Original NOS Autolite coils for C-C, Falcon, Gramm, Kermath, Lathrop, Lycoming, Palmer and others. Also available; points, rotors, distributor caps, and coils too)

MACK BORING & PARTS COMPANY
130 Route 110
Farmingdale, NY 11735
(516) 293-2719

(Carry gaskets for Gray Marine engines from mid 1930's to late 1950's. Also have parts and retrofit kits for Sherwood water pumps)

(African Mahogany Wood Source)
CRAFT WOOD
on Old Deerfield Road
Highland Park, IL 60035

(Stock good selection of hard to fine African mahogany wood)

(Western Refinish Shop)
FLYING BOAT COMPANY
153 Lincoln Street
Twin Falls, ID 83338

(Restore and repair wooden speedboats)

(New Boat Book)
"THE BOAT BUILDERS OF MUSKOKA"
by A. H. Duke & W. Gray

(An all new book available now, covering many of the old-time wooden boat builders of the Muskoka Lakes chain in Canada. Aude Duke, one of the former owners of Duke Boat Co. and W. Gray, put together this excellent book. I highly recommend this book to all antique speedboat buffs everywhere)

(Gray Marine Engine Maintenence Manual)
DON HINES
Gray Marine Company
339 W. 20th Avenue
Oskosh, WI 54903
(414) 231-4560

(Have #665 marine engine manual available at $7.50 postpaid, covers most flathead 4 and 6 cylinder engines)

(Replacement Gar Wood Tach. Cables)
DICK ELTON
1651 Maplewood
Sylvan Lake, MI 48053

(Has source of original AC Tach cables that fit Gar Wood instruments perfectly. Cables run $15.00 each plus $5.00 shipping. Contact directly for more information)

(Cotton Rope Fenders & Mooring Lines)
DENMAR
Box 999
Gravenhurst, Ontario, Canada P0C 1G0
(705) 687-5464

(Fenders and mooring lines of cotton for all types of wooden boats, all sizes 10" x 3½" fenders to 26" x 4" and rope in sizes from ½" and ¾" size, 10' to 20' in length)

(Chris-Craft catalogs)
JIM SNELL
1290 S. 11th Street
Beaumont, TX 77701
(713) 838-6655

(Will share copies, for a small fee, of nearly every Chris-Craft catalog from 1935 to present. Includes; Sea Skiffs, Cavaliers, Marine engines and price sheets. Has parts list and service bulletins from 1947 through about 1962. Contact for more specifics)

(Literature, Photos, etc.)
TIM COLBERT
2250 N. Triphammer Road U2F
Ithaca, NY 14850
(607) 257-6807

(Has available full-color photos of Chris-Craft brochures for 1936, 1937, 1939 and 1948. Sold in 3 different sizes, suitable for framing. Also has b/w reproductions of the 1934, 1935 and 1936 C-C brochures and spec. sheets. Contact for further information)

MOBILE MARINE SERVICE, INC.
73 Railside Road, Unite 3
Toronto, Ontario, Canada M3A 1B2
(off Lawrence, east of Don Valley)
(416) 444-1116

(Fully equipped mobile van and workshop, experts in diesel, gas and outdrives. Specializes in engine rebuilding, transmissions and outdrives. They stock lots of parts, orders shipped C.O.D.)

M. BALDSON TRUCKING LTD.
Pickering, Ontario, Canada
  (416) 683-5917
  (416) 839-5885

(Lumber Sources)
ATLANTIC MARINE
Newcastle, ME 04553
  (207) 563-5570

(Chris-Craft "lady" & posters from 1940's etc.)
GARY WOLLARD
13188 Latourette
Fenton, MI 48430
  (313) 750-0205

(Fuel pump repair kits)
DENEAL GOTTESMAN
2187 Bluegrass Lane
Cincinnati, OH 45237
  (513) 731-4134 after 6 p.m.

REAL RUNABOUT BOATS
Box 343
Geneva, NY 14456

(Model Boat Builders)
THE MODEL BOAT WORKS
P.O. Box 241, Station "M"
Toronto, Ontario, Canada M6S 4T3

(Hand and Power Tool Source)
SEVEN CORNERS ACE HDW. INC.
216 W. 7th Street
St. Paul, MN 55102
  (612) 224-4859
  1-(800) 328-0457 toll free number

(Lumber Source)
YUKON LUMBER COMPANY
520 W. 22nd Street
Norfolk, VA 23517
  (804) 625-7131

(Wood Lapstrake Boat Builder)
MURPHY BOAT WORKS
220 N. Front Street
LaCrosse, WI 54601
  (608) 782-7650

(Marine Wood Finishes)
WATCO-DENNIS CORPORATION
1756 22nd Street
Santa Monica, CA 90404
Dept. R-5

(Boat haulers, PCV Class D & X Ontario and U.S.A. Hydraulic Trailer Service)

(Stock and sell cedar, mahogany, teak, longleaf yellow pine, exotics and others. Custom resawing and planing)

(Exact reproduction of original Chris-Craft "Lady" from 1940 painted by Don Spalding. Also up to 25 other posters etc., painted by Spalding, all prior to 1946. Write for prices, specs. etc.)

(Fuel pump repair kits for AC pump #4478 used on Gray 225 and others, $35.00 plus U.P.S. Also hard to find electrical and carburetor parts)

(A good selection of 15' to 18' inboard wood runabouts for sale. Send a s.a.s.e for current list)

(A miniature scaled down from its prototype in the 3rd dimension is the nearest thing to possession of the real thing. Custom built scale models, power or sail plans not necessary)

(Excellent source for all sorts of hand and power tools, useful for boat building, repairing, etc.)

(Lumber supplier of such varieties as: mahogany, teak, cherrywood, spruce, marine plywood, oak, maple, poplar, birch and many more)

(Build beautiful mahogany lapstrake 18' to 24' wooden lapstrake runabouts and cruisers. Write for folder)

(Manufacturers of WATCO marine wood finishes. Great for all types of wood. Write for free color folder on WATCO finishes)

(Dry Rot "Medicine")
TUGON CHEMICAL CORPORATION
Box 31
Cross River, NY 10518
(203) 762-3953

(Manufacturers of "Rot-Fil" for dry rot in your boat. Packed in high pressure injector syringe)

(Out of print nautical items)
TONA GRAPHICS
P.O. Box 306
North Tonawanda, NY 14120

(Suppliers of out-of-print nautical books, manuals, catalogs, magazines, emphemera, etc. New catalog now available for $1.00 refunded with first order)

CLUBS, MAGAZINES AND BOOKS OF INTEREST

APPENDIX

Listed below is an expanded selection of clubs to join as well as books you, the reader, might wish to purchase for your own libraries. Also, there is a new and current list of magazine articles written since *Volume III* was published, which concern themselves with antique and classic boats. Rumors of new clubs are popping up almost daily. I am sure before very long, there will be "fan clubs" organized for all the major wood boat builders in this country and elsewhere.

ANTIQUE BOAT CLUB
P. O. Box 1386
Tallahassee, FL 32302

(A fine club, made up of mostly Chris-Craft owners. Publish *The Brass Bell*. Dues are $20.00 per year. Trace their roots back to the original Chris-Craft Club of the 1970s.)

ANTIQUE & CLASSIC BOAT SOCIETY
Box 831
Lake George, NY 12845

(Club formed in 1975, now boasts over 700 members with eight national chapters established in the United States and Canada. Publishes an excellent quarterly magazine and an annual membership directory)

ANTIQUE BOAT SOCIETY
E. R. Wells, Admiral
Learning Place
Manset, ME 04656

THE ANTIQUE OUTBOARD MOTOR
 CLUB, INC.
Shipyard Museum
750 Mary Street
Clayton, NY 13624

(A unique club of those who collect, restore, use and maintain antique and classic outboard motors as well as boats. Dues are $12.00 per year. Publishes quarterly magazine and newsletter—contact for more information)

CENTURY BOAT CLUB
Bob Speltz
505 Albert Lea Street
Albert Lea, MN 56007
(507)373-2145

(A new club formed for Century wood boat owners, including all boats built of wood by Century through 1968. Newsletter, etc., published. Contact for dues and more information. Need not own a boat to belong)

CLASSIC YACHT ASSOCIATION, INC.
Box 3039
Terminal Island, CA 90731

(Formed in 1969 to promote and encourage interest in the preservation, restoration and maintenance of fine old power-driven pleasure craft. To qualify, a vessel must be of good design, construction and maintenance, built before December 31, 1942, and showing no exterior alterations to distract from the designer's original intent)

CLASSIC YACHT CLUB OF AMERICA
c/o Al Kmiec, Commodore
1433 Walker Avenue
Baltimore, MD 21239

CLAYTON ANTIQUE BOAT
  AUXILIARY
Clayton Shipyard Museum
Clayton, NY 13624

(This fine organization operates an exceptional museum full of antique power and sailcraft, plus other displays of outboard engines, old gas engines, etc. Publish the *Gazette* every four months. Staged first antique boat show in the United States in 1961)

DISAPPEARING PROPELLER BOAT
  CLUB
Joe Fossey, president
305 Duckworth Street
Barrie, Ontario, Canada L4M 3X5

(Brand new club for owners and buffs of the disappearing propeller boats)

THE ELCO CLUB
c/o Dudley Lewis
Rural Delivery 2, Box 135
Egg Harbor, NJ 08215

(Informal group of Elco boat owners who issue newsletter and hold annual get-to-gethers)

THE GAR WOOD SOCIETY
Box 6003
Syracuse, NY 13217

(A new organization dedicated to the great Gar Wood speedboats of the past. The club issues a monthly newsletter called the *Gar Wood News*, and will issue a quarterly magazine called *The Trophy Fleet Times*. Contact for dues schedule. This group really has big plans, and I hope it is very successful)

LYMAN OWNER'S ASSOC.
Dale T. Hooper, Pres.
27294 2nd St.
West Lake, OH 44145
  (216) 835-5685

(Owners of all types of Lyman wood boats—here's a club you should join!)

MATTHEWS BOATOWNERS
  ASSOCIATION
Sound Avenue
Box 13
Mattituck, NY 11952-0013

(New club formed in 1978 for Matthews owners and fans—write directly for more information)

MIDWEST ANTIQUE & CLASSIC
  BOAT ASSOCIATION
435 Lake Street
Mukwonago, WI 53149

(Approximately 50 members made up of antique boat fans and owners. Hold meetings, occasional swap meets and generally help those interested in antique boating. A fine new club founded in 1978)

RICHARDSON BOAT OWNERS
  ASSOCIATION
John Dubickas
270 S. Meadow Drive
North Tonawanda, NY 14120

(Organized to promote the preservation of Richardson cruisers. Publish newsletters and hold annual rendezvous)

WOOD CANOE HERITAGE
  ASSOCIATION
Box 5634
Madison, WI 53705

(A new organization consisting of persons interested in or owning wood and birch bark canoes. Publishes newsletter and stages annual wood canoe assembly each year. Dues are $10.00—write for more information)

INLAND EMPIRE WOODEN
  BOAT CLUB
1523 N. 2nd St.
Coeur d'Alene, ID 83814
  (208) 667-1253

(A new club formed for wooden boat owners in northern Idaho and eastern Washington state.)

ADDITIONAL NEW CLUBS

MONTANA WOODEN BOAT CLUB
Box 1822
Dept. #5
Kalispell, MT 59901

(Here's an all new club for you folks up Montana way. This club sponsors an Annual In Water Antique Boat Show on Flathead Lake, Mt. each summer. Call Gary Cockrell at (406) 755-3302 for more details)

ALABAMA ANTIQUE & CLASSIC
  RUNABOUT CLUB
c/o Alan Coupland
8817 4th Avenue North
Birmingham, AL 35206
(205) 836-9481

(A local club situated in the great southeast for owners and buffs alike who love all makes and styles of mahogany speedboats)

MAC CRAFT BOAT CLUB
171 Margaret Avenue
Dept. #5
Wallaceburg, Ontario, Canada N8A 2A3
(519) 627-3296

(Club for owners of Mac-Craft Canadian-built runabouts, utilities and cruisers. Free Mac-Craft burgee to registered owners)

OREGON CLASSIC WOODEN BOAT
  CLUB
c/o Jim Piercey
195 Sunshine Acres Drive
Eugene, OR 97401
(503) 687-8811

(New club set up for wooden runabout and cruiser owners in Oregon and Washington states. If you live in that area and are interested, contact Jim at once)

BOAT MAGAZINES OF INTEREST TO WOOD BOAT ENTHUSIASTS

ANTIQUE & CLASSIC
  BOAT MAGAZINE
P.O. Box 1634
Colton, CA 92324

(A premier full color magazine covering the world of mahogany inboard runabouts. U.S. subscriptions $20.00 per year! A must for *all*.)

NAUTICAL QUARTERLY
141 Lexington Avenue
New York, NY 10016
(212) 689-8232

(Superb new quarterly full of color photos; hard covers. It comes in its own protective hard box. Will cover both power and sail. Probably the finest as well as most expensive publication on the market today. Write for prices and more information)

MESSING ABOUT IN BOATS
29 Burley Street
Wenham, MA 01984
(617) 774-0906

(A new bi-monthly newsletter for those who enjoy messing about in boats. Contact for current subscription fees etc. It is a fine little publication and deserves your support)

SMALL BOAT JOURNAL
Box 400
Benington, VT 05201

(A new magazine aimed at the reader-owner of small wooden boats. Have been publishing for about a year. Subscription fee for this monthly magazine is currently $12.00 a year)

THE WOODEN BOAT
Box 78
Brooklin, ME 04616

(Excellent slick paper quarterly with color covers and all types of reports on sailing, building and maintaining all sorts of wooden work and pleasure craft. Also, reports on the use of tools, methods of repair, etc. A must for the boat owner, builder and designer. Write for subscription fees, etc.)

CURRENT MAGAZINE ARTICLES OF INTEREST — OUTBOARDS

"Antique Boating," *SMALL BOAT JOURNAL* (Apr./May '82), pp. 65-70.
"1916 Evinrude Model AA," Antique Corner, *TRAILERBOATS* (May '81), p. 60.
"1930 Johnson Model J-25," Antique Corner, *TRAILERBOATS* (Aug. '81), pp. 38-39.
"1954 Mercury Mark 20," Antique Corner, *TRAILERBOATS* (Sept. '81), p. 39.
"Oldtime Racing Vocabulary," Antique Corner, *TRAILERBOATS* (Nov./Dec. '81), p. 15.
"1917 Caille 5 Speed," Antique Corner, *TRAILERBOATS* (Jan. '82), p. 44.
"1958 16' Lyman Outboard Runabout," Antique Corner, *TRAILERBOATS* (Feb. '82), p. 52.
1937 Evinrude Sportfour," Antique Corner, *TRAILERBOATS* (Mar. '82), p. 48.
"1954 Martin 200 Silver Streak," Antique Corner, *TRAILERBOATS* (Apr. '82), pp. 54-55.
"Hand-Driven Outboards," Antique Corner, *TRAILERBOATS* (May '82), pp. 48-49.
"1939 Clarke Troller," Antique Corner, *TRAILERBOATS* (June '82), pp. 18-19.
"A New Lyman Lapstrake in Wood," *LAKELAND BOATING* (Oct. '81), pp. 34-35.
"A Skiff for the River," *CANADIAN YACHTING* (Jan. '82), pp. 43-44.
"A Survey of Rowing Craft—Rowboat Renaissance," *LAKELAND BOATING* (Feb. '81), pp. 66-69.
"A Thousand Islands Romance Rekindled," *SMALL BOAT JOURNAL* (Apr./May '81), pp. 18-21.
"Crafting Canoes in Maine," *SMALL BOAT JOURNAL* (Aug. '79), pp. 11-14)
"Looking for Bargains in Wooden Boats," *SMALL BOAT JOURNAL* (Apr./May '81), pp. 46-49.
"New Life for Ancient Motors," *OUTBOARD* (Oct. '60), pp. 16-17.
"Rebuilding the Wood & Canvas Canoe," *WOODEN BOAT* (July '79), pp. 68-75.
"Repairing Motors Keeps Him Busy," *SOUNDINGS* (Jan. '82), pp. 1-11.
"Build Your Own Strip Canoe from a Box," *SMALL BOAT JOURNAL* (Jan. '82), pp. 33-34.
"Stock Outboards," *NAUTICAL QUARTERLY* (Spring '82), pp. 106-115.
"Society Dedicated to Preserving Gar Wood Boats," *SOUNDINGS* (Feb. '81), p. 10.
"The Backyard Boatyard," *CANOE* (Nov. '78), pp. 70-72.
"The Outboard and Its Early Days," *TRAILERBOATS* (Feb. '81), pp. 32-33.
"The Rangley Tradition," *WOODEN BOAT* (Apr. '81), pp. 26-30.
"The Stonongton Pulling Boat," *SMALL BOAT JOURNAL* (June/July '81), pp. 40-41.
"They Don't Spook Fish," *SMALL BOAT JOURNAL* (July '80), pp. 16-18).
"Those Beamy Army Storm Boats," *SMALL BOAT JOURNAL* (June/July '81), pp. 44-45.
"Canoes According to Galt," *SMALL BOAT JOURNAL* (July '82), pp. 22-27.

CURRENT MAGAZINE ARTICLES OF INTEREST — INBOARDS

"Ace Speedboat," *WOODEN BOAT* (Mar./Apr. '82), pp. 65-70.
"A Wooden Winner, Skiff Craft 26 SF," *LAKELAND BOATING* (Mar. '81), pp. 52-53.
"Antique Boating," *SMALL BOAT JOURNAL* (Apr./May '82), pp. 65-70.
"Antique Boating—Is It For You?," *SMALL BOAT JOURNAL* (Feb./Mar. '82), pp. 21-25.
"Building in the Grand Manner," *LAKELAND BOATING* (Feb. '82), pp. 32-36.
"Clarke, Dick," *DELTA & BAY YACHTSMAN* (Nov. '81).
"Commuters," *NAUTICAL QUARTERLY* (Spring '81), pp. 66-79.
"Chris-Craft Expanding in Michigan," *LAKELAND BOATING* (Feb. '82), p. 35.
"Chris-Craft Prefers Northern Work Ethic," *SOUNDINGS* (May '82), p. 21.
"Dauntless Shipyard Revived This Old Salty," *SOUNDINGS* (Feb. '81), pp. 41-42.
"Golden Pond Floats a Real Golden Oldy," *SOUNDINGS* (Apr. '82), p. 6.
"Grand Craft," *WOODEN BOAT* (Jan./Feb. '82), pp. 80-85.
"*Gypsy,* a 1905 Launch Takes Top Honors at Clayton," *SOUNDINGS* (Oct. '80), p. D.
"Hacker and His Craft," *NAUTICAL QUARTERLY* (Summer '81), pp. 2-17.
"Handyman, Building a Century Dinghy," *LAKELAND BOATING* (Mar. '81), p. 16.
"Ladies of the Lake," *DELTA & BAY YACHTSMAN* (Oct. '81), pp. 62-63.
"My Uncle the Boat Builder," *CANADIAN YACHTING* (Oct. '81), pp. 52-57.
"Nostalgia for Steam Power," *LAKELAND BOATING* (Jan. '81), pp. 75-79.
"Plain City's Amish Craft Wood Boats," *SOUNDINGS* (Feb. '82), p. 1-4.

"Planking Repairs," *SMALL BOAT JOURNAL* (Feb./Mar. '82), pp. 70-73.
"Riva, A Pioneer's Story," *SYMBOL* (Fall '80), pp. 44-49.
"Restoring the Classics," *BAY VIEWS* (Apr. '81), p. 38-42.
"Building a 1937 Century Sea Maid," *SCALE MODEL SHIP BUILDER* (Jan. '82), pp. 56 plus.
"Steamboating," *TRAILERBOATS* (Nov./Dec. '81), pp. 26-27.
"Summer in Muskoka," *NAUTICAL QUARTERLY* (Summer '80), pp. 10-25.
"The Power & The Glory," *MOTORBOATING & SAILING* (Feb. '82), pp. 78-83.
"They're Still Building Them of Wood," *POPULAR MECHANICS* (Feb. '82), pp. 94-96.
"The Wooden Boat Revival," *NAUTICAL QUARTERLY* (Winter '81), pp. 2 plus.
"Thunderbird," *NAUTICAL QUARTERLY* (Summer '81), pp. 92-95.
"The Skiff Craft Story," *LAKELAND BOATING* (Mar. '81), pp. 54-57.
"The Great Canadian Dispro," *CANADIAN YACHTING* (May '82), pp. 38-42.
"When It Needs Some Work," *SMALL BOAT JOURNAL* (July '82), pp. 45-56.

CHAPTER IX
Current Builders of Mahogany Inboard Runabouts

As the title suggests, this final chapter of Volume V will take a brief look at the four builders who currently produce either standardized or custom wooden inboard speedboats. I am sure most of you are familiar with at least a couple of the following builders. The first firm we shall review is the Ace Speedboat Company of Amesbury, Massachusetts.

THE ACE SPEEDBOAT CO.
Amesbury, Massachusetts

The Ace Speedboat Company has been in business for about five years. They have taken an old 1920 John Hacker runabout design and kept the best of it, while building the boat via the W.E.S.T. system of construction. The first photo here shows an overhead view of the twin-cockpit beauty being displayed at a famous East Coast antique boat show some years back. You will immediately note the extreme amount of curve built into the hull sides, decks and transoms. At first glance the Ace runabout very much resembles a Greavette Streamliner, only smaller in size. As you know, back about 1920, a few runabouts came equipped with any type of windshield. Correct? Well, the Ace 21-footer has none either, but does sport a beautiful wooden swept-up front deck which diverts the wind up and out of the eyes of the captain and crew.

The Ace Speedboat Company's 21-foot runabout, as I already mentioned, is built using the W.E.S.T. system of construction. With this type of construction the Honduras mahogany planking is blind fastened to the mahogany and spruce frames. It is then sealed with Epoxy to form a stable structure and a perfect surface for the numerous coats of varnish. By saturating both the inside as well as the outside of the boat with Epoxy resin, the wood absorbs the finish, then sets up hard, dry and strong. It does not need to be soaked each season as the boat becomes one solid piece of wood rather than a bunch of singular planks held together by fastenings and caulking.

Any boat built by the W.E.S.T. method of construction is not only strong but also lightweight, and will in no way leak or suffer from dry rot. This type of construction has been around for some years, mostly used in sailboat and hydroplane construction where lightness and strength is paramount. Owners of Ace advise me that they keep their runabout on a saltwater mooring

1981 21' Ace speed boat. John Hacker replica runabout, approximately 270 h.p.

eight months a year, and the only maintenance they perform is a light sanding each spring to the hull, followed by two coats of varnish, plus fresh bottom paint. Ace runabouts kept on a freshwater lake, in a boat house, or on a boat lift would require very minimal care as compared to conventional wooden inboards.

James Forrest of Ace Speedboat Company tells me that the firm currently builds only the one model, the boat we shall take a close look at next, but they can build whatever type or style of boat the customer prefers. If you have a favorite design, feel free to call Ace and chat with them concerning your ideas and designs.

Now for the boat itself. As mentioned, it was designed by John Hacker, N.A., about 1923. John's idea was to design a craft that would not only serve as a pleasure boat, but one that could be raced as well. It was a small-size "gentleman's" runabout; 26' and 28' versions were also offered. Specifications of the Ace 21' are as follows:

DESIGNER	LENGTH	BEAM	DRAFT	WEIGHT	SPEED
J. Hacker, N.A.	21'	5'	18"	2200 lbs.	60 m.p.h.

ENGINE	FUEL	STEERING	SAFETY
Crusader 270 h.p. V-8 2-pump cooling w/thermostat. Alternator, oil filter and cooler. Equipped w/tachometer, engine oil pressure, water temperature, and oil temperature gauges, Borg-Warner 1:1 transmission, neutral safety switch, 1:25" stainless steel shaft, 13 x 17 cupped BiBral propeller.	30-gallon stainless steel tank, w/baffles, bronze fuel filter, electric fuel pump, and Type A fire-resistant fuel hose.	Edson bronze pulleys and quadrant, $3/16$" S.S. wire rope. Bronze wedge rudder.	4 life jackets, Halon protected engine compartment. 21-lb. dry chemical fire extinguisher. Electric bilge pump, engine driven bilge pump, bilge blower. 8-lb. Danforth anchor and line, paddle, horn and flares.

21' Ace 2-seater runabout with Crusader 270 h.p. V-8 engine.

Snug cockpit of the custom "Ace" mahogany runabout.

The hardware used on the Ace 21' runabout is custom-made from 316 stainless steel and chrome-plated cast bronze. The seats are covered with the best grade naugahyde available in a rainbow of colors. Floors are covered with black rib matting as was used in many boats back in those early years. A locker is built under the seat for storage of life jackets, mooring lines, etc. If ever the owner need give attention to sea cock or shaft log, a handy floorboard hatch gives you excellent access to that area. The beautiful teak handmade steering wheel fits the driver's hand to a "T," and the shift lever is conveniently placed on a control quadrant in the center of the wheel. The throttle is floor mounted, and the foot pedal is made of tough, durable bronze.

If you are a fan of inboard speedboats with the driver's station mounted aft as in years past, then Ace Speedboat Company's 21-foot runabout will be right down your alley. For more details on the above-mentioned boat, please contact the following: (Tell them you read about their boat in *Real Runabouts Volume V*, won't you?)

Ace Speedboat Company
9 Merrill Street
Amesbury, MA 01913
Phone (617) 388-3891

Poised and ready for action—this beautiful 21' Ace runabout will reach a top speed of 60 m.p.h.

Our second firm we shall look at is currently building wooden speedboats again as the Hacker Boat Company. Yes, Hacker Boat Company located at Silver Bay, New York, on the shores of Lake George.

HACKER BOAT COMPANY

One of my most exciting memories of my visit to the Toronto Boat Show in July, 1981, was my meeting a man whom I have admired for many years. I consider Bill Morgan to be the "dean" concerning Hacker Craft inboards. In fact, I often funnel calls and inquiries out to Bill. Bill is soft spoken, a gentle man in every sense of the word. I enjoyed our short visit at Toronto. By the time the beautiful awards were presented that Saturday afternoon of the show, poor Bill was worn out just running up to the award display to carry off all his winnings.

Back in 1981 or 1982 Bill Morgan decided that it made good sense to start building old-style inboards since the replica boats he had built over the years were so popular and customers were anxious to have new runabouts built by this woodmaster of boat building. In 1982, three Hacker Craft runabouts were offered. They included a 26-foot Gentleman's Roadster, a 26-foot three-cockpit runabout, and a big 30-foot three-cockpit runabout.

Bill Morgan has operated his Morgan Marine Base at Silver Bay, New York, for over 30 years. He repaired, restored and sold wooden boats right through the years when fiberglass all but took over the industry. Bill stuck with wood, and today he is more glad than ever that he did. Collectors still consider the Hacker Craft one of the top brands of boats to own, especially the big three-cockpit babies. Because it was getting harder and harder and more expensive to find old Hackers to redo, William J. Morgan decided to embark on building new Hackers, wedding the beauty of the old Hacker with the space age construction materials of today. The "wedding" appears to be a big success. In chatting with a Morgan employee recently, I was informed that only one boat remained to be sold for 1984 and the schedule would be filled for that year. I was given this information in the first week of January, 1984. In 1983, 15 Hacker Crafts were built. The majority were the 26' and 30' three-cockpit models. Let's look at some of the features on the "new" Hacker Craft runabouts by Morgan. The specifications for the three runabouts are shown here.

Bill Morgan, left, and crew check progress in new Hacker-Craft runabout.

Front to back: 26' gentlemen's roadster, 26' three-cockpit runabout, 30' three-cockpit runabout.

	LENGTH	BEAM	DRAFT	FREE BOARD FORWARD	ENGINE	SPEED
26' Gentleman's Roadster	26'	7'	24"	32"	Crusader 350 h.p.	50 m.p.h.
26' Three-cockpit Runabout	26'	7'	24"	32"	Crusader 350 h.p.	50 m.p.h.
30' Three-cockpit Runabout	30'	7'1"	24"	32"	Crusader 350 h.p.	50 m.p.h.

All side and bottom frames are sawn from white oak at Hacker-Craft.

A new 3-cockpit Hacker-Craft runabout really starting to take shape!

Decks about to be installed, ½" Honduras mahogany.

Prices, though far from cheap, are very competitive with other wooden inboards in the same class. Bill said interested parties should contact him directly at Hacker Boat Company for current prices, as more than likely they would be different from those I may quote when this book is printed. You will be surprised, though, as the price will be less than you think.

Construction information for all three Hackers is as follows: Side and bottom frames are sawn white oak 1" x 3". Keel is of white oak, 2" x 4" size. Bottom is 1" triple planked Honduras mahogany and cyprus. Hull sides are planked with ½" Honduras mahogany with all stainless steel fastenings used on each boat. Decks are also ½" Honduras mahogany finished with 12 to 17 coats of hand-rubbed varnish. The side and bottom frames, keel, stem and bottom are completely encased in Epoxy, using the "West System." This means that both the inside and outside of bottom, plus all the above-mentioned parts of the boats, are covered with Epoxy resin which keeps the wood dry and strong, preventing any chance of dry rot attacking the boat at a later date. Used for many years in the construction of wooden sailboats, canoes and other small craft, the "West System" of boat building has now reached into the powerboat arena and has enjoyed good acceptance so far.

Other new construction features found on all three Hackers include 25 percent more frames than on original Hacker Crafts, double the number of floor timbers, stronger side battens, fore-foot, stem frames and engine stringers. Even a new improved steering system is standard, which allows for better maneuverability for the driver. The list of standard equipment found on all new Hacker Crafts looks like the optional equipment list for other boats. Bill has decided to equip these boats in a way that would even make old John Hacker proud.

Though I shall never own a Hacker, be it old or new, I am thrilled that the man who is the expert on this make of pleasure boat is the fellow who is building them again and not cutting corners, as happens so often when replicas are made. Hats off to my friend, Bill Morgan, and all the gang there at Hacker Craft of Silver Bay, New York. One final note: Bill also still operates his custom boat division and can build racing hulls and custom runabouts built to your specifications.

This concludes our look at the "new" Hacker Craft runabouts. We shall now move west and review the Marinacci "torpedo" style inboard runabouts. They are built by the man who built the famous Fairliner Torpedo runabouts back in the 1940s and early '50s. I think you will like the new edition.

A beautiful new Hacker-Craft 30' runabout idling along for its proud owner.

20-FOOT "TORPEDO" RUNABOUT BUILT BY JULIUS MARINACCI

Many readers have commented on how much they wished they could own a Fairliner 17' inboard runabout like the one we looked at back in *Volume II*. Perhaps it was the boat's rounded torpedo stern that made it such a popular one. Whatever the reason, the original 31 Torpedos have decreased in number to the point now where only about six or seven still exist. Of all the firms we have discussed throughout these four inboard books, we would be hard pressed to find more than a couple who are back building the same type boat they did over 30 years ago. Well, in the case of the Fairliner Torpedo, you are in luck.

The original builder of all the Torpedos built by Western Boat Building of Tacoma, Washington, was Julius Marinacci. It was my extreme pleasure to meet this wizard of boat building at the 1983 Con Cours' de elegance Boat Show at Lake Tahoe. Julius was at that show displaying his first "new" Marinacci 20'2" Torpedo. Julius had thought for some years about building a Torpedo but finally got going on it when he read an article about Curt Erickson of Tacoma who was restoring one of the original Torpedos.[1] Since then, Julius and Curt have joined forces and are working together in the sale of these fine mahogany inboards.

Curt Erickson proudly poses before the first 20' "Torpedo" runabout by Julius Marinacci. Photo taken at Lake Tahoe, California, July 30, 1983.

---

[1] "A Sleek Torpedo Runabout Coming Back," *The News Tribune* (March 3, '83), p. 4.

Original factory view of frame setup over which planking was installed on the original 17' Fairliner Torpedo.

Planking on bottom and sides all in place, time to turn boat over and install decks, etc.

When I arrived at the Lake Tahoe show back in August of 1983, the first two people I met on the show grounds were Curt and Julius. They proceeded to lead me over to see their "pride and joy" rakishly displayed on its trailer, drawing large crowds all weekend. I was most impressed by what I saw.

Before we go further I wish to thank Curt Erickson for the large packet of old and new color and black and white photos he gave me concerning the Torpedo. All the photos used in this report are from the Curt Erickson archives. The first photos shown are old factory shots showing how the original Fairliner Torpedos were built. Several others show the original 17' Fairliners under power. Note the flat planing angle these beauties run at, will you?

The new 20'2" Torpedo is three feet longer and one foot wider than the original model. This was done to allow for the seating of six rather than four or five adults, plus the use of a new 270 h.p. V-8 powerplant.

By adding the three feet to the boat's length, the builder tells us, it is more stable and faster than the original 17-footers ever were. The new runabout will be marketed for around $25,000 each, but the price will fluctuate. You will have to contact the builder to get a current price quote.

Restored Fairliner Torpedo driven by Curt Erickson.

The Marinacci Torpedo was built of Honduras mahogany with frames of Philippine mahogany. The bottom sports an inner planking of ¼" marine plywood with an outside hull of 7/16" mahogany. Another change on the larger Torpedo is a beautiful one-piece rolled mahogany dashboard, rather than the old flat style used on earlier models. The decks are all bleached Honduras mahogany with narrow inlaid strips of black walnut for trim. One of the things I liked best on the new Torpedo was the bright, blue bottom paint used on that #1 boat. In the clear, cold waters of Lake Tahoe, California, this is a good color as it shows right through the water just as nice as can be.

If you would like more specifics on the Marinacci Torpedo, please feel free to contact Curtis Erickson of Tacoma, Washington, at the following number: 1-(206) 879-5429.

Our final builder is located back East, and is known by the name Black Bottom Runabouts, Inc.

Curt sits proudly atop the new 20'2" Marinacci "Torpedo" runabout—270 h.p. V-8 engine.

1983 20' Marinacci Torpedo runabout 270 Crusader. Built by original builder of the Fairliner Torpedo.

BLACK BOTTOM RUNABOUTS, INC.
of Rocky Point, Long Island, New York

Patrick Carney, Jr., president of Black Bottom Runabouts, says it's all in his firm's slogan, "The Tradition Lives On." Pat has been a wooden boat buff for years. After restoring a number of various older wooden craft, he could see that the process of redoing an older boat was getting harder each year. Also, boats to be redone were harder and harder to find all the time, and engine parts and hardware often caused an owner gray hair trying to find everything he needed. Although the old boats have charm, grace, and more, our modern designs and construction offer a lot as well.

Pat decided back in 1979 or so to build a replica of the mid- to late 1930s 16' Gar Wood split-cockpit runabout. In looking at various views of the new *Phoenix* as it was to be called, you will see the close resemblance of it to an older Gar Wood. Pat's own boat, *"10¢ a Dance,"* is making the antique boat show circuit each year. Maybe you have already seen this beautiful craft with its bright red naugahyde interior and, of course, her black bottom.

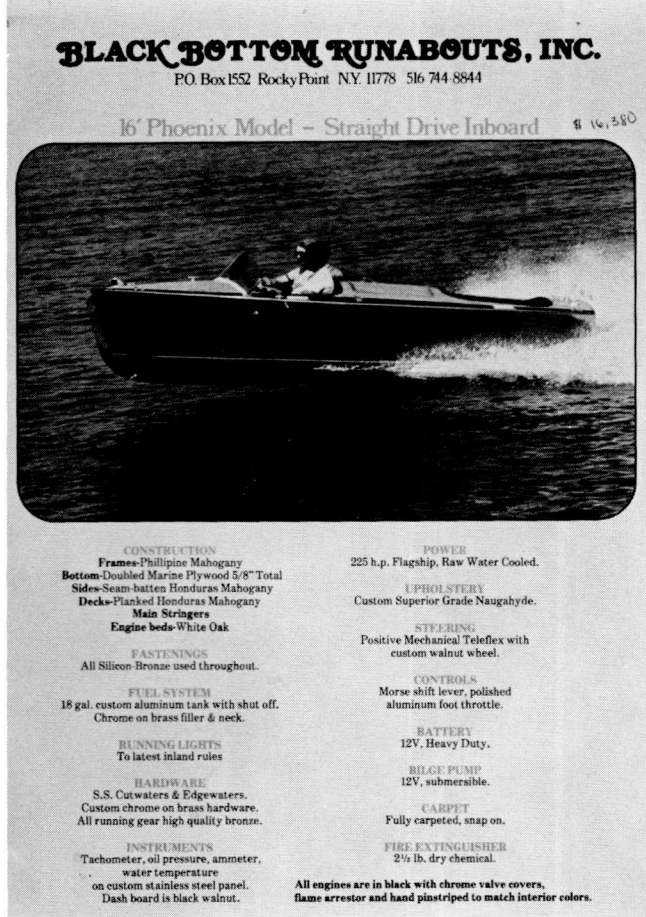

Black Bottom runabout—front cockpit.

Pat Carney's Phoenix 16' runabout, *10¢ a Dance.*

Carney first displayed the *Phoenix* at the 1980 Winter Miami, Florida Boat Show. Acceptance of the craft has been excellent. For awhile Carney toyed with the idea of adding a larger, 3-cockpit runabout along the lines of the Fitzgerald & Lee, *Foot Loose and Fancy Free,* but those plans have been shelved as Black Bottom Runabouts, Inc. plans to continue building only the *Phoenix* for now, along with engaging in some limited restoration work on older boats when the workload will allow it.

The accompanying chart gives you the basic breakdown of information on the *Phoenix*. Being a custom-type inboard, Carney advises that every boat built so far is different, finished to the wishes of the owner as far as interiors and options are concerned.

Gar Wood owners and fans have been very pleased with the boat that Black Bottom Runabouts is turning out. Sometime back the entire story of this unusual little boat was written up in the *Gar Wood News* for March, 1982. Rather than go into any more detail about this little jewel, I will tell you who to contact if the *Phoenix* looks like a boat you might like to own.

Please contact: Patrick Carney, President
Black Bottom Runabouts, Inc.
P.O. Box 1552
Rocky Point, L.I., NY 11778
(516) 744-8844

This concludes *Volume V*. I hope you have enjoyed this book as much as I have enjoyed preparing it for you. When I began work on it back in 1982, I could see that it was going to be too large a volume, so I decided at that time to cut the book in half and make a *Volume V* and a *Volume VI*. This is what I have done, and I am already working the second half of this set. There are a lot of exciting things planned for that volume as well. I think you will really enjoy what's coming up. Just as an example, or might I say preview, the following current builders of wooden speedboats will be included: Gar Wood Speedsters, Grand-Craft from Holland, Michigan, Morin Mahogany Marine also of Michigan, and Stan-Craft of Post Falls, Idaho.

Thanks to everyone who has written or called these last several years. Your encouragement and help have made my life much more enjoyable. If you are a member of any of the numerous boat clubs now in operation, I ask that you please check to be sure my name and address is on the mailing list as I like to keep up on all the goings on around the U.S. and Canada in the field of antique wooden boats. If you have material on firms we have not discussed as yet, or other new material on firms we have already looked at, especially old photos, drop me a line or call me and maybe we can work it into a future edition. So long for now, and may God bless you and yours.

BLACK BOTTOM RUNABOUTS INC.
"THE TRADITION LIVES ON"
P.O. BOX 1552 • ROCKY POINT, L.I., N.Y. 11778

16' PHOENIX MODEL
Straight Drive Inboard

Construction:	Frames— Phillipine Mahogany Bottom— Doubled Marine Plywood ⅜" Total Sides— Steam-batten Phillipine Mahogany. Decks— Planked Phillipine Mahogany Main Stringers & Engine beds—White Oak	Power:	225 h.p. Flagship, Raw Water Cooled.
		Upholstery:	Custom Superior Grade Naugahyde.
Fastenings:	All Silicone Bronze used throughout.	Steering:	Positive Mechanical Teleflex with custom walnut wheel.
Fuel System:	18 gal. custom aluminum tank with shut off. Chrome on brass filler & neck.	Controls:	Morse shift lever, polished aluminum foot throttle.
Running Lights:	To latest inland rules.	Battery:	12V, Heavy Duty.
Hardware:	S.S. Cutwaters & Edgewaters. Custom chrome on brass hardware. All running gear high quality bronze.	Bilge Pump:	12V, submersible
Instruments:	Tachometer, oil pressure, ammeter, water temperature on custom stainless steel panel. Dash board is black walnut.	Carpet:	Fully carpeted, snap on.
*All engines are in black with chrome valve covers, flame arrestor and hand pinstriped to match interior colors.		Fire Extinguisher:	2½ lb. dry chemical.

OPTIONAL EQUIPMENT: Tonneau covers, mooring cover, custom leather interior. Dual batterys, gear driven water pump, automatic oil changer, remote oil filter, bilge blower, shipping cradle.

Conclusion

Well, here we are at the end of *Volume V!* Where does time fly? I hope that you have enjoyed this latest edition of *The Real Runabouts*. As I mentioned earlier, I could see while writing this book that it was going to be too large so I decided to divide it into two volumes. As you read this conclusion, work is already in progress on yet another, *Volume VI,* which will cover many other firms not discussed in the previous books.

The world of antique boats and boating has mushroomed over these last seven years. I can recall when I did *Volume I* seven years ago that interest in the old wooden beauties was pretty limited in size. With the founding of the Chris-Craft Antique Boat Club, The Antique & Classic Boat Society, the Century Boat Club, The Gar Wood Society, The Antique Outboard Motor Club, and a score of other groups, continued interest and growth in our hobby and sport is assured.

Antique boat shows are blossoming all over this nation, Canada, and even in Europe. In 1984 alone, I figure there will be over forty shows, both large and small, being held from April through September. Attending such a show with your trusty camera is the best way to view large groupings of old, restored wooden boats all in one location. Each show has its own special features and you can figure on spending a day or perhaps a weekend enjoying all the events.

Since the writing of *Volume IV,* I had the extreme pleasure of being an honorary judge at the 1983 Lake Tahoe Concourse de 'elegance Boat Show this past August. The boats at Lake Tahoe are almost beyond belief, as is that beautiful mountain lake. Thanks to everyone connected with bringing my mom and I to Tahoe for that show. I will never forget the great time we had. Glen Wilson, one of the real wooden boat fans on Tahoe, told me there are over 1,100 wooden boats of many sizes and types plying that beautiful lake. If ever you get a chance to go to Tahoe, be sure to see the beautiful boats there. Sierra Boat Company is the local haven for most of the wooden boat restoration and care on the lake. Their shops, sales facilities and harbor are among the greatest anywhere.

During the summer of 1984, I plan to attend the Second Annual Montana Antique & Classic Boat Show on Flathead Lake. That lake is larger than Lake Tahoe and much less populated. Interest in wooden boats there is just starting to reappear again. Up into the 1960's, Stan Craft Boat Company built all kinds of runabouts, utilities and cruisers. I also plan on attending the 20th Annual Clayton (New York) Shipyard Museum Antique Boat Show & Parade, as well as the Chris-Craft Jamboree being held there two days previous.

So much is happening in this sport that I can't mention it all.

There are several firms that I hope to include in *Volume VI* but I am still in need of history, photos, etc. They are: Welch Boat Company of Milwaukee, Wisconsin; Pacesetter Boat Company of Waxahachie, Texas; and Rochester Boat Company of Rochester, New York. Several Canadian firms I still need more information about include Hatley Craft, Kings Craft Marine, Brougham Boat Company, and Matlo Boat Company; one other builder is Dawcett Boat Company of Portland, Ontario. If any of you readers can help me with information on any of the above builders, feel free to call or write me anytime. Anyone providing material used in these books will have their name listed in that book as a contributor.

Volume VI will be called *The Real Runabouts, International Edition.* You can look forward to more Canadian and American builders as well as stories on firms from England, Germany, Sweden and Italy. We will also have more colored photos. Color photos really do justice to these beautiful old wooden masterpieces.

In conclusion, thanks to you all for your continued support in the production and purchase of my books. May God bless you all. Keep watching for *Volume VI.* It will be out before you know it!

CONTRIBUTORS TO VOLUME #5

Thanks to everyone who so graciously shared with me the material used in this book. I apologize if anyone was left out; it was unintentional on my part. Some of you who sent material to me and expected to see it in *Volume V*, don't despair. If material you sent in applied to firms discussed in *Volume II* or *III*, your items should appear in *Volume VI* which I have already started. God bless you all and take care in whatever you do. Now, on to friends who contributed material appearing in this book:

Anderson, Ken—Northbrook, Illinois
Bartos, Mark—S. Deerfield, Massachusetts
Besemer, John S.—E. Moline, Illinois
Black, Jay C.—Des Moines, Iowa
Bratlouf, Dick—W. Milford, New Jersey
Brown, Tony & Rita—Lake Tahoe, California
Bucci, George—Mobile, Alabama
Burgess, George M.—Pearl Beach, Michigan
Carney, Pat Jr.—Rocky Point, Long Island, New York
Chisleti, John—Perry Sound, Ontario, Canada
Ciesielski, J.—Cheetowaga, New York
Clarke, Gwen & Dick—Carnelian Bay, California
Cockrell, Gary—Lakeside, Montana
Coffin, Terry E.—Boise, Idaho
Craig, Clayton—E. Vassalboro, Maine
D' Earth, Al Mrs.—Harsens Island, Michigan
Deibel, Wm. T.—Seattle, Washington
Ellis, Wm. C.—Lake Forest, Illinois
Erickson, Curt—Tacoma, Washington
Fairbanks, Gordan—Ft. Lauderdale, Florida
Fangman, Rose—Britt, Iowa
Ferguson, Mike—Peterborough, Ontario, Canada
Fischer, Paul—Fond du Lac, Wisconsin
Forrest, James—Amesbury, Massachusetts
Fox, Stephen M.—Aylmer, Quebec, Canada
Garelick, Ken—St. Paul, Minnesota
Gast, Chuck—Sonoma, California
Gatter, L. Gene—Baja, California
Hafer, Glenn—Spirit Lake, Iowa
Halvorson, Vic—Ishpeming, Michigan
Hamblin, J. Carl—Barton, New York
Hardy, Larry—Dayton, Ohio
Harnes, George—Winnipeg, Manitoba, Canada
Harper, Charles & Jane—Meredith, New Hampshire
Holvay, Greg—Palatine, Illinois
Homma, R.—New York, New York
Humburg, Don—Clear Lake, Iowa
Johnson, Jim—Plano, Illinois
Johnson, Lance—Fargo, North Dakota
Jones, Don G.—Toronto, Ontario, Canada
Koehler, F. J.—Long Valley, New Jersey
Knight, Charles—Saratoga Springs, New York
Kramer, Vern J.—Fox Lake, Illinois
Ladue, Wm. L. M.D.—Plattsburg, New York
Leathers, Randy—Hillsborough, California
Lewin, Marcella & Ed—Mound, Minnesota

Logan, Don—Soudan, Minnesota
Loop, Robert J.—Kingsville, Ontario, Canada
MacPherson, Lrone—Magog, Quebec, Canada
Macal, Ken—Downers Grove, Illinois
Machuca, Juan—Malaga, Spain
Mann, Alan—Wallaceburg, Ontario, Canada
Martin, Mike—Ankeny, Iowa
Marinacci, Julius—Tacoma, Washington
Menth, Jon—Excelsior, Minnesota
Miklos, Chuck, Paul—Pittsburgh, Pennsylvania
Millar, A. C.—New York, New York
Moore, Robert I.—Averill Park, New York
Morgan, Bill—Silver Bay, New York
Morrison, Joe—Algonac, Michigan
McCarthy, D. J. W.—Stuart, Florida
Ogilvie, Wm. G.—Lakefield, Ontario, Canada
Pierce, Bruce—Leesburg, Indiana
Pike, Doug—Portland, Oregon
Polek, Jerry—Lake Geneva, Wisconsin
Ray, Alan C.—Ft. Lauderdale, Florida
Rio Nautica—Sarnico, Italy
Routh, John—Muncie, Indiana
Riva Boat Company—Lake Sarnico, Italy
Sills, G. A.—Peterborough, Ontario, Canada
Sligh, Dick—Holland, Michigan
Smith, Chris—Holland, Michigan
Smith, George—Holland, Michigan
Smith, Riggs—Endicott, New York
Stork, Gil—Hoquiam, Washington
Storz, Kurt—Woodland, California
Streblow Boat Company—Kenosha, Wisconsin
Tassell, Dale—Mt. Dora, Florida
Teasdale, Dave—Cannifton, Ontario, Canada
Therrien, Ross—Bancroft, Ontario, Canada
Thomas, John H.—Cincinnati, Ohio
Thompson, Wm. J.—W. Wareham, Maine
Viccone, Jeff—Decatur, Illinois
Waddell, E. W.—Windsor, Ontario, Canada
Wallace, J. H.—Scarborough, Ontario, Canada
Warner, F. Todd—Mound, Minnesota
Whatley, Leonard—Canton, Texas
Watson, Monty—Pawleys Island, South Carolina
Wilcox, Cam.—Cobourg, Ontario, Canada
Wilson, Glenn—Homewood, California
Wright, Wilson W.—Tallahassee, Florida
Young, Terry & Mary—Minneapolis, Minnesota